To the Worthy and Independant Electors of the Town of Three-Rivers.

GENTLEMEN,

ENCOURAGED by feveral of my Fellow-Citizens to offer myfelf as a Candidate to reprefent you in the next Provincial Parliament:

Permit me to folicit your Votes and Patronage on *Wednesday* the *4 party next* the day fixed for the Poll by the Returning Officer.

I have always been, and you fhall find me, Gentlemen, on every wishes and prosperity.—*My interest is connected with yours*, and should I succeed in attaining so important a station, be assured my exertions shall be to fulfil the duties thereof, to the utmost of my abilities, and that of the interest of this my *native Place*.

I have the honor to be,

Gentlemen, and Fellow-Citizens,

Your faithful and

Most Obedient Servant,

EZEKIEL HART.

Three Rivers 22 June 1807

Baraka
Books

The First Jews in North America

The Extraordinary Story of the Hart Family (1760-1860)

By Denis Vaugeois (Translated by Käthe Roth)

Denis Vaugeois

E FIRST JEWS IN NORTH AMERICA

The Extraordinary Story
of the Hart Family

1760-1860

Translated by Käthe Roth

Telling the captivating story of the Hart family over 100 years, historian Denis Vaugeois situates the drive of Jews to achieve justice and equality among the major events that shaped the politics and geography of North America. The work of a lifetime, he has combined great story-telling skills and more than 50 years of research to produce an intriguing and accessible book.

Filled with original documents and vintage illustrations, this history chronicles the lives of the Hart family—a Jewish family from New York who settled in the French-speaking and predominantly Catholic Trois-Rivières, Quebec, in 1761, but maintained links with New York. Aaron Hart was, according to Irving Abella, "the most influential of the early Jewish settlers in Canada."

Following Aaron Hart and his descendants for a century through the political upheavals that shaped North America, this account not only bares the Jewish struggle for equality and freedom, but also delineates the contributions made by the various family members. These include the election of Ezekiel Hart, first Jew elected to parliament in the British Empire, the passing of the Jewish

368 p | Tradepaper $34.95
978-1-926824-09-3

Trophy for the National Hockey League's Most Valuable Player. A fascinating and comprehensive read, this book breaks new ground in its examination of the Jewish experience in North America.

Preface by the Honorable **Herbert Marx**, former Minister of Justice and Attorney (1985-88) and former Justice of the Quebec Superior Court (1989-2007).

Awards/Praise

Winner of the 2012 Canadian Jewish Book Award for History sponsored by the Koffler Centre of the Arts, The Helen and Stan Vine Award.

Runner-up for the Marcel Couture Award at the *Salon du livre de Montréal* (Montreal Book Fair)

"The First Jews in North America 1760-1860 is an exceptional work, abundantly illustrated, the result of vast research…" *Voir*, Montreal

"A book that will be cited by scholars… it is also a story well told, easy to read… a good read." The Honorable Herbert Marx.

Denis Vaugeois is a historian, a publisher, and the author of many books on North American and European history, including *America: The Lewis & Clark Expedition and the Dawn of a New Power* and *Mapping a Continent*. He is also Quebec's former minister of cultural affairs. He lives in Quebec City.

Käthe Roth of Montreal translated the book into English and Baraka Books is pleased to announce that *The First Jews in North America* will be available in bookstores on June 15, 2012.

CONTACT: Robin Philpot – 514-858-6333, extension 226.

Baraka Books | 6977, rue Lacroix | Montréal, Québec | H4E 2V4

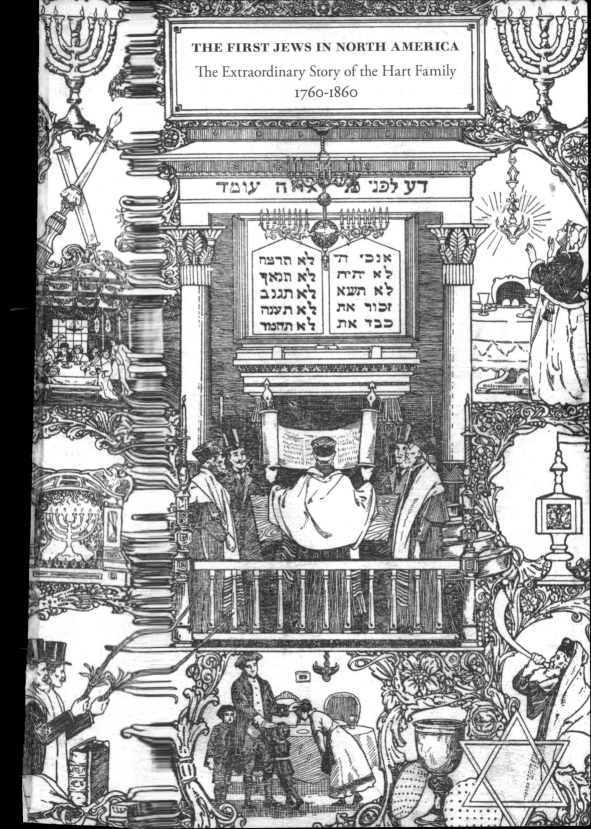

THE FIRST JEWS IN NORTH AMERICA

The Extraordinary Story of the Hart Family
1760-1860

דע לפני מ אתה עומד

אנכי ה׳ לא תרצח
לא יהיה לא תנאף
לא תשא לא תגנב
זכור את לא תענה
כבד את לא תחמד

"Biographical history and anecdotal history is the least explanatory; but it is the richest in point of information for it considers individuals in their particularity and details for each of them the shades of character, the twists and turns of their motives, the phases of their deliberations. . . . The historian's relative choice, with respect to each domain of history he gives up, is always confined to the choice which teaches us more and explains less, and history which explains more and teaches less."

(Claude LÉVI-STRAUSS, *The Savage Mind*, 1962)

Denis Vaugeois

THE FIRST JEWS IN NORTH AMERICA

The Extraordinary Story of the Hart Family

1760-1860

Translated by Käthe Roth

Baraka
Books
Montreal

Cover illustration: James Duncan, *Steamboat Wharf* (Lithograph by Matthews), National Maritime Museum, London, c1843, PAD 2018.

Editorial director: Robin Philpot
Project manager and photograph of the author: Sophie Imbeault

Canada Council for the Arts We acknowledge the support of the Canada Council for the Arts which last year invested $20.1 million in writing and publishing throughout Canada. We acknowledge the financial support of the Government of Canada, through the National Translation Program for Book Publishing for our translation activities.

Société de développement des entreprises culturelles
Québec

Baraka Books acknowledges the support received under the Programme de crédit d'impôt pour l'édition de livres du Gouvernement du Québec.

Original title: *Les Premiers Juifs d'Amérique, 1760-1860, L'extraordinaire histoire de la famille Hart*
Copyright © 2011 by Les éditions du Septentrion
Publié avec l'autorisation des Éditions du Septentrion, Québec (Québec)

Translation Copyright © Baraka Books 2012

Cover by Folio infographie
Book design by Folio infographie
Translated by Käthe Roth

Legal Deposit, 2nd quarter, 2012

Bibliothèque et Archives nationales du Québec
Library and Archives Canada

Published by Baraka Books of Montreal.
6977, rue Lacroix
Montréal, Québec H4E 2V4
Telephone: 514 808-8504
info@barakabooks.com
www.barakabooks.com

Printed and bound in Quebec

Trade Distribution & Returns
Canada
LitDistCo
1-800-591-6250; ordering@litdistco.ca

United States
Independent Publishers Group
1-800-888-4741 (IPG1);
orders@ipgbook.com

Table of Contents

Chronology

1759	Short battle on the Plains of Abraham. Wolfe and Montcalm die and a few days later, Quebec capitulates.
1759	Samuel Jacobs is at Québec.
1760	General Amherst obtains the capitulation of Montreal. Arrival of the first Jews, including Aaron Hart, considered to be the father of Judaism in Canada.
1760-63	Negotiations in Paris concerning the future of New France.
1763	A treaty is signed in Paris on 10 February under which France cedes Canada to England. Louisiana was secretly ceded to Spain a few weeks later.
1763	James Murray is appointed Governor of the Province of Quebec. Canada no longer exists, but there are still *Canadiens*, as Historian Guy Frégault wrote.
1774	The Quebec Act is voted in London in an aim to accommodate the *Canadiens* to ensure their loyalty in the context of agitation in the Thirteen Colonies. French Civil Law is reinstated and freedom of religion for Catholics is increased. The seigneurial regime is maintained.
1775-76	American insurgents invade the Province of Quebec.
1776	American Congress votes for independence. American declaration of independence.
1783	Arrival of several thousand Loyalists who provoke the division of the Province of Quebec into Lower Canada and Upper Canada.
1791	The Constitutional Act introduces the Parliamentary System.
1808-10	Political crisis under Governor Craig.
1830-32	Jewish Emancipation Act passed in Lower Canada.
1837-38	Rebellion in Lower Canada and Upper Canada.
1838	Durham Report
1840	The Act of Union creates the United Canadas.
1848	Responsible Government is established.
1849	English-speaking Tories provoke the burning of the Canadian Parliament in Montreal.
1849	Movement in favour of annexation to the United States develops.

Preface by Herbert Marx*

I FIRST MET DENIS VAUGEOIS in the early 1980s when we were both members of the Québec National Assembly. As well, I knew him as a historian. With time I learned of his interest in the history of the Jews as he had written some biographies for the *Dictionary of Canadian Biography* as well as a book entitled *Les juifs et la Nouvelle-France.*" He is an expert on the subject.

While driving to a meeting last year, I was listening to Denis Vaugeois being interviewed on Radio-Canada. He was discussing the French edition of the book under review. In his reply to questions put to him by the interviewer, he was exceptionally knowledgeable and animated. I was impressed by his expertise and passion for the subject that dealt with the first Jews in North America. As soon as I left my meeting, I stopped at a book store to purchase a copy of the book. I was not disappointed.

Under French rule only Roman Catholics were permitted to settle in Canada. All non-Catholic Christians as well as Jews were barred from settling in this country. However, Jews were permitted to immigrate to English colonies. Aaron Hart arrived in Québec with the British army in 1760. He was soon followed by his two brothers and some other Jews.

Aaron Hart, age 36, settled in Trois-Rivières, which had a population of 672 people. In 1763 there were only twenty Jews and 113 Protestants in all of Québec. This small group of English people settled in a country where everyone spoke a different language and practised a different religion.

In 1768 Aaron went to England to marry his friend's sister, Dorothy Judah. He returned to Trois-Rivières with his bride where they raised a family. They had eleven or twelve children, of whom eight survived to adulthood, four girls and four boys.

---

* The Honourable Herbert Marx is a graduate of the Université de Montréal and Harvard Law School. He was professor of law at the Université de Montréal (1969-1979), Member of the Québec National Assembly (1979-1989), Minister of Justice and Attorney General of Québec (1985-1988), and a Justice of the Québec Superior Court (1989-2007). He has published many articles and books on constitutional law, civil liberties and poverty law.

The book traces the history of the Hart family, especially that of Aaron and his offspring, until the third generation, that is from 1760 to 1860. It is a remarkable story.

Hart was very well integrated into the French community. Vaugeois cites a document in which Mother Thérèse de Jésus of the Monastère des Ursulines, which was in dire straits, is thankful to Hart for lending them a large sum of money without interest. He also apparently provided the Ursulines with hot meals.

The most outstanding issue of early Jewish settlement in Québec was the election of the first Jew to the Québec Legislature. Denis Vaugeois deals with this issue in detail.

Ezekiel Hart, Aaron's son, had studied in the United States and he was an English-speaking Quebecer. He decided to run for election to the Québec Legislature. Aaron had told him that he would be "opposed as a Jew." His father was both right and wrong!

He was wrong insofar as the French Canadian voters of Trois-Rivières gave him a majority vote in 1807. However, the law in place required that before he could take his seat in the legislature, he had to take an oath ending with the words "on the true faith of a Christian." He refused. A new election was called and Ezekiel won a second time.

However, it was only in 1832 that "An act" was passed "to declare persons professing the Jewish religion entitled to all rights and privileges of the other subjects of His Majesty in this Province." This law had the support of the Speaker of the Legislature, Louis-Joseph Papineau. It is significant that it was almost thirty years later that Jews were first admitted to the House of Commons in England. Québec had set a precedent.

In the census of 1831, Québec had a population of 403,000 Catholics, 34,000 Anglicans, 15,000 members of the Church of Scotland, 7,000 Methodists and 107 Jews, 85 in Montréal, 19 in Trois-Rivières and three in Québec City.

Eventually many of the Harts and their offspring intermarried with French Canadian Catholics. For example, Ezekiel-Moses Hart, one of the founders of the Seminary in Trois-Rivières, married Marie-Joséphine Domithide Pothier. Ezekiel was baptized and subsequently married in the Cathedral of Trois-Rivières. His daughters attended school at the Ursuline Convent. His brother some time later married his wife's sister.

The Hart blood flows in the veins of hundreds if not thousands of Quebecers of all religions. For example, the Hart Trophy, given to the most valuable player in the National Hockey League, was named after Cecil Mordecai Hart who was the son of David Alexander Hart and Sarah Matilda Hart.

The book is very well illustrated, with interesting photos of people, paintings and objects mentioned in the text. This is a book that will, no doubt, be read and cited by scholars interested in Québec and Canadian history. However, it is also a story well told, easy to read, that the general reader will find very interesting. In short, it is a good read.

Honorable HERBERT MARX, Montreal, 20 April 2012

North America: A Wonderful Land of the Future

S INCE QUEBEC WAS FOUNDED IN 1608, Canada was a Catholic colony, like France, where Protestants and Jews were excluded. Unsurprisingly therefore, just six weeks after the capitulation of Montreal in September 1760, Jews in New York celebrated "the reducing of Canada to His Majesty's Dominions" in a ceremony held "at the at the Jews Synagogue in the City of New York."

Jews in New York were often descendants of pioneers originally from Amsterdam, a refuge city for Jews, and they had dreamed of gaining access to the vast lands of France's empire that stretched from Quebec to New Orleans.

After British troops invaded the Great Lakes region, Jewish merchants followed close behind as sutlers (purveyors). They were undoubtedly drawn to the intensive fur trade, which was the basis of New France's economy. The Indians had formed a formidable alliance with the French and were waging war throughout the area. Some Jewish merchants almost lost their lives. That was the case of Chapman Abraham, Aaron Hart's future brother-in-law. Historians consider Aaron Hart to be the father of Judaism in Canada.

Aaron Hart was received at the Trinity Lodge in New York on 10 June 1760 and, by all indications, the Masonic certificate given to him served as his passport when he joined the British troops en route to take the last bastion of France's North American empire, Montréal. Another Jew, Samuel Jacobs, had already arrived at Quebec. Hart came down the St. Lawrence with Amherst's troops, while Jacobs came up the St. Lawrence with an armada of more than 150 ships headed by Admiral Saunders. That armada was bringing nine thousand soldiers who, under James Wolfe's command, would lay siege to Quebec in summer 1759 and take over in September.

The conquest of New France was complete when Montreal capitulated on 8 September 1760 and when France ceded Canada under the Treaty of Paris on 10 February 1763.

By taking over New France, which included Canada or that part of the French empire encompassing the St. Lawrence Valley, the British Conquerors acquired a fourteenth colony to be added to the Thirteen Colonies to the south. It became the "province of Quebec," or the colony of Quebec. The *Canadiens*, generally descendants of French settlers who had adapted to the new continent, were given eighteen months to decide whether or not to move to France. That option was out of the question for the vast majority of the *Canadiens* who were no more French than the American inhabitants of the Thirteen Colonies were English.* The British were realistic; they tolerated French laws and the French language, but placed the Catholic Church under close scrutiny. They allowed people to practise the religion inasmuch as was allowed under British law.

The first Jews arrived one at a time, usually from New York. The first congregation was created in Montreal in 1768 and was an extension of the Shearith Israel of New York, which in turn was under the influence of London. The Sephardic rite was adopted even though most of the Jews present were of Ashkenazi tradition.

Aaron Hart was an exception. Undoubtedly originally from Germany, Hart never attended the Montreal synagogue, nor did his sons. That is except for Benjamin Hart whose wife was from New York and who decided in the 1820s to reorganize the Montreal Jewish community. Benjamin Hart was an authoritarian and a determined man. With support mainly from Moses-Judah Hays and Hays's brother-in-law, Isaac Valentine, he had a new synagogue erected, which revived the Montreal congregation. Together with his nephews Samuel-Bécancour Hart and his brother Aaron-Ezekiel Hart, sons of his brother Ezekiel, who was elected to the House of Assembly in 1807, Benjamin Hart began a struggle to obtain the right officially to found a congregation, keep registers, and hold property. The ultimate goal was to obtain equality, which was achieved when the Parti Patriote, dominated by French-speaking *Canadiens* and Irishmen, voted for it in 1832.

The opening of the new synagogue, inaugurated in 1838, coincided with the arrival of a new wave of Jewish immigrants mainly from Poland and Germany.

* The English-speaking inhabitants of what became British North America only began calling themselves "Canadians" about seventy years later. The *Canadiens*, as they are called in this book, then became "French Canadians."

Benjamin reacted to the new immigrants with distrust and became aggressive, combative, and intransigent towards those he described as "foreigners." In September 1846, the newly arrived Jews incorporated the Congregation of English, German, and Polish Jews, which later became the Shaar Hashomayim Congregation. They inaugurated their new synagogue on Rue Saint-Constant on 22 May 1860.

Benjamin Hart did not live long enough to see what resulted from his opposition to the "foreigners." Disappointed by the course of events, he moved to New York where he died in 1855.

Without intending to, Benjamin had indirectly accomplished what his father had only dreamt of, namely create a synagogue in the Ashkenazi tradition.

As of 1860, Montreal Jews had two synagogues corresponding to Judaism's two great traditions. The city would become a leading Jewish centre in North America and would always maintain close ties with the New York Jewish community.

From the beginning, travel was constant between Montreal and New York. For example, the family of Aaron Hart's wife, Dorothea Judah, settled in New York and one of her brothers, Samuel Judah, was close to George Washington and helped fund the revolution. Aaron Hart's brother was in Albany, New York, and his sons studied in Philadelphia and New York where they met their future wives. Jews in Montreal were divided during the American Revolution with many choosing to side with the insurgents. Benjamin's children would later move to the United States. The Jews in Lower Canada who chose to live under the British took an active part in all the political struggles of the day. They were British subjects involved in different activities. These included painters like William Raphaël; entrepreneurs like Moses-Judah Hays; lawyers Aaron-Ezekiel Hart and Aaron-Philip Hart; doctors Philip Hart and David Alexander Hart, whose son Cecil became coach of the Montreal Canadiens Hockey Club; brewers or bankers like the Harts of Trois-Rivières; city councillors such as William Benjamin; police officials like Jacob Kuhn; chimney inspectors like John Franks; and later, a pioneer of telephones and electricity in Quebec City named Sigmund Mohr, whose two sons enjoyed careers in public works in New York City.

Just as the first years are crucial in an individual's life, the first years of a community are decisive. From the beginning, the Americas were a land of promise for Jews. That is what can be learned from the wonderful collections of documents conserved in Cincinnati, New York, Boston, Ottawa, and Montreal, especially thanks to the historian and collector Ephraim Hart, great great grandson of Aaron Hart and Dorothea Judah. The same can be said of Trois-Rivières where upwards of one hundred thousand documents make it possible to follow the lives of three generations of the Hart and Judah families.

That first century, 1760 to 1860, enabled the North American Jewish communities to develop fully in all areas of human activity.

Denis VAUGEOIS, May 2012

Acknowledgements

I would like to thank those who braved the sometimes forbidding task of reading a first draft. Prime among these is André Ménard, the skilful producer of a series broadcast on Quebec's Canal Savoir, who convinced me to take a personal, storytelling tone. His advice enabled me to relive all my years of research and bring to the work the rather intimate knowledge of the characters and the period that I had developed. Honour to whom honour is due: Gilles Herman told me "There are many books within this book! It's interesting to follow the evolution of the research and the fantastic progress in the means available to researchers." The historian and publisher Sophie Imbeault followed; she limited the damage while carefully pointing me in the direction of useful works. After that came my longtime colleagues: Gaston Deschênes, René Hardy, Jacques Lacoursière, and, particularly, Pierre Anctil. On more specialized questions, I turned to the advice and assistance of Jean Prince, Christian Lalancette, Nora Hague, Denis Lacasse, Rénald Lessard, Claude Kaufholtz-Couture, René Chartrand, Claude Bellavance, France Normand, Lucia Ferretti, Claude Rétat, René Beaudoin, Hélène Levesque, and Anthony Deshais, who revealed to me the magic of digital photographs in archives. It has been quite a road travelled since handwritten transcription and photostats! Käthe Roth translated the book, but she also made revisions to the overly personal tone that might be unfamiliar for an English readership. Robin Philpot, publisher of Baraka Books, provided many useful comments and details while Josée Lalancette designed the book with her usual flair. This book is easier to follow thanks to the detailed index prepared by Jeannette Larouche.

IMPORTANT NOTE (for serious readers)

In the three hundred or so pages that follow, I introduce three generations of the Hart family. That is a lot of people! To complicate matters, the same first names return again and again, shared by different family members. And so, here's a key to some of the main characters.

THE CAST

Aaron Hart was the patriarch. He arrived with the British troops in 1760 and decided to settle in Trois-Rivières. He quickly made contact with Jewish merchants Samuel Jacobs and Eleazar Levy, who arrived in Quebec at about the same time.

Aaron was soon joined by two of his brothers: Moses, who moved to Montreal after a short stay in Trois-Rivières, and Henry, who settled in Albany. They did not have Aaron's stature and are not often mentioned in this book. However, Aaron's oldest son was also named Moses— a possible source of confusion.

Another Jew, Uriah Judah, was in Aaron's orbit; Aaron was responsible for the immigration of many members of the Judah family, including his wife, Dorothea Judah, whom he married in London. Her parents and siblings later immigrated to North America. Aaron was also responsible for the immigration of the three Joseph brothers, his nephews, who settled in Berthier.

Three of Aaron and Dorothea's sons are at the centre of this family saga.

Moses, the oldest, was unpredictable and extravagant. He had a finger in every pie, made many connections, and left a considerable estate to some of his natural children. Although most of his female conquests were passing fancies, one became important late in life: Mary McCarthy, whose sister, Margaret McCarthy, married one of Moses's natural sons, Aaron Moses Hart.

Moses had one legitimate son, Areli Blake, who survived him. After a trip to Italy, where he married Rosalinda Fiachhi, Areli returned to Canada and married Julia Seaton, with whom he had four children, including one daughter, Amelia Henrietta, and one son, William Blake, who left descendants. Among Moses's other children, Alexander Thomas married his cousin, Miriam Judah, the daughter of Moses's sister, Catherine Hart.

Ezekiel, Aaron's second son, was responsible for the Hart name going down in history. Elected a member of the House of Assembly of Lower Canada in 1807, he was barred from taking his seat. He married a New Yorker, Frances Lazarus, whom he had met while studying there, and they had children who continued their father's struggle for equal rights. They were Samuel Bécancour, Aaron Ezekiel, and Adolphus Mordecai. Only the last two had children.

Benjamin married a wealthy heiress whom he had also met while studying in New York, Harriott Judith Hart (her maiden name). After a time in Trois-Rivières, they lived in Montreal, where he and Moses Judah Hays, an extraordinary entrepreneur, became leaders of the Jewish community.

Nine of Benjamin's children survived him, but the only one I have been able to trace is Constance Hatton, who married her cousin Adolphus Mordecai, one of Ezekiel's sons.

Three of Aaron and Dorothea's daughters married Jews. **Charlotte** and **Sarah** married Moses and Samuel David who were brothers; **Catherine** married her cousin Bernard Judah (son of Samuel Judah, Dorothea's brother).

The action takes place mainly in Trois-Rivières, Montreal, and Quebec, between 1760 and 1860.

The historian Albert Tessier, founder of the archives at the Séminaire de Trois-Rivières, was also a filmmaker and photographer. He willingly sat for photographs, particularly for his nephew, Yves Tessier. This photo has a place of honour at the archives; the reflection in the glass is the consultation room. Tessier communicated his passion for visual documents, of which this book is one example.

Father Tessier (1895–1976) was a historian and cultural leader. The Séminaire archives include collections on the history of the institution and the region. Some particularly important collections have been categorized as cultural properties by the Quebec department of cultural affairs, including the Hart collection in 1979 and the Montarville-Boucher de la Bruère collection in 1980.

Introduction

O**N THE DAY IN** S**EPTEMBER** 1960 when Dr. Jacob Rader Marcus, director of the American Jewish Archives at Hebrew Union College in Cincinnati, sat in the archives room at the seminary in Trois-Rivières and saw for himself the richness of the collection of Hart documents, he had to turn away. He looked at me, absolutely dumbfounded and quite desperate. He had little time. The seminary archives were going to close around five o'clock.

In the top drawer of the filing cabinet were the Hart family papers and documents about religion. On that day, Marcus didn't realize that there were another five drawers stuffed with papers by or about the Hart family. To impress him, the archivist, Father Herman Plante, had decided to show him letters that Aaron Hart wrote to his sons when they were studying in the United States. In some, there were words in Hebrew. In others, their mother, Dorothea, had added greetings for Jewish families in New York. We also showed him numerous drafts by Moses, the oldest son, who had thought long and hard about religion—so long and hard that he founded a new one and, to spread the word about it, published a short treatise called *General Universal Religion*. Marcus shook his head, incredulous and nonplussed, for Moses Hart had had no love lost for the Catholic Church. Father Plante observed him impassively. Closing time had passed, and it was impossible for Marcus to return the next day; he had to leave for Montreal that evening.

I took him to my home to show him some of the documentation that I had brought back from recent stays in Ottawa. He followed me to the basement, where I had my study, and settled in with my papers. "May I take some notes?" he asked after a moment. I was flattered that my work seemed to interest him. He talked little and wrote much, almost too much for my liking. He knew that he was taking advantage of the situation, and he asked me from time to time if he could also note down this or that. He asked me questions. Communication was not easy as my English was a bit sketchy, but we found a way to make ourselves understood. Time passed, and I remarked that we had to think of getting to the train station. He

Father Herman Plante (1907–78) lost the power of speech after he suffered from cancer of the larynx, which destroyed his vocal chords. A historian and professor of theatre rhetoric, he met this sad challenge with courage and found refuge in the Séminaire archives. He learned to express himself using his esophagus with his close friends and by gestures with strangers. Dr. Marcus quickly grasped the tragic situation of this very dignified man, who had retained all of his theatrical demeanour.

took notes feverishly up to the last minute, accumulating a plethora of references to photostats that I had brought back from my research at the National Archives (today Library and Archives Canada).

Of course, Marcus already knew about the existence of Aaron Hart, especially through the family branch of his son Ezekiel, who was elected to the Legislative Assembly of Lower Canada, and Ezekiel's sons Samuel Bécancour and Aaron Ezekiel, who fought for the equality of Jews in Lower Canada. He told me about another Hart, from the fourth generation, Gerald Ephraim, the well-known historian and numismatist; his interesting collection of papers is conserved at the American Jewish Archives in Cincinnati and at the American Jewish Historical Society, whose archives had once been housed at Brandeis University and were now at the Center for Jewish History in New York.

Jewish Archives in a Catholic Seminary

On the way to the train station, Marcus, a Reform rabbi, asked me if the priest who managed the seminary archives might eventually agree to have the Hart archive microfilmed. I sensed that he was a little uneasy to have ventured to the heart of the Catholic province of Quebec, a "priest-ridden society," as historians used to say. I knew the book that he had written, *Early American Jewry,* published in Philadelphia in 1951. The last two chapters were about Canada, which he dubbed "the fourteenth colony," and covered the period from 1763 to 1794.[1] I really liked the expression "fourteenth colony," but was less impressed by his description of the anti-Semitism that Aaron Hart likely faced in Trois-Rivières from his arrival around 1760 to his death in 1800: "Aaron must have run up against a great deal of anti-Jewish sentiment in the forty years in which he lived in French-Canadian Three Rivers. Only a man who had taken many a hard knock, had been cursed as a 'Jew' by the drunken *engagés*, or politely snubbed by the rural aristocracy would have written to his politically ambitious son: 'You will be opposed as a Jew. You may go to law, but be assured, you will never get a jury in your favor nor a party in the House for you.'"[2]

Without realizing it, Marcus had succinctly expressed deep-rooted prejudices about the French-speaking *Canadiens*.[3] Yet, he knew nothing about Trois-Rivières in the eighteenth century and not much about the history of the Harts. His knowledge about the founder of the Hart dynasty was limited mainly to what he had been able to glean from the papers of Samuel Jacobs, another Jewish merchant who was Aaron Hart's contemporary, conserved at the National Archives of Canada.

In that late summer 1960, Marcus was rather shocked to have walked into a seminary, where members of the Catholic clergy were trained. I tried to make him understand the difference between "petit" and "grand" seminaries—the former leading as much to the liberal professions as to the priesthood. The presence in this college of a collection dealing with Jewish history intrigued him. He was a bit dubious.

Marcus seemed to me to be very old. In fact, he was in his early sixties then. Over time, I realized that he understood some French (he had married a Frenchwoman, Nettie Brody). In 1967, he made abundant comments on my master's thesis, "Les Juifs et la Guerre de Sept Ans" (The Jews and the Seven Years' War).* He had not much appreciated my comments about the Gradis family of Bordeaux, accomplices of Intendant Bigot.

---

* "The thesis has been written from the point of view of a French nationalist," he wrote to me on 8 July 1967. "It is my contention that a historian has no religion, no country, no ideal save the truth in an absolute sense. I realize that there is no such thing as absolute objectivity, but one should strive for it." His letter was accompanied by four pages of suggestions, many of a grammatical nature but others on my glossary and on the Gradis family. "Your treatment of Gradis is in my opinion unnecessarily harsh. I think that you have set out to denigrate him." I will not here reprise the argument that I laid out in my book *Les Juifs et la Nouvelle-France* (Trois-Rivières: Éditions du Boréal Express, 1968; this book was adapted from my master's thesis in history, "Les Juifs et la Guerre de Sept Ans," submitted to Université Laval in March 1967), but I consoled myself by observing that he made use of my argument about the importance of the Gradis and Franks families "in bringing supplies." "An army moves on its stomach," he wrote, "and the commissaries made a great contribution to the war. Most historians neglect to mention this fact." But I have not.

The Ultimate Conservation: Microfilm

On 13 September 1960, Marcus confirmed his institution's interest in preserving the Hart papers on microfilm. "We are not interested in microfilming the entire Archives of the Seminary," he wrote to me. "We are interested, however, in microfilming every item of Jewish interest that they have. I doubt whether they will have, at the most, more than five thousand items." We then realized that, in the excitement surrounding his visit, we had neglected to show him the inventory of the Hart collection. Thus began a long correspondence. Finally, I sent him the microfilmed ninety-eight-page repertoire prepared by Hervé Biron. "I want to congratulate Mr. Biron on a fine job well done," he wrote me on 14 November 1961. He agreed with our assessment of at least 100,000 documents, perhaps double that number, directly related to Jewish history. Raymond Denault, of the Canadian Microfilm Society, estimated that performing the transfer would cost around $3,000, on condition that there was someone on site to handle the documents. Marcus suggested that we "split the cost" and offered to compensate me for supervising the work. He rightly insisted on the importance of putting the collection beyond the risk of fire, "God forbid!"

Aware that the decision to make the microfilms would take some time, Marcus returned to spend two or three days in Trois-Rivières. I expected him to ask about the notes that he had left at my house, but he seemed to have forgotten about them, or maybe he thought he had lost them on the way to Cincinnati. I had found them when I returned home from taking him to the train station—with some relief, I must admit. But I quickly overcame my early reluctance and began to exchange information with Marcus and, especially, with the archivist David Rome, director of the Jewish Public Library in Montreal.

Arrangements were made between the authorities at the seminary and the directors of the Archives nationales du Québec and the National Archives of Canada. It was agreed that copies of the microfilms would be deposited at both places. Suddenly, everyone became aware of the significance of the Hart collection, which Marcus considered to be the most important to North American Jewish history between 1760 and 1860. Rome, to whom I had shown the letters with the words in Hebrew, shared this opinion, and he also explained various words to me: Pesach, *chametz*, matzo, Rosh Hashanah. He shared Marcus's enthusiasm and was pleased about the funding for the microfilm project.

DIRECTOR OF ARCHIVES: JACOB R. MARCUS, Ph. D.
   Adolph S. Ochs Professor of American Jewish History, Hebrew Union College-Jewish Institute of Religion
ASSISTANT TO THE DIRECTOR: STANLEY F. CHYET, Ph. D.

AMERICAN JEWISH ARCHIVES

CLIFTON AVENUE · CINCINNATI 20, OHIO

November 14, 1961

Mr. Denis Vaugeois
2245 6e Avenue, Apt. 2
Trois-Rivieres, P.Q.
Canada

Dear Mr. Vaugeois:

      I have gone through the "Fonds Hart" index
very carefully, and I want to congratulate Mr. Biron
on a fine job well done.

      We are very much interested in securing a
microfilm copy of practically all of the papers listed
in the index, with just one or two minor exceptions.
We want only one copy of the testament of Mordecai Hart
(page 11, top), and only one copy of J-a-8 (page 31).

      Do you think that some arrangement can be
made with the seminary whereby we would split the cost
of microfilming? This would make it cheaper for both
of us. Also, the seminary would be protected because,
in the event of a fire, God forbid, there would be an
available copy on microfilm.

      Will you please get in touch with the
authorities of the seminary to make such an arrangement.
I am deeply grateful to you for your interest in this
matter.

      May I have the pleasure of hearing from you
soon?

      With all good wishes, I am

          Very cordially yours,

          Jacob R. Marcus

JRM:jw

DEDICATION OF ARCHIVES BUILDING — May 31 · June 1, 1962

Dr. Marcus was an extremely courteous man who immediately encouraged me to continue my research, even though he was aware that the subject was quite foreign to me. He did not mollycoddle me, as his critique of my master's thesis shows. He had been warned about French-Canadian nationalism. Nevertheless, he always supported me, going so far as to put me up at his house during one of my research trips to Cincinnati. I remember his German-born housekeeper. I learned later that he had done his doctoral studies in Berlin from 1922 to 1925. Born in 1896, he remained active until 1995, the year of his death.

    Opening each letter from Dr. Marcus was an emotional moment for me. Here, I reproduce the one of 14 November 1961, concerning the microfilm project.

Dr. Mo

I se no way for you to keep פסח at Willm Henry thear fore you had Better Come Over hear the Sunday Before than you Neat not Due any thing to your House to git the חמץ out of your House it will be attanded with no Lass as its all Holy dayes that Pople Bay noting. I have wrote to H Judah and to Ben and Alex to Sell of for new yark the ... of may next as i am Determent to have tham hear if you Came at any rate Go afrats the Lakes for tham i will Pay all Expence you may be at as i hope you well not faile Baing hear פסח than Shall Say more to you on that Jurny it well Save you truble and Expence of Bakeing of מצה to Come hear

I had only one Letter by Decr Packt of ... of 5th Dear noting new the fall not than arrived haveng further to Mention tell i Se you And am Dr Mo your Loveng father Aaron Hart

28th March

This letter from Aaron Hart to his son Moses, in William Henry (Sorel), is dated 28 March 1794. It is interesting in several ways. It shows a father's concern about the slightest details. Aaron uses several Hebrew words to remind Moses of the holidays to come and their associated rituals. However, the letter is in English, a language that Aaron definitely had not mastered. Aaron ends the letter, "Noting new the fall not than arrived having further to Mention till i se you and am Dr Mo your Loving father Aaron Hart." Understanding this sentence is a triumph, but one might imagine that for Aaron writing each sentence was a victory combined with humiliation. He was never certain that his sons weren't ridiculing him for his poor English. This time, he begins the letter reminding his son that Passover is coming soon: "I se no way for you to keep PESAKH (HE MEM FEH) at Willam Henry," for which he would have to remove yeast from the house—". . . get the KHAMETS out of your house." As he mentions that he has written to H. Judah (in New York) and to Ben and Alex, I believe that he was counting on Moses to go and get them and bring them home for the holiday. "I will pay all Expence you may be . . . as i hope you will not fail being hear PESAKH." We could talk about it more and "it will save you trouble and expense of baking of MATSA to come hear." It is obvious that Aaron observed *Hag Ha-matsoth*, the feast of unleavened bread, and he wanted to be certain that Moses would respect it, too.

The Merits of Father Tessier

Father Tessier, the true founder of the seminary's archives, was very happy about the sudden interest in his Hart papers, which had barely escaped destruction. A tireless cultural organizer, Tessier had long been preparing for the celebrations for the tercentennial of Trois-Rivières in 1934. After returning from four years of studying theology in Rome and literature in Paris (1921–24), he began to publish in the Trois-Rivières weekly newspaper *Le Bien public* a series of articles called "La Grande et la petite histoire." Among his attempts to mobilize the population, he regularly encouraged people to let him know before they destroyed old documents.

In his memoir, *Souvenirs en vrac*, Tessier proudly recounts the history of the Hart collection.[4] "This rescue," he writes, "took all my free time for three or four years. After the death of Senator Jacques Bureau, his son Édouard advised me that he had found in the attic two large wooden crates filled with Hart papers.[5] He offered them to me for the archives. I accepted enthusiastically. They were a mine of dust and history. We found with the Harts' entire family, political, and business life—Aaron, Moses, Ezekiel, and more. Hundreds of packages tied with string, dated, containing official papers, contracts, correspondence, piles of paper that took me months to unfold, smooth out, and flatten under presses. There were more than 100,000 documents. I didn't throw out a single scrap of paper, not even the ones that seemed to be of no interest."

Tessier had occasionally demonstrated to me, in the archives hall, how he had stretched out clotheslines to dry the documents before making a preliminary classification, which the journalist and historian Hervé Biron would review. Biron sorted this mass of letters, contracts, invoices, legal papers, and drafts and plans of all types into twenty topics, identified from

Father Albert Tessier (1895–1976) was a historian, filmmaker, and cultural leader. The Séminaire archives include collections on the history of the institution and the region. Some particularly important collections have been categorized as cultural properties by the Quebec department of cultural affairs, including the Hart collection in 1979 and the Montarville-Boucher de la Bruère collection in 1980.

\\

Hervé Biron (1910–76), journalist, historian, novelist, and poet, was a man with a vast culture. Father Tessier asked him to inventory and sort the Hart papers. It was an enormous task, but Biron had four mouths to feed, including a disabled child who was extremely dear to the family and lovingly cared for. Journalism didn't pay well, and Biron liked history. He took on the challenge. On the cover page of the index to the Hart collection, Father Tessier wrote by hand, "Compiled by Mr. Hervé Biron. Revised and annotated by Father Gabriel Beaudoin and Jean-Marie Houle, 22 May 1950." Beaudoin and Houle were devoted to Father Tessier and were at his side in the Tavibois project (see René Hardy, *Tavibois, 1951– 2009* [Sillery: Septentrion, 2010, pp. 67 ff]).

\\

A to T. In the *Bulletin des recherches historiques*, he wrote a broad overview of the richness of the Hart collection—and the richness of the Harts as a subject.[6]

At the end of his article, Biron gave some details on Moses Hart, Aaron's oldest son:

He owned a number of seigneuries and held interests in a large number of others. I compiled large dossiers on the Bélair, Courval, Gaspé, and Grondines estates; the Marquisat du Sablé; the Longueuil baronate; the Sainte-Marguerite, Sainte-Marie, Saint-Maurice, Vieux-Pont, de Carufel, Dorvilliers, Dutord fiefs; and other fiefs in twenty townships, forty parishes, where Moses Hart had business relations.

This man was a fierce litigant. He must have brought several thousand lawsuits over the course of his career. The papers of this nature . . . indicate that Moses Hart did business with at least eighty-three law firms and thirty notaries' offices. . . .

If we look only at international business, I grouped almost one thousand documents (letters or detailed invoices) from thirty English companies supplying valuable details on the importation of British goods in the last century.

There was enough material to overwhelm almost any researcher, and in fact the Hart papers lay fallow for years, with two or three exceptions.

The Jewish Identity

The 1930s brought Jews into the Canadian news. A wind of anti-Semitism was blowing from the United States and, especially, Europe. In Montreal, a deep crisis was shaking Anglo-Protestant schools, which were flooded by tens of thousands of Jewish students.[7] Meanwhile, the Catholic Church maintained a sort of mistrust of Jews. In school, Catholic children learned that Christ had been killed by Jews. People also learned that there were good and bad Jews. This alone did not generate anti-Semitism, but such a weed didn't need fertilizer to spread, especially when certain politicians found it in their interest. For instance, the federal Conservatives, led by R. B. Bennett, funded the movement of Adrien Arcand, the "Canadian Führer."[8] Fortunately, the people of Quebec did not follow. "As the anti-Semitic trend gained strength in [Arcand's newspaper] *Le Goglu*, advertising by small businesses disappeared," writes Jean-François Nadeau.[9] Only one advertiser remained after 1933: the party in power in Ottawa—the Conservatives.

Nevertheless, a chasm existed between the Jewish community and French Canadians. Ignorance was rampant, and reciprocal. Prejudices were well anchored on both sides. Writings by novelists such as Mordecai Richler bring this world to light.

As for myself, I had no idea what a Jew was. In my master's thesis on Jews in New France, I tried to find out. First of all, I needed a way to identify Jews in the historical documents. Family and first names provided clues, but I had encountered men named Jacob, Levi, Moses, Benjamin, and David who apparently had no Jewish background.

Nevertheless, names from the Old Testament were widespread among Jews. They were used as both first names and family names. To avoid confusion (or, at least, to limit it), they would specify a filial relationship—for example, Isaac ben David, meaning Isaac, son of David. In various languages, "ben" was replaced by the suffix "sohn," "vitch," "vici," "sky," or "esco." Names such as Mendelsohn, Kaganovitch, Abramovici, Levinsky, and Tedesco came into existence. In Montreal, the names Samuelson, Rabinovitch, and Velasco, and many others follow this tradition. Itinerant or stateless Jews often wanted to identify with a city or a country and took names such as Rome and Pollack. Metals and gemstones inspired some family names: Goldberg (mountain of gold), Silberstein (silver stone), Rubenstein (ruby) or Ruby, Steinberg (mountain of stone). Names after colours included Weiss (white), Braun (brown), Roth (red), and Schwartz (black), and ensigns became the names Adler (eagle), Rothschild (red shield), and Stern (star).

It is always chancy to rely on family names as a source of Jewish identity even when they are inspired by functions performed at the synagogue: rabbi (*shohet* or *schohet*, giving the name Schechter) or cantor (*hazzan*, giving the names Singer, Cantor, Cantarini). It can be a sensitive subject. For instance, Marcus coldly informed me that the name Cohen comes from the Hebrew word *kohen* (priest), whereas I thought that it—as well as the names Cahen, Cohn, Cahn, Kohn, Kahn, and Kuhn—was derived from Cain. Levi is the source of the names Levy, Levis, Levin, Levine, Levinsky, Levinsohn, and other variations. Again, Dr. Marcus corrected my statement to the effect that Weil is an anagram for Levi and suggested that the name comes, rather, from *villa*.

In general, how can Jews be identified in archival documents? It must be hoped that at a certain point, an individual declares himself or herself to be a Jew. According to Jewish tradition, one is Jewish if one's mother is Jewish. Since Jews may identify themselves as non-practising, nonbeliever, or atheist, I had to consider the notion of belonging to a "tradition that creates Jewish awareness."[10] The French writer Raymond Aron called himself a French citizen of Jewish origin. "I use this term," he explained, "for lack of a better one, to designate Jews, among whom I place myself, who are neither religious nor practising, but who have nevertheless kept the Jewish culture."[11] Aron returned to his Jewish roots during the Six-Day War (5–10 June 1967).

Awareness of being Jewish was never completely subsumed. Here is an example: when I began working on the subject of Jews in Quebec, I spent time researching the life of Samuel Jacobs, who arrived in Quebec City in 1759 accompanied by children from a first union. He later married, before

For his most important letters, Samuel Jacobs often wrote his name in Hebrew under his signature. The owner of a schooner, he followed Admiral Saunders to Quebec in the summer of 1759 and supplied the troops with liquor. Jacobs, according to his own version, was getting ready to restock his supplies in Portugal when Murray requisitioned his small ship. Jacobs settled in Quebec, where he met Eleazar Levy, a friend of Aaron Hart's. The three quickly formed a partnership. They were the first Jews to set foot in the St. Lawrence Valley. When the fate of Canada was decided in 1763, creating a new British colony called the Province of Quebec, Jacobs moved to Saint-Denis-sur-Richelieu, a village on the river route to New York.

a Protestant minister, a French-Canadian woman with whom he had more children, who were baptized. His daughters studied at the Ursuline convent in Quebec City. Yet, Jacobs never stopped calling himself Jewish. He often signed his letters with the addition of his Hebrew name, Shemuel, a way of reaffirming his sense of belonging despite the circumstances. If he had distanced himself from the Shearith Israel synagogue in Montreal, it was perhaps to avoid the disapproval of his fellow Jews with regard to his family situation, even though there were precedents of this nature among the synagogue's members. Or perhaps it was the rites followed that kept him away.

Aaron Hart, the Trois-Rivières merchant, also avoided the Montreal synagogue. Did he reject the Sephardic rites practised there? It is possible, but almost all of the Jews who attended the synagogue in Montreal (which was founded in 1768) were apparently in the Ashkenazi tradition. In any case, Hart was very religious. He married a Jewish woman and educated his children in his forebears' traditions. An examination of the Hart collection leaves no doubt in this regard.

An Archival Treasure Trove

Declining interest in event-based history and biography has helped to keep historians away from the Hart collection. Furthermore, the sheer volume of material—the thirteen bobbins of microfilm full of anecdotes and details of daily life—is intimidating, and the collection contains nothing to attract proponents of the field of "new history."

Hervé Biron had taken on the Hart collection somewhat in spite of himself. Once he had finished his work on the collection, he had no desire to become the historian of the Harts. His primary interest was religion. In 1947, he published *Grandeurs et misères de l'Église trifluvienne, 1615-1947.* From his work on the Hart collection, he had kept aside a little secret that he left lying in a drawer until October 1948, when he published in the Trois-Rivières newspaper *Le Nouvelliste,* for which he was a journalist, a long article on Moses Hart, founder of a new religion. Moses Hart, as we have seen, was the oldest son of Aaron Hart and Dorothea Judah.

The editors of *Le Nouvelliste* did Biron the honour of devoting a full page to his article, under the headline "The tribulations of a Canadian author in the last century." The subhead read, "Mr. Hervé Biron evokes the difficulties faced by Moses Hart, author of a treatise on universal religion." The article

In the Saturday, 16 October 1948, edition of *Le Nouvelliste* of Trois-Rivières, journalist Hervé Biron shared with his readers his knowledge of the Hart family papers. Interested in religious questions, he concentrated on Moses Hart, the self-proclaimed founder of a new religion and author of a short treatise on the subject. Residents of Trois-Rivières must have been absolutely dumbfounded. Some no doubt dug into the depths of their local library for the short biography of Aaron Hart written by Raymond Douville.

The feature published in October 1948 had been long forgotten when the editors of *Le Nouvelliste* reprinted it (*Le Nouvelliste*, 16 May 1953). This time, to return to the Hart family history Biron used the pretext of a book published by the American rabbi and historian Jacob Rader Marcus, who devoted several pages of his work to the Hart family in Trois-Rivières. The newspaper's editors cut costs by reusing the pictures from the 1948 feature. A portrait of Moses Hart again dominated the page, even though Marcus had barely mentioned his pamphlet, *General Universal Religion*. In fact, Marcus wrote only a few lines about Moses, associating him with Enlightenment-influenced American deists (Marcus, 1952, p. 490).

(which appeared on Saturday, 16 October 1948) was accompanied by a montage of photographs showing Moses Hart and the cover page of Biron's "little secret," Hart's pamphlet titled *General Universal Religion* published in New York in 1815, as well as the invoice from the printer, a handwritten letter by the politician and historian Robert Christie, a document signed by Moses Hart in 1847, and a note in Hebrew.

Several years passed, and Biron had no doubt completely forgotten the Harts when he learned that Marcus had published the first volume of *Early American Jewry*. (The book was dedicated to Pretty Nettie Brody, to whom he had been married for twenty-five years. Marcus was born in 1895 and died in 1995; he was active up to the end of his life.) Since the book dealt at length with the Harts of Trois-Rivières, the editors of *Le Nouvelliste* decided to devote a full page to it (Saturday, 16 May 1953). Elements from the 1948 photograph montage were reused. No one questioned the place of honour accorded to Moses Hart, although Marcus had made only the briefest mention of him and his *General Universal Religion*. Moreover, Biron had obtained a good photo of Marcus, who looked youthful for his fifty-eight years.

In his long account, Biron recognized that Marcus might "give a much better interpretation of the character of the Harts than we French Canadians might," given "the great body of knowledge that he has on the question and his knowledge of the Jewish mentality, which for the most part escapes us." Biron may have had in mind the great commotion provoked by Raymond Douville's biography of Aaron Hart ten years earlier—a subject to which I shall return—but he did not want to discuss it further.

However, Biron could not ignore Marcus's comment about the "hard knock" that Aaron suffered squeezed between the "drunken *engagés*" and a "rural aristocracy."[12] To each his prejudices!

Father Tessier under the Influence of Valdombre

Even before Biron undertook his painstaking work, Tessier had begun what he called the salvage operation. One document quickly drew his attention: the inventory after death of Aaron Hart's property. In his way, Tessier was a tycoon. He liked to figure things out—a quality that he needed to be a successful publisher, photographer, and filmmaker. He recognized the scent of money.

Tessier was also the son of a farmer. He had seen his own father, or certainly his neighbours, make their pilgrimages to the village moneylender[13].

Left to right: Conrad Godin, Marcel Couture, Paul Dupuis, Albert Tessier, Raymond Douville, and Jean Pellerin, all members of the Société d'histoire de Trois-Rivières. The photo dated 5 March 1956 is by H.-A. Beaudoin of Studio Lumière in Cap-de-la-Madeleine. The meeting took place in the archives hall.

My grandfather, Ernest Massicotte of Saint-Prosper, regularly took his "offering" to the Germain brothers in Saint-Stanislas. This was before Quebec Premier Maurice Duplessis established the agricultural credit program. Only much later did I learn the meaning of this sad reality, which always procured me the pleasure of a little buggy ride.

Claude-Henri Grignon captured the popular imagination in 1933 with his novel *Un homme et son péché*. The author himself was touched by his protagonist, Séraphin Poudrier, and professed personal contempt for all moneylenders. Writing under the pseudonym Valdombre, Grignon associated Jews and greed in his *Pamphlets*. In Sainte-Agathe around 1937, a poster appeared declaring, "Jews are not wanted here." Undeniably, there was anti-Semitism in the air in those years. Tessier breathed in its stench, as did André Laurendeau and Pierre-Elliott Trudeau.

"It is not admiration," Tessier wrote in the third issue of the journal *Cahiers des Dix* (1938), "that dictates the subject of my article this year," which was titled "Two Wealthy Men: Aaron Hart and Nicolas Montour." As a first act of dissimulation, he likened Hart to Montour. The former was Jewish; the latter, Protestant. The exact origins of both men were not known. This is still true of Hart, but not of Montour: he was a descendant of Pierre Couc of Trois-Rivières, who married an Algonquin woman in a union registered in the diocese of Trois-Rivières.

Tessier, treading carefully, describes the work of notaries Badeaux and Renvoyzé: "The first two days [14–15 January 1801], the investigators must have thought they had been transported to a fabulous country. They spent hours opening coffers and bags the contents of which in *cash money* would have astounded a pirate most blasé in the facts of treasure. In a small, discreet, dark bedroom, Aaron Hart had carefully hidden in a suitcase and an iron trunk twenty-eight bags and bundles of coins of all denominations. More than $15,000 (or £3,600) in hard cash! Wonderful moments of voluptuous pleasure for a miser—to touch these coins of the realm and make them jingle." Grignon's influence was in the air.

Raymond Douville's "Historical Account"

Raymond Douville, a native, like Tessier, of Sainte-Anne-de-la-Pérade, was co-owner with Clément Marchand of *Le Bien public*. Douville was an excellent historian, accustomed to archival research; Marchand was a well-known poet who had twice won the Prix Athanase-David for literature. Douville was one of the few researchers who responded to Tessier's appeal. He even had the privilege of taking home armfuls of documents, which were thus lost to Hervé Biron's inventory. When he returned them to the archives, in the late 1950s, they delighted Jacques Lacoursière, then a young archivist just beginning his journey into history. I have kept the transcriptions that Lacoursière generously made for me, to which I have been able to add those made by Raymond Douville himself, which were deposited at the Trois-Rivières centre of the Bibliothèque et Archives nationales du Québec.

When Tessier described the masses of documents that Édouard Bureau had given him, Douville was all ears. The memory of the Harts was still very much alive in Trois-Rivières, "although," Douville wrote, "it was mixed with murky inaccuracies, the rotten fruit of the years. . . . When one realized that one was going to say the name Hart out loud, the idea of wealth immediately came to mind. All that remains of the name today is the memory of a fortune that has become legendary. A fortune made of money, land, power, prestige, and fear."[14]

"The name of Hart is all of that, indeed," Douville continued in the introduction to what he called a historical account dedicated to Aaron Hart. "But he was above all the ancestor, the starting point, solid enough to found a dynasty that has not yet breathed its last. . . . Aaron did his part. And it is not his fault if his descendants did not realize his dream. He laid the solid foundations for the edifice, knowing that a single man's life is not enough to build it. But he did his part fully, with pride, assurance, and genius."

Good intentions were not enough; Douville triggered a storm. Aaron Hart had arrived with the British conqueror. This did nothing to make him a sympathetic character. A conquest is more than a signature at the bottom of a treaty; to be meaningful, it must be accompanied by a change of masters and transfers of riches. The conqueror does not intervene for the wellbeing of the conquered. The conquered must be dispossessed. I hear someone protest: "No! The English wanted the best for us!" While another will reply, "And they took our best."

By his success, Hart gave meaning to the conquest of 1760. But readers need not worry; this is not my point. In a biography of Hart,[15] I have already explained how the conquered—or, at least, their descendants—have had the last word.

To put those who deny the consequences of the Conquest more at ease, I summarize the adventure of people who dealt with the Harts as follows: "You want my eggs, here they are; my chickens, here they are; my farm, fine; my house, it's yours. Ah! Now, you want my daughter . . ." In other words, it was a question of time before the Canadiens recovered everything. "Firmly attached to their properties, [tens of Aaron Hart's descendants] refused to lose everything by leaving [the] region"[16] of Trois-Rivières, where no one cared about their origins or their religion.

The Hart descendants themselves came to forget their Jewish origins. One day, Roger Marchand, Clément Marchand's oldest son, announced that he was marrying the very pretty Suzanne Houde. Impressed by my own cleverness, I said, as a joke, "You're marrying a Jewish girl?" He shrugged. Like most people in Trois-Rivières, he knew nothing about Jews. Suzanne didn't either! She asked her parents and discovered the secret of the Houde family's wealth: large real-estate holdings inherited from the Harts.

Douville reconstructed Aaron Hart's life very skilfully, putting his main character in a very good light. He committed just one error, and it was a significant one. One of Dorothea's nieces, Dolly Manuel,[17] who served as a maid at the Hart house, was found hanging in the attic. An official inquiry concluded that it was suicide. Wagging tongues accused Hart of sexual harassment. He "could not see a woman without burdening her with dishonest propositions," wrote Douville.[18]

"At the end of his life, Hart . . . to make up for his amorous adventures . . . questioned urchins who, naming their mother, reminded him that they might well be owed something from his life. And, putting his hand in his pocket, he took out a coin to give to such problematic descendants."[19] People from Trois-Rivières who are somewhat literate still tell this anecdote today. It must be said that Douville insisted that Hart, aside from his dalliances, was a "good family father," and he did his best to convince his readers of this.

Yes, all indications are that Aaron Hart was a good husband and father. The same cannot be said of Moses, his oldest son, whose philandering defies description. In my view, Douville mixed up father and son.

Jewish circles did not receive Douville's book favourably, but I found no indication that this disapproval was because of allusions to Aaron's supposed affairs. The discomfort lay elsewhere.

A Spark

There is one sentence in Douville's biography that was particularly offensive to Jews. The day after Aaron's death, the inventory of property led the notaries into "an old, dingy store." "It was a shapeless bazaar, smelling of Jews and plundering,"[20] wrote Douville, "for the Jews always come, at an opportune moment, to pick through the savings of sedentary citizens, who toil and sweat to fill the treasury of Israel."

Douville was drawing on the thoughts of Chevalier de Tonnancour, the principal victim in Trois-Rivières of the British Conquest, but many readers thought that these were Douville's own reflections. Hart seemed to Chevalier de Tonnancour to "have been expressly placed in this town by England to seize everything. . . . Hart, he no doubt told himself, was only a cog in the great monopolizing machine, but a necessary cog who worked, unaware, for the prestige of the conquerors. Hart himself, perhaps, did not know this. Above all, he was working for himself, he was getting rich, and he did not ask for more."[21]

Aware that he was sometimes on the brink of being offensive in the eyes of the Hart descendants, Douville tried, in conclusion, to redeem himself: "Superior men—and I believe that Aaron Hart was one of them—are always, owing to their qualities and their faults, at the edges of common humanity."

It was too late; the harm had been done. It took me a number of years to discover it. The newspapers of 1939 were not part of my required reading. I first was surprised to find in an essay by David Rome, the peaceful archivist of the Canadian Jewish Congress, the expression "the unfriendly Douville."[22]

It was an article by B. K. Sandwell, published in February 1939 in *Saturday Night*, that opened my eyes. Sandwell did not know the story of Aaron Hart, and he was no doubt ready to take Douville at his word, but "at this precise moment of Canadian and world history" it had been inappropriate, in his view, to publish this biography, and especially in French. "The attack upon the Jews, that easiest and most unscrupulous of all methods of undermining the fundamental concept of democracy, that the rights of human beings are not dependent upon race, creed or color, is

Realizing his youthful errors, André Laurendeau later reconciled with the Jewish community. In May 1955, he addressed the members of the Cercle juif de langue française. His speech was titled "The Evolution of French-Canadian Thought." To the right of the speaker are Moses Myerson and David Rome, director of the Jewish Public Library; to the left, Samuel D. Cohen. Myerson and Cohen were representatives of the Canadian Jewish Congress. Laurendeau was assistant editor-in-chief of the newspaper *Le Devoir,* where he had been working as a journalist since September 1947. (CJCCNA PC1-4-22A-9)

so widespread and so successful at the moment, that those who wish democracy to survive will beware of adding to the weapons of the attackers."

"Mr. Douville," Sandwell added, "possibly without intending it, has certainly added to the antisemitic armoury in French Canada." And what was the reason for Aaron Hart's successes that was likely to shock all French Canadians who would read the book? The reason may have been Hart himself, his origins, or the medieval system that prevailed in Canada before 1760, Sandwell posited. He had his own idea in this regard: the Conquest, in his view, was a real tragedy, but it also made the transition from a feudal system to a market economy possible.

Douville's friends, particularly a certain Jacques Renaud, defended him.[23] The most significant review of Douville's article came, however, from

André Laurendeau: "This little Jew, who one imagines with slanted features, a lolling head, and long-winded speech, had a genius for business. . . . He was a textbook usurer, but, more than that, a sober paean to tenacity, industriousness, and agile intelligence." Laurendeau concluded, "Among the recently published books, [Douville's] is one of those that is the most pleasurable to read."[24]

In 1948, Raymond Douville joined the historical society, La Société des Dix. He returned to the subject of the Harts in 1952, when he wrote an interesting article on Moses Hart's political and religious opinions,[25] followed, in 1958, by an enlightening account of his youth and family life.[256] Had Douville realized, in examining Moses Hart's life more closely, that it was he rather than Aaron who had drawn gossip following the death of Dolly Manuel? If he had, he did not breathe a word of it. However, his tone was clearly more prudent. He wrote of a "taste for risk," "financial flair," and the Harts having become "truly a national institution." In his view, Moses remained an upstart. "His stormy temperament, his lack of scruples, and his cynicism did not allow him, alas, to give his fullest, and for a number of years his faults and eccentricities surrounded the name of the Harts with a discredit that did not do justice to the true value of this family."[27]

My Interest in the Hart Collection, then in Jewish History in General

In 1957, I accepted a one-year position as a teacher at Séminaire Saint-Joseph de Trois-Rivières. It was only the second year that laymen were among the institution's faculty. Chance brought me to Father Tessier. He invited me to visit his archives and introduced me to his friend Raymond Douville, who was finishing his second article on Moses Hart. He took advantage of my presence to scold Douville, who was returning, after twenty years, important pieces of the Hart collection. I then witnessed a passionate exchange on the Harts. One thing led to another, and Father Tessier persuaded me to apply for a grant from the Canadian Jewish Congress to undertake research that would highlight the bicentenary of the arrival of the first Jews in Canada.

I have copies of a letter addressed to Samuel Bronfman, president of the Canadian Jewish Congress, and of exchanges with Saul Hayes, chief organizer of the National Bicentenary of Canadian Jewry. On 28 January 1961, I thanked Hayes for the assistance I had received: the sum of $200. This

David Rome was born in 1910 in a Lithuanian shtetl called Zasliai, some 100 kilometres from Vilnius; he immigrated to Canada in 1921. After first living in Vancouver, then studying literature in Seattle, he moved to Montreal in 1938. There, he earned a degree in library science at McGill University in 1939. He was editor of the Canadian Jewish Congress's *Congress Bulletin*, published in Montreal, until 1953, when he became director of the Jewish Public Library in Montreal, a position that he held until 1972. He then became the archivist for the Canadian Jewish Congress. He published a number of books in Yiddish and English, which Pierre Anctil describes in *Cent ans de littérature yiddish et hébraïque au Canada* (Sillery: Septentrion, 2005, pp. 366–67). As will be noted from the many references in this book, the collections of documents that Rome published have been extremely useful to me, as were our long discussions during which he taught me about Judaism. In the photograph to the left, he is proudly addressing guests at the opening of the new library on Rue de l'Esplanade on 4 October 1953. (Source: CJCCCNA-PC1-4-21K).

was the cost that I had naively estimated for my early research. I had not yet figured things out! It was, I believe, the only grant that I applied for in a half-century.

My visits to the Jewish Public Library had put me in touch with its director, David Rome, who I suspected had given a thumbs-up to my application for financial aid. It was the beginning of a marvellous friendship. I had much to learn. I have so many memories of that time. One day, I was at the counter of the Jewish Public Library, then situated on Esplanade Street in Montreal, and a lady asked me in a distrusting tone, "Are you Jewish?" I quickly responded, "No, no, no!" I am still ashamed of that. At the downtown Saint-Sulpice Library, they invariably asked me, "Are you an anti-Semite? You must be, to ask for so many documents on Jews."

David Rome, Lithuanian by birth, was a man of exquisite delicacy and utter kindness. We frequently went to an inexpensive Chinese restaurant. One Friday, I saw him attacking some spare ribs. "Dr. Rome," I exclaimed, "that's pork!" He smiled, looked at the spare ribs on my plate, and retorted, "It's Friday!"

At the time when microfilming of the Hart collection was underway, Rome was impatient to have in his hands copies of some of the documents that I had told him about. He rarely left Montreal, due to a difficult family situation. With the blessing of Father Tessier, I became his courier. Furthermore, he helped me to understand what I was bringing him.

Rome was working with Louis Rosenberg, who, in 1955, had begun to publish documents in a newsletter called *Canadian Jewish Archives*. He showed me an 1829 statute that authorized Jews to keep their own civil registers. Three registers had been planned, one each for Montreal, Quebec City, and Trois-Rivières.

Douville had never found anything of the sort in Trois-Rivières. He advised me to go to the legal archives of the city of Montreal and to ask Jean-Jacques Lefebvre about it. Mr. Lefebvre sullenly told me, "We don't have a register like that here." I pressed the matter, trying to explain the legislative context to him. "If we had such a document, wouldn't you think I would know!" was his response. Nevertheless, he let me look at a few files. As luck would have it, I found exactly what I was looking for. Incredulous, he stared at the valuable document. After some hesitation, he agreed to provide me with photostats of the first few pages.

I was waiting for an opportunity to show my find to Rome when I received a note from Rome telling me to stop my research on the registers.

In volume 1, issue 6 (May 1962) of the *Canadian Jewish Archives*, Rosenberg reproduced seven pages of the register, thanking "Mr. Jean-Jacques Lefebvre, Chief Archivist of the Superior Court of Montreal, whose co-operation and assistance made it possible to find it." I showed Dr. Rome my own photostats. He could not believe his eyes, which went from the latest issue of the Canadian Jewish Archives to the photostats that I was showing him. Mr. Lefebvre wanted to earn points in Rosenberg's eyes and was unaware of my own work with the Jewish Library.

Rome was delighted with the various documents that I brought him. When he saw the certificate signed by John Franks in 1768 on which "Upon the true faith of a Christian" has been replaced by "Upon the true faith of a Jew," I realized that I could never bring him greater satisfaction.

Over the years, I regularly wrote articles on Jewish history and some biographies for the *Dictionary of Canadian Biography*: Aaron Hart, Moses Hart, Ezekiel Hart, Aaron-Ezekiel Hart, Samuel Jacobs, and, my favourite, Sigismund Mohr (1827–93).[28]

The time has come to celebrate 250 years of the Jewish presence in Quebec. I missed the bicentenary, so I will now pay my debt to the Canadian Jewish Congress. It is one of the many things I learned from Aaron Hart, who, among other things, introduced me to the world of business.

According to Benjamin Sulte, Aaron Hart was born in Germany, possibly in the Palatinate near the Haardt Mountains, or somewhere in Bavaria. If this hypothesis is true, one may presume that he had been subjected to anti-Jewish prejudice in his country of origin. This illustration shows a thug throwing stones at a "wandering Jew" or simply a homeless Jew, whose head is clearly at the centre of a series of concentric circles forming a target. It is a truly sinister image. The poster is dated 1747; Aaron Hart was born around 1724.

CHAPTER I

The Arrival of Aaron Hart: A Dynasty Is Born

I N 1492, JEWS WERE FORCED to flee the horrifying persecution of the Spanish Inquisition. Five years later, they were forced out of Portugal for the same reason. At the same time, the Europeans were "discovering a new world"—"discovering" as if the continent that they had found, situated somewhere between Europe and Asia, existed only once they arrived on its shores. Named America following a misunderstanding among a small group of intellectuals in Lorraine,[1] this landmass was to become an important refuge for victims of political and religious conflicts.

In the sixteenth century, Jewish people found a tolerant atmosphere in Amsterdam. They came from Spain and Portugal, then from Lithuania, the Ukraine, Germany, Poland, and Russia. Sephardic and Ashkenazi Jews lived side by side while trying to preserve their differences. At the time, Amsterdam was the hub of international trade. The Dutch were extremely active in conducting maritime trade from the Indian Ocean to the Atlantic Ocean. When they landed at the mouth of the Hudson River, a few Jews were among the pioneers who settled in Manhattan and Fort Orange (Albany). In 1667, through the Treaty of Breda, these settlers became British subjects, a situation that was confirmed by the Treaty of Westminster in 1674.

Following the example of the French who settled along the St. Lawrence River, the Dutch made an alliance with the Indians living along the Hudson River. This treaty, signed in 1618, was the forerunner of the Covenant Chain, a series of alliances that were later concluded between the British and the Agniers, who were called Maquas by the Dutch and then Mohawks by the British.

For more than a century, New England and New France were at war. The latter, through a vast network of alliances with countless Indian nations, gradually surrounded the English colonies. French exploration enterprises were largely financed and supported by the fur trade, and the Great Lakes region quickly became their preserve.

The war that was to put an end to French hegemony in North America broke out in 1754 in the Ohio Valley. During the first three or four years of the conflict, the Anglo-Americans incurred one defeat after another. When the wind changed, around 1758, English merchants, including some Jews, prepared to invade the territory that had been closed to them up to then. Among those banned from New France, Jews, particularly those in New York, were waiting impatiently. The grass always appears greener on the other side of the border.

Jeffery Amherst, Commander in Chief

After winning the battle of the Louisbourg fortress in the summer of 1758, General Jeffery Amherst earned the supreme command of the British forces in North America. His superiors had noted his methodical mentality. Some historians, in fact, see him as a little "slow," in that he preferred calculation to military engagement. He advanced at a cautious pace. If he captured a fort, he took care to make sure that it was rebuilt before continuing on his way. He always laid out a path of retreat in case it was needed. Given his deliberate state of mind, he had every chance of dying in his bed and none of perishing on the Plains of Abraham.

Amherst's army left New York in early June 1759 and headed for Lake Champlain, but, thanks to the commander's usual hesitations, his troops barely got past Crown Point. Amherst started to erect fortifications and build boats; then, learning of the defeat of the French at Quebec, he returned to his winter quarters. He took up pen and paper and wrote a plan for the meeting of three armies in Montreal in the summer of 1760.

Amherst had missed a rendezvous with General Wolfe in the summer of 1759. Leading a battalion of thirty thousand men, some ten thousand of whom were soldiers, Wolfe, at the cost of his life, had managed to eke out a victory over Montcalm in September 1759. The following year, 1760, therefore promised to be decisive. James Murray, now in command of Quebec, was impatiently awaiting reinforcements. In the spring of 1760, after a long battle, Chevalier de Lévis forced Murray to take refuge within the town's fortifications. Finally, British reinforcements came up the St. Lawrence and this forced Lévis to end the siege of Quebec and return to Montreal, which was the target of the final assault planned by Amherst.

On 14 July, Murray left Quebec for Montreal leading some three thousand men. At the same time, a small company of 3,500 men, led by William

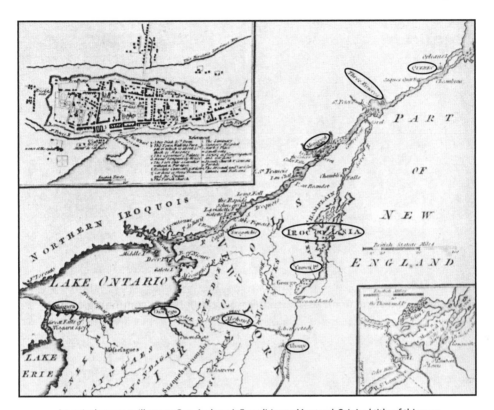

A particular map to illustrate Gen. Amherst's Expedition to Montreal. Original title of this map published in the *Gentleman's Magazine* as early as early October 1760. On 8 September 1760, Amherst noted in his journal: "I believe never Three armys, setting out from different & very distant Parts from each other joined in the Center, as we intended, better than we did." This map illustrates the routes followed by De Haviland via Lake Champlain, Murray coming up the St. Lawrence from Quebec to Montreal, and Amherst himself travelling down the St. Lawrence from Oswego with a stop at Swegatchy.

Haviland, was making its way across Lake Champlain and down the Richelieu River. Amherst, meanwhile, took the Upper St. Lawrence; he reached Oswego on the south shore of Lake Ontario, the meeting place, on 9 July. It was a strategic location, linked to New York via the Oswego, Mohawk, and Hudson rivers.

Amherst's plan was a classic three-pronged attack, and this time it was certainly the right one! In New York, celebrations were being prepared for a decisive victory over what remained of the French forces.

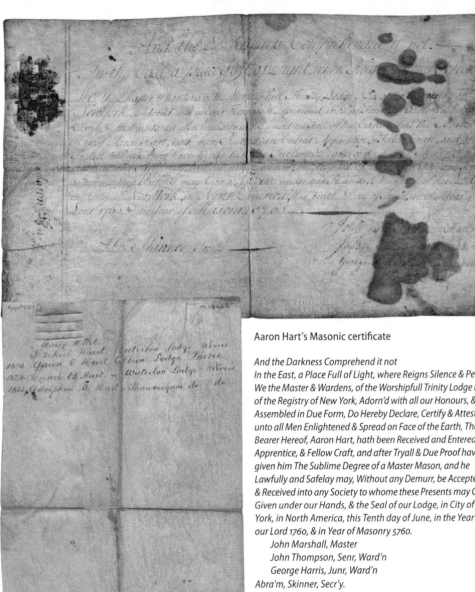

Aaron Hart's Masonic certificate

And the Darkness Comprehend it not
In the East, a Place Full of Light, where Reigns Silence & Peace.
We the Master & Wardens, of the Worshipfull Trinity Lodge No. 4
of the Registry of New York, Adorn'd with all our Honours, &
Assembled in Due Form, Do Hereby Declare, Certify & Attest,
unto all Men Enlightened & Spread on Face of the Earth, That The
Bearer Hereof, Aaron Hart, hath been Received and Entered
Apprentice, & Fellow Craft, and after Tryall & Due Proof have
given him The Sublime Degree of a Master Mason, and he
Lawfully and Safelay may, Without any Demurr, be Accepted of
& Received into any Society to whome these Presents may Come.
Given under our Hands, & the Seal of our Lodge, in City of New
York, in North America, this Tenth day of June, in the Year of
our Lord 1760, & in Year of Masonry 5760.
   John Marshall, Master
   John Thompson, Senr, Ward'n
   George Harris, Junr, Ward'n
Abra'm, Skinner, Secr'y.

Aaron Hart wrote his name below the lodge seal. The
original is conserved at the McCord Museum in Montreal.
The certificate is written on vellum.

On the back appear the names of Aaron's son Ezekiel
and three of Ezekiel's sons. It is likely that this document
was kept in Ezekiel's family and that his grandson, Gerald
Ephraim, a historian and collector capable of
appreciating its value, donated it. Ezekiel and Samuel
Bécancour belonged to the Waterloo lodge; Aaron
Ezekiel, to the Albion lodge; Adolphus Mordecai, to the
Shawenegam [Shawinigan] lodge.

This portrait of Aaron Hart is of unknown origin. It is taken from *The Jew in Canada* by Arthur Daniel Hart. A copy of the portrait, with the title *Commissary Aaron Hart*, was reproduced in the brochure published for the 150th anniversary of the foundation of the Spanish and Portuguese Jewish Congregation, also called Shearith Israel. This community was an extension of the Shearith Israel congregation of New York, which also gave rise to congregations in Philadelphia, Savannah, Richmond, and Charleston.

Aaron Hart: The First Jew in Canada?

On 10 June 1760, Aaron Hart, having solemnly taken all the prescribed steps, was granted the status of "Sublime Degree of a [Master] Mason" by Abraham Skinner, secretary of Trinity Lodge No. 4 of New York.[2] This is the oldest known document concerning Aaron Hart. He had made up his mind that he would be in Montreal on the day of its surrender. This Masonic certificate would serve as his passport.

Long considered the first Jew to settle in Canada, Hart was actually preceded by at least one other, Samuel Jacobs, who was in Quebec in the summer of 1759. As the historian Jacob Rader Marcus has written, "The careful historian soon comes to the unfailing rule that no Jew is ever the first Jew in any town: there is always one who had been there before him."[3]

Numerous historians have set out, with varying degrees of success, to trace the beginnings of the Jewish presence in New France. The story of Esther Brandeau, a pitiful young woman who fled to Quebec, has been told many times, but for serious scholars, Aaron Hart and Samuel Jacobs were clearly the first.

A Masonic certificate attests to Aaron Hart's presence in New York in early June 1760. Amherst was no doubt also in New York, making his final preparations to march on Montreal. He had chosen Oswego as his base of operations, and he began to gather men and munitions there in mid-May. He arrived on 9 July and observed Haldimand's excellent organization. Obviously, such an undertaking posed numerous challenges for those supplying the troops. Aaron Hart's role was as sutler. On 10 August, Amherst set off for Montreal. The route was full of obstacles. The St. Lawrence River was a succession of rapids.

Jacobs settled in the British colony of Nova Scotia, formerly Acadia taken over from the French after the Treaty of Utrecht in 1713. There was already a small Jewish community. For example, there is a price list printed for the merchants Nathans and Hart in 1752 by Bushell, the printer of the *Halifax Gazette*. That price list became an important historical document in itself, but also for other very specific reasons[4].

For his part, Jacobs decided to follow Sir Charles Saunders's fleet in the summer of 1759. After the surrender that autumn, Murray requisitioned his small schooner. Jacobs complied; he could always ask for compensation later. Since he was not able to make his planned voyage to Portugal, he set up a business in Quebec, profiting from the reconstruction that was taking place in the town.

Aaron Hart in the Wake of Amherst

Although no document has yet surfaced that establishes this as fact, it is plausible to think that Aaron Hart was among the eleven thousand men who descended the St. Lawrence in August 1760. It has been claimed that he belonged to a small group of sutlers (purveyors) who provided support to the intendants charged with supplying the troops. Historians are a little like magicians: with a stroke of a pen they move thousands of men hundreds of kilometres. The reality is more prosaic. The provision and transportation of war munitions, equipment, food, and services of all sorts had to be planned. The authorities could not, or would not, make provisions for all of these logistics; much was left to private initiative. There was therefore room for resourceful small businessmen.

A few later documents give us a glimpse of a certain friendship between Frederick Haldimand, one of Amherst's lieutenants, and Aaron Hart, who was clearly under the protection of this high-ranking officer. We might imagine that they got to know each other as they headed down the St. Lawrence. Both were foreigners among the British troops: Hart was Jewish; Haldimand, Swiss. They both spoke a bit of German. Marcus, who carefully studied the letters written by Hart, mentions "a German-accented phonetic English."[5] The historian Benjamin Sulte, who lived near Aaron's descendants in Trois-Rivières, claimed that the Hart family was originally from the Hartz Mountains in Bavaria.

Some historians portray Hart as one of Amherst's officers, rather than a sutler. "Aaron Hart," wrote Benjamin Sack, "was a member of his staff and when, following the city's surrender (September 8, 1760), Amherst triumphantly rode through the old city gates, Commissary Hart was one of the officers who rode by his side.[6] Sack was repeating, almost word for word, what the historians J. Douglas Borthwick[7] and Martin Wolff[8] had written. Anne Joseph, in *Heritage of a Patriarch*, quotes a newspaper clipping from 4 May 1907—no doubt *The [Montreal] Star*, she writes—in which are mentioned, "among the officers of the British invading armies," "Commissary Aaron Hart, Emmanuel de Cordova, Hananiel Garcia and Isaac Miranda."[9] This complicates things further: Aaron Hart had no doubt arrived in Canada by that time, but who were the three with Sephardic names? Other authors, writing between 1892 and 1945, also mention Uriel Moresco and Fernandez Da Fonseca, who seem to have left no trace. In any case, it seems certain that Aaron Hart accompanied Amherst's army when it arrived in Canada.

Taking his cue from Benjamin Sulte's interest in the Hart family, Sulte's nephew, Gérard Malchelosse, wrote extensively on the first Jewish families in Canada at the time of the British Conquest. At first, he simply reprinted, without checking them, the lists of names that were circulating among scholars at the time.[10] He also depicted Aaron Hart and several other Jews as officers in Amherst's army.

A meticulous historian, Francis J. Audet, wrote in *Le Bien public* on 23 February 1939 to correct his friend Malchelosse, who had begun to publish a series of articles on the first Jewish families in Quebec in that newspaper. "At the time," Audet noted (our translation), "no Israelite could obtain a rank in the English army." The commissaries of food supplies were simple purveyors whose names did not appear in the Army List, he noted; they belonged to a civil branch of the army.

Malchelosse took note and corrected himself in a synthesis article published in 1939 in *Les Cahiers des Dix*. Although he had apparently been led astray by many authors, it must be noted, in his defence, that he had found in the notes of Émilie Sulte, Benjamin's sister, a persistent legend that a number of Aaron Hart's descendants had perpetuated: in exchange for services rendered, the Harts had obtained permission to form a regiment named the Hart N.Y. Rangers. "In 1759," Émilie wrote (our translation), "Aaron Hart was its colonel, when General Amherst came to inspect the regiment that was posted in the vicinity of Albany. Amherst proposed that Aaron join him in besieging the town of Quebec, promising to have him promoted to

This pin is an enigma. The McCord Museum has only a photograph of it. It is therefore impossible to conduct a careful examination of the piece itself. It is presented as a "Hart family militia badge." The conservator dated it in the twentieth century. In the centre, the deer is the emblem of the Hart family and is found on the family coats of arms (see p. 70).

brigadier general." Apparently, Aaron accepted, but the king of England later refused to give his assent.

Aaron Hart's biographer, Raymond Douville, accepted the fact that Aaron led a regiment that joined Amherst's army in the summer of 1760.[11] He was aware of Audet's opinion, but he persisted in believing in the existence of Aaron Hart's regiment. Documents prove that Aaron was in fact a commissary officer in Amherst's army. According to Douville, Garcia, Cordova, Miranda, Moresco, and others belonged to the regiment.[12] The Hart family came to be convinced that their ancestor had directed a regiment composed of Sephardic Jews. Émilie Sulte told Douville that she had information "straight from the mouth of one of Aaron's descendants."

The McCord Museum in Montreal conserves two items supporting this version: a photograph of a pin marked *Harts Reg't Militia* (the pin is owned by an unknown collector) and a portrait of Aaron Hart in an officer's uniform. The miniature that supposedly portrays Aaron Hart has been reproduced many times. The writer Michel Solomon used it for the cover of his novel inspired by Aaron Hart's life.[13] Solomon's protagonist, Aaron Hart, states that he recruited a battalion at his own expense, which he put at the service of His Majesty—that is, Amherst. Thus, Solomon skilfully circumvents the difficulty: his Aaron Hart did not wait for an officer's appointment but took the initiative.[14]

Irving Abella, who organized a beautiful exhibition called "A Coat of Many Colours: Two Centuries of Jewish Life in Canada," reproduced the same portrait in his book, *A Coat of Many Colours,* with the simple legend "Aaron Hart, 1724–1800, the most influential of the early Jewish settlers in Canada." Abella claims that Aaron was a sutler and adds, "He was not, as some early historians would have us believe, a British officer—no Jew was—and he certainly did not ride into Montreal alongside Amherst, as

The McCord Museum long presented this very handsome portrait as being that of Aaron Hart, the founder of the Hart dynasty. Now, it is thought to be a portrait of Aaron Ezekiel Hart (1803–57), attributed to Dominique Boudet and painted around 1831 (M 18640). Aaron Ezekiel was the first Jew in Lower Canada to pass the bar exams. He became a highly respected lawyer and was well integrated into French Canadian society. No doubt aware of the support that he had received from the Parti Patriote for bills that he had backed with his brothers Samuel Bécancour and Adolphus Mordecai, he later drew close to the Parti Patriote led by Papineau.

other early versions claim."[15]

For a long time, the McCord Museum considered this miniature to be a portrait of Aaron Hart. Recently, experts consulted by the museum's directors attributed it to the painter Dominic Boudet,[16] who apparently had painted not Aaron Hart but one of his numerous grandsons, Aaron Ezekiel Hart (1803–57). According to René Chartrand, a military historian and expert in uniforms of that era, the figure in the miniature is wearing "the uniform of a general (of a brigade, I believe) of the French army in the Napoleonic era." Chartrand dates the portrait to around 1810. Asked about the likelihood of a Jew being an officer in the British army, he answered, "Jews (and Catholics) were not legally entitled to receive an officer's commission in the British regular army. The situation changed for Catholics— that is, the Irish regiments—in the 1830s, and much later for Jews. They had the reputation of following the armies as sutlers. They were shopkeepers." He added, "In the late seventeenth century, a commissary was an administrative department of the army that fell under the Lords of the

Gerald Ephraim Hart (1849–1935), son of Adolphus Mordecai Hart, made a career in insurance; his vocation was historical research. He published *The Fall of New France, Notes of 1837,* and *The Quebec Act of 1774,* and left an uncompleted manuscript titled *Corrections in British, American, French and Canadian History,* conserved among the Gerald E. Hart Papers at the McCord Museum. He was also very active in the Society for Historical Studies, of which he was president, and the Antiquarian and Numismatic Society of Montreal. He was a member of the Spanish and Portuguese Synagogue.

Treasury and not the military authorities."*

Before coming to the firm conclusion, in light of the known documents, that Aaron Hart was but a simple sutler, I turned to the writings of two of his descendants, Adolphus Mordecai Hart and Gerald Ephraim Hart. Of course, I followed in their footsteps and tried to gather every document that they had produced. I reviewed my own documentation once again.

I had at hand a series of notes intended no doubt for the *Annales* published by the Ursuline nuns of Trois-Rivières. One nun, probably Mother Adelina Bois de Saint-Ignace, had summarized a letter of 10 May 1870, written in English, received from one of Aaron's grandsons, Adolphus Mordecai Hart, in which he recounted the origins of his family.[17] He specified that Aaron Hart "had followed General Haldimand to Canada." Adolphus Mordecai belonged to the intellectual branch of the Hart family; he was a lawyer and the author of various essays about the United States. Unfortunately, he had neglected to write about his illustrious ancestor, and I found nothing other than the notes conserved by the Ursuline nun.

I had one remaining hope: Gerald Ephraim Hart. This renowned numis-

---

* A number of researchers have examined the lists of British military troops hoping to uncover some Jewish soldiers. One name constantly arises: Alexander Schömberg. The son of a Jewish doctor who had emigrated from Germany, he enlisted in the navy in 1743 and was promoted to captain in 1757. As commander of the frigate Diana, he facilitated the landing of Wolfe's troops at Quebec in September 1759. Educated in the Jewish traditions, he had to be baptized to have a career in the British navy. This was certainly not the case for Aaron Hart, who remained faithful to his forebears' religion.

THE

F O R M

O E

P R A Y E R,

Which was performed at the

JEWS Synagogue,

IN THE

City of N E W-T O R K,

On Thurſday Ocʒober 23, 1760;

Being the Day appointed by Proclamation for a
General Thankſgiving to Almighty GOD, for
the Reducing of Canada to His Majeſty's
Dominions.

Compoſed by D. R. JOSEPH YESURUN PINTO,
In the Hebrew Language :

And-tranſlated into Engliſh, by a Friend to Truth.

───────

N E W-Y O R K:

Printed and Sold by W. WEYMAN, at his New Printing-Office, in
Broad-Street, not far from the Exchange, 1760.   (Price 4d.)

The Form of Prayer. This document shows that New York Jews were, by all evidence, faithful and loyal British subjects and the target of a propaganda war (Frégault, 1955, pp. 18–22). Canada was the enemy to be fought; the French, the Canadiens, and their Indian allies represented a terrible threat to the inhabitants of the Thirteen Colonies. In addition, New France was a territory closed to Jews. The surrender of Montreal in September 1760 was celebrated enthusiastically by the Jews of New York. Samuel Jacobs, Eleazar Levy and Aaron Hart then made their first forays into this future British colony. It should be noted that the prayer was written in Hebrew—a way for Jews to affirm their distinctive nature.

matist, one of Adolphus Mordecai's sons, wrote a book called *The Fall of New France, 1755–1760*, published in 1888. It occurred to me that he might have chosen this subject as a pretext for glorifying his ancestor. Many years before, I had purchased a copy, somewhat out of a sense of family loyalty, for, little by little, as I read letters from parents to children, I had come to feel a part of the Hart family. When I had bought the book, I had briefly examined it and admired the quality of the illustrations, which were utterly worthy of a collector. Now, I read it carefully, slowly, even though I was eager to meet Amherst on his march to Montreal in the summer of 1760. On each page, I expected to find Aaron Hart in the company of Frederick Haldimand. Finally, realizing how little there was left to read, I became uneasy. The convergence of the three armies was settled, by the author, in seven pages.[18] In another couple of pages, spanning twenty-four hours of history, the terms of the surrender of Montreal had been decided upon and the document had been signed. On 8 September 1760, without a single gun being fired, "the complete surrender of the Province was made. . . . Colonel Haldimand, afterwards Governor, being the first to enter the city and plant the British Ensign of Possession."[19] Gerald Ephraim Hart had written not a single word about his great-grandfather, Aaron Hart. This silence seemed eloquent.

So, where was Aaron Hart in the summer and autumn of 1760? It is not possible to establish this with certainty, but I hypothesize that he was not far from Haldimand, who was responsible for organizing the immediate repatriation of the French troops.

News of the surrender of Montreal reached New York quickly. There was rejoicing. On 23 October, one Jewish congregation gathered at their synagogue and brought out a "Proclamation for a General Thanksgiving to Almighty GOD, for the Reducing of Canada to His Majesty's Dominions."

Levy Andrew Levy, partner of William Trent

The British victory brought down barriers and borders. Drawn by the fur trade, some Jewish traders travelled in the wake of the British troops as they pushed westward. William Johnson's successes at Fort Niagara in July 1759 finally opened the floodgates. Merchants rushed into the Great Lakes region. Some were caught up in the turmoil created by Chief Pontiac's uprising; others were major suppliers of the troops, including Jacob Franks and his son, David Franks,[20] as well as Joseph Simon, Gershom Levy, and Levy Andrew Levy. The latter Lévy was William Trent's partner. Trent was later identified as having provided the indigenous people with blankets contaminated with smallpox. Though they were partners, Lévy might have been unaware of what Trent was actually doing.

This diabolical idea of spreading smallpox was Amherst's. Although crowned with glory after the surrender of Montreal, he was completely inept with the Indians and sought to change radically the relations with them that had been established by the French. To say that Amherst feared the Indians would be understating the situation; he was scared to death of them and fervently wished for their extermination.

Informed of Pontiac's uprising, the ministers in London found it difficult to understand how Amherst, the conqueror of the French forces, could be humiliated by bands of barbarians. His honour was at stake—and he lost it completely by ordering Henry Bouquet, his officer dealing with the rebels, to distribute contaminated blankets and handkerchiefs. By all accounts, however, Bouquet does not seem to have executed such an order.

In *The Conspiracy of Pontiac and the Indian War after the Conquest of Canada*, published in Boston in 1870, Francis Parkman revealed Amherst's instructions to Bouquet; he urged him to use "every stratagem" including

Dr The Crown to Levy, Trent & Comp: for Sundries had by
Order of Capt: Simon Ecuyer Commandr

1763
June 3 — To Sundries for the Militia Vizt

8 Tom hawks	. . . .	d 10/	£42.0.0	
6 large Tin kittles	. . . . .	10/	3.0.0	
1 Canteen	. . . .		0.3.0	45.3.0

To Sundries deliv: the following & prisons Vizt

Nossa & his Comerad	2 pr Leggins a 6/	0.12.0		
	1 Breech clout	0.8.0		
	Cash	1.0.0	£2.0.0	
Yaaly 2 dress'd Deer skins	a 15/	1.10.0		
	1 Blanket 20/ & Cash 3/6	1.3.6	2.13.6	
Thompson & Johnston 1 dress'd Deer skin			0.15.0	
Isaac & John Cox	2 pr Leggins a 6/	0.12.0		
	2 Breech clouts 8/	0.16.0		
	2 pr garters 1/6	0.3.0		
	3 Indian Hand kr	0.10.6		
	1 dress'd Deer skin	0.15.0		
	2 Ruffles &c	15.0.0	17.16.6	
Abrm Bidles 1 pr Moccersons	. . . .		0.7.6	23.12.6

To 1 Box Candles for the Guard &c wt 121 lb N: a 2/3 . . . . . £13.12.3

To Sundries got to Replace in kind those which were taken
from people in the Hospital to Convey the Small pox
to the Indians Vizt

| 2 Blankets | . . . . | a 20/ | £2.0.0 | |
| 1 Silk Handkerchef 10/ & 1 linnen do: 3/6 | . . . . | | 0.13.6 | 2.13.6 |

£ 85.1.3

Fort Pitt Augt 13th 1763
I do hereby Certify that the above Articles amounting to Eighty five
Pounds One Shilling & three pence Pennsylva Curry: were had for the
uses above mentioned
S. Ecuyer Capt Commandt

Philadelphia May 22d 1764
Deduct for 27/ of the Kings Droves employed eight days } 27.0.0
carrying your Stone from Fort Pitt to Fort Bedford £6 Shillrs }

£ 58.1.3

The claim is entitled, "**The Crown to Levy Trent & Company for sundries had by orders of Capt Simeon Ecuyer Commandant.**" Ecuyer accepted the charges: "I do hereby Certify that the above Articles . . . were had for the uses above mentioned." (Jones, 2004, p. 97. British Library, Bouquet Papers, ADD.21654f168.)

As soon at the Great Lakes region was opened up to English merchants, William Trent (1715-87) became partner with three Jewish merchants from Pensylvania, Joseph Simon, David Franks, and Levi Andrew Levy. The partnership lasted from 1760 to 1769. In May 1763, Chief Pontiac led an uprising against the British. Trent formed a company of militiamen to support the regular troops led by Captain Ecuyer who was charged with the defence of Fort Pitt. Trent was the son of a Pennsylvania pioneer and was aware that history was being made. He kept quite a detailed diary from 28 May through 16 October 1763. In addition to very useful information on life in the different forts of the region, Trent kept an account of the intensity of the conflict. The situation was dramatic and forts were falling one after the other: Michilimackinac, Detroit, Fort Ligonier, Fort Sandusky, Fort St. Joseph where the garrison was massacred, etc.

Trent talked about the discussions, negotiations, scheming, attacks, small skirmishes, and more. On 24 June, he reported an exchange with two chiefs, Turtle's Heart and Mamaltee (Maumaulttee). " . . . They returned and said they would hold fast of the Chain of friendship. Out of our regard to them we gave them two Blankets and an Handkerchief out of the Small Pox Hospital. I hope it will have the desired effect." (William Trent's Journal at Fort Pitt, edited by A.T. Volwiler, Historical Society of Pennsylvania, vol. XI, no 3. Notes and Documents, p. 400). According to Francis Parkman (*Conspiracy of Pontiac*, II, 44), Amherst wrote to Bouquet, "We must on this occasion use every stratagem in our power to reduce them."

Four days earlier, on or about 24 May, Levy Andrew Levy was taken prisoner less than a league away from Fort Pitt. He would be freed shortly after but several of his employees were killed. He prepared a claim with Trent for an amount of 85£ including 2£ 13s 6p for "sundries got to replace in kind those which were taken from people in the Hospital to Convey the Smallpox to the Indians."

"to inoculate the Indians by means of blankets" to spread smallpox among them. For more than a century, experts analyzed this issue from every angle. There was in fact a smallpox epidemic, but historians hesitated to attribute its cause to Amherst's orders.

The late Bernard Assiniwi, a Cree writer and historian, once told me that such actions had definitely taken place at Fort Pitt. He died before bringing me his proof. I found it in a book by David S. Jones.[21] The author went so far as to reproduce William Trent's expense account, in which he claimed reimbursement for "sundries got to replace in kind those which were taken from people in the Hospital to Convey the Smallpox to the Indians."

At Fort Pitt, on 24 June 1763, the commandant, Siméon Écuyer, a Swiss-born mercenary, was negotiating with two Delaware chiefs, Turtle's Heart and Maumaulttee. He gave them some merchandise and a little liquor. Trent added a small personal gift: "We gave them two Blankets and an Handkerchief out of the Small Pox Hospital. I hope it will have the desired effect."[22]

Included in Trent's expense account for the time of the siege of Fort Pitt was £2 13s6d for the contaminated merchandise that he had given to the Indians. On 13 August 1763, Siméon Écuyer approved the expenditure for these articles "for the uses above mentioned." On 24 May 1764, Quarter-master L. S. Ourry rejected the transportation costs and a claim for candles but accepted the rest, a total of £58 1s3d. Thomas Gage, Amherst's successor, authorized the payment on 13 August 1764.

Jewish Merchants Following the Troops

The Jewish merchants who ventured into the region, most of them following the troops as sutlers, were harshly dealt with. No one lost his life, although legend has it that Chapman Abraham barely escaped the whipping post. A few years later, six of them—Isaac Levi, Levi Solomons, Benjamin Lyon, Gershom Levi, Ezekiel Solomons, and Chapman Abraham—signed a memorandum asking Governor Carleton for compensation. In Amherst's correspondence for the year 1761, there is mention of a "Levi a Merch't at Montreal" and a "Levy's Goods stop at Tuscarora by the Indians."[23]

The authorities generally recognized the assistance that the Jewish merchants provided to the advancing troops. The procurer general, Francis Masères, who was generally favourable to the merchants, including the unfortunate Pierre Du Calvet, defended Levi Solomons as "a Jew of a very good character."[24] Masères apparently hoped that Solomons, insolvent, would take advantage of a future bankruptcy law and pleaded for the creation of a "commission of bankrupts."

The military occupation of the St. Lawrence Valley began with the surrender of Montreal and ended with the institution of a civil government on 10 August 1764. These four years of military rule gave British merchants a chance to explore business opportunities. Amherst quickly left for New York, leaving Thomas Gage, Ralph Burton, and James Murray responsible, respectively, for the administrative regions of Montreal, Trois-Rivières, and Quebec. There were obvious rivalries among the three military officers.

In August 1764, Murray was finally chosen as governor general in an atmosphere of friction and animosity. Not only did he not get along with Burton and Gage, but he gave the cold shoulder to most of the English merchants who surrounded him. In his report of 29 October 1764, he denounced the "unbalanced fanatics doing business." "Nothing will satisfy them," he wrote, "except the expulsion of the Canadiens who constitute perhaps the bravest race and the best on Earth."[25] In fact, things had gone poorly since June 1762, when he had expanded British efforts to relieve the misery of the Canadiens, who were victims of "the calamities of war and a bad harvest." "The English merchants and traders," he wrote, "joined this generous movement quickly and with good spirit" to calm and reassure this "conquered people."[26]

But quickly, the wind shifted. Some merchants denounced "a military government so oppressive and intransigent," were concerned about the French "paper money" in circulation (see chapter 2), asked that the governor be recalled, and demanded nothing less than a "House of Representatives . . . as in all other of His Majesty's provinces." "There are here," they stated, "a more than sufficient number of loyal and interested Protestants . . . to form a Legislative Assembly. . . . And the new subjects [the Canadiens] could be authorized, if His Majesty felt it appropriate, to elect Protestants without their having to say the oaths that their conscience will not permit them to say."[27] Among the twenty-one signatories were three French names and that of one Jew, Eleazar Levy. Levy was quite a character. Burton had requisitioned a large amount of his merchandise in Montreal in January 1764, and he spent years claiming reimbursements and damages. He appealed to the Privy Council in London and even went to England himself. He won his case, but Burton was no longer in the picture and so he was unable obtain justice. Perhaps as a consolation prize, he received a notary's commission on 24 December 1766.

The first Jews to land in the Province of Quebec spread out through the

6209

In this carefully written document (8 February 1768), the signatories related their misadventures in the Great Lakes region during "the late war with France and the subsequent Indian War." They demanded assistance from Governor Carleton. The signatories were Levy Solomons, Benjamin Lyons, Gershom Levy, Ezekiel Solomons, Isaac Levy, and Chapman Abraham. The last signatory, Dorothea's future brother-in-law, had barely escaped being tortured.

territory, as if by reflex. Isaac Levy, John Franks, Elias Solomon, Lazarus David, and Eleazar Levy settled in Quebec in 1760 and 1761; Hyam Myers regularly travelled between Quebec and New York; and Samuel Jacobs, understanding the importance of the route to New York, chose to go to Saint-Denis-sur-Richelieu.

There was a good deal of traffic through Montreal. Merchants from the Great Lakes set up shop there. Although many of them returned to New York, including Isaac Levy, a partner of Aaron Hart's, others arrived to take their place, including Levy Simons, Myer Michaels, and Andrew Hays.[28] I learned of their presence by chance, as I perused business papers conserved mainly in the archives of Samuel Jacobs, William Johnson, and the Hart family. They formed business partnerships to share risks and keep abreast of market conditions.

Aaron's Choice

No doubt influenced by Haldimand, Aaron Hart chose to live in Trois-Rivières, where he was joined by his brother Moses and at least one cousin, Uriah Judah, his future brother-in-law. In the years that followed, he would encourage other relatives to settle in Yamachiche, Rivière-du-Loup (now called Louiseville), and Berthier.

A total of twenty Jews were living in the Province of Quebec around 1763. That doesn't seem like many. In fact, Sheldon J. Godfrey and Judith Godfrey, in their remarkable book *Search Out the Land*,[29] established that there were only 133 Protestants present living under the governments of Quebec and Montreal in 1764.

In a letter to Thomas Gage written in July 1764, Frederick Haldimand, posted in Trois-Rivières, indicated that "the Group of British merchants" in this city comprised a Jew, a sergeant, and an Irish soldier. Ralph Burton, in his report of April 1762, had counted in Trois-Rivières 114 "heads of household" and a total population of 672. The district of Trois-Rivières had a population of 6,472, including 1,217 "heads of household."[30] All of them did business with Aaron Hart . . . for better or for worse.

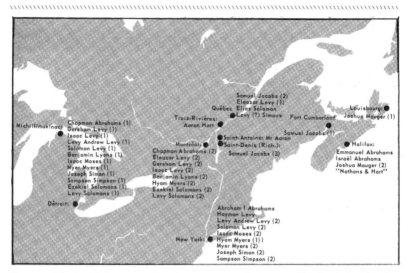

This map, "The Jewish Presence in New France, 1760–63," was created by Claude Bouchard and is taken from *Les Juifs et la Nouvelle-France* (Montreal: Boréal, 1968). Looking at the names listed, I have serious doubts that Sampson Simpson was Jewish. The name "New France" is justified, at least until 10 February 1763, when the Treaty of Paris was signed. Notable is the attraction of the Great Lakes region to Jewish merchants. They travelled in the wake of the invading troops and occasionally acted as sutlers.

Trois-Rivières, 1784. The perspective chosen by James Peachey is quite impressive. Has he exaggerated the size of this large village? No doubt, but nevertheless Trois-Rivières was being transformed by merchants such as Aaron Hart. Peachey was employed as a surveyor, which would lead one to believe that this painting is relatively accurate. The mill on the left can be found on old maps, such as Bouchette's of 1815. Between this mill and the houses was a commons that gave its name to the Saint-Philippe neighbourhood called La Commune.

CHAPTER 2

"The Little Jew of Trois-Rivières": Secrets to Success

After the surrender of Montreal, while Frederick Haldimand was overseeing the departure of the French troops, Jeffery Amherst was supervising the British take-over of the country. The negotiators of the Treaty of Paris were not able to firmly establish the boundaries of the conquered territory. At the last minute, the French secretly ceded to Spain the watershed west of the Mississippi River, as well as New Orleans. Amherst had a border problem on his hands. Nevertheless, he sent troops to the Great Lakes forts to advise the garrisons of the French defeats.[1] Meanwhile, he finally made his way to Quebec, where he surveyed the Plains of Abraham, the site of two famous battles, one in September 1759 and the other in April 1760.[2] He could now return to New York with complete peace of mind.

On 16 September, Ralph Burton, a career military officer, was made responsible for the government of Trois-Rivières. He was not very pleased with this assignment. He would have preferred Quebec or Montreal, but James Murray was already filling the position in Quebec, and Thomas Gage had been picked over him for Montreal.

On 23 September, Burton called the residents of Trois-Rivières together to "take the oath of loyalty and submission due to His British Majesty George Second"; he also announced that their weapons were being confiscated. He met with them in the parlour of the Récollets convent, into which the British had moved; they later replaced the Catholic church with an Anglican church.

The military occupation lasted until 10 August 1764. The population docilely agreed to participate in the various work parties that Burton organized. According to Amherst's instructions, the inhabitants were to "settle their affairs according to their own laws"—that is, the Custom of Paris.

Burton tried to verify the presence of English "deserters or prisoners" who might have hidden among the population, especially in two nearby

This decorative Polish sheet
of paper is particularly evocative.

The oldest document in the Hart collection that concerns Aaron Hart is dated Quebec, 12 August 1761. Eleazar Levy, on behalf of Hugh Finlay, acknowledges receiving from "Mr Aaron Hart" the sum of "twenty-six pounds, eight shillings, and seven pence in full." The receipt does not indicate where Aaron was at the time. In the Samuel Jacobs collection conserved at Library and Archives Canada, we found a document dated 28 March 1761 that bears the names of Aaron Hart and a certain Levy, who could be Eleazar or Isaac. Very soon after their arrival in this colony occupied by British troops, Hart, Levy, and Jacobs had forged a business relationship, which they maintained throughout their lives.

Abenaki villages; he counted, in passing, several dozen Acadian refugees, who were thereafter deprived of the pension paid to them by the French authorities. In the end, some three hundred English soldiers were billeted at Trois-Rivières or in nearby parishes.

Aaron Hart's Arrival in Trois-Rivières

When did Aaron Hart settle in Trois-Rivières? It is reasonable to think that he was with the troops commanded by Burton. On 21 October 1761, and again on 14 November of that year, Samuel Jacobs wrote to Hart in "Three Rivers." He mentions their good friendship, which led him to part, at cost price, with mittens purchased from Eleazar Levy. In fact, Hart, Jacobs, and Levy were in close contact.

On 4 July 1762, a fire broke out in Trois-Rivières. Haldimand, who was temporarily replacing Burton,[3] reported to Amherst that the fire had been caused either by cinders that escaped from the pipe of a negligent smoker or by candles that were not properly extinguished. "The Jewish English Merchant Hart, who suffered the most, may have lost £400 or £500, the Others much less, but as they are very poor, the loss is considerable for them, and even more so for homeowners."[4] On 7 July, three days after the fire, Hart rented a house from Théodore Panneton, Jr., and declared himself an "English Merchant living in this town." For an annual rent of £300, he occupied "a house and lot situated in this town, yard, garden, stable, and appurtenances." Conserved in the registry of the notary Dielle, this first official document signed by Aaron Hart was concluded in the presence of Sieur Jean-Baptiste Badeaux "serving as interpreter."[5] Hart arranged the ground floor of the house as a general store and moved his personal effects to the second floor.*

Marcel Trudel, in his interesting study *Le Régime militaire dans le Gouvernement des Trois-Rivières 1760-1764*,[6] notes purchases of "forge furnaces" by Aaron Hart[7] and mentions a loan of £100 that he made to the government, for three months, at an interest rate of 5 percent.[8] In a letter to Gage on 29 July 1764,[9] Haldimand, who had returned to Trois-Rivières, reported, "Everything is calm." He specified that "the corps of British Merchants of 3 Rivières Composed of a Jew & an Irish reformed sergeant and soldier is easier to lead than that of MontRéal. However"—he added enigmatically—"my trustee admits to having naught but a few confused notions about a certain Magna Charta on which are based limitless privileges; and as Ideas that may favour licence spread easily, my Jew misses no opportunity to remind me of his rights as a British Subject, and I admit that he has frequently raised my ire. But I have always kept him to his duty without objection."

Haldimand was more subtle and patient than Murray and Carleton in dealing with the English merchants, those "wild fanatics." Hart was no doubt more reasonable than the others, but by all evidence he was not shy to argue with Haldimand. In his correspondence after 1764, Haldimand no longer mentioned Hart, in whose premises the authorities had opened a post office in compliance with an order publicly issued by Ralph Burton on 23 August 1763. Hugh Finlay, the postmaster in Quebec, already had a business relationship with Hart.

---

* On 7 September 1764, a deed of sale for a lot on Rue Notre-Dame, in Trois-Rivières, was concluded between Aaron Hart and Jacques Perrault, merchant of Quebec, before the notary Saillant de Collégien, the defender of the famous Marie-Josephte Corriveau, dit La Corriveau. Perrault was acting on behalf of the de Noyelle family. The widow of Nicolas-Joseph de Noyelle held powers of attorney for Charles-Joseph de Noyelle, knight of the Ordre royal et militaire de Saint-Louis, and for Fleurimont de Noyelle and Lanoix de Noyelle. The Treaty of Paris, signed 10 February 1763, gave the vanquished population eighteen months to sell their property to subjects of His British Majesty.

"As per act of Parliament . . . a general post office has been established for the countries belonging to the British Empire & the superintendant of said bureau having judged appropriate . . . to establish a post office in Quebec and to commit Mr. Finlay to manage it, in compliance with the content of said act, who has opened a post office in the town of 3 Rivers, in the house of Mr. Hart, merchant. Ordered in 3 Rivers this 23 August 1763. [signed] R. Burton."

During the American Revolution, which gave rise to an invasion of the "province of Quebec," the mail was tightly controlled. By this time, Hart had given up the job of postmaster. On 16 February 1780, Hector Theophilus Cramahé reported to Haldimand about some letters that he had in hand, including one from "Henry Hart, addressed I believe to his brother, the little Jew of Trois-Rivières."[10] Cramahé, the governor's secretary, belonged to the small group of French-speaking Huguenots who settled in the new British colony at the time of the conquest.[11] The Huguenots were French-speaking Protestants who served as intermediaries between the Canadiens and the British administrators. Cramahé had been there since 1759. He had many times travelled to all parts of the colony. He knew everyone.

It was very rare for Aaron Hart to be designated by the word "Jew." Canadiens in general had no opinion about Jews. There hadn't been any in New France, and after 1760 they were seen as English or, simply, foreigners.* The British themselves rarely used the word "Jew"; Hart, who had picked up English on the fly, did not himself know how to spell the word. In a letter written in March 1786[12] to his son Moses, he recommended, "You will say as lettle as passeble about your businiss to any of the jues in New York."[13] He then warned him about a "jues House."

---

* French Canadians have always remained at arm's length from Jewish reality. When North African Sephardic Jews began to immigrate to Quebec in the 1960s, people spoke of them as Catholic Jews, because they spoke French. When I began my research on the Harts, in the 1960s, I conducted a little survey, with journalist Yvon Thériault, among the population of Trois-Rivières. To the question "Can you name any Jewish retailers?" people responded by mentioning Nassif, Baraket, Courey, and Boumensour, all of them Lebanese or Syrian, but no one named Steinberg, the name of a supermarket chain with outlets in Trois-Rivières.

How should we comprehend Cramahé's expression "petit juif" or "little Jew"? At the time when this note was written, Haldimand and Cramahé were on chilly terms. Was he making fun of Haldimand's sometimes embarrassing protégé? Was he simply alluding to Hart's small stature? Did many people call Hart that? Regardless of what was said about him, or why, Hart carved out an important place for himself in Trois-Rivières. In less than twenty years, he became a prosperous merchant. How did he achieve this?

Paper Money

The period of the military regime was one of uncertainty. The war was continuing; peace negotiations dragged on. Some Canadiens dreamt of returning to France. The more time passed, the worse the news got. The British were racking up the victories. In the end, the French wanted just to save their islands—the Antilles and the French Shores of Newfoundland. The islands were synonymous with wealth. Santo Domingo alone enabled France to control 40 percent of world sugar production and more than 50 percent of coffee production. Compared to sugar, furs faded in importance![14]

William Pitt, the victor in the Seven Years' War, was not sure that England would decide to keep Canada. From the beginning of negotiations, rumours were circulating that London might return Canada to France in order to keep its sugar islands, especially Guadeloupe and Martinique. The sugar lobby, composed of wealthy British planters, was concerned. Above all, the British planters did not want to face competition from the French planters, who sold at much lower prices. Addicted to sugar in their tea, the British were willing to pay a high price to feed their habit. Pitt also knew that if England kept Canada, it would remove from the English American colonies a threat at their borders that had justified, up to then, the maintenance of links with the homeland. Choiseul, the French foreign minister, followed the same reasoning. At the time of the signature of the Treaty of Paris, 10 February 1763, he is said to have murmured, "We have them!" Twenty years later (1783), a new Treaty of Paris was signed, recognizing the independence of the United States.

At the time that Choiseul signed the first Treaty of Paris (1763), the British emissaries were concerned about the fate of the paper money in circulation in the former French colony. An addendum was immediately written assuring that "His most Christian Majesty, entirely disposed to

Playing-card Money

The use of playing-card money was introduced to New France to make up for the shortage of coins. The history of playing-card money is well known. Introduced by Intendant De Meulles in 1685, this money consisted of playing cards on which face values were printed and the intendant's seal affixed. At first, the cards were converted into cash when the king's ships arrived but, over time, an imbalance arose. In 1713, after France was defeated in the Spanish War of Secession, there was so much playing-card money in circulation that the authorities were unable to convert all of it into money. The king bought it up at half of its face value. History was repeated when war broke out again in 1756. At the French department of foreign affairs, under the title "Mémoires et documents, Amérique," there are a series of council judgments concerning payments for "Canadian paper." Mixed in with these are documents showing the state of inflation. By all evidence, the repeated delays were related to the concern with keeping track of the unreal value engendered by the conflict. Neither did the king want to enrich speculators nor was the necessary money available.

On 16 July 1759, Abraham Gradis wrote to his son, "God willing . . . that we can save this colony," and repeted it elsewhere. The French archivist Claude de Bonnault sees this as a sign of the patriotism that motivated the two shipowners from Bordeaux. However, Gradis also wrote, "If we lose this colony, this paper will not be paid out." Gradis and his son were worried, and justifiably, about the fate that awaited the "Canadian paper," which they held in enormous quantities. They were not the only ones in this situation (see Vaugeois, *Les Juifs et la Nouvelle-France* [Montreal: Boréal, 1968], pp. 74–75). The authorities had to reassure the population and, especially, the businessmen. There was extreme mistrust. For instance, Intendant Bigot had to pay cash if he wanted to purchase wheat. Payment of bills of exchange was suspended in October 1759. In the spring of 1760, His Majesty issued new reassurances to the colony: "Bills of exchange drawn in 1759 and 1758 will be paid exactly three months after the peace, with interest starting from the due date until payment; that those drawn in 1759 will be paid in 18 months, and cash notes or orders will be withdrawn and well paid as circumstances permit" (Shortt, 1925, p. 940).

render to every one that justice which is legally due to them, has declared, and does declare, that the said bills, and letters of exchange, shall be punctually paid."[15] In other words, France guaranteed "the payment of bank notes and bills of exchange that were issued to Canadiens for the supplies provided to the French troops." Would this ensure reimbursement "within a suitable time"?[16]

In May 1763, the residents of Montreal made an inventory of their paper money: cards, warrants, and bills of exchange. The people of Trois-Rivières did the same the following month. They gave Burton a register with a total of 1,735,370 *livres*, 16 *sols*, and 11 *deniers*. This was a considerable sum, and heavy speculation clouded the issue. France's commitment soon provoked shameless trafficking, and money changed hands under fraudulent conditions. Alerted, the French government issued a set of conditions: it would reimburse only "paper money actually in the possession of Canadiens" and would demand to know "by what means the bearer had acquired it."[17]

Sarah Solomon

The McCord Museum possesses important documents on the Harts and a number of portraits of family members, including many photos by William Notman. I found this portrait of Sarah Solomon, by Louis Dulongpré, on the museum's Web site. Of course, I was pleasantly surprised to find a Jewish woman and a little intrigued. Why her? It turns out that she was the wife of Thomas McCord, the grandfather of the museum's founder, David Ross McCord (1844–1930). The biography of Thomas McCord in the *Dictionary of Canadian Biography*, written by Elinor Kyte Senior (volume 6), notes that Sarah was the daughter of Levy Solomon(s) and Louise Loubier. I knew of several Levy Solomon(s), but I had not known that one of them had married a non-Jewish woman. According to Kyte, Louise Loubier had previously had a long relationship with the goldsmith Jacques Terroux. The DCB also contains an article on Terroux, written by José Igartua, and this biography led me to Marcel Hamelin's doctoral dissertation on Terroux, who was a fierce speculator in "Canadian paper."

In his dissertation (Université Laval, 1961), Hamelin examined Terroux's speculation activities. Terroux had taken advantage of the disarray created by the surrender of Montreal to purchase, at a low price, certificates, *billets d'ordonnance*, and bills of exchange, which he turned to good profit. In the fall of 1760, a number of properties were put up for sale. Terroux purchased them, but he paid with "Canadian paper." On 13 May 1761, for instance, Samuel Jacobs paid 200 pounds sterling for a stone house situated in La Canoterie that Terroux had acquired for "30,000 pounds in money *billets d'ordonnance* printed by the French treasury and signed Bigot" (Minutier de Sanguinet, no. 1403, 1 April 1761; no. 1417, 13 May 1761). Terroux had required cash payment from Jacobs. What was the value of the *billets d'ordonnance* with which Terroux had paid for the property? One thing is certain: Louis Dunière, the initial seller, had received Monopoly money. Terroux could not keep making similar transactions at the pace at which he amassed paper money. According to Hamelin, he had accumulated a value of 1,333,681 pounds, a good portion of which he foisted on Francis Rybot, a London merchant. Even though he had paid very little for the paper money, he still needed some coins. He became indebted and, in turn, fell prey to Rybot. In 1765, he joined the ranks of Rybot's victims and discreetly left the colony.

In early 1764, a second inventory was taken in Trois-Rivières, and holders of paper money in that town began to file past Conrad Gugy, secretary of the government, who was assisted by Jean-Baptiste Perrault, Hertel de Rouville, and Godefroy de Tonnancour. Declarations were accepted until 8 June. On the 14th, Haldimand approved a register containing 759 declarations for a total of 1,561,330 *livres*, 18 *sols*, 11 *deniers*.[18] This extraordinary document, offering a snapshot of the population immediately after the British conquest, is still waiting to reveal all of its secrets. Among the holders of paper money were two "English merchants": Aaron Hart, 2,341 *livres*, and Jeremiah Daily, 1,285 *livres*. The churchwardens of various parishes declared a total of 58,735 *livres*, 13 *sols*, and 6 *deniers*. Members of the clergy also came in their own names, as did a number of seigneurs. At the top of the list was Godefroy de Tonnancour, who declared that he held 153,359 *livres*, 0 *sols*, and 5 *deniers*.

The issue of repayment was a long, drawn-out affair. In fact, the Canadiens were never to see the colour of the equivalent of 16 million *livres* in paper money bearing "the stamp of the arms of France and Navarro."

There remained, buried under mattresses, enough cash to confound the best exchange expert. In 1759, Murray had established an equivalency between the French six-*livre* écu and the Spanish *piastre*.[19] After 1763, he tried to bring a bit of order to the coins in circulation: Johannes, guineas, gold Louis, and French and Portuguese *pistoles*. In 1760, the English had introduced new currency aligned with the pound sterling; these were added to the silver Louis, the white écu, the gold Louis doubloon, the farthing— all fading memories of France and now valued in relation to the Spanish *piastre*, which was widely used in North America and the Antilles.

"Without an equivalency table or an assay balance," wondered Fernand Ouellet, "how would a resident in the market in the town of Quebec quote the price of his foodstuffs in three different, sometimes non-averaged currencies?"[20] Murray was even forced to forbid the cutting up of Spanish *piastres*, pieces of which were used as small change. "How," continued Ouellet, "could one give change in French currency to a customer who had paid for his goods in English currency?"

Once, in a Marrakesh souk, I saw a child trading with tourists who held out U.S. and Canadian dollars, Moroccan *dirhams*, French francs, Spanish pesetas, Portuguese escudos, Italian lire, and more. He quickly made change for customers who were nervously fingering their calculators. It made me think of Aaron Hart jingling pieces of change, a habit he picked

Note on money

Although this document isn't terribly legible, the inflation is very clear. Between 1755 and 1759, the cost of a quintal of flour rose from 14 to 60 *livres*; a pound of butter, from 8 *sols* to 3 *livres* and 10 *sols*; a turkey, from 2 *livres* to 12 *livres*; a pound of candles, from 12 *sols* to 3 *livres*; a pair of wool socks, from 7 *livres* to 20 *livres*; a barrel of wine, from 100 *livres* to 1,200 *livres*. The *livre tournois*, the French pound, was worth much less than the pound sterling introduced by the British. It should be noted that the *livre* was an accounting instrument; it had no equivalent in hard cash.

The *écu* was the basic cash piece. It was worth ten *lives tournois*. The *écu* was called the silver Louis, the French *piastre*, and the *pistole française*. The *demi écu* (three pounds) was nicknamed the little silver Louis or *petit écu*. Collectors consider it the ancestor of the fifty-cent piece. The *quart d'écu* was worth thirty shillings or thirty cents in New France; it is the ancestor of the twenty-five-cent piece. This explains the old expression that is still used, "*4 trente sous font une piastre*" or four quarters (four thirty cents) is equal to one dollar. The 1/12 *écu* was worth ten cents (a dime), and the 1/24 *écu* was five cents (a nickel). The twelve-*denier* piece was worth one cent, the famous copper penny, and the *liard* was worth three *deniers* (if it could be said to be worth anything!); it took four to make a penny.

Finally, several gold coins were in circulation in New France: the Louis (24 *livres*), the *pistole* (21 *livres* and 10 *sols*), and the Portuguese guinea (48 *livres*). There were also some silver coins: the little Louis, the *petit écu* or *écu blanc* (3 *livres* and 6 *sols*). Imagine the difficulties facing the notaries charged with establishing the value of Aaron Hart's after-death inventory (see chapter 4)!

Here are excerpts from the microfilm consulted at the Archives diplomatiques de La Courneuve in suburban Paris (vol. 10, bobbin P.12092; volume 11, bobbin P.12093).

Coat of arms that opens the microfilm titled "Mémoires et Documents. Amérique" (P. 12092 and P12093) conserved at the diplomatic archive of the French department of foreign affairs. These documents no doubt come from the collection of Moreau de Saint-Mery, who was a major collector—or raider—of historical archives. At least, he conserved documents well. Adam Shortt reproduced several of them in his *Documents Relating to Canadian Currency, Exchange, and Finance during the French Period* (Ottawa, 1925).

VIII.

A l'égard des lettres de changes tirées de Canada, tant fur l'exercice 1760, que fur les exercices antérieurs, Sa Majefté fe réferve de prendre d'autres arrangemens pour pourvoir à leur acquittement de la manière la plus équitable. Ordonne Sa Majefté que le préfent arrêt fera publié & affiché par-tout où befoin fera. FAIT au Confeil d'État du Roi, Sa Majefté y étant, tenu à Verfailles le douze décembre mil fept cent foixante-un. *Signé* LE DUC DE CHOISEUL.

A PARIS, DE L'IMPRIMERIE ROYALE. 1761.

"With regard to the bills of exchange in Canada, for the year 1760 and for the previous years, His Majesty reserves the right to make other arrangements to provide for their payment in the fairest manner possible." Versailles, 12 December 1761, signed Choiseul. Despite this commitment, France did not compensate people with bills in Canada. After the Conquest, speculation was rampant on the money left by France. Hart's legacy was first in cash and then in real estate obtained during a financial breakdown following the Conquest.

ARREST
DU CONSEIL D'ÉTAT
DU ROI,

Portant prorogation d'un nouveau délai pour les déclarations à faire par les Porteurs de Papiers de Canada.

Du 15 Mai 1763.

Extrait des Régîtres du Conseil d'État.

LE ROI, étant en son Conseil, s'étant fait rendre compte de l'exécution de l'arrêt de son Conseil du 24 décembre 1762, par lequel, entre autres dispositions, Sa Majesté auroit ordonné que tout particulier, ayant entre les mains des Papiers de Canada, soit qu'ils lui appartiennent, ou qu'ils lui aient été remis en dépôt ou

"Decree . . . regarding propagation of a new deadline for declarations to make by Bearers of Canadian Paper," 15 May 1763. Such notices were issued from month to month, from year to year. In December 1765, the notion of interest was introduced, deadlines were announced and then modified, and new devaluations occurred. Bills of exchange drawn "for the subsistence of the army" were to be paid in their entirety, but the other types of paper money might be depreciated down to a quarter of their value. The following year, a new decree: "To end the difficulties that have lasted for too long a time, with regard to the liquidation of this Paper, belonging to Subjects of Great Britain," the two sovereigns designated plenipotentiary ministers. An agreement was signed on 29 March 1766. Officially, the conditions of the liquidation were settled. As to the liquidation itself, I found no traces of it in Canada. In March 1769, yet another decree set out new provisions! (ill. 1060329.) The amounts owed were converted into interest-bearing (at 4.5 percent) notes or annuity contracts. At the time of the American Revolution, France and England went to war. The last claims by British holders were swept away in the turmoil, and the French revolution completed the wiping away of all traces of "Canadian paper."

At the end of the French regime, in circulation were cards, certificates, *ordonnances*, and treasury bills. A certificate was an account certified by the storekeeper who had written an amount; an *ordonnance* was a promise to pay signed by the intendant on a printed form, writes Marcel Trudel (*Initiation à la Nouvelle-France* [1968], p. 201). Finally, a bill of exchange was a form of money midway between the above-mentioned instruments and the cash distributed by the Navy Treasury. In other words, paper money had to be converted into bills of exchange, which were paid in cash. However, increases in expenses and the greed of some merchants caused amounts largely above the authorized budgets to be put into circulation.

The British administrators immediately understood the seriousness of the situation. Ralph Burton, governor of Trois-Rivières, encouraged the Canadiens to reject "this imaginary money in exchange for real and useful merchandise" and threatened the "defrauders" with sanctions (order by Burton to militia captains, 22 September 1760, RAC, 1918, app. B: 84 ff). Gage, in Montreal, and Murray, in Quebec, shared his suspicions.

In this book, I summarize the declarations made by the Canadiens, and I present the sums in question (see pp. 65–66). The amount of speculation was huge. Canadiens lost enormous sums, and speculators had to wait a long time to see any compensation whatsoever. Around 1770, it was judged that the liquidation of Canadian papers was completed. English holders did not see it that way; they continued to make claims and denounce the many irregularities.

It is not unlikely that any Canadiens were directly compensated. When possible, all those who were able, as well as the religious communities, dispatched their paper money to France, convinced that it would be easier to receive compensation from the mother country. Historian Sophie Imbeault, who studied the case of the Tarieu de Lanaudière family, relates the difficulties encountered by Charles-François de Lanaudière, who entrusted his French agents, Thouron Frères, with the task of obtaining reimbursement. The affair ended badly: "The reduction of Canadian Papers," wrote Charles-François's wife later, "had considerably weakened his fortune" (quoted by Imbeault [2004], p. 164, our translation). Imbeault adds that Charles-François no longer had his officer's income or income from the fur trade, but he still had enough to maintain his way of life. In addition, he had agreed to serve the new governor, Carleton, and he filled various salaried positions as a result. In Trois-Rivières, de Tonnancour, de Niverville, and Richerville were not as lucky.

up during the long journey that took him to Trois-Rivières. In examining the countless coins and bills that he handled in his life as a lender, I realized that he had mastered the different exchange rates used in the Province of Quebec: the Halifax exchange rate, the York exchange rate, sometimes the London exchange rate. He specified the exchange rate in which each loan made was to be repaid. It was as if a lender today were to demand repayment in U.S. dollars for a loan made in Canadian dollars, or the reverse, depending on the value of the respective currencies.

Hart had another important advantage: he was the main supplier to the army. The British government paid its balance in hard cash for supplies for the troops, as well as the salaries of the functionaries and all of its employees. Most of the money that came into the Trois-Rivières government went through Hart's hands, and he therefore had "real money" with which to take advantage of any good opportunity. He became a devotee of sheriff's sales and was almost always able to outbid the competitors, who were still waiting, in vain, for repayment of their paper money.[21] Hart became a lender to seigneurs who were trying to keep up their former way of life. He always gave them credit—even offered it to them. He did the same thing with the Indians.

The Fur Trade

The British wanted to control trade, including the lucrative fur trade. For this to happen, transactions had to take place in posts in the shadow of the garrisons. The authorities were concerned about, among other things, alcohol abuse; there were strict regulations, both to keep the order and keep the Indians from being duped. With his well supplied general store, Aaron Hart was in a good position to benefit from the situation, but this was not enough for him. He wanted to be in direct contact with the Indians.

Raymond Douville[22] mentions an agreement made in 1765 by Joseph Chevalier, Louis Pillard fils, and Joseph Blondin, who were to go and meet with the Têtes-de-Boule nation.[23] It is not known whether they obtained clearance or a permit for this purpose or the authorities simply closed their eyes to the affair. The important point was that the furs would have to transit through Trois-Rivières on their way to England. Hart had contacts with Phyn, Inglis & Co., Forsyth & Co., and Bainbridge, Ansley & Co., which purchased his furs and supplied him with various products for trade needs and retail sale.

The above document is an *Engagement* contract made between Pillard, royal notary, involving Joseph Chevallier and Aaron Hart. See Claude Gélinas, *La gestion de l'étranger. Les Atikamekw et la présence eurocanadienne en Haute- Mauricie, 1760-1870* (Sillery: Septentrion, 2000), pp. 155 and 167; "Commerce des fourrures et société autochtone en Haute-Mauricie à la fin du XVIIIᵉ siècle," *Recherches amérindiennes au Québec*, 30 (2): 23–32.

Aaron Hart quickly got involved in the fur trade with the Têtes-de-Boule Nation. One document mentions more than thirty names of Indians who were likely Algonquins, according to Claude Gélinas. "The Indian names found in this document are Algonquin and not Cree, which would lead us to believe that it was Algonquins who hunted in the Rivière-aux-Rats sector; at the time, the term 'Têtes de Boule' was a generic term used to describe Indians from the interior and not only those who were later known as Atikamekw" (personal communication with Claude Gélinas, 8 September 2010). The statement is one of the few documents signed by Moses Hart, Aaron's brother. The terms used seem to indicate that the Indians had refunded the merchant who had given them credit or agreed to bring the pelts listed (ASTR, Hart collection, non-classified). Thanks to Douville, an excellent paleographer, I can give their names: Avoine, 8abitane; Okimane; Niako; Hekima Canôenam; Eshebaume; Atotine; Alatchouy; Couthikis; Tihis hebanne; Oskiba; Mannataie; Kanitchabidjean; Piscoukense; Kigouche; Orangouane; Molin; a8etchitché; Ayakikepitch's son; Tintépé known as Oskinomatch; Tintépé son of Oskinomatch; Cabertaune; Papamoulas; Tchatchaman; Sitanne; Kichénabé; Arontitchitché; Sareaux fils de Kichénapé; Pilotré; and Mangoucha (Douville, 1938: 49–50).

The 1765 experiment of engaging in the fur trade with the Indians yielded good results. Having had a taste of success, Aaron let himself be convinced to go and meet with the Indians. In the meantime, however, he got married. In the summer of 1767, he went to England, where he met Uriah Judah's sister Dorothea and decided that she would make a good wife. He left it up to his brother Moses, who had recently arrived in Trois-Rivières, to make the preparations for his expedition the following year.[24] He made what was no doubt his first expedition into the forest in the summer of 1768, and returned with two canoes filled with furs in time to attend the birth of his first son on 26 November. Meanwhile, Moses was making his own fur-trade deals on the outskirts of Trois-Rivières at a place still today called Cap-aux-Corneilles.

Although Trois-Rivières offered good business opportunities, this proved that there wasn't enough room for two entrepreneurs. Both Moses and Uriah Judah ended up moving on to find new opportunities. Aaron was no doubt hoping to set up a network to complement the one that he had started with Samuel Jacobs and Eleazar Levy.[25] He started by moving close relatives into the parishes between Trois-Rivières and Montreal: the Manuels to Yamachiche, the Pines (or Phineases) to Louiseville (Rivière-du-Loup), and the Josephs to Berthier.

First and Last Real-estate Acquisitions

February 7, 1764, was a big day for Aaron Hart: he purchased forty-eight *arpents* of land from the heirs of Fafard Laframboise.[26] He paid the £350 in cash. On May 6, 1765, he bought part of the Bruyères estate. He paid the seller, Simon Darouet, two instalments of £500. Possessing land was a priority for Aaron. He was dreaming of starting a dynasty in North America and understood instinctively that real estate had real value. He learned about the seigneurial system and, like the Scottish, began to covet the beautiful estates in the vicinity. But he was patient.

On October 6, 1791, Sheriff Thomas Coffin auctioned off part of the Bécancour estate. Aaron, flush with cash as a result of his dealings with the British troops, purchased half of the estate, "the part along the Rivière Puant or Bécancour," the islands that included "with all seigneurial rights, honors and Knowledge annexed to the said François P[o]mmereau[27] share of the said seigneury," about one league of frontage and one league and eighteen arpents in depth. Pommereau was the neighbour of Ralph Henry

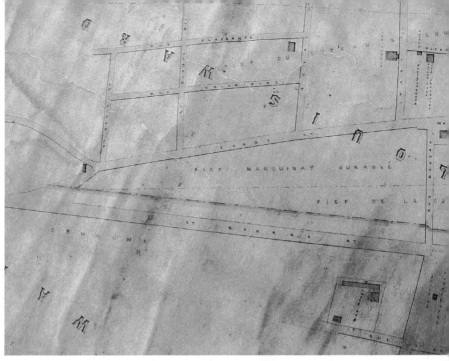

My own family arrived in Trois-Rivières in the summer of 1942. My father rented an apartment at 327, rue Saint-Georges, facing the former Marquisat de Sablé. The existence of this marquisate was a well-guarded secret in Trois-Rivières. This detail taken from Macdonald's map (1860) shows the central location of this small site (see Marcel Trudel's description of it in chapter 4). The street names shown on this map are still in existence except for Rue Plaisante, which has become Rue Radisson, cut by Parc Champlain, and Rue Alexandre, which has also lost its original name to become the extension of Rue Radisson. "Alexandre" was in memory of Alexander Hart, Aaron's youngest son. The first Jewish cemetery was at the corner of Rue Alexandre and Rue Notre-Dame. Rue Plaisante was as enjoyable as its name indicates, but it lost its name during a morality campaign. The market at the corner of Badeaux and des Forges was moved a bit, and the hay market disappeared for obvious reasons. When I was a boy, it was our playground. At the corner there was a huge scale, or "weigh," for hay bales.

Bruyères fils and the heir of Jean Bruyères.[28] On 11 April 1795, Hart acquired from Reine Pommereau part of the rest of the estate.

Up to the very end of his life, Hart continued to make acquisitions. The jewel, in his view, was the Marquisat du Sablé, in what is now downtown Trois-Rivières, which he acquired at auction from the Boucher de Niverville family in September 1800 for the ridiculous sum of 21 *livres*.[29] This land did not bring in seigneurial rents; its owner would have to wait patiently for Trois-Rivières to grow. Nevertheless, he didn't hesitate. Would it be possible that he went to the auction? Would he have been courageous enough to look into the eyes of Joseph Boucher de Niverville, the much-decorated soldier? De Niverville was a man of legend. Aaron knew his story.

Until his death Aaron Hart kept receipts for merchandise supplied to the Americans during the occupation of Trois-Rivières.

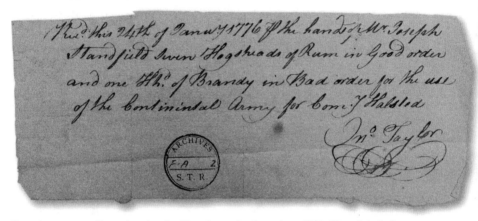

On 24 January 1776, "Seven hogsheads of Rum in good order and one Hh'd of Brandy in Bad order for the use of the Continental Army . . ."

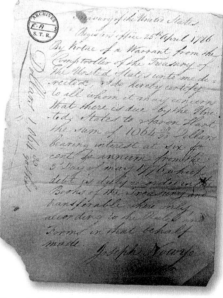

A more detailed invoice of what Colonel Levingston owed to Aaron Hart, written by the latter: various garments and 24 gallons of rum.

On 25 April 1786, Joseph Nourse acknowledged, on behalf of the United States, a debt of $1,064 bearing six percent interest per year, starting May 1776. The bills themselves, presented for payment, have disappeared.

As a young man, he had fought the Fox Nation, then the Chicachas, on expeditions that had taken him to the far reaches of French America. He had served in Louisiana and Acadia; he had fought the British in Acadia and at Lake Champlain; he had been at the battle of the Plains of Abraham in the fall of 1759, then at the battle of Sainte-Foy in the spring of 1760; he had been present at the surrender of Montreal.

De Niverville decided to return to France to continue his military career. There, his immense service was recognized and he received the supreme decoration, the Croix de Saint-Louis. But he quickly realized that there was little future for a "Canadien" in the former mother country. Nor was there one in the British colony resulting from the Conquest of 1760. Thus the man known as Chevalier De Niverville resigned himself to the new order. But that was not enough.

Chevalier De Niverville returned to Trois-Rivières, where he tried to maintain a way of life that was no longer possible in the new political context. He became relatively easy prey for Aaron Hart, who discreetly advanced him small loans. The unfortunate war hero had to give up the Saint-Marguerite seigneury,[30] and then the marquisate. This was only the beginning; this family, direct descendants of Pierre Boucher, the founder of Trois-Rivières, saw their real estate gradually pass into the Harts' hands.[31]

More Paper Money: This Time From the American Congress

Aaron Hart didn't win every bet he made. He had an unfortunate experience with another kind of paper money. During the American invasion of 1775, Trois-Rivières was besieged by the Americans. The owner of the Saint-Maurice ironworks, Christophe Pélissier, was a Frenchman sympathetic to the rebels. He chose to collaborate. In his history of the Saint-Maurice ironworks, historian Albert Tessier noted proudly that the siege of Quebec was made possible by goods produced in Trois-Rivières: shovels to dig trenches, stoves to heat the assailants, and cannonballs to rain down upon the town.

Hart sided with the British; he had little choice in the matter. Carleton made him one of the purveyors for the British troops and prepared the following passport for him: "The bearer, Hart, is permitted to pass and repass between the Army at Three Rivers and Quebec."[32]

The Americans occupied Trois-Rivières in the fall of 1775;[33] they had a good junket at Hart's expense. After their failure at Quebec in late December, they returned to Trois-Rivières, where they suffered a humiliating defeat. Chevalier de Niverville brilliantly repelled their advance guard, and the people of Trois-Rivières stood their ground awaiting the rest of the British company. The Americans turned tail, leaving behind some twenty injured men. These soldiers were nursed back to health by the Ursuline nuns, who were paid in new paper money issued by the U.S. Congress. Aaron Hart received similar payment. But the Americans had welshed on their bill; the money wasn't worth the paper it was written on.[34]

For years, Hart tried everything he could think of to obtain payment of this debt. Of course, he had supplied not arms, but merchandise and drink—that is, fabric and rum, much rum.[35] He had also been foolhardy enough to settle a note for Mr. Price and Mr. Haywood, who were demanding £600 11s7d from General Wooster.[36] He had in hand receipts from General Wooster, Colonel Livingstone, Captain Goforth, and Lieutenant McDougall. He had made their lives easier and had even become friends with some of them. On 5 June 1785, having received no response from the U.S. government, he asked his "friend" Captain Goforth to intervene with the authorities personally, reminding him that he had accepted this paper money on the insistence of General Wooster and General Arnold.

Finally, he asked his brother Henry, who lived in Albany, to handle all the accounts due from the U.S. government. He badgered Henry, urging him to take every effort: "There must be one honest man left in the United States government."[37]

In the Hart collection is an official document issued on 25 April 1786 by Joseph Nourse [Nowye], registrar of the United States treasury: "By virtue of a warrant from the Comptroller of the Treasury of the United States unto me directed, I do hereby certify to all whom it may concern that there is due by the United States to Aaron Hart the sum of 1064.88/90 dollars bearing interest at six per cent per annum from the 3rd Day of May 1776 which debt is duly recorded in the Books of the Treasury and transferable here only according to the Rules and Forms in that behalf made."[38] This recognition of debt was the result of ten years of efforts.

But no reimbursement followed. Aaron continued to harass his brother and mandated his oldest son, Moses, in December 1796, to continue the pursuit. On 8 March 1797, Moses gave a power of attorney to Ralph Mather of Philadelphia to act in his name. In Aaron's inventory after death, the notaries found four certificates from the United States bearing interest of between three percent and six percent starting in 1792, for a total of

$2,001.63. They were signed by Joseph Nourse. The heirs continued to take steps. Around 1831, an offer of $15,000 was made by President Andrew Jackson, but it was deemed insufficient. Aaron Philip[39] Hart, one of Aaron's grandsons, demanded $60,000. Aaron may have consoled himself by thinking of the much larger claims by Samuel Jacobs and by his cousin Samuel Judah, who in fact, fancied that he had the friendship of General George Washington.[40]

The Harts' initiatives appear pathetic. Aaron Hart took it personally. The amount in question represented a fairly small loss, but it must have dredged up Hart's anxiety about dealing with the invader. Like many others, he had supported the British but believed that the Americans would win. In short, he had played both sides against the middle. Christophe Pélissier, the owner of the ironworks, had taken much greater risks, bordering on treason, by openly supporting the Americans. Haldimand and others had closed their eyes to Hart's affairs, and Pélissier's difficulties were of a different nature.[41] In the end, Hart refused to admit that it would have been better to just let things go.

One Person's Misfortune . . .

If Aaron Hart suffered at all from the speculation in paper money, he suffered less than others and was in a better position to turn the situation to his advantage. In fact, the lack of reimbursement for holders of paper money paved the way to his fortune; the impoverishment of the Canadiens served him well. [42]

Manoir Tonnancour is named after René Godefroy de Tonnancour, seigneur of Pointe-du-Lac, built in 1723. In 1795, the Honourable Pierre-Louis Deschenaux had the house reconstructed after it was damaged by fire eleven years earlier and he added a storey. In succession, it was a military barracks, a presbytery, a bishop's residence, and a residence for the Filles de Jésus. Today it is a historical monument.

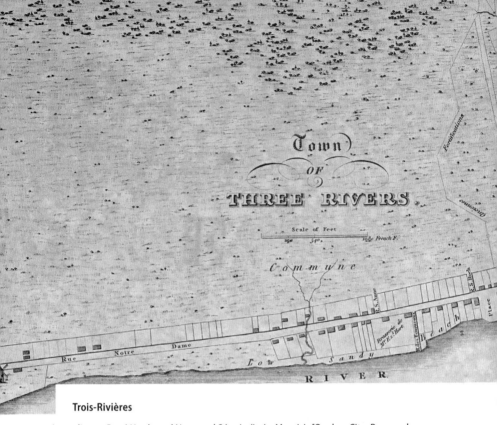

Trois-Rivières

According to René Hardy and Normand Séguin (in *La Mauricie* [Quebec City: Presses de l'Université Laval, 2008], p. 48), Trois-Rivières' population was 672 in 1762; 1,213 in 1790; and 3,118 in 1831. Other towns in the Mauricie region—Yamachiche, Louiseville (Rivière-du-Loup), and Sainte-Anne-de-la-Pérade—were similar in size.

A census completed in March 1762 gives slightly different figures: 5,871 for the government of Trois-Rivières as a whole. This figure was divided into smaller units: Trois-Rivières and environs, 586; Yamachiche, 566; and so on. See also Marcel Trudel, *Le régime militaire dans le gouvernement des Trois-Rivières, 1760-1764* (*Le Bien public*, 1952), pp. 28–30; Canadian Archives, Series M 375 and 893; Haldimand Papers, Series B, vol. 21-1, p. 37, Report 1918, p. 158; Census of Canada, 1931, vol. I (Ottawa, 1936), pp. 142–45.

"Trois-Rivières is very small in comparison to Montreal or Quebec City. . . . I have never been able to verify the exact number of houses and residents, but I believe that the former is not over 250 and the latter 1,500. There are only a few presentable houses. The rest are miserable wood houses with a few rooms on the ground floor and an attic." John Lambert, *Travels through Canada and the United States of North America in the Years 1806, 1807 & 1808,* vol. 1 (London, c. 1810), p. 291. "Trois-Rivières is seen as the third-largest city in the province; but in comparison to the two others, it is very small, containing only about 320 houses, and the population is barely more than 2,500." "A number of potash and pearl-ash factories, two or three breweries, and a huge brick-yard have expanded considerably the general commerce of this town; a large number of bark canoes are built there. . . . As a port, this town is well situated, with water depth sufficient for large vessels to approach the docks and to lade and discharge their cargoes. . . . The streets are narrow and unpaved; the main street is Rue Notre-Dame. . . . After these come des Forges, du Fleuve, du Rempart, St. Maurice, du Platon, des Casernes, St. Louis, St. Jean, and St. Pierre streets, which form almost all of the inhabited part of the town. There are many boutiques and stores, and English merchandise of all types is found; a number of inns offer travellers very well-maintained lodging." Joseph Bouchette, *Description topographique de la province du Bas-Canada...* (London, 1815), pp. 307–09.

Pierre Boucher's first wife was Marie Ouebadinskoue, an Indian woman who had been a student with the Ursuline nuns in Quebec. She died giving birth to their first child, who did not survive. In 1652, Boucher remarried. He and Jeanne Crevier had fifteen children, who received names borrowed from his homeland of Perche. Most have been perpetuated up to the present day. Aside from Niverville, they are Grandpré, La Bruère, Boucherville, Montarville, Montbrun, Grosbois, Montizambert, La Perrière, and La Broquerie. The daughters married Gaultier de Varennes, LeGardeur, Sabrevois de Bleury, and others. The descendants settled all over the continent. In them, Aaron Hart had a model for his dreams of a future dynasty.

The above photo, conserved in the archives of the seminary, shows the manor as it was in 1933. Today, the city of Trois-Rivières uses it for cultural activities.

In his 1938 biography of Aaron Hart, Raymond Douville summarizes how Chevalier de Tonnancour, who lost the most in 1764, became Hart's victim: "He based his expenses on his prestige, which was great, more than on his income, which was not its equal."[43] Hart made a large number of small loans to de Tonnancour. He did the same thing with Chevalier Joseph Boucher de Niverville, Jean-Baptiste de Courval, and Jean Drouet de Richerville.[44] When the time for repayment came, usually when the owner of the seigneury died, the notary presented to the heirs the total of the sums borrowed. Of course, the deceased's assets were worth more than the accumulated debt, but the debt still outstripped the heirs' resources. Their first reflex was to contest the small notes that the notary placed before them. It was not a total surprise; they had seen the blow coming as they had witnessed the seizures. Faced with the hard evidence, where would they find the money to pay the debt? Hart had a solution. The notary explained his proposal to the heirs: he would agree to pay the difference between the debt and the value of the property in question, which would then belong to him. The heirs, relieved to extract themselves from the situation with a little cash in hand, gratefully accepted.

SCHNELLFÜSSIG UND FREY

CHAPTER 3

The Hart Clan: Introductions

Aaron Hart's descendants were always very proud of their origins, and of their patriarch. They accepted, no doubt with a mixture of resignation and pride, the escapades of some family members and chose to remember, instead, the accomplishments of others, which clearly dominated the first century of the Jewish presence in Quebec.

In the Harts' family history, truth and legend became intertwined. The family had a coat of arms, which quickly disappeared from the Seminary archives, except for a copy found among the unclassified documents. It shows a bounding deer above a banner displaying the words "Rapid, Graceful, and Free." In his letter of 10 May 1870 addressed to the Ursuline nuns of Trois-Rivières (see chapter 1), Adolphus Mordecai Hart related that his forebears came from the Hartz mountains of Bavaria and that the family's name was Hertz at the time. According to him, the coat of arms had been copied by his cousin Aaron Philip when he travelled to Germany, and he had had it validated by experts in London. In the 11 March 1893 edition of *Le Monde Illustré*, Benjamin Sulte wrote that the Hart ancestors had been born "in the vicinity of the Haardt Mountains of the Palatinate" in south-western Germany.

Adolphus Mordecai noted that he had found in the family papers a death notice published in the March 1801 issue of *European Magazine* published in London: "Dec. 28, 1800. At Three Rivers, in Canada, Mr Aaron Hart, in his 76th year. He was the first British merchant who settled at Three Rivers after that place was taken by his friend General Haldimand in the year 1760." The news of Aaron's death had therefore circulated as far as

This coat of arms belonged to Charles Theodore Hart, the oldest son of Theodore Hart, who was one of the sons of Benjamin Hart and Harriott Judith Hart. Theodore's second marriage was to a non-Jewish woman (Mary Kent Bradbury), and Charles Theodore was their son. His family distanced itself from Jewish tradition but not from a sense of family. Theodore immigrated to France, where he died in 1887. He was proud of his origins; the family motto is written in German: Schnellfüssig und frey (Rapid, Light, and Free).

London, though it is not known who supplied this information to the magazine.

From Germany, the Harts had moved to London, Adolphus Mordecai wrote, whence some members of the family went to North America. When he arrived in Trois-Rivières, Aaron Hart was appointed treasurer of the government of Trois-Rivières (Adolphus Mordecai was inflating Aaron's importance here; he was in fact the paymaster for the British troops) by Murray or Haldimand. In this role, he was responsible for the convoys headed for the western posts, including Frontenac and Hochelaga (no doubt an error, as there was no Hochelaga post). Turning to more recent history in his letter, Adolphus Mordecai recalled that the election of his father, Ezekiel, to the House of Assembly had left a bitter taste: "His sons had more trouble than profit from these bitter struggles starting around 1808," he wrote. As he pointed out, the English were divided, and it was the Canadiens who elected his father as a representative. The only tangible and positive souvenir of this episode was a portrait that Governor James Henry Craig gave of himself to the family before his departure for England. Again according to Adolphus Mordecai, Governor Craig visited his father in the summer of 1809; a new son was born at the time and was named James Henry Craig Hart, later known as Ira Craig Hart. The author of *Histoire des Ursulines des Trois-Rivières* uses Adolphus Mordecai's version in her account.[1] One thing is certain: that author did not invent the visit to the monastery by Governor Craig, who was touched by "the religious poverty and the modest cells."[2]

I have previously quoted the warning that Aaron wrote to his son Moses upon learning his intention to run in the election of 1796: "What I do not like is that you will be opposed as a Jew." This warning has been interpreted in various ways. In the view of Sheldon J. Godfrey and Judith C. Godfrey, it may have been a reminder of the Jewish tradition that "an observant Jew should not seek secular positions of leadership"[3] and should become involved only in cases of strict necessity. He "understood," writes Irving Abella, "that despite his prestige, wealth and philanthropy, there were limits beyond which a Jew could not yet venture." Abella adds, "By 1800 the handful of Jewish settlers had already achieved much, but a great deal remained to be achieved."[4] I do not know Jewish culture well enough to assess the Godfreys' comment, but I do know the history of the period well enough to second Irving Abella's analysis.

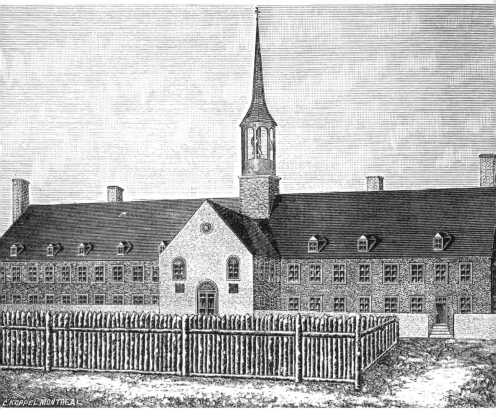

The Ursuline nuns of Trois-Rivières suffered a number of devastating fires. Each time, they rebuilt a bigger and more spacious building. The nuns were skilful entrepreneurs and operated a seigneury at Rivière-du-Loup (Louiseville), where they had a mill built. In Trois-Rivières, their establishment was both a hospital and a school. A number of Aaron's and Dorothea's daughters and granddaughters were students there. Aaron himself was attentive to the needs of the nuns, who considered him one of their benefactors.

The Promised Land

Aaron Hart arrived in Trois-Rivières when he was about thirty-six years old. He moved freely among a population impoverished by years of war. There were dead to mourn, buildings to reconstruct, crops to replant, herds to rebuild, an economy to re-establish. The occupying army called upon his services. He was thrilled. He had finally reached his promised land, he was sure of it. In 1764, he acquired his first piece of land.

Aside from the occupying army, Aaron encountered only an ineffective political authority. He quickly noted the existence of another type of authority, the Catholic Church. But it too was in disarray. Catholics, like Jews, had their problems with the British regime. The requirement to take various oaths blocked them, in principle, from access to public office. I will return to this subject in chapter 5, in which I discuss the election of Ezekiel Hart.

Aaron had the feeling that the British would have to ensure some form of cohabitation between Protestants and Catholics. The latter were going to have a serious recruitment problem; their bishop, the only one authorized to ordain new priests, had died. Under the terms of the surrender of Montreal, men's communities had an uncertain future. This had no immediate consequences for Aaron, although he understood that the Jesuits and Recollets had more than their share of problems.* In Trois-Rivières, there was a well-established religious community, the Ursulines, composed of astute, skilled, intelligent women. They were women of power. Aaron made them his allies. He helped them financially when the time came.[5] One day, he told himself, his daughters would go to their school.

Until then, Aaron had never found a better place to start a family than the small town of Trois-Rivières. All he needed was a wife. A friend and cousin, Uriah Judah, told Aaron about his sister, Dorothea. Born around 1747 (according to family tradition and evidence in notarized acts), she was twenty years younger than Aaron. But this age gap pleased him. He feared that an older woman might be a handicap; moreover, a younger wife would give him more children, and Aaron wanted a lot of children.

---

* In section 33 of the surrender of Montreal, Vaudreuil's proposal to protect the men's religious communities was rejected and the decision was reserved for the king's prerogative. Finally, the British authorities forbade the Recollets and the Jesuits to recruit. Once the last of them died, the community's assets would be turned over to the Crown, which would dispose of them according to its best judgment. Part of the Jesuits' assets, consisting of 800,000 arpents of land, would be used to establish the Royal Institution for the Advancement of Learning, which would finance English-language schools. The last Jesuit died in 1800, and the Royal Institution was created the following year. Jeffery Amherst's heirs received compensation in the form of a large parcel of Jesuit land that had been promised to the general. The rumour spread that they had taken possession of the Jesuits' assets and were seeking to dispose of them. On 2 May 1802, the young Moses Hart wrote to the firm Villet & Ansley asking it to offer £8,000 to Amherst's heirs and proposed a 10 percent commission. ASTR, Fonds Hart, 0009-K-g. Samuel Holland and John Collins give a description of the Jesuits' assets. BAnQ, E21, SS6, 101, and LAC, CO 42, 116.

This portrait of Dorothea Judah is attributed to James Sharples and was likely painted in 1809. After Aaron died, Dorothea moved to Rue Saint-Gabriel in Montreal. Her parents, Abraham and Zelda, had lived in New York (Godfrey, 1995: 120). Her father died around 1784 and her mother may still have been alive when this portrait was painted. In any case, she had friends there. Dorothea also had a large family network in North America: Uriah, Samuel, Isaac, Elizabeth, Henry, and Miriam. Miriam married Emanuel Manuel who sought his fortune in Yamachiche. It is interesting to note that this portrait is conserved at the New York Metropolitan Museum of Art.

The First Generation

As I have mentioned, Aaron Hart had two brothers in North America, Henry and Moses. Henry lived in Albany and left an estate that was difficult to untangle and gave Aaron no end of problems. The brothers were in almost constant contact, and all indications are that either Henry did not have Aaron's talent or Albany did not offer the same business opportunities as Trois-Rivières did. Aaron sometimes threatened to put Henry's accounts into collection and warned him, in at least one letter, written on 4 January 1787, to mistrust the Dutch of New York.[6]

The other brother, Moses, lived in Trois-Rivières for some time and took care of Aaron's interests while Aaron was in London to get married. Moses seemed to be neither very talented in business nor very stable. Aaron arranged his marriage to Esther Solomons, the sister of Ezekiel, who had been caught up in Chief Pontiac's rebellion. Ezekiel Solomon was very active in the Shearith Israel synagogue, where his fellow congregants had agreed to close their eyes to his marriage, before a Protestant minister, to Elizabeth Dubois in July 1769.

Aaron's Covenant
A NOVEL BY CHARLES LAW

"Seeding the Hart Dynasty"

Charles Law, *Aaron's Covenant: Seeding the Hart Dynasty* (Trafford Publishing, 2006). The cover features the portrait long considered by the McCord Museum to be of Aaron Hart. On my remark to Law about a supposed affair between Dorothea and Moses, Aaron's brother, he answered, "It's a novel." Nevertheless, this novel is in general solidly documented and accurate.

Aaron and Dorothea were probably among those reluctant to accept an inter-faith marriage, and one of their concerns would have been to find Jewish spouses for their children. Both were very religious, and they formed a responsible, unified couple. Dorothea liked the finer things in life, and Aaron acquired them for her; his inventory after death is eloquent proof of this (see chapter 4). In the will that she wrote after Aaron's death, Dorothea left to her daughters "diamond rings, " "gold watches," "gold earrings," and "three large silver spoons," and to her sons "a gold snuff box," other silver spoons with a silver pot," "a mahogany table," and other such items.[7]

I must mention in passing a very unexpected portrait that Charles Law, in his recent novel *Aaron's Covenant*, painted of the couple—in fact, of a love triangle involving Aaron, Dorothea, and Moses. When I expressed my surprise, Law retorted, "It's a novel!" However, the novel is remarkably well documented historically, and the characters depicted are real. Law had researched the Harts' private life and leaves nothing out of his book. However, it seems to me that the only time he did not respect the truth, or even likelihood, was in certain details concerning Aaron and Dorothea. In the novel, Dorothea has a falling-out with her brother-in-law and is not enthusiastic about her successive pregnancies. This doesn't seem to ring true, as it is customary for an observant Jewish wife to want to bear her husband many children.[8]

In this case, the couple had eleven (or perhaps twelve) children. This does not surprise me. As a part-time resident of Outremont in Montreal for almost half a century, I can vouch that for religious Jewish families having many children is very normal. I would also add however that the traditional French Canadian family would very often have as many or more children. For example, Joseph Boucher de Niverville and Marie-Josephte Châtelin had eleven children.

Aaron and Dorothea were in good health and kept a clean home;[9] four boys and four girls reached adulthood.[10]

The Absence of Registers

This is where my main problem as a historian starts. Jews were not included in the civil registers kept by Catholics and Protestants during this period, and there were no Jewish registers. I can therefore give only approximate ages for Aaron and Dorothea. In fact, this has also been a constant problem for Jews; taking it to an extreme, one might almost say that legally they didn't exist at that time!

This difficulty with registers, in fact, led me to have a healthy dose of scepticism about historical civil registers in Quebec. I feel that these sheets of paper cover only part of the reality. They record very few people of mixed French and Indian blood, for instance. Luce Jean Haffner's study *Quatre frères Jean* highlights some of the gaps.[11] Today, the Université de Montréal's Research Program in Historical Demography has begun to publish notarial acts to complement the "parish" registers. The marriage of Moses Hart and Sara Judah (1799) (see below) appears in an act registered before the notary Joseph Badeaux. For records of the births of their three children, however, information must be sought here and there.

What does "here and there" mean? For Jewish boys, circumcisions were noted by the rabbi in his journal. (Aaron's sons were circumcised in Trois-Rivières by a rabbi passing through.) Some boys were circumcised during a ceremony at the synagogue, and this was recorded in the synagogue's minutes. More generally, and for girls in particular, the researcher turns to family correspondence or various notarial acts. This is how I reconstructed families to present a more or less complete portrait of three generations of Harts and their connections with other major Jewish families: the Davids, the Judahs, the Josephs, the Hays, and the Solomons.

The Second Generation: Born in Quebec

Aaron and Dorothea apparently got married in Portsmouth, England, on 2 February 1768, according to archivist David Rome, who possessed notes from Aaron's prayer book to which he sometimes referred, for lack of a better source.[12] Anne Joseph, however, author of a monumental work called *Heritage of a Patriarch* (the patriarch being Henry Joseph), refuses to accept this kind of source. I share her mistrust with regard to a few notes written in a Bible that Theodore Hart gave to his wife, Frances Michaels David, as they contain too many obvious errors. Theodore, Aaron's grandson, was no doubt unwittingly responsible for this. Despite his best intentions, he was not reliable.[13] Evidence must be sought elsewhere.

My preferred source is a document written by Lewis Alexander Hart, dated 24 November 1919. He supplied very interesting information on the Hart and Judah families. Lewis Alexander was a notary—in other words, a solid reference. His son, Alan J. Hart, gave the McCord Museum a copy of the document and sent a slightly different version to the American Jewish Archives in Cincinnati.

In both versions, I found the same proud comment: "Aaron Hart and Samuel Judah were men of means when they came to Canada in 1760." Lewis Alexander surely added the regretful comment, "Before leaving St. Lambert to return to Montreal, I destroyed several boxes of old letters and papers." I am inconsolable, especially because this was one of the most formidable branches of the Hart-Judah family. It included Mrs. Seymour Elkin, née Vera Hart, the child of Alan Judah Hart and Eva Vineberg, the second daughter of Harris Vineberg and Lily Goldberg, and Cecil Hart, a partner in the Montreal Canadiens hockey club. Cecil Hart's father, David A. Hart, donated the trophy that bears the family name, awarded each year to the National Hockey League player most valuable to his team.*

---

* Cecil Mordecai Hart (1883–1940) was the son of David Alexander Hart and Sarah Matilda David and the grandson of Alexander Thomas Hart and Miriam Judah; thus, he was the great-grandson of Moses Hart and the great-great-grandson of Aaron Hart. Cecil Hart made his start in baseball, forming a team of stars that played exhibition games. He then became manager of the Montreal Maroons hockey team and went to the Canadiens after a dispute with management. Year after year, he took his team to the playoffs. Cecil's father, born in Trois-Rivières on 22 June 1844, is said to have been the second physician with a degree earned in Canada. Cecil's mother, Sarah Matilda, was the oldest daughter of Dr. Aaron Hart David and Catherine Joseph. Aaron Hart David was the son of Samuel David and Sarah Hart, one of Alexander Thomas Hart's aunts.

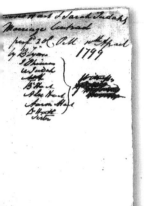

On the back of his marriage certificate (10 April 1799, BAnQ, TR, 2-AC-4), Moses wrote the names of the witnesses: B. Lyons, I. Phineas, U. Judah, B. Hart, Alex. Hart, Aaron Hart, D. Hart (sister). The contract, written by notary Badeaux, is in French. It unites Moses Hart, trader, and "Miss Sarah" Judah, a full adult twenty-one years old. Both parties agreed to be bound by a joint agreement "notwithstanding all laws, customs, and conventions to the contrary, which they waive and renounce by the present" in the presence of Mr. Bernard Lyons and Mr. Isaac Phineas. The agreement is written in English. Essentially, it deviates from "what is meant by the French word communauté." In case of Moses's death, Sarah was to receive a pension of £20 per year, or double that if she had a child, or for as long as she remained a widow. I am not sure I understand the rest, but there appears to be little emotion.

The Hart Trophy, Yesterday and Today

Cecil Hart (1883–1940) was the coach of the Montreal Canadiens in 1930 and 1931, years in which the team won the Stanley Cup. He was then fired following a dispute with Léo Dandurand, the club's owner at the time. In 1936, he was rehired by the new owner, Ernest Savard, as coach and general manager. He recalled Howie Morenz, who then suffered a broken leg, an injury that was to prove fatal. Hart coached the team to first place in the Canadian division, but it lost in the semi-finals. He resigned during the 1938–39 season.

This branch's ancestor was Aaron Hart's oldest son, Moses, born on 26 November 1768. He was the black sheep of the family—sheep didn't come any blacker. His natural son, Alexander Thomas, re-established the family's Judaism by marrying his cousin, Miriam Judah, with whom he had three sons: Moses Alexander, David Alexander, and the above-mentioned Lewis Alexander (see p. 169).

Moses Hart was an impossible character. His parents' wealth went to his head. Very young, he believed that he could do anything. His parents wanted the best possible education for him, as they did for their other three sons. He was to study in the United States. A family friend, Eleazar Levy, was concerned about this: why not simply Montreal or Quebec? In fact, he was concerned about the Hart sons' behaviour—especially that of Moses.

Aaron and Dorothea did everything they could, including sending recommendations in all their letters. Their first intention was to have

Aaron's brother, Henry, keep an eye on Moses in Albany. Apprenticeships in Plattsburgh or Burlington were also envisaged. But Moses took it upon himself to head for New York, a city that he loved, in 1784 or 1785. In 1786, he went again. Aaron suggested that he return home for the Pesach seder or the beginning of Passover. Some "pertickeler bussiness," unbeknownst to Aaron, kept Moses in New York, where he attended the theatre rather than synagogue. His personal diary, in which he kept track of his expenses, at his father's request, reveals that he made payments to barbers and tailors and handed out tips to chambermaids. The plays that he saw, John Vanbrugh's *The Provoked Husband* and Oliver Goldsmith's *She Stoops to Conquer,* dazzled him. Finally, his pockets empty, he returned home.

Moses Tries His Luck in Nicolet, and then in William Henry (Sorel)

In 1778, Aaron and Dorothea moved to a dwelling much larger than the apartment above the store on Rue du Platon, which Aaron had rented in 1762. The house on Rue Notre-Dame was swarming with children; Dorothea gave birth to the last three in 1782, 1783, and 1784. Moses alone, however, required more attention than the rest of her brood; the letters that she sent him indicate that she treated him like a spoiled child.

In his travels, Moses learned not only about life, but also about business. He had established useful contacts. He now had to sink or swim, Aaron told himself. He offered to set his son up in Nicolet, on the south shore of the St. Lawrence River, to open a small store. With his father's model in mind, Moses set out to be the master of the small town. He had his mail addressed to Moses Hart, Hartville.[14] But he overextended himself and had to beat a retreat. Aaron told himself that Nicolet didn't offer enough opportunities for Moses, and he moved him to William Henry or Sorel (named after the future William IV), a strategically located town on the route to New York. He had seen his friend Samuel Jacobs, who had recently died, succeed in Saint-Denis-sur-Richelieu, and he was convinced that it was the right choice.[15] Moses stayed there for five years before returning home to Trois-Rivières. He had constantly travelled, including to England in 1792. His business network was impressive.

Aaron was beginning to feel his age. He wanted to bring his sons into the family businesses, and he created a company with his three oldest. But the oldest son held a special place in the Jewish family. Moses had to marry. He had "shopped around" quite a bit over the years but had never found

Letter of 27 March 1799. "Dear Hart and Dolly (Dorothea), Last January your son Moses came here & renewed the old subject of marrying Sally (Sarah). I would not consent to it without a certificate under his own hand that he was lawfully married to her (words in Hebrew) which he refused to do."

his soul mate. He may not have been fundamentally interested in marriage, but the obligation was there. Dorothea had in her sights the two daughters of her brother, Uriah, who had moved to Verchères. Uriah was not made of the same stern stuff as Aaron. He was fainthearted, and Moses took advantage of this. When one of Uriah's daughters was proposed to him, he spread humiliating rumours, such as that Uriah was insolvent.[16] Uriah complained to Aaron, bringing up their old friendship and their good years in Trois-Rivières. However, he was realistic enough to admit that despite Moses's detestable and provocative character, it was still a good match for his daughter. He took his responsibility as a father. On 27 March 1799, he wrote to Dorothea and Aaron, "Last January your son Moses came here & renewed the old subject of marrying Sally [Sarah]. I would not consent to it without a certificate under his own hand that he was lawfully married to her [words in Hebrew] which he refused to do." Uriah also told Aaron and Dorothea that he required their consent, which Moses had promised to obtain, and their presence at the marriage. And so, a few days before the festival of Purim, Moses arrived with a contract written in his own hand "wherein instead of love and affection" he offered financial arrangements in case of death or separation, for he reserved the "liberty to separate himself from her bed & board whenever he thought proper." Outraged, Uriah declared himself ready to display this contract to the entire world. "In short," he concluded, "he wants her at the price of a good negro wench."

Moses had an even more outrageous scenario in mind. He proposed that Sarah leave her parents' home and take up residence somewhere on

The marriage of Moses Hart and Sarah Judah was doomed to failure. Moses did nothing, and Sarah could do nothing, to save it. He had an important affair with Mary Cline, who, in 1804, bore him a son of whom he was particularly proud, Alexander Thomas. In 1807, Sarah Judah asked the court for "a separation of body and habitation" although she returned to Moses hoping that he would keep his promise to remove from their house the two women who were living there. In 1814, she left him again, this time for good.

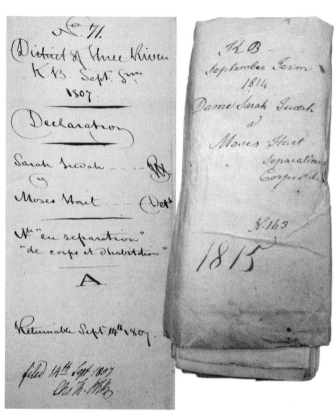

The court's ruling came in two parts: on 15 March 1816, justices James Kerr, Edward Bowen, and Pierre Bédard awarded the plaintiff "three hundred pounds as an alimentary provision" retroactive to 23 September of the preceding year. Two weeks later, the separation of body and property was awarded. Moses Hart assuaged his conscience by promoting a new religion and penning violent attacks against the Catholic Church, documents that have remained buried among his business papers to the present day.

the other shore of the St. Lawrence: Berthier, Louiseville (Rivière-du-Loup), or Trois-Rivières. When Uriah learned about this plan, he was livid.

Nevertheless, on the following 10 August, as unlikely as it may seem, Sarah and Moses signed a marriage contract at the office of notary Joseph Badeaux. It was not a happy union, although they had three children: Louisa Howard, Orobio, and Areli Blake.

On 14 September 1807, Sarah asked the court for a legal separation due to her husband's bad treatment of her and poor behaviour. She took refuge with her father, who had returned to Trois-Rivières to live. Three months later, she proposed to Moses that they live together again "if you will send your two women and child away." It seems that she made her point; she returned to live with Moses and stayed for another seven years. In 1814, she applied again for legal separation. Her life had been hell, as court testimony eloquently revealed. A servant in their household, Marie Leblanc, told about one of Moses's rages: he threw a clay sugar bowl and a bottle of milk at Sarah's head and was barely kept by a servant from "throwing a teapot full of boiling water in her face."

"The defendant told the witness that he thought nothing of taking the plaintiff's life," the bailiff noted, "and that women mean nothing to Jews."

Moses, having launched a number of lawsuits, was quite at home in court. He likely wrote to James Reid, a judge in Montreal and a friend of the Hart family, to ask for advice. Reid sent a letter to Pierre Bédard, a judge in Trois-Rivières, to ask for further information about the case. Bédard replied at great length to Reid on 6 January 1816; this letter is now conserved in the Baby archive at the Université de Montréal. Bédard was not sparing with explanations, but his handwriting was so execrable that it has confounded many historians, myself among them.

On 15 March 1816, the judges of the Court of King's Bench, James Kerr, Bédard, and Edward Bowen, awarded Sarah an annual pension of three hundred *livres*. Two weeks later, the legal separation was granted.[17]

Sarah was both relieved and devastated. Was Moses satisfied with the outcome? Certainly, he had matured. His reflection led him to the subject of religion. When something was not to his liking, he was determined to find a solution. He had ideas about reform on practically every subject, and he now founded a new religion. This issue is so important and unusual that I will discuss it in detail in chapter 7.

Ezekiel, the Second Son

Ezekiel was a complete contrast to his brother Moses—so much so that I sometimes wonder if they had the same parents. Charles Law's novel *Aaron's Covenant* comes to mind.[18]

Ezekiel, the second son, was born a year and a half after Moses, on 15 May 1770. His biographers recount that Aaron wrote this date in his prayer book, but I found it in Ezekiel's death notice in the 22 September 1843 issue of *Le Canadien*. This is also the date that Ezekiel's son Aaron Ezekiel gives in a letter to John Neilson dated 18 September 1843 informing him of his father's death.

Since Moses did not return to Trois-Rivières until 1795, Ezekiel worked closely with Aaron, although he did spend some time studying in New York, possibly hoping to meet his future wife there. In 1793, he moved in with Ephraim Hart, a prominent New York businessman, in whose home he met Frances Lazarus, the niece of Ephraim or of his wife, née Frances Noah. The two young people were well matched, but Ezekiel was not very forthcoming about the subject.[19] In his letters home, he wrote mainly about his younger brothers, Benjamin and Alexander, born on 10 January 1779 and 30 January 1782, respectively, who were studying in Philadelphia and New York. Their parents were concerned about their academic progress— and their health. In September 1793, rumours of a serious epidemic were circulating. The news that he was receiving, Aaron wrote to Ezekiel, "made me unhappy and uneasy in my mind and body." "Shall not have any comfort," he added, "tell [till] I hear from you that my dear boys Benjamin and Alexander are in some place of more safety and more that disorder does not range. . . . I cannot write at this present time; my trouble is too much for me tell [till] I hear from you and Ben and Alex."[20] Despite his anxiety, Aaron did not lose sight of his business concerns. He learned about David Franks's precarious financial situation, and he expressed his anger about Uriah Judah, who was trying his luck in New York. But for Uriah, luck was elusive. Aaron was categorical: "Not a single shilling. If he wishes money let him write to me."

The letters that Aaron received from New York were affectionately addressed to Dada. "As the postage is high," Aaron wrote to his sons, "a letter will do for me and mummy." But Dorothea was no doubt in greater need of news than was Aaron. He suggested that they address their letters "to hir [her], if you fear it will affront hir your not writing to hir, I shall not take it amise." Aaron's English had clearly not improved, nor had mine. I needed a dictionary to understand that he meant to write "amiss."

Aaron's written English was not very good, and it sometimes took me several hours to decipher his letters. Nevertheless, they are valuable because they brought out his human side. Whenever one conducts historical research on individuals, there are thousands of hours that remain secret between the people concerned. One of my history professors, Guy Frégault, once told his students that we should keep the documentation in our published works to a minimum, rather than making readers wade through all of our sources. I see his point, but on the other hand I don't want to deprive readers of knowledge that brings to light the true nature of the people studied. Some have demonized Aaron Hart and his son Moses even more. (By their innuendos, Douville and, especially, Law, contributed to this demonization.) The latter deserved this reputation, but I am happy to correct the portrait drawn of Aaron as a husband and father.

Here is one last example before returning to the main subject, Ezekiel's marriage. Aaron wrote Ezekiel that he had received word from Ben and Alex: "They both write worse than they did when [they] left here. But I was happy to read [their letter]."

Dorothea and Aaron tried to discern in Ezekiel's letters the existence of a woman in whom he might be interested. They thought that they had found a hint in a mysterious allusion to an "unknowing story of some girl." Aaron was impatient: "I have wrote to you to know [more about] her and family."

Although he was preoccupied by his son's future, Aaron had not forgotten the unpaid American debt. He never stopped trying to obtain payment. In a letter to his mother, Ezekiel mentioned a Mrs. Haysen. The light bulb went on inside Aaron's head, even at the ripe old age of seventy. He immediately wrote his son, "You write to your mother about a Mrs Haysen. Her husband, if you see him, Col. Hayzen [Hazzen] he can be of greatest services to me about the paper money to get it paid." And Aaron now recounted for the thousandth time, plaintively, the events of 1775 and the valuable assistance that he had provided to the Americans, dredging up yet again the names and details.

Ezekiel's mystery woman resurfaced in a subsequent letter: "You say there is no handsome girls in New York," wrote Aaron ironically, "only one, and that girl you wish to marry. You ask my consent." Ezekiel was serious, and he began to negotiate. He asked Aaron £100 for wedding expenses and "half the business"—no doubt, half of the shares in Hart and Sons, the family firm.

But what Aaron learned brought him back down to earth: he wanted to know "what her family is." Then, "she must be of very mean family if her friends cannot be at the expense of the wedding." Finally, "your expense should be no more than the shule expense [and] a new suit of clothes." That Aaron was irritated was obvious: "You will answer me the first of this, and then I shall be able to write you more fully."

As often happens, we have here only part of the correspondence: the letters received by Ezekiel. Those that he sent to Aaron and Dorothea were not conserved. All things considered, I prefer having the parents' letters. I can easily guess what Ezekiel wrote. It is obvious that he was hesitant to tell them that Frances Lazarus was not a blood member of his host's family but had been taken in as a charity case by Ephraim Hart and his wife.

Aaron did not abandon his inquiry. "I should be very glad," he wrote, "you was married to a Jew girl of a good family and character." Alas, he added, "all that your letter does not inform me of."

A marriage was "an affair for life." Precautions had to be taken. Aaron continued to prod, asking questions in different forms and formulating hypotheses. "I do not think you will get one with money," he wrote to Ezekiel. But then he softened his tone: "But one without money should have as much as her wedding clothes and expense of the wedding." Aaron was dying for details. He couldn't contain himself: "My head is not easy." Then, almost a cry of anger: "You will mention fully about your marriage."[21]

On 3 December, Aaron and Dorothea waved the white flag. They told Ezekiel that they accepted "your choice of a wife," and they added, "If you marry, do it soon." They also agreed to send him more money. Ezekiel and Frances were wed in New York in February 1794.

It seems that Aaron and Dorothea travelled to New York for the wedding. Although I have no proof of this, Raymond Douville confirms it in his biography of Aaron Hart. "It was a big celebration," he writes. "For the first time, Aaron had an opportunity to show off his wealth in a social setting, and Dorothea, the no less valuable windfall of seeing all of her relatives."[22]

David Rome consulted with great interest the list of wedding guests and an announcement by Isaac M. Gomez addressed to his friend E. Hart "to partake of a family dinner and will take no denial."[23] It was a wonderful opportunity, for both Rome and me, to get a picture of a part of the New York Jewish community.

"List of gifts offered at the marriage of Ezekiel Hart in 1794" was the title of this document. In fact, it is the list of gift givers that is interesting. All indications are that Dorothea and Aaron were present at the marriage of Frances Lazarus and their son. Both had family and friends in New York. For a long time, I believed that Dorothea was the only member of her family to have immigrated to North America. This is not the case. She had a large family network, as did Aaron (see pp. 75 and 91).

The guest list included all of the gifts presented. According to a Sephardic tradition, Rome explained, the gift was an equal amount of money from each—in this case, £1 6s. First came the *cala* (the bride). Then came the bride's father, mother, and brothers; this confused me, as I thought that Frances was an orphan. Since Ephraim's name does not appear, I deduce that he stood in for Frances's father. Then came the groom's parents, brothers, and sisters; Uncle Uriah and his family; Mr. & Mrs. Hart (the mystery of Frances's parents reappears); Eleazar Levy; the *hazan* (cantor) and his family; Mrs. Judah (and perhaps her family); Kitty Manuel; Hester Gomez; Phil. Phillips; Leah Abraham; Bernard Hart; Samuel Hart, who was likely a brother of Ezekiel's, born 6 May 1774, of whom I have found no trace; Bernard Judah, Samuel Judah's son and thus Dorothea's nephew, who married Catherine Hart, born 26 January 1776, in Trois-Rivières on 30 August 1797; Asher Hart, also called Alexander, Ezekiel's younger brother; Benjamin [Phillips]; and all the foreigners; finally, a Mr. Nathan.

Ezekiel and Frances moved to Trois-Rivières. They lived there happily and had thirteen children, seven of whom, four boys and three girls, reached adult age. Most remained in Trois-Rivières. The family lived in an immense house situated on Rue des Forges, about where the city hall is today. Benjamin Sulte has written that this house had belonged to the Anglican minister Jehoshaphat Mountain, who left Trois-Rivières several years after Ezekiel got married.

I found Ezekiel and Frances's children in the 1851 census with the help of France Normand and Claude Bellavance of the Centre interuniversitaire d'études québécoises. The oldest, Samuel Bécancour, inherited the Bécancour seigneury; Aaron Ezekiel was the first Jewish lawyer in Lower Canada; James Henry Craig Hart became an entrepreneur interested mainly in maritime business; and Adolphus Mordecai, who was, at times, a historian, was a particularly active lawyer. The couple's three daughters were Esther, Henriette, and Caroline.

I found this rather titillating note about Esther in the *Bulletin des recherches historiques,* vol. 28, p. 276. "Esther Elora, second wife of Vallières de Saint-Réal. She was not unaware of her worthy husband's 'outings' but she consoled herself easily with his valet, a fine specimen of a man, who, over time, became tired of the demands of his spirited mistress and left her employ saying that he had not been hired for that." In the *Dictionary of Canadian Biography,* vol. 7, James H. Lambert and Jacques Monet contribute interesting information. See also Raymond Douville, "La Maison de Gannes," *Cahiers des Dix,* no. 21 (1956). A marriage licence was issued in July 1831 by the solicitor general, C.R. Ogden, for Esther Elora (Eliza) Hart and Justice Vallières de Saint-Réal, but the marriage certificate has not been found. Vallières de Saint-Réal married the widow Jane Kiernan while Esther Elora was still alive; she was said to be single at the time of death of her father (1843) and her brother, Samuel Bécancour (1859).

Two of the sons left descendants through marriages to cousins. None of the daughters seems to have married. Esther, however, lived with Joseph-Remi Vallières de Saint-Réal, a widower who eventually left her to marry a widow, Jane Kiernan (or Keirnan).

Vallières de Saint-Réal was one of the most flamboyant personalities in Lower Canada at the time. His relationship with Esther Hart was significant in that, at the very least, it revealed his free nature and independent spirit. They lived together in the Gannes house (see page 89) and had planned to marry. As a politician, Vallières de Saint-Réal was very familiar with story of Esther's father and his electoral misadventures (which are addressed in chapter 5). The fact that she was Jewish was the least of his concerns.[24] In fact, the elite in Trois-Rivières seems to have accepted the Harts without manifesting the slightest prejudice. Or perhaps the prejudice was manifested in a different way: a number of Hart girls had difficulty, for whatever reason, with finding a husband.[25]

Since I have brought up the subject, I shall mention here that three of Aaron and Dorothea's four daughters married Jewish men: Catherine, as mentioned above, married her cousin, Bernard Judah; Charlotte and Sarah married two brothers, Moses and Samuel, sons of Lazarus David, one of the first Jewish settlers in Montreal.

Until recently, I thought that Elizabeth (known as Bilhah), another of Aaron and Dorothea's daughters, born on 27 March 1783, had remained single. The Jewish archives made no mention of her. Brand-new research by Serge Goudreau on the Algonquins in the Trois-Rivières region has revealed the existence of a certain Georges Laveau, who married Agathe Koska, a Huron woman from Lorette, on 11 February 1828. Laveau drowned in 1848 and was buried in Trois-Rivières on 29 July of that year. He was the son of Augustin Laveau and Elizabeth Hart.

Ben and Alex

Benjamin and Alexander were born three years apart, in 1779 and 1782 respectively. Their parents sent them to study together in the United States. They were in New York at the same time as Ezekiel, and they likely spent time with Ephraim Hart's family.

Of Aaron's four sons, Benjamin seems to have been the most determined—and the most impatient. He knew what he wanted and he was ambitious—which does not mean that success came easily. He decided to take short cuts, such as marrying into a rich family, to become truly wealthy.

Aaron's estate was substantial, but most of it went to his two oldest sons. The Sainte-Marguerite and Bécancour seigneuries went, respectively, to Moses and Ezekiel. Benjamin inherited the store on Rue Notre-Dame—at least, the building—and Alexander had to be content with two parcels of land, one on Rue Notre-Dame and the other on Rue Des Forges.

Here is part of Aaron's last will and testament, which was originally written in French. Although it is not scintillating reading, it is of interest for its content:

> Mr. Moses Hart will be able to take possession of [the Sainte-Marguerite sei-gneury and the Marquisat du Sablé] in usufruct only for his lifetime, the property and the fiefs and rights attached to it will belong to the oldest son in a legitimate marriage of Mr. Moses Hart, and in the case that said Mr. Moses Hart dies without male child born or to be born in legitimate marriage, said testator wishes and orders that the property of said fiefs and all rights attached to them be bequeathed to the male child born in legitimate marriage of Mr. Ezekiel Hart, and in the case of the death of this last without male child born or to be born of said marriage, the property of said fiefs and the rights attached to them shall pass into the hands of the oldest male child of the legitimate marriage of Mr. Benjamin Hart, and in the case of said Mr. Benjamin Hart without male child born or to be born in legitimate marriage, said testator wishes and orders that said fiefs and the rights attached to them become the property of the oldest male child issued in legitimate marriage of Mr. Alexander Hart, and finally in the case of death of this last without male child born or to be born of his said marriage . . .[26]

And on it went. One might well imagine that Aaron Hart's notary was paid by the word! The descriptions in the inventory after death do nothing to dispel this notion. And it's a good thing that Aaron had only four sons![27] The question is, if Alexander did not leave a male child as prescribed in the will, what was to happen?

I am in possession of a handwritten will made by Aaron, dated 16 November 1793. It is short. He leaves money to his wife and children and the rest to the executors of his will: Moses, Ezekiel, Benjamin, and a certain Judah Joseph. This last was a new character on my canvas. At first I thought it was the son of one of Aaron's sisters, who married Naphtali Joseph and set down roots in Quebec; he would thus have been in the country long enough

A few years after her husband died, Dorothea (Judah) Hart moved to Rue Saint-Gabriel in Montreal, in the vicinity of the Champ-de-Mars, near two massive buildings that bordered this vast square where military manoeuvres took place. In the foreground, two Indians; a bit farther away, a French Canadian and his ever-present pipe. Dorothea died here in 1827. We know that she was buried in Trois-Rivières on the initiative of her son, Benjamin. According to Godfrey and Godfrey (1995: 122), Elizabeth Judah had joined her sister in Montreal after the death of her second husband, Moses Myers, son of Hyam Myers. Her first husband had been Chapman Abraham. She died in 1823. Although the Judah family is less well known than the Hart family, they were very present in Montreal and New York. The patriarch, Abraham, lived in Montreal for some time and died in New York, as did his wife, Zelda. One of their sons, Samuel, was very active in business during the American revolution.

to have earned Aaron's trust. Suddenly, I wondered if the names had been inverted—could it have been Joseph Judah? Perhaps a person related to Dorothea? However, I never found anyone by this name in my research.

In the 1793 will, there is thus nothing that resembles the tangle of instructions in the will of 11 December 1800, written when Aaron was at death's door. Between 1793 and 1800, there had been three marriages in the family: those of Moses, Ezekiel, and Catherine. Catherine's union had caused frustration (see below), and the behaviour of Moses aroused uneasiness, at the very least. Ezekiel presented a more reassuring character, no doubt, but Aaron was taking no chances.

What was to be done if these sons did not provide the desired heir? Notary Badeaux continued to read what had been dictated to him: "The ownership of said fiefs and all rights attached to them will be entailed to the oldest daughter resulting from the marriages of said Moses, Ezekiel, Benjamin, and Alexander Hart, to whom said assets will remain entailed one to the other in said cases, with this express defence by said testator, who states that Mr. Moses Hart, usufructor of said fiefs and all the rights attached to them, shall in no way sell, engage, and alienate and mortgage said fiefs, the property being reserved as stated above."

Two days before his death on 26 December, Aaron called for the notary and added a codicil in which he confirmed his "intention and last will" and added Dorothea Judah to the four executors already appointed, among them Robert Lester, who had replaced Judah Joseph.

The will was *too* well thought out. Quarrels erupted. I will return to this when I discuss the litigiousness of the Harts (see chapter 5). I had never seen anything like it. In my view, there are never true winners in court cases. There are always wounds that refuse to heal. In 1802, "amiable" settlements were hammered out. The family was broken apart. The blood ties remained, but nerves were very frayed.

Benjamin resigned himself to the situation and turned to a "better half," Harriott Judith Hart,[28] heir to one of the wealthiest men in New York. They wedded on 1 April 1806 in New York with a separation as to property, in compliance with a marriage contract "written in the Hebrew language." Following apparent family quarrels and reversals, they declared bankruptcy in 1848 and filed lawsuits against each other, in order to have others settle what they could not settle between themselves. On 30 March 1849, Harriott Judith countersued her husband. The complaint is an extraordinary document that tells the story of their marriage. It lists, with dates of birth, the living children: Frances, Samuel Arthur Wellington, Frederick Webber, Jonathan Theodore, Henry, Benjamin Moses, Emily Abigail, Constance Hatton, Dorothea, and Catherine. They had a total of sixteen children, including Aaron Philip (see chapter 6), who died in 1843. Constance Hatton was to marry the remarkable Adolphus Mordecai Hart, and they were the parents of Gerald Ephraim Hart. Theodore Hart reported on the settlement of the estate of Harriott Judith Hart before the notary A. D. Jobin on 6 April 1876. This is another document chock-full of information.[29]

Finally, Alexander, the last and the least of Aaron and Dorothea's sons. Soon after Aaron's death, he followed his mother to Montreal, but he became involved with other circles. He had a mixed marriage. His wife, Mary-Anne Douglas, survived him by a number of years. Alexander was the only Hart of the early generations to die relatively young, at the age of fifty-three.

Alexander likely resembled Ezekiel. Affable, calm, discreet, and pleasant, he got along with his in-laws and had a successful marriage of which I found no record either in the registers or, of course, at the synagogue. The couple had a son named Alexandre or Alexander, nicknamed Bay, who married Louisa Bouchette, the daughter of the well-known surveyor Joseph Bouchette. She belonged to high society, and there is no indication that her family saw this union as scandalous. After her husband died, Louisa married Sir Ambrose Shea, a journalist, publisher, and governor of Newfoundland and then of the Bahamas. At the time of this marriage, she bore the name Louisa M. Hart. I would be very curious to know how she was presented in her marriage contract.

Bay had a sister named Louisa. I know nothing about her. I fear that Alexander's line was extinguished with Bay and Louisa.

A few remarks are in order about this chapter on the second and third Hart generations. I listed the children of Moses Hart and Sarah Judah, and the reader will understand why when I return to the subject of Moses himself. I spent a little more time on the children of Ezekiel Hart and Frances Lazarus, who were to play a more important role in the obtaining of political rights, a subject that I will delve into when I write about the election of Ezekiel Hart. In passing, I mentioned nine of Benjamin Hart's and Harriott Judith Hart's sixteen children because by chance I laid my hands on a legal document from 1849. Finally, I wrote only briefly about the youngest of Aaron and Dorothea's children, Alexander Hart, who did not play a prominent role and who, in any case, I know little about.

Of course, one might reproach me for my silence concerning the off-spring of Aaron and Dorothea's four daughters: Catherine, Charlotte, Sarah, and Elizabeth. The fact is, in traditional Jewish families, the sons took precedence over the daughters, for whom the primary concern was to find them a good Jewish husband.

This was the case, more or less, for Catherine's husband, who did not find it easy to respect his marriage contract. Aaron took account of this in his will. There is no documentation on the offspring of Charlotte and Sarah. I do know that these two sisters went to live with their husbands, Moses and Samuel David, in Montreal, and that the David brothers were chided by their brother-in-law Benjamin Hart about the community's properties.

Finally, a fact that I found striking: Aaron and Dorothea's two youngest children did not marry Jews. This was not a coincidence. Alexander and Elizabeth were less influenced by their parents. They did not reject the family but they did turn their backs on the religion of their ancestors. Neither their older brothers and sisters nor their offspring took this route.

CHAPTER 4

Aaron Hart's Estate

Aaron Hart died early on Sunday, 28 December 1800. He had likely spent the Sabbath day in a state of semi-consciousness. On the previous Friday, he had had a burst of energy and summoned notary Joseph Badeaux to take dictation of a codicil to the will that he had made on 11 December. He added his wife, Dorothea Judah, to the list of executors[1] and introduced further details to paragraph 2 of the will, which "contained the bequest [to his wife] of all furniture, silverware, and household utensils found in said house on the day of his death/cash money not included/also the merchandise in the store and the warehouse, which will belong to the said four male children of said testator."[2]

I reread this codicil several times, but was unable to figure out the intention behind the forward slashes that precede and follow the words "l'argent monoyé non comprise" which might be translated by "petty cash not included." I envy the skill that Raymond Douville had in decoding old documents; although I believe that I properly transcribed Aaron's will, I feel that part of its meaning has escaped my grasp.

The historian Jacques Mathieu once cautioned me about the punctuation of old documents. He gave me an example of the dispute between François Guyon, a resident of Beauport, and Joseph Giffard, son of Robert Giffard and seigneur of Beauport. The former read in the concession certificate, "À chacun, deux mil arpens de terre" (To each, two thousand arpents of land), while the latter read it as "À chacun d'eux, mil arpens" (to each of them, a thousand arpents). An arpent is about 3200 square metres. Mathieu noted that the difference between one thousand and two thousand arpents represented the equivalent of ten average parcels of land granted to residents. René-Louis Chartier de Lotbinière, civil and criminal lieutenant general, had to interpret the text that was the source of the dispute. Chartier de Lotbinière referred to the certificate made before Roussel, the royal notary at Mortagne, on 14 March 1634. An analysis of the documents led him to conclude that "the concession contracts granted by the deceased Sieur

Detail of a cut-out paper sheet conserved at the Musée d'art juif in Paris.

Giffard to Jean Guion [Guyon] Senior and to Zacharie Cloutier explained clearly that he granted only one thousand to each, this word 'deux' being separated by a comma from the word 'mil' and having an apostrophe between the 'd' and the 'e,' which makes it read 'each of them.'"[3] This is a good illustration of the importance of the comma and the apostrophe. In the case of Aaron Hart's will, the forward slashes must mean something, but we have not yet definitively deciphered it.

In my opinion, aside from this specification made to paragraph 2, Aaron Hart's will poses several difficulties. There were some ten other changes

Text of the addendum: "The second article of said will, which contains the bequest of all the furniture, silverware, and household utensils that are found in said house on the day of his death / cash money not included / also the merchandise that are in the store and shed which shall belong go to said four male children of said testator..." (*"Le deuxième article du dit testament, qui contient le legs de tous les meubles, argenterie & ustencils de ménages qui se trouveront dans la dite maison au jour de son décès / argent monoyé non comprise / aussi les marchandises qui sont dans le magasin & hangard lesquels appartiendront & seront aux dits quatre enfants males du dit testateur"*). It was difficult to transcribe the French in this document. One of the problems was the words found between forward slashes, which seemed to exclude his wife from inheriting any money. This transcription is as accurate as possible.

The notary took the freedom of style as with the word "comprise," which is written as "compris" in the will itself as follows: *"Secondement, donne et lègue le dit Sieur Testateur la Jouissance et l'usufruit à Dame Dorothé Judah son épouse***: l'emplacement sur lequel ils sont construits [...] tous les meubles, argenterie et ustencils de ménage qui se trouveront au jour et heure de son décès dans la maison [sans] les animaux et voitures qu'il délaissera, toutefois / l'argent monnoyé non compris /*** de la maison, emplacement et dépendance d'écurie..."* (Secondly, the said testator gives and bequeaths the enjoyment and usufruct to Dame Dorothé Judah, his wife***: the place upon which they are built (...) all the furniture, silverware, and household utensils that are in the house on the day and hour of his death (without) the animals and carriages that he leaves, however the cash money not included: *** from the house, the place, and stable building..."

made or details added throughout the twelve pages of the document, as well as many deletions. The will is written in French, which provided Aaron with an additional difficulty. He must have been sweating—even in a panic. The subtleties of French had always escaped him. He had worked his entire life to provide his descendants with considerable assets; he wanted to lay solid foundations for the dynasty about which he had dreamed with his dear Dorothea, for whom he also wanted to provide as a good husband.

He had long been looking for ways to foresee every eventuality. In 1793, he had handwritten his will in English and chosen to let the executors make most of the decisions, but he no longer saw this as an option. He had tried to educate his sons with a view to bringing them into his business. He was uneasy about this prospect, whence the refrain "to the oldest male son of a legitimate marriage" of Moses or, if not, "the oldest male son of a legitimate marriage of Ezekiel" and so on, as far as allowing that ownership of the fiefs might be "entailed to the oldest daughter issued from the marriage of said Moses, Ezekiel, Benjamin, and Alexander . . ."[4] For weeks, for months, ideas and intentions had jostled in his mind. When one rereads the will that he had dictated, half in English, half in French, and takes account of the explanations given by his two notaries, Badeaux and Étienne Renvoyzé, it may be surmised that he asked questions and felt the need to add details, and he energetically initialled each addition or modification. The final signature was also made with a firm hand. These are my last wishes, he seems to have said, in an ultimate gesture.

In compliance with Jewish tradition, Aaron was likely interred quickly, no doubt in the cemetery that he had created at a location that today corresponds to the corner of Rue Notre-Dame and Rue Radisson, which was once called Rue Alexandre in memory of Alexander Hart. Had a first son named Alexander been buried at this spot? One thing is certain: this cemetery was created when a first child died. The street name was probably changed from Alexandre to Radisson when a perpendicular street was opened along one of the Harts' lots, today Parc Champlain. The lot was given to the city by Aaron's four sons on condition that the new street bear the name Hart.[5]

The first Jewish cemetery in Trois-Rivières was likely situated at the corner of Alexandre (Radisson) and Notre-Dame streets (site 1). It was then moved to what is now the parking lot for the Capitanal building (site 2). In my opinion, Rue du Haut Boc is not properly situated. The Friar's School, which became the Académie de La Salle, was at the corner of Saint-Pierre and Laviolette streets. At first, Rue Hart began at Rue des Forges and ended at Rue Bonaventure. The extension indicated as Rue Saint-Joseph was for a long time called Rue des Groseilliers, after Radisson's partner. Today, this section of the street is also called Rue Hart and has two monuments to Hart 100 metres apart. The most recent location of the cemetery is site 3 (see p. 224).

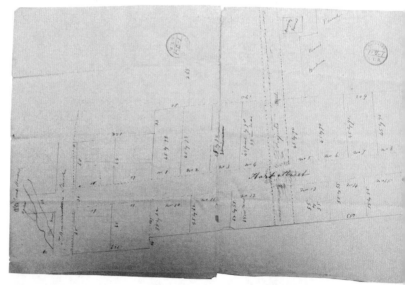

The Property Inventory

On Wednesday, 14 January 1801, the inventorying began in the presence of the executors and three witnesses, Benjamin and Charlotte Hart and Henry Joseph, a cousin who lived in Berthier and had been duly elected curator on 31 December 1800. Pierre Ignace Daillebout and Jacques Delepine were also present as witnesses. Notary Badeaux, accompanied by his colleague, Étienne Renvoyzé, carefully identified the people present, their roles, and whom they represented. Thus we learn that Charles Blake, a Montreal businessman,[6] was the guardian of the three minor children, Sarah, Alexander, and Elizabeth, who were designated as heirs. Of course, Dorothea Judah was present, but I don't know whether as an executor or a guardian. She was no doubt wearing several hats. She also had to keep track of her squabbling children, two obsequious notaries, and curious witnesses.

After a preamble that no doubt seemed overly long to those present, everyone followed Dorothea and Badeaux into "a small bedroom." The notary removed the seals "deliberately placed by said parties after the death" on a first suitcase and withdrew from it "four bags, each containing four hundred Spanish *piastres*." The two notaries registered a value of £400. Then they opened six bags containing 500 Spanish *piastres*, worth 750 *livres*, and another bag containing, among other things, a *portugaise* (Portuguese crown or dollar) with a value of £104 3 shillings, 5 *sols*. In a metal trunk were twenty bags, as well as a package (no. 21), the contents of which I list as an example: "One hundred and fifty Spanish *piastres*, one hundred and eight *demi-piastres* & two French *piastres*, three half and thirty-seven shilling coins, fifteen coins worth twenty-six *sols*, two coins worth fifty *sols*, one coin worth forty *sols*, five coins worth fifteen *sols*, five coins worth twelve *sols*, and two coins worth twenty *sols*, all forming fifty-six *livres* five shillings seven and a half pence."

The notaries seemed to have a method for making these calculations and establishing the corresponding values. In 1793, when Aaron wrote his first will, he also penned a document in which he established the value of a wide variety of coins, as if to guide his heirs. In early August 1800, he repeated the exercise with coins the names of which I can't decipher, as well as "joes" (Portuguese johannes), guineas, moidores, double Louis, doubloons, and other coins, for a total of £1,516 10s10d.[7]

Old Money, Course 101

A *demi-écu*, coin struck in 1644, value: 3 francs.

A *pistareen*. Many believe that this coin is the ancestor of the 25-cent piece. It was worth 2 *réals*.

On the evening of 14 January 1801, the notaries attacked the inventory of Aaron's goods yet again. They opened "a canvas bag containing two hundred sixty and a half gold *portugaises*, forty guineas, and six half-guineas, weighed all together one hundred twenty seven ounces, ten gross and twelve grains, following the weight used in this province, making the sum of five hundred sixty-five pounds, eleven shillings, and ten pence (£ 565..11..10). . . .

"Another bag, no. 25, containing twenty-fight guineas, eight hundred half-guineas, three *portugaises* and quarter-*portugaises*, & one eight, twelve *moidores*, and five American eagles, weighed all together thirty-one ounces, forming the sum of one hundred thirty-six pounds nineteen shillings, and nine pence (£ 136..19..9). . . .

"Another bag, no. 26, containing forty gold double Louis, fifty gold single Louis, twenty doubloons, four half-doubloons, and nine quarter-doubloons weighed all together fifty-three ounces, three gross, worth two hundred thirty pounds, nine shillings, one and a half pence (230..9..1 1/2)."

The notaries expressed no emotions. They identified, counted, weighed, and added to the best of their abilities. Before writing his article on Aaron Hart, Father Tessier transcribed or had transcribed by typewriter the entire inventory of the house and the store. This was a good point of departure. I started to concentrate on the notaries' work. I consulted various authors but I couldn't figure out their calculations. Marcel Trudel supplied valuable information in his *Initiation à la Nouvelle-France* (HRW, 1968); Fernand Ouellet added more information, including equivalency tables, in his *Histoire économique et sociale du Québec, 1760-1850* (Fides, 1971); and the works by Adam Shortt (1925) and A. B. McCullough (1987) complemented my documentation. Finally, I called my friend Denis Lacasse to come to my rescue. A quiet but inquisitive man, hungry for knowledge, he had a wide variety of interests and the soul of a researcher. I found out by chance that he was interested in old money.

We started with the bank notes issued by the Harts. I later asked him about the coins in circulation at the beginning of the British regime. After a first lesson, I began again to analyze the inventory of Aaron Hart's goods, believing that I was now well equipped. I was quickly brought down to earth. Humbly, I once again called Lacasse and invited him over to look at the inventory with me.

He read in silence. I watched him. "Spanish *piastres*," he murmured, nodding his head decidedly. When he reached bags 17 and 18, he read out loud, "A hundred and sixty-two French *piastres*, eighty-seven French half-*piastres* . . . What was the population of Trois-Rivières at the time?" he asked me. I hesitated and looked in my notes. "In 1762, the population of the government of Trois-Rivières was assessed at 5,871, with almost 600 in Trois-Rivières and the same number in Yamachiche. . . . Around 1807, John Lambert spoke of fewer than 1,500 residents and 250 houses; in 1815, Joseph Bouchette suggested about 2,500 people living in some 320 houses."

Lacasse was silent for a moment. "When was this inventory made?" he then asked. "Hart died in late December 1800," I told him, "and this was early January 1801. "That's surprising," Denis said. "I am hypothesizing that he collected all the French *piastres* and half-*piastres* in circulation in Trois-Rivières and the surrounding area. Over forty years, Aaron Hart collected, gathered, pocketed, and harvested everything that remained of the old New France. What was his main business? How was he able to amass all this hard cash? In the lack of hard coin money, people did a lot of bartering. He had a way to find coins. It's amazing. From the coins listed in the inventory, we can see that he harvested all of the French coins that remained in the colony, then he grabbed much of the new money that arrived from England and the American colonies."

Lacasse explained to me that people hoarded their few precious silver and other metal coins. To get them back into circulation, the authorities overvalued them, so that almost every coin had its own valuation. Most were of Spanish and Portuguese origin and were worn or were missing bits that had been deliberately ground away. And so the grain (weight) and the pennyweight appeared. In fact, coins had been lightened or altered so much, McCullough (1985: 53) relates, that in 1780, merchants in Quebec offered a premium of 100 pounds sterling "for any information leading to the conviction of individuals performing this practice," known as sweating.

Looking at the inventory, my first question had to do with the notaries' calculations. Even with Trudel's and Ouellet's tables and various public notices at hand, I was not able to understand their calculations. "It is obvious that they made mistakes and there was no one to correct them, but above all they constantly had to weigh certain coins in order to establish their value," Lacasse told me.

I will spare you the equivalences in these tables, which for me were very unclear, among Johannes, English guineas, gold Louis, and *moidores*, American eagles, doubloons, *écus*, *pistareens*, and the rest, but it is my pleasure to show you some digitized illustrations from the collections belonging to the Quebec City numismatics society and Parks Canada. I asked Lacasse a final question: "The notaries valued the coins accumulated by Hart at £3,659 9s. Was this a large amount?" "I would say that he had in cash the equivalent of what 6,000 average families might hold together" was Lacasse's answer, delivered with an enigmatic smile. "Legend has it that families hid somewhere one or two *écu* coins (for their golden years!). Hart had the equivalent of more than 12,000 *écus*." Hart knew how big his fortune was. He knew that the British conquest had played in his favour. It was inevitable that regime change had penalized the conquered.

The 8-*real* piece, or *piastre*.

The Spanish *Piastre*

These coins were struck in silver. There were 2-, 4-, and 8-*real* coins. The *real* was the basis of the Spanish monetary system, and Spain was becoming the minter for the world. The piece of eight, *real de la ocho* or *peso de plata*, was the famous Spanish *piastre*. Its head bore the coat of arms of Spain or a portrait of its sovereign. The tail was particularly interesting to the origin of today's dollar sign. It featured two columns called columns of Hercules, around each of which was wound an S-shaped banner. The two columns became the two vertical bars through the S, and then one bar disappeared. There are other hypotheses about the origin of the dollar sign, the most interesting being that it is a combination of the letters U and S, which does not explain why the dollar sign is also used by the Mexicans for the peso.

An assay balance, a tool that was absolutely necessary for establishing the value of various coins. In New France, some gold coins were in circulation: the Louis (24 *livres*) and the Portuguese guinea (48 *livres*); some pieces of silver: the *petit* Louis, *petit écu*, and *écu blanc* (3 *livres* and 6 *sols*), in comparison to the large *écu à couronne* (6 *livres* and 12 *sols*) and the Spanish *piastre*; billon (alloy of copper and silver) coins in the form of marked shillings (12 *deniers*); and copper coins, *liards* (3 *deniers*).

Aaron Hart's silver bags contained Spanish *piastres* evaluated at 100 pounds. Were these *livres tournois* or pounds sterling? The notary wrote "current pounds."

At four in the afternoon, the notaries, their fingers no doubt cramped, proposed a break until six that evening. They had registered a total of £2,100.15.4 1/2, to which they added £39.19.4.

By nine o'clock that evening, the total was £3,659.9. The notaries then turned to the accounts receivable, among which appeared the famous American certificates. Moses and Ezekiel no doubt caught each other's eye as they thought of all the times their father had made them attempt to recoup this money. The notaries stopped again and agreed to meet the next morning at nine o'clock. "The cash in gold and silver listed above and in paper inventoried above has been placed in an iron trunk and locked with a key," which was entrusted to Robert Lester.

The list of accounts receivable confirmed the breadth of Aaron Hart's business affairs. Albert Tessier evaluated at more than $15,000 the sums due to Aaron by people of all social classes. He was owed money by his brother Henry Hart; his brother-in-law Uriah Judah; Isaac Phineas and Barnet Lyons, two Jewish merchants in Louiseville (Rivière-du-Loup); a certain George Lyons; his nephews Joseph and Henry Joseph of Berthier; and David David and his brother Samuel David, the future husband of Aaron's daughter Sarah.

In passing, I note a not unimportant detail. At the end of the military occupation, in August 1764, the authorities decided to abolish the government in Trois-Rivières and divide it in two. The part west of the Saint-Maurice River was, naturally, annexed to Montreal, and the part to the east was annexed to Quebec. There was a Jewish presence in Yamachiche,

Louiseville, Maskinongé, and Berthier, to the west of Trois-Rivières. These were strategic locales, and I suspect that Aaron Hart encouraged fellow Jews, especially his close relatives, to settle in them. The names included Manuel, Lyons, Pines (or Phineas), and Joseph. Naphtali Joseph married one of Aaron's sisters, and together they started a large family.

With the exception of the Josephs in Berthier, these people quickly abandoned their activities, but Aaron nevertheless tried to establish a chain of Jewish partners from Trois-Rivières to Montreal. He lent them money and, when the time came, helped them liquidate their businesses.

After the "petty cash" (*argent monoyé*) the notaries began to inventory Aaron's goods. The list that they compiled gives a fairly accurate idea of what a general store and a middle-class house in eighteenth-century Trois-Rivières might have contained. The two-storey house had nine well-furnished rooms, including two kitchens. This suggests that the family respected the Kosher custom of not cooking meat products with dairy products. It would be interesting to look for implements that may have been used for the ritual slaughter of animals.

A Carron stove was installed in the "big bedroom," and six other stoves were distributed around the house. The notaries, who sometimes took care to list every object in detail, at other times were laconic, simply noting "paintings or prints" and "two suitcases full of books." We know that Aaron's neighbours included the Reverend Jehoshaphat Mountain and the ex-Récollet Léger Veyssière, known as Father Emmanuel, the last serving Catholic at the Récollets chapel and then the first Protestant pastor at the same chapel. Veyssière, called the "poor little creature" by Monsignor Charles Inglis, who teased him for his lack of height (he was 4 feet 10 inches tall) and his intellectual stature, died on 26 May 1800. It seems that the Harts divided his library among themselves.

In the Harts' yard, the notaries noted two horses, two cows, about fifty chickens, four geese, two turkeys, and two ducks. There were also a caleche on a spring frame, a silver-plated double harness, two old carriages and two harnesses, a sleigh, a cart, a yellow caleche, a *berouette* (wheelbarrow), and garden tools.

It took almost a month for the notaries to complete their inventory. The store's activities had been brought almost to a standstill, and all of these goods still had to be divided according to the testator's wishes.

Ritual Slaughter

Aaron Hart's after-death inventory revealed that his house had two kitchens, which suggests Aaron and Dorothea had food-related concerns and were trying to respect the laws of *kashrut*. It is written in the Old Testament (Exodus 23: 19), "Do not cook a young goat in its mother's milk"; the corresponding kosher law required dairy products and meat to be cooked separately. I consulted experts, who tried to determine the extent to which the Hart family was able to comply with these laws.

Kosher laws restrict the choice of animals that can be eaten, and ritual slaughter would have posed difficulties to a Jew in Trois-Rivières in the late eighteenth century; indeed, Ira Robinson, an expert on Judaism, felt that it would have been impossible. My research led me to this Italian miniature from a 1435 Hebrew manuscript attributed to Jacob ben Asher, known as Rabbi Yaakov, who devoted his life to studying the Torah and was famous for his encyclopedic book *Arba'a Turim* (Vatican Library, Codex Rossiana 555, folio bis verso. Illustration taken from "Histoire du judaïsme" by Sonia Fellous. File 8065. La documentation française, September–October 2008).

As is typical of images from this epoch, various scenes and moments are portrayed on the same page. In the foreground is the *shohet*, who is leaning over a cow and holding it on its side. With his left hand, he holds the animal's head in a position that enables him to cut its throat with a large knife. All of the texts emphasize that the knife must be perfectly sharpened, as the animal must be slaughtered quickly so that it doesn't suffer.

On the right, an inspector examines the beef entrails and ensures that there is no disease. The animal was suspended head down to allow the blood to flow out, as its consumption was forbidden. The animal has cloven hooves, making it an animal fit to eat.

In the background, two men slaughter poultry as a woman watches. Here again, the animals are suspended by the feet so that the blood flows freely.

vvv

Eating Kosher

Jewish people are often asked, "What can you eat?" This is God's answer in Leviticus 11 (Old Testament, New Living Translation [2007]): "Of all the land animals, these are the ones you may use for food. You may eat any animals that has completely split hooves and chews the cud. You may not, however, eat the following animals that have split hooves or that chew the cud, but not both. The camel chews the cud but does not have split hooves, so it is ceremonially unclean for you. The hyrax chews the cud but does not have split hooves, so it is unclean. The pig has evenly split hooves but does not chew the cud, so it is unclean. You may not eat the meat of these animals or even touch their carcasses. They are ceremonially unclean for you.

"Of all the marine animals, these are the ones you may use for food. You may eat anything from the water if it has both fins and scales, whether taken from salt water or from streams. But you must never eat animals from the sea or from rivers that do not have both fins and scales. They are detestable to you. This applies both to little creatures that live in shallow water and to all creatures that live in deep water. They will always be detestable to you. You must never eat their meat or even touch their dead bodies. Any marine animal that does not have both fins and scales is detestable to you.

"These are the birds that are detestable to you. You must never eat them: the griffon vulture, the bearded vulture, the black vulture, the kite, falcons of all kinds, ravens of all kinds, the eagle owl, the short-eared owl, the seagull, hawks of all kinds, the little owl, the cormorant, the great owl, the barn owl, the desert owl, the Egyptian vulture, the stork, herons of all kinds, the hoopoe, and the bat."

Foods of plant origin "must be verified to ensure the absence of parasites visible to the naked eye." Finally, precautions must be taken to keep utensils and dishes from becoming "impure."

In her essay "L'Histoire du judaïsme," Sonia Fellous (2008, p. 42, our translation) concludes, "Beyond ritualized hygiene, the goal of the kosher laws is to make people aware that the authorized foods are those that have no spiritually negative aspects, such as pain, illness, or dirtiness."

vvvvvvvvvvvvvvvvvvvvvvvvvvvvvvvvvvvvvvvvvvvvvvvvvvvvvvvvvvvvvvvvvvvvvvvvvvvvvvvvvvvvvvv

Disputes and Agreements

Difficulties, disagreements, and even quarrels were to be expected. It took me some time master the obvious. In fact, it was war.

In the directory of the Hart archive, Hervé Biron modestly summarized the papers pertaining to Aaron Hart's estate: "Six folders labelled from a to f. Large file containing all the papers from the trials incurred following the death of Aaron Hart. By his wife against his sons; by Aaron Hart's sons among themselves, etc., then arbitration and amicable settlement."

Before becoming interested in Aaron Hart's estate, I had examined those of Moses and Ezekiel when I was writing their biographies for the *Dictionary of Canadian Biography*. I thought I had seen everything. Moses's

Carron Stoves

René Hardy, a historian of the Mauricie region, drew my attention to the mention of a Carron stove in the inventory. "These were seen only among the wealthy," observed Hector Berthelot (quoted by Marcel Moussette, *Le chauffage domestique au Canada* [Quebec City: Presses de l'université Laval, 1983], p. 136, our translation).

The Scottish company Carron began to export stoves to Canada soon after the Conquest. The early models may have been copied by the craftsmen of the Forges du Saint-Maurice, just as it seems that the motifs produced by the moulders of Trois-Rivières inspired foreign competitors, including Carron. On this subject, see Roch Samson, *Les Forges de Saint-Maurice*, pp. 232–34. The expert on this subject is Marcel Moussette, who is very circumspect about the rivalry between the two companies. About this stove illustrated by Jefferys, he writes, "Because of the decorative motifs and the slender legs, it seems to be a Carron stove," especially because it does not bear the "FStM" stamp that normally appeared on the front plate of Forges de Saint-Maurice stoves. See Mousette, *Le Chauffage domestique au Canada*, pp. 135 and 208. (Photo: Jean Jolin.)

property inventory was two hundred pages long, took one year to make, and involved a "widow" whom he had not married (see chapter 10) and children resulting from various unions. In contrast, Ezekiel's estate perfectly reflected his character: orderly and respectful. How can the free-for-all that surrounded Aaron's estate be explained?

In his attempt to plan and order everything, Aaron had created complications. In 1793, when he was reaching seventy, Aaron had decided that it was time to make a will, as was normal for a man of his age. I find wills almost as interesting as inventories. I have already summarized Aaron's three-page will from 1793, penned in English in his own hand. The writing is clear; here and there, a word is jotted in the margin. He was concerned with the future of everyone, especially his wife, to whom he willed a pension of "two thosend pounds Hallifax [Halifax] Currincy . . . during [her] life." He repeated this amount twice, and each time he added "five hundred" to "two thosend" to make "two thosend five hundred."

The 1793 will contained nothing contentious. But the 1800 will, with its refrain concerning the male children issuing from a legitimate marriage, was provocative. And the codicil threw everything up in the air; in fact, I believe that the will of 11 December immediately launched arguments and anxieties. On 11 October 1800, Benjamin Hart summarized one of his father's wishes:

> Whereas our dear father Aaron Hart has this day signed his last will and testament by which we understand he has left our dear mother Dorothea Judah the enjoyment after his decease of two thousand five hundred pounds currency of this province which will yield her but one hundred and fifty pounds currency per annum.—This therefore serves to bind and obligate us that after the decease of our said Father (which we hope may not happen for many years) if the said will should continue in force, that we will equally put out at interest a sum of money so to produce our said mother fifty pounds current money per annum during her life so that she has two hundred pounds currency per annum in whole and at same time—another—to further—it to her.[8]

I found it difficult to understand how Aaron had cobbled together a pension for his wife. I finally found the explanation when I went through the list of his debtors. I noted several seigneurs mainly in the Trois-Rivières region, but a certain Grant from Longueuil stood out. I was stunned to find this well-known figure in debt to Aaron. The amounts involved were considerable.

The arrangement set out by Aaron is explained in a signed contract notarized by Louis Chaboillez and Charles Prevost on 25 July 1803, in the presence of Benjamin Hart, acting as proxy for his three brothers. Here is the tenor of the contract (our translation): "David Alexander Grant, seigneur of the Barony of Longueuil and other locations, living in his manor on St. Helen's Island, who has voluntarily recognized and confessed by this contract to legitimately owe to Mr. Moses Hart, Mr. Ezekiel Hart, Mr. Benjamin Hart, and Mr. Alexander Hart, merchants in Trois-Rivières," the sum of £2,500 on which "the pension or interest will be paid annually and will belong to Mrs. Dorothea Judah." When Dorothea died, "the principal will be paid" to the four brothers. The contract set out the terms and deadlines, specifying the amounts of £1,000 and £1,500 for a total of £2,500 constituting a mortgage "on the present and future goods and especially the Barony of Longueuil without one obligation infringing on the other."

Aaron Hart was used to dealing with seigneurs. Nonetheless, when Baron David Alexander Grant reeled off his titles, Aaron quite respectfully acknowledged them. He likely was unable to keep himself from thinking that one day one of his own descendants might call himself a baron. He knew Grant's story. It was through his marriage to Marie-Charles Le Moyne, the only daughter of Charles-Jacques Le Moyne, that this Scotsman had snagged the title.*

Aaron had always coveted land—a normal reaction for someone aware of the restrictions faced by Jews in various countries throughout time. It had taken him forty years to acquire two seigneuries; not long before he died he added a marquisate. His two oldest sons would have the title of seigneur. And would the oldest be a marquis? Moses, who was this heir, was more pragmatic; he first requested information about the borders of the marquisate and the income attached to it. On 4 March 1801, he wrote to P. E. Desbarats, "My father has left me the Marquisat du Sable, situated in the town, along the Coteau St. Louis, belonging to the Jesuits. I am not certain whether I can exact lods & rents or not, also where it begins."[9] In his *Terrier du Saint-Laurent en 1663*, Marcel Trudel gives a good description of this property, situating it in relation to today's Trois-Rivières streets: from Rue Badeaux to the "five corners" between 5 Rue Des Forges and roughly Rue Saint-Antoine.[10]

Before agreeing to this contract with Grant, the Hart heirs went through much internal combat. What a surprise to learn that Dorothea sued her two eldest sons, and they countersued her. Even Moses, who had warned her about those who could turn against her, was a party in the lawsuits! That appeared to me to be particularly odious. A first step toward settling the disputes was taken in January 1802. On the 13th, Dorothea accepted the will—specifically paragraph 2. Essentially, the notary Badeaux used the same terms: house, hangar, and appurtenances, silverware, household "utensils," and animals and carriages. Finally, the pension drawn from a sum of £2,500 was confirmed. "After having received the opinion of her friends, and having deliberated, Dorothea Judah declares that she wants, intends, and agrees that said testament of her husband be hereafter dated, be executed in its full form and content," her agreement read. "She renounces all of the rights that she may have had, today and forever."

---

* William Grant, David Alexander's uncle, had married (twice: first before a Catholic priest and then before a Protestant minister) Marie-Anne-Catherine Fleury Deschambault, the widow of Seigneur Charles-Jacques LeMoyne de Longueuil. Grant was one of those who had profited from the disarray of the Canadiens to acquire superb residences in the town of Quebec and in Montreal and to appropriate beautiful seigneuries. He was also an extreme speculator on paper money. He should not be confused with William Grant of Trois-Rivières, who married Marguerite Fafard, known as Laframboise.

The next day, 14 January, exactly one year after the inventory taking had begun, Dorothea Judah renounced ownership of the merchandise that was found in "the store of the house" "without the need for further enumeration" in exchange for capital of £1,500 that she would have available "to do with as she wishes for the rest of her life." At her death, the remainder and the results of investments would go in equal shares to the four Hart brothers, as would the merchandise that was the subject of the dispute.[11] It is to be noted that the four daughters were excluded from this agreement. And what was the source of the dispute? In fact, the last-minute changes made to paragraph 2 had introduced some ambiguities that were amplified by anxiety and covetousness.

The Four Brothers

The strangest was yet to come. The negotiations with their mother concealed a myriad of tensions among the four brothers. The two oldest were the executors, as Alexander was not yet of legal age and Benjamin was urging Charles Blake, who appeared as Benjamin's lawyer in the papers of Mr. Beck, lawyer in Montreal, to oversee his interests. Benjamin was in fact Ezekiel's partner in one of the family's stores.

Finally, fed up with the whole thing, Benjamin decided to go to Europe, where he intended to establish his own contacts. On 14 October 1801, he wrote a will in which he made Alexander his appointed heir and named his mother, Charles Blake, and Robert Lester his executors. He bequeathed £500 to his mother, £250 to his three single sisters, and £250 to a nephew named Samuel Judah, the son of Catherine Hart and Bernard Judah. Either he felt that his two older brothers didn't need his money or he was expressing his bitterness toward them.

Time passed, and the Hart brothers realized that it was in their best interest to complete the settlement of their father's estate. On 21 March 1803, they went to the offices of notaries Joseph Badeaux and Étienne Renvoyzé and agreed to submit their dispute to arbitration. They made a list of their personal claims. The text of their agreement is preserved in the Hart archive.[12] It is long and difficult to read, both because of its poor state of preservation and because of its particularly convoluted wording.

The arbitrators, David Ross and James Reid, took their job seriously. (The latter, future chief justice of the Court of King's Bench, would be regularly consulted by the Harts. Immediately after his election, Ezekiel wrote him for advice.) Moses was claiming £300 "for his time, trouble and expenses in keeping the Books of Account of the said Estate, managing the affairs of the same . . . and making a Journey to Albany." This sum was the equivalent of a good annual salary. But he didn't stop there. "Also for a sum of five hundred pounds promised him by letter from the said Aaron Hart if the said Moses should marry to the liking of the said Aaron Hart-And Lastly for the sum of two hundred and twenty pounds for conducting Harman Fisher Hart an orphan, nephew of the said late Aaron Hart." Moses noted that Aaron had entrusted this child to him in 1794 and that he had paid "for the board cloathing [sic] and education of the said Harman Fisher Hart since that period." This child was no doubt the son of Henry Hart, Aaron's brother. In total, Moses was claiming £1,020 from the estate.

Ezekiel was either less greedy or had less imagination. He claimed £100 for his work as an executor and for having balanced the books of Hart & Sons. Enigmatically, he claimed "a sum of money which he the said Ezekiel demands Under certain letters from the said late Aaron Hart to the said Ezekiel Hart respecting the marriage of the said Ezekiel." I admit that I am tempted to figure out how he formulated this claim, but I am resisting that temptation.

Finally, Alexander claimed the paltry sum of £100 for having acted as clerk for eight months, from 1 May 1800 to 1 January 1801.

It was also established that Moses owed the estate £505 and Ezekiel owed £287 7s6d.

The two arbitrators, who had been chosen and appointed by the four interested parties, concluded, "The said Moses Hart is not entitled nor ought be, to recover or receive from the Estate of the said Aaron Hart for or by reason of his claims aforesaid or of any or either of them any of the sums of money by him the said Moses Hart thereby demanded or any part thereof, the said claims appearing to us ill-founded and not supported, and we do therefore hereby disallow the same and every part thereof." Moses must have smiled and shaken his head at all the words that Ross and Reid had used to say, simply, no.

Ezekiel had no better luck. His claims "for his trouble as one of the Executors" and for "settling the accounts of the partnership of Aaron Hart and Sons" were judged inadmissible. On the other hand, the arbitrators concluded that the money that he owed to the estate would not be claimed, as Aaron had given it to him in consideration of his marriage. Finally, Alexander's claim was declared inadmissible.

There remained the matter of the £505 that Moses owed the estate. This debt was to be split into four. Instead of the £126 due to each of them, the other three brothers agreed to accept £75. Moses negotiated right to the last farthing.

The Remainder of the Estate

Moses received as his inheritance the Sainte-Marguerite seigneury and the Marquisat du Sablé; Ezekiel, the Bécancour seigneury; Benjamin, a two-storey stone house on Rue Notre-Dame; and Alexander, the lot on Rue Notre-Dame and another on Rue des Forges. As to the other pieces of land that Aaron Hart owned, there is a document that divides them among Moses, Ezekiel, and Benjamin.[13]

Aaron had not forgotten his four daughters. To each, he left £1,000, which they could access when they got married. Until then, they could collect the interest. If they remained single, the money would go to the male children, their brothers. Catherine, who was already married, also had the right to £1,000, but she had received £625 when she wed.

Out of curiosity, I looked into the fate of a slave purchased by the Harts on 7 September 1779 in Montreal. What had happened to Phoebe, a black woman, bought from James Finlay for £45 "to be paid on delivery"?[14] The contract made in front of two witnesses, Uriah Judah and Andrew Hays, specified, "The said James Finlay for myself my heirs and Executors against any person or persons whatsoever Do for ever warrant and defend and further warrant and guarantee the said Negro wench sound free of all Sickness and disorders whatsoever at the day of the date hereof upon this further special Condition that the said sum of Forty five pounds current money of this Province be paid on delivery of the said Negro wench."

Several years later, Moses brought back from Albany another black slave, Jane, about twenty-six years old, and her daughter Mary, about six months old. The papers had been drawn up on 23 May 1786 in the name of Aaron Hart and the sale consented to by James Bloodgood at the price of £72 10s.[15]

Were these two women purchased to assist Dorothea or were they intended for resale? Raymond Douville believes that Aaron and Dorothea wanted to impress the people of Trois-Rivières. He imagined Dorothea doing her shopping with Phoebe in tow.

On 19 July 1787, one year after Jane's arrival, the Hart family was shaken by a tragedy that triggered a major inquiry, and Aaron had to call upon

Pour par mon d. sieur aaron hart, jouir, faire et
disposer dud.e nègre comme bon lui semblera, comme
de son propre; La présente vente ainsi faite pour ce

The Purchase of Pompée

The black figure proudly holds up the globe made by Vincenzo Coronelli (1688). This exceptional piece is in the collection of the Stewart Museum (1979-33-1). It adorns the cover of the work devoted to earthly and celestial globes, *Sphaerae Mundi* (Sillery: Septentrion, 2000), written by Edward H. Dahl and Jean-François Gauvin, with the collaboration of Robert Derome. The globe is supported by four figures that may represent the cardinal points. They are scantily clad in loincloths and turbans. Behind each is a support to provide the sculpture with solidity. The globe measures 108 centimetres in diameter. See Dahl and Gauvin (2000), pp. 24, 33, 118, 131.

In 1774, did Aaron have any scruples about purchasing a slave? Likely it was the opposite. With the purchase of young Pompée, the Hart family rose a rung on the social ladder. Owning a slave was well regarded, as surprising as that might seem today. One of the oldest practices in the history of humanity, slave owning was nevertheless coming to an end. In Quebec, it was at the point of "dying of old age." There were fewer and fewer transactions. Nevertheless, here are the terms for the sale of Pompée.

Jérémie Dugand "of Saint-Ours on the River Chamblie," "by these presents Bargained, Sold and Confirmed, now and forever, promised and promises to guarantee all claims whatsoever to Mr. Aaron Hart merchant . . . a negro boy of the age of thirteen years named pompée, that said Mr. Dugand declared having acquired from Jean Thomas of New England." Dugand gives himself six weeks to deliver the slave to his new master. "So that Mr. Aaron Hart, *jouïv*, does with and disposes of said Negro as he sees fit." Price, 1,050 shillings paid "in good current coins," which Dugand declared to have received. Aaron Hart being able to "act fully as owner and true master . . . made and passed at three rivers, house of said Mr. Hart afternoon the twenty-third of September one thousand seven hundred seventy four" (notaries Dillet and Badeaux, BAnQ, Trois-Rivières).

The word "jouïv" completely puzzled the notaries. They wrote it as they had heard Aaron pronounce it. They no doubt did not know the word and had no idea how to spell it.

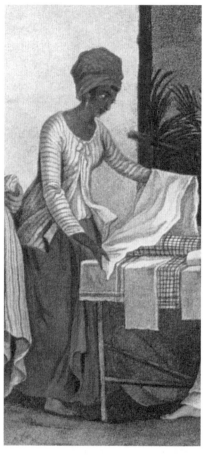

Phoebe and Jane

I don't know what happened to Pompée, but four years later Aaron bought "a negro woman named Phoebe with all her wearing apparell" for forty-five pounds sterling. She was declared "free of all sickness and disorders." Uriah Judah, Aaron's brother-in-law, and Andrew Hays, a Jewish Montreal merchant, served as witnesses.

Did Pompée and Phoebe work together in the Hart household? We know nothing about them. However, we do know, through two other transactions, that Aaron bought and resold slaves. On 23 March 1786, Moses brought Jane, twenty-six, and her daughter, Mary, about six months old from Albany. Two years later, the mother and child became the property of Jean Macpherson, who purchased them from Monsieur le Chevalier de Tonnancour [Charles Antoine] (Badeaux, BAnQ, 2 AC-5.31/314S). The seller stated that he had purchased them from Mr. Aaron Hart. He declared that he was "content and satisfied . . . to have had them in his home for about ten months." The price paid by de Tonnancour is not known, but we know how much Macpherson paid: "40 guineas equivalent 46 pounds, 13 shillings and 4 pence." Jane's name was changed to Gennie and she aged by three years over a two-year period, as did her daughter, who was now identified as a three-year-old. Aaron had paid "75 pounds 10 shillings" in New York currency. Unless the New York pound was weaker than the "Province de Québec" pound, someone got a bad deal. There is something else intriguing. In July 1787, Dolly Manuel was found dead in the Harts' home. At the time of the inquiry, no one questioned Jane. She had been with de Tonnancour since the summer of 1787 (May or June)—she had left the Harts shortly before the tragedy. In any case, this was Aaron's last transaction involving a black person.

Preceding page: left, the transaction concerning Phoebe; right, the transaction involving Jane and her child.

his influential friends to come to the rescue. A young servant, Dolly Manuel, had hanged herself in the Harts' attic. The inquiry led by the commissioner of peace, Chevalier de Niverville, ultimately concluded that it had been a suicide. Doubt remained in the minds of the town's residents for a long time, and Moses was the object of their suspicions.[16]

Curiously, Jane and her young daughter no longer seemed to be with the family.[17] If she had been, it would have been normal for the investigator to question her.[18]

Finally, an inevitable question: were such quarrels over an estate common? To make a comparison, I looked into the Molson family, rivals of the Harts in the brewery, shipping, and banking sectors. (Sophie Imbeault has made a thorough study of the Lanaudière family on this subject.) Late in his life, John Molson Sr. wanted to alter his will by introducing the obligation for his three sons to work together in the same firms. He had not succeeded in this during his lifetime, and his last wishes produced no greater success. "Each of them, as both residuary legatee and executor of the will," writes Alfred Dubuc, "was accountable to his brothers."[19] Discord arose. The legal battles lasted five years, and it took another two to reconcile John Jr., Thomas, and William. Their father, in a desire to control the future, forced his three sons to become partners; Aaron tried to do more or less the same thing—with the same result.

In the end, thanks to the arbitrators David Ross and James Reid, the four Hart brothers took a little less than three years to wrap up their father's estate. Did that mean that they were reconciled with each other? I think not, as later events bear witness.

In the short term, however, a very special event would bring them together: the 1804 elections. The four brothers decided to close ranks. Their father had bequeathed to them an enviable social status, and they agreed to form a common front to test it among their fellow citizens.

CHAPTER 5

Ezekiel Hart, House of Assembly Member from Trois-Rivières

IN 1807, EZEKIEL HART WAS THIRTY-SEVEN YEARS OLD and a successful man. Married for a dozen years, he already had a nice flock of children: Samuel Bécancour, Esther, Harriet, Aaron Ezekiel, and Caroline; two others would follow. The oldest had received the name Bécancour. Ezekiel intended him to inherit the seigneury of the same name, a part of which had been left to him by his father (as we recall, Aaron's will obliged him to bequeath it to his oldest son), and which he was restoring. The second youngest of his children, born 22 August 1809—the date is important—was named James Henry Craig Hart or, shortened, Ira Craig Hart. The youngest son was Adolphus Mordecai.

Bécancour and Craig—these two names were points of reference in the life of Ezekiel Hart. The former bore the promises of the future in this new land; the latter recalled the difficulties of a path that was to lead to equal rights, the Harts' political victory—especially those of the third generation.

Ezekiel Hart, the First Jewish Elected Representative

Ezekiel's name went down in history on Saturday, 11 April 1807. On that day, he triumphed over three solid adversaries—Mathew Bell, Thomas Coffin, and Pierre Vézina—and became an elected member of the House of Assembly of Lower Canada for Trois-Rivières. The three candidates whom he defeated that day would later each take their turn in this seat: Bell was to be elected in 1809; Coffin, in 1810; and Vézina, in 1816. At the time, Trois-Rivières had the right to two members; however, none of these three held on to his seat for very long at a stretch. Getting elected was a challenge for these successful men, but remaining there was another kind of challenge. The position, unpaid, was in the end quite disappointing, as much for the bureaucrats who supported the governor as for the Canadiens who were trying affirm their prerogatives as elected representatives.

This is the only known copy of a portrait of Ezekiel Hart.
I was unable to find the original.

Matthew Bell, born in England, was an extraordinary businessman who was involved with the operations of the Saint-Maurice ironworks located close to Trois-Rivières. Thomas Coffin, born in Boston and a Loyalist, had invested in the ironworks in Batiscan. Thus, Bell and Coffin were already business competitors. Pierre Vézina had chosen to use a law career as a social springboard.

Ezekiel had the means to meet them head-on. Through his extended family, he belonged to a vast network in both North America and England. He was confident. His mother, Dorothea Judah, had family in London and New York and at least two brothers, Samuel and Uriah, living in the Province of Quebec, which had been formed in 1763 and had become Upper and Lower Canada in 1792. His father, Aaron, had been among the first Jews to settle in the new British colony. He had succeeded beyond all expectations. It was as if the British had forgotten about the Jews. What was forbidden in England seemed to go unnoticed in North America. Besides, the British had enough to contend with in dealing with the French-speaking and Catholic Canadiens. At the beginning of the British regime, in principle—there were exceptions—anyone who wanted to enter public service had to take the Test Oath, denying transubstantiation and abjuring the authority of the pope. Oaths of this type posed very different problems for Jews. First, there was the issue of swearing on the Bible—that is, both the Old Testament and the New Testament; Jews rejected the latter and therefore would not swear an oath on it. Second were the phrases "the true faith of a Christian" and "in the Year of Our Lord." The former was, of course, inapplicable; as to the latter, the Jewish calendar is not based on the birth of Jesus Christ.[1]

The First Attempt in 1804

Ezekiel first tried to run for office in 1804. His older brother, Moses, had already made his political aspirations known. Ambitious, self-assured, even a little cocky, Moses had offered his services in 1796 in the town where he was living at the time, William Henry (Sorel), strategically located on the route to New York. Did he really campaign? In any case, he was not elected, to his father's relief. Aaron had sent Moses a warning: "What I do not like is that you will be opposed as a Jew. You may go to law, but be assured you will never get a jury in your favour nor a party in the House for you."

Out of respect for his father's wishes, Ezekiel waited until after his death in 1800 to give free rein to his political ambitions. It is doubtful that he

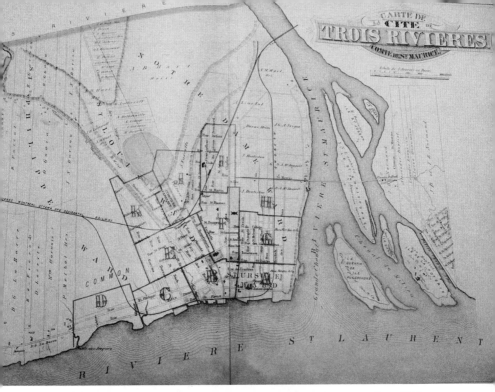

At the time Ezekiel Hart was elected—in fact, from 1792 to 1838—the county of Trois-Rivières had the right to two members in the House. The county was bordered to the east by the Saint-Maurice River and to the south by the St. Lawrence River. Until the municipal mergers took place, in 2002, the county and the city had the same borders.

ran for office to prove his success in life, but he had clearly understood his father's message. He also understood that equal rights were a possibility in this new country. Ezekiel was an educated man; his personal library (which took up seventeen pages of his property inventory) was one of the largest of its time. Freedom had to be earned; equality as well.

As the 1804 elections approached, the Hart family assessed its chances of having a member elected. Moses's behaviour was often scandalous, whereas Ezekiel was a gentleman in every sense of the term. He would be the candidate. Nevertheless, a victory would not be easy. He had to run against John Lees, who had been elected without interruption since 1792; Louis-Charles Foucher, who, with an impressive political career, had just been promoted to a judgeship in the provincial court; and Pierre Vézina, a thirty-two-year-old lawyer with no particular allegiance.

The Harts formulated their strategy. Each elector could vote for two candidates, and the two with the greatest number of votes would be elected.

In the 1980s, I discovered in the archives of the American Jewish Historical Society, then situated at Brandeis University in Waltham, this extraordinary document classified under "Hart Family, Miscellaneous Material, Box 2." At the time, I didn't know that Ezekiel Hart had run in the 1804 election—information that was very useful to me for the biography that I was writing for the *Canadian Dictionary of Biography*. At the time, voting was done by a show of hands, and I wasn't surprised that a member of the Hart family carefully recorded the votes cast. Although they are difficult to read, the names recorded confirm that Ezekiel received the support of many French Canadians and of his neighbour, Veyssière. The names of five women are on the list, including Miss Laguereche (?) and Miss Boucher (?), a Mrs. Tonnancour, and a Mrs. Denaut (?). They came together and declared their votes toward the end of the session. All five voted for Vézina.

Moses would vote for just one: his brother. He understood that the two candidates who obtained the most votes would be elected.

Around 1987, when I was easing back into the world of history after a few years in politics, the editors of the *Dictionary of Canadian Biography* asked me to write the biography of Ezekiel Hart. I knew that I would have to look elsewhere than the archives of the Séminaire de Trois-Rivières to shed light on his election. I suspected that Gerald E. Hart, Ezekiel's grandson, a historian and collector, had kept for himself the most significant documents; he certainly had not discarded or destroyed them. I found some of them at the McCord Museum in Montreal, the American Jewish Archives in Cincinnati, and at the American Jewish Historical Society, housed, at the time, at Brandeis University in Waltham, near Boston.

By a stroke of luck, I found a document, the ancestor of a tally sheet, on which were written the votes of each elector. It was not an official document but a personal initiative taken, very likely, by one of the Hart brothers, who recorded everything and left nothing to chance. This valuable document bears neither a date nor identification, and it is barely legible. I deciphered the names of the candidates, although I could not ascertain that the Hart registered was in fact Ezekiel Hart. Since neither his name nor those of the other candidates appeared among the electors, I deduced that the candidates did not vote in this election. I also read with a fair amount of certainty the name M [Moses] Hart on the list of electors, written just above the name McCarthy, which intrigued me. I thought that this could be Mary McCarthy, Moses's last wife, until I found out that she gave birth to two boys in 1838 and 1840. I did note that several women were on the electors' list, including a certain Mrs. Tonnancour.

A broadsheet that Ezekiel Hart had posted for voters in Trois-Rivières, a copy of which I found at Brandeis, finally convinced me that, in fact, in 1804 Foucher won a seat and Lees was re-elected. Despite his commitment to fulfil the tasks of his position "to the utmost of my abilities, and that of the interest of this my native place," Ezekiel came in fourth, with 44 votes out of a possible 144.

It is also to be noted that Ezekiel's two younger brothers, Benjamin and Alexander, voted for both Lees and Hart; they did not follow the lead of Moses. This would not have affected the results, but they did end up giving two votes to an adversary.

> *Aux Dignes et Indépendants Electeurs de la Ville des Trois-Rivières.*
>
> MESSIEURS,
>
> ENCOURAGE' par pluñeurs de mes Concitoyens à m'offrir comme Candidat pour vous repréfenter dans le prochain Parlement Provincial :
>
> Permettez-moi de folliciter vos voix et votre influence, *Mercredi* le *4 Juillet Prochain* jour fixé pour la tenue du Poll par l'Officier Rapporteur.
>
> J'ai toujours été, comme je me flatte, Meffieurs, que vous me trouverez être en toutes occafions, animé par une attention la plus zélée et fans affeftation à tout ce qui peut remplir vos vœux, et contribuer à votre profpérité. *Mes intérêts font liés avec les vôtres*, et fi je fuis affez heureux pour obtenir cette fituation importante, je vous prie d'être affurés que mes efforts feront dirigés à m'acquitter, autant que mes foibles talents le permettront, des devoirs qu'elle exige, et plus particulierement lorfqu'il s'agira des intérêts de ce lieu où j'ai pris naiffance.
>
> J'ai l'honneur d'être, très refpeftueufement,
>
> Meffieurs et Concitoyens,
>
> Votre très fidèle,
>
> *Trois Rivières 22 Juin 1804* Et obéiffant Serviteur,
>
> EZEKIEL HART.

In the autumn of 2009, I intended to return to the American Jewish Historical Society archives; the papers that I wanted to see had been moved from Waltham to the Center for Jewish History in New York. My friend and publisher of Baraka Books Robin Philpot paid a visit to the archives, which was fruitful. He photocopied documents that I had consulted in Waltham. In particular, he brought a French version of the broadsheet addressed to voters written by Ezekiel, who left the date of the election blank. Ezekiel had had extra copies made, no doubt aware that he wouldn't win on the first attempt.

The Next Attempt in 1807

On 2 March 1807, John Lees died. A by-election was called for Saturday, 11 April. Thomas Coffin was running for Lees's seat. Foucher decided to throw his support behind Coffin, who had represented the Saint-Maurice riding from 1792 to 1804. He was from a Loyalist family and was a formidable opponent. He had married a wealthy heir, Marguerite Godefroy de

Tonnancour, in 1786 but had had financial reversals and wanted to cosy up to political power. His father-in-law, Louis-Joseph Godefroy de Tonnancour, had been one of the most influential men in the Trois-Rivières region, and one of those who had lost the most due to France's almost total lack of reimbursement of paper money. Aaron Hart had often advanced the unfortunate seigneur small, discreet loans that his heirs had to pay off in the end. They had major real-estate holdings, but little money. Thomas Coffin may have had an account to settle with Ezekiel; at any rate, Coffin was relentless.[2]

Bothered by Foucher's support of Coffin and realizing that he had little other backing, Vézina pulled out of the race and threw his support behind Coffin. Ezekiel nevertheless held on. Out of 116 electors, 59 voted for him. The chairman announced his victory.[3] A legend maintained by historian Benjamin Sulte suggests that Ezekiel was reluctant to sign papers on the Sabbath day. It seems that he quickly changed his mind, however; he signed where he was asked, notwithstanding the wording "in the year of Our Lord."

On 14 April, Hart wrote to his former lawyer, James Reid, who was now chief justice on the Court of King's Bench, to ask his advice.[4] He had won the first round, but what should he do next? In his letter, he mentioned Justice Foucher's challenges to his eligibility, described the situation in England and in the English colonies, and expressed his anxiety about taking the oath of loyalty to the Crown.

Ezekiel understood the opposing forces in the House of Assembly. The British had started a newspaper, *The Mercury* (1805); the Canadiens had responded by starting their own, *Le Canadien* (1806). In recent months, the tone had escalated dangerously. There was much absenteeism among the "Canadien" representatives, who did not have the means to stay away from the sources of their livelihoods for long.[5] Furthermore, they had been fiercely opposing the eligibility of magistrates to sit as members of the House, because they were in the pockets of the Tories. Ezekiel's allegiance was with the Tories.

Since they had arrived in North America in 1760, Jewish people had always supported the claims of the "old subjects"—the British in the colony. They had managed to sign their numerous petitions, while avoiding confrontation with the Canadiens, with whom they had cordial relations. They had put down roots throughout the province, discreetly settling in with a population almost all of whom were French-speaking and Catholic. They blended into the background. Almost fifty years had passed without a single voice criticizing their presence. Like Protestants, Jews had been banned from New France. Anti-Semitism had no roots in the St. Lawrence Valley. For the Canadiens, Jews simply did not exist as Jews. Restrictions and exclusions to which they were subject in Europe, especially England, simply were not part of life in North America.

"I have now to congratulate you on your late success," Reid wrote to Ezekiel in a letter of 20 April, "and I am happy to find that the confidence of the majority of your electors had placed you in the responsible situation of their representative." He professed his surprise at Justice Foucher's involvement in the matter and his declarations concerning Hart's ineligibility. He noted that, in fact, magistrates were forbidden to sit in the House of Commons in England. Assuaging Ezekiel's anxiety, he concluded, "There can be little doubt on the question you propose:– Your right to be elected and sit as a Member of the House I consider to be equal to that of any other Member in it."

"Sir James Henry Craig was almost at death's door when he debarked in Quebec on 18 October 1807," wrote Jean-Pierre Wallot (1973, p. 148). "Short but with a majestic bearing, he arrived basking in the glow of an enviable military reputation." He had already served in the "Province of Quebec" and had contributed to the defeat of the Americans in 1775. Legend has it that he became friends with Aaron Hart. From there to being Ezekiel's protector was, in the view of some, a short step quickly taken. However, Ezekiel had been elected on 11 April 1807—well before the arrival of his supposed protector. He was re-elected the following year in a general election, but Wallot is categorical: Craig did not leave Quebec before 1808 (1973, p. 164). He went to Trois-Rivières in 1809, according to the Ursuline author (see p. 127), but this time it was Moses Hart who was planning to run for office. Ezekiel was saving himself for other battles. In fact, he was preparing his sons. It was thus with an easy mind that he hosted Governor Craig at his residence. Craig therefore had an opportunity to see the path taken by the merchant Aaron Hart, whom he had met in 1775. He could also observe the situation of the French Canadians and certainly wonder about the debate raging in the newspapers. Ezekiel not only subscribed to the *Quebec Mercury* but was its agent in the town. Together, they might have read the diatribe by a certain Scevola: "The French Canadians are needlessly prolonging a backward, feudal, decadent society incapable of changing. Instead of whining about the distinction between the races, they could simply erase this distinction by assimilating, in becoming English" (quoted in Wallot, 1973, p. 152 [our translation]).

Ezekiel did not rejoice too quickly about this legal opinion. He knew that neither jurist had addressed the most important question: that of the oath (or oaths) to be taken.

Reflecting on his next move, Ezekiel decided not to rush to Quebec City to take his seat; the House had, in any event, adjourned on Thursday, 16 April. He would therefore have ample time to consult with more people and ask for advice from all of his contacts. One of his business partners obtained an opinion from Sir Vicary Gibbs, the new attorney general of the British government, known for his strictness and rigour. "I see no legal objection to the eligibility of a Jew who was elected and sits in the House of Assembly after having taken the usual oaths," pronounced the erudite jurist, according to a document found by David Rome. In fact, neither jurist had truly addressed the most delicate question—the nature of the oath or oaths to be taken.

Ezekiel knew what was at stake. He had not forgotten his father's warnings, but he had not heeded them. Or, rather, he had weighed them. In his view, the time had come to take the final steps toward equal rights. The opinions that he received from Reid and Gibbs strengthened his determination. He made his decision; when he arrived at the House of Assembly, he would take the prescribed oath in his own way, his head covered, his hand on the Pentateuch.[6] At least, that is my conviction: he knew what he was doing.

Legend versus Fact

The Hart affair has been told many ways, some of them with a whiff of anti-Semitism. Although it was very important, the case of Ezekiel Hart has been treated lightly. As often happens in history, people repeat things without taking the time to go back to the documents and check. It is quite annoying to read the judgments and interpretation based on intuition or, worse, false information, of which there is no lack in this case. Some of these accounts are of no consequence, whereas others keep us from understanding what really went on.

Until the biography of Ezekiel Hart was published in the *Dictionary of Canadian Biography,* researchers and scholars who were interested in him were unaware of his participation in the 1804 election. Most thought that he had run for the first time in the by-election of 1807 and then in the general elections of 1808 and 1809.

The governor, James Henry Craig, had prorogued the Parliament on 27 April 1808, and then again on 2 October 1809, in both cases leading to general elections. Why had he done this? Was he enamoured of the pomp and circumstance that went with inaugurating a new parliament? Or was it due to a deep disagreement between him and the majority group in the House? Some believe that these two prorogations took place following the expulsion of member Ezekiel Hart and have built a scenario on the links between Craig and the Harts. In this view, Ezekiel's father, Aaron Hart of Trois-Rivières, had been a close friend of the governor's. At the time of the intervention by the British army in 1776, Craig was in the regiment that had expelled the American invaders from Trois-Rivières and had stayed at Aaron's house. It was said that Craig never missed an opportunity to stop in at Ezekiel's house on Rue des Forges in Trois-Rivières. And Ezekiel named his fourth son, born on 22 August 1809, James Henry Craig Hart.[7] Of course, Ezekiel could count on Craig's support. That is what one reads between the lines. One thing led to another. Many things were said by people who didn't know the facts, especially the extremely tense context in which the "Hart affair" took place.[8]

Ezekiel did indeed run for office three times: in 1804, 1807, and 1808, and not in 1807, 1808, and 1809. But there was a candidate named Hart in 1809, who received 32 votes, compared to 86 for Matthew Bell and 86 for Joseph Badeaux. In its issue of 2 November 1809, the *Gazette de Québec* gave the explanation: the defeated candidate was Moses Hart, Ezekiel's older brother.

For those who know about Aaron's sons, the fact that Moses ran for office is not surprising. As we know, he had previously planned to run in William Henry (Sorel), and one may suppose that he was reluctant to step aside in favour of Ezekiel in Trois-Rivières. Moses was no doubt aware that his various escapades did not stand him in good stead. Convinced gradually to adopt a more orderly life, he tried several times to get elected in ridings in the Trois-Rivières region, and running for Ezekiel's seat seemed a logical step in 1809.

On How to Take an Oath

The Hart family had been right to line up behind Ezekiel. The owner of part of the Bécancour seigneury, a well-established merchant, forming an exemplary couple with Frances Lazarus, he was a respected and respectable man. On Friday, 29 January 1808, he presented himself for the opening of the fourth session of the Fourth Parliament. The new governor, James Henry Craig, had arrived in Quebec the previous 18 October and was concentrating his energies on his state of health. He had stroked the ego of the parliamentary leader of the Parti canadien, Pierre-Stanislas Bédard, by naming him a militia captain in December 1807.

The House was brought to order with unusual pomp. Craig had asked that the necessary steps be taken. Elected in a by-election, without the support of the governor for obvious reasons (he had not yet arrived), Ezekiel had to present himself for the swearing-in. With resolution and faith in his convictions, he took the oath. Michel Amable Berthelot d'Artigny took responsibility for informing the House.[9] An unidentified member was uneasy about how the member from Trois-Rivières had taken his oath. Berthelot specified, "Mr. Hart took the oaths on the Bible with his head covered." Member Louis Turgeon added that the oath seemed to have been taken in the "manner described" by Berthelot, which doesn't tell us much. Member John Mure, a businessman who was no doubt a friend of Ezekiel's, realized what was about to happen and proposed that the session be adjourned to the next day—a Saturday.

On Monday, 1 February, Berthelot added a detail: "Ezekiel Hart, esquire, had taken the oath and not the oaths." Jonathan Sewell, seconded by Justice Amable De Bonne, tabled a motion to the effect that Hart "had not take the oath in the customary manner," with consequences that can be guessed.[10]

Jonathan Sewell and Amable De Bonne both participated in the debate over the election of Ezekiel Hart. Sewell, however, was in a bind. Even though Hart would clearly stand with the Tories, Sewell, a Loyalist by background, could not forget about his religion. Sewell had lived with his family in England and then had returned to North America, where he had studied law. His university education made him one of the key men in Lower Canada. He voted to keep Hart out of the House of Assembly. De Bonne, obliging the Tories, followed Sewell's lead. This is the paradox of the Hart affair that has bothered many historians. In fact, De Bonne could have sided with Hart, for as a judge he also had to confront the Parti canadien, which was trying to expel magistrates from the House of Assembly.

Whatever it Takes to Protect a Fragile Majority

Since 1792, the House of Assembly had had an average of thirty-five "Canadien" members and fifteen "English" members who were favourable to the Tories—that is, the governor's party. Despite a majority that seemed comfortable, the Canadien members were on the alert. Their ranks shrank as each session progressed. The members received neither salaries nor reimbursement for their expenses, and many had jobs that required them to be at home. To consolidate their position, the Canadien members had already chosen to exclude magistrates from the House. As Ezekiel Hart was perceived as a partisan of the Tories, his religion became a pretext for attempting to exclude him as well. In parallel with the debate over the eligibility of magistrates—more concretely, justices Foucher and De Bonne—another began on the validity of the oath that he had taken.

The ball got rolling at the beginning of the session. Thomas Coffin, a poor loser, started the hostilities. On 9 February 1808, he presented a petition, seconded by his colleague Benjamin Frobisher, member from Montreal, to recall the report made by returning officer Charles Thomas on the result of the recent election in Trois-Rivières in which Ezekiel Hart had received fifty-nine votes while he, Coffin, had received forty-one votes. Furthermore, the petitioner asserted, "Ezekiel Hart is of the Jewish Religion and is therefore not capable of being elected to serve in the House of Assembly, or of taking the oaths required, or sitting or voting in the House Assembly." As a consequence, his election ought to be considered "null and void." The House was asked to annul Hart's election and to ask the "clerk of the Crown in Chancery" to correct the result "by erasing the name of the said Ezekiel Hart, and inserting that of the petitioner in lieu thereof." The newspapers quickly picked up on Coffin's ploy, and the *Gazette de Québec* of 11 February and *Le Canadien* of 3 February carried stories on them. Coffin's petition was summarized thus: "Ezekiel Hart, Esquire, being Jewish, cannot take the oath required by Members and as a consequence cannot be admitted to the Chamber," and therefore "said Ez. Hart's name must be crossed out of the Election return and replaced by that of the Applicant."

Hart was not slow to react. On the 12th, he demanded to submit his own petition. A vote was taken to establish whether it should be received or rejected. The vote was twenty-four in favour and nine against. There was obviously confusion. The members were interpreting the request differently.

Hearing the petition—or not hearing it—did not mean being in favour of Hart or against him.

Hart was petitioning for the right to take his seat. He said that he had "duly taken the oath ordered by the statute of the 31st year of His Present Majesty Chap. 31, Section 29, which oath renders him eligible to take his seat in Said House. . . . He regards his oath as legal and is bound to it in all regards. Whether he has taken the said oath in compliance with the Constitutional Law of this province, there is no objection to taking it again in the usual manner. [That is] why the applicant humbly begs that it please this Chamber to permit him to take his seat as a consequence."

In the following days, various manoeuvres took place. The members voted repeatedly, but it is not clear on what. The content of the debates was not reported in the House minutes.

The Expulsion of Ezekiel Hart

Finally, on 15 and 16 February, the entire House became a committee studying Ezekiel's petition. On the 17th, it came to the conclusion that the oath that he had taken would be accepted in the courts ("is that practised in the Court of Justice when Oaths are administered to persons professing the Jewish religion"). The members then heard three of their number—John Mure, Jean-Marie Mondelet, and Justice Foucher—testify that, to their knowledge, Ezekiel was in fact of "Jewish religion." On Friday the 19th, the members again heard from Hart. The House minutes are silent on the exchanges. Fortunately, the newspapers, including the *Quebec Mercury* (22 February), decided to report on the affair.

The House had taken on the demeanour of a courtroom. Ezekiel felt as if he had been summoned to testify. "Mr. Speaker," he said, with firmness and dignity, "I neither required nor did I wish to take oath in the form it was administered. I took it in the words of the Act of the 31st year of His Majesty and in a manner binding on my conscience. I profess the religion of my father; a religion tolerated by my King and Country and not forbidden by the Constitutional Act. Mr. Speaker, I think I have a right to take my seat in this Honourable House, and I am now ready to do my duty therein, and I wish to have the opportunity of returning the obligations I have to those who elected me. I have no further observations to make."

As was its habit, the House decided to adjourn and meet again the following day. Some members noted that it was the Sabbath. Ezekiel's political

This magnificent painting by Charles Huot depicts the language debate of 1793. This is a recent photograph taken by Francesco Bellomo for the book written by Gaston Deschênes and published by Stromboli in 2007, *L'Hôtel du Parlement. Mémoire du Québec*. Ernest Gagnon wrote a booklet, *Tableaux d'histoire*, in which he identifies the members present in the Chamber. I was therefore able to find John Lees, whom Ezekiel ran against in 1804 and succeeded in 1807.

adversary, Justice Foucher, who liked to make fun of Ezekiel's small stature, was forced to recognize that he was standing tall. Nevertheless, he insisted on an adjournment until the next day, alleging that in his opinion nothing was stopping a Jew from satisfying his curiosity on the Sabbath and recalling that in fact Ezekiel had been elected on a Saturday.

This innocuous exchange led member Joseph-Bernard Planté to remark that the question of the Sabbath was in itself a difficulty for the session to come if Hart was to be admitted. The House minutes do not mention any further comment.

On Saturday, 20 February, after examining the various documents that had accumulated since 29 January, the House arrived at the conclusion that "Ezekiel Hart, Esquire, professing the Jewish Religion, cannot take a place, nor sit, nor vote in this House." Justice Foucher was the author of this ultimate resolution, which was seconded by the member from Surrey (named Jacques-Cartier).

Reading the House documents, one has the impression that this was simply procedure. Fortunately, reports in the newspapers of the time have enabled me to partially reconstruct the debates. John Mure indicated to

Justice Foucher that it seemed "disloyal to make war in the House with the very one that he had fought during his election." Jonathan Sewell was interested in the nature of the oath; John Richardson discussed the privileges of subjects born in the colonies, which was the case for Ezekiel Hart. He even brought up the possibility of omitting the words "upon the true faith of a Christian." Mure and Ross Cuthbert (Warwick [Berthier] riding) shared Richardson's opinion, while Sewell sought refuge in canon law to state, "The oath must be taken on the Holy Gospel."

The "Scholarly" Discourse of Pierre Bédard

Since the beginning, Pierre Bédard, leader of the Parti canadien, had not said a word. He did his research, his nose deep in his books. Despite his eloquence, he was not very convincing on the question of oaths. *Le Canadien* (28 May 1808), which allowed for a bit of humour from time to time, reported that an orator "realized, in the middle of his speech, that sleep had crept up on his audience. He suddenly went quiet, changed tone, and three times appealed to one of his colleagues, 'Milord, I am sorry to interrupt your nap, but I must ask you not to snore so loudly, as you might wake His Majesty.'"

Almost three months earlier, *Le Canadien* (2 March 1808) had, with all the respect due to the leader, reported at length on Pierre Bédard's "schol-

Pierre Bédard was by no means a small-time quarrelsome politician. Nevertheless, he wanted to engage in politics and was elected to the first Parliament in 1792. Studious and intelligent, he became leader of the Parti canadien. He was deeply involved with the disturbances of 1809–10 and imprisoned in 1810, with members Blanchet and Taschereau and some journalists from *Le Canadien*, of which he had been one of the founders in 1806. He refused to be freed and demanded a trial. He was let go, against his wishes, after thirteen months of captivity. He had been re-elected to the House despite the circumstances and retained his seat until December 1812, when he accepted a magistrate's position for the Court of King's Bench in Trois-Rivières.

arly discourse" on the formulation of oaths, naturalization, the Jews' historical situation in England, and their status in the world. On this last subject, Bédard said that their condition was no better in the other Christian countries, as nowhere were they granted the right of citizenship; this was not doing them an injustice, however, because they did not want to be citizens of any country. They were present in every country, because they had to be somewhere, but they did not regard any country as theirs; they lived in the country where they conducted their business and they gave it no title other than that of the country of their residence. They were held by their beliefs to act thus, they were waiting for the Messiah their Prince, and while waiting they could not engage their faith to any Prince other than the one that they had reserved for themselves.

"All this reasoning is simply sophism," retorted Richardson. Speeches by members Mure, Blackwood, de Salaberry, and Cuthbert followed suit. But in a democratic and parliamentary system, the majority holds the truth—unless the king gets involved.

The Reply

On 29 February 1808, Ezekiel Hart addressed the governor directly. There are various published versions of his speech. He claimed his right to take his seat and, above all, humbly observed that he and his fellow Jews would be deprived of their rights if the position adopted by the House was maintained.

On 14 March 1808, Herman Witsius Ryland, the governor's secretary, sent this reply: "The Governor in Chief . . . having given the subject the most mature consideration in his power . . . cannot think it expedient that he should interfere with the proceedings which the House of Assembly has thought proper to adopt in your case."[11]

In his petition, Ezekiel had alluded to his fellow Jews. In fact, where were they during this debate? At first, the Hart affair had no doubt seemed a minor quibble. In the early nineteenth century, the Jewish community in Lower Canada consisted of about one hundred people, dispersed and not organized. Over the years, no cause had mobilized them. In public debates, they aligned themselves with the British and made the same demands. No doubt if Ezekiel had consulted them, they would have given him the same advice that Aaron had given his sons: stay out of politics, for as a Jew you will not be welcome in the House.

Now that the question had been raised, some Jews became active. On 14 March, as Ryland was writing the governor's reply, John Mure tried to make the Chamber aware of a petition by "several Jews." The majority of the members present were opposed to hearing it. The document was not tabled. In the Hart archive conserved at the Archives Pierre-Boucher in the Séminaire de Trois-Rivières, among the tens of thousands of documents that await researchers, is a draft memorandum.[12] It is unsigned and may have been written by Ezekiel. The signatories denounce the resolution voted by the House—"It would be a truly hard and injurious case to your petitioners"—and demand a law recognizing and affirming their rights. This would come with the efforts of Ezekiel's son. For the moment, Ezekiel planned to run for office again at the first opportunity.

Ezekiel Hart: Expelled Again

On 27 April 1808, the Fourth Parliament was prorogued. On 17 May 1808, Ezekiel Hart, once again a candidate in Trois-Rivières, was re-elected; he had retained his fifty-nine voters from the previous election. According to the results published in the *Gazette de Québec*, Joseph Badeaux finished first, with sixty-seven votes, and won the other seat in the riding. Pierre Vézina and Justice Foucher earned, respectively, forty-six and thirty-two votes. The message was clear for Foucher: his political career was over. He had not been very devoted to it, having won three mandates in three different ridings. As for the "Jewish question," it had not raised any debate. *Le Canadien* (28 May 1808) published another humorous item, this one titled "The Jew and the Christian."

A Jew and a Christian were chatting on the edge of a well, when the Jew, by chance, fell in, without injury. The Christian ran to find a ladder, and, as he was making every effort to lower it into the well, the Jew said, "It's not worth it, I won't use your ladder; it's Saturday today." He stayed in water up to his chin until the next day, when his friend came to see how he had spent the cold night. "The ladder! The ladder!" cried the Jew, "for the love of God bring the ladder!" "May God keep me," replied the Christian, "it's Sunday today."

When the session opened, on 14 April 1809, Hart was no doubt a bit reassured. One of his adversaries, Foucher, was no longer around; the other, Coffin, elected in the Saint-Maurice riding, seemed calmer. On 10 April, the members met to choose their speaker. They chose Jean-Antoine Panet

Jean-Antoine Panet was one of the most skilful parliamentarians of his times. In 1784, he was won over to the ideas of Pierre Du Calvet and declared himself in favour of a House of Assembly. He became one of the leaders of the reform party. Wealthy and educated, he had a flawless career. He knew how to make useful compromises; his successive elections as Speaker of the House are evidence of this.

by thirty-five votes to eight. Hart voted for Denis-Benjamin Viger. It was clear that he had not yet figured out the parliamentary game! If he wanted to soften up the Parti canadien, he had to support its candidate.

On 15 April, and during the sessions that followed, Ezekiel again had opportunities to participate in votes. The question of his presence was raised only on 17 April. Once again, the procedure was labyrinthine. Days passed, and Ezekiel no doubt began to hope. Finally, on 5 May, the House decided to examine the Hart case: how had the oath been taken? Members Bourdages and Duchesnay had been present at Ezekiel's swearing-in. He had taken the oath, bareheaded, hand on the book. Which book? The New Testament. Mr. Blackwood had taken the oath at the same time; he had kissed the book and presented it to Mr. Hart, who did the same.

Now, Mr. Mondelet and Mr. Martineau protested. By taking an oath on the Holy Gospel, Mr. Hart, who was of the Jewish religion, "cannot be bound by this oath, he has profaned the religion of the oath and cannot take his place, nor sit, nor vote in this House."

And so the debate began again. Everyone had his say. Finally, on that very day, Ezekiel Hart was excluded by resolution, and on Monday, 8 May 1809, his seat was declared vacant. A final attempt by members Planté and Caron to save him, on 6 May, had not been not successful. These two, out of solicitude for Ezekiel, asked him if he would be willing to convert. Might this have been the solution?

History is not made with "ifs," but I cannot keep from wondering whether Ezekiel could have undertaken at least a symbolic political conversion. After all, a majority of his electors had no doubt hoped that he would

The Napoleonic Wars left in their wake a conflict between England and the United States. Even though they were poorly prepared, the Americans invaded Upper and Lower Canadas. They first attacked Upper Canada and set fire to part of Toronto. An expedition sent to attack Montreal was blocked at Châteauguay by militias led by Charles de Salaberry. "Old" and "new" subjects fought side by side against the invader.

vote with the Parti canadien in favour of their candidate for speaker, Jean-Antoine Panet. Politics is not for the pure; it requires flexibility, planning, a sense of compromise.

Ezekiel missed his chance, especially given that he was not subjected to party discipline. In the "good old days," parliamentarians enjoyed a wide margin to manoeuvre.

Climate of Crisis with Threat of War

In parallel with the Hart affair, another debate was ongoing about the eligibility of magistrates. On 15 May 1809, a vote was held to decide their fate, and Justice Amable De Bonne was expelled. On that day, Craig suspended work in the House; finally, on 2 October 1809, he prorogued the Fifth Parliament, which was in only its first session. This time, he decided to become involved in the election campaign. For the first and only time in his mandate as governor, he left Quebec City, which led the historian Jean-Pierre Wallot to observe that the governor's frequent visits to his friend Ezekiel Hart were the stuff of legend.[13]

The results of the 1809 election campaign changed nothing for the Tory Party. The opinions received from London solved nothing. In a confidential letter of 7 September 1809, Lord Castlereagh supported the House of Assembly on the ineligibility of magistrates and the expulsion of Hart, a practising Jew. The members wanted to expel the magistrates immediately. On 1 March 1810, exasperated, Craig dissolved the Sixth Parliament, which had gone into session on 29 January, cancelled the Canadien militia officers' commissions, seized the presses of *Le Canadien,* and threw into prison some twenty of the newspaper's managers and employees. Party leader Bédard was to stay in prison for a year without going to trial. Even had he been re-elected, he could not have been present at the opening of the Seventh Parliament on 12 December 1810.

The Tories held only twelve seats, but Craig took advantage of the absence of the leader of the Parti canadien to manoeuvre skilfully. Many of the British felt that the 1791 constitution had been an error. Craig was convinced that it was based on an illusion. He went to London himself to explain in the summer of 1811. He asked for the two Canadas to be united, although he would have preferred to see the elimination, pure and simple, of the House of Assembly. Jonathan Sewell and Herman Witsius Ryland, the governor's secretary, had more or less convinced him that the House had to be controlled by a majority of members favourable to the governor, even if it meant falsifying representation in the ridings to reach this goal. The true solution, in Sewell's view, would be massive English immigration to Canada.

In the short term, a new American threat—the War of 1812 between the United States and Britain—returned calm to the colony and crowded out the memory of one of the worst crises in Canadian parliamentarianism. It is really in this context that we must see the Hart affair. Ezekiel's religion had served as a pretext, and the protection that Governor Craig offered him was a decoy. It was his secretary who acknowledged receipt of Ezekiel Hart's petition, while Craig decided, on 5 June 1809, to solicit the opinion from London. On 7 September, as we know, the Secretary of State, Lord Castlereagh, confirmed that a Jew could not sit in the House of Assembly. Sewell had thus been right to distance himself from the Tories and vote with the Parti canadien against Ezekiel Hart's eligibility, except that this excellent jurist had alienated his ally while the *Canadiens* had removed a political adversary.

One day, not too long thereafter, the question of Jewish rights would return before the elected members of Lower Canada. It would be an opportunity to see what Canadiens truly felt. The Hart affair had sown the seeds of justice and equality.

ONE HUNDRED AND FIFTIETH ANNIVERSARY
OF THE
SPAN... AND PORTUGUESE JEWS
OF MONTREAL

CHAPTER 6

Jews Win a Victory Thanks to the Patriotes: The Laws of 1831–32

IN THE SUMMER OF 1960, under the delusion that I had exhausted the subject, I decided to wrap up my research on the Harts and the Jews at the beginning of the British regime. Each week, I went to Ottawa, where I had become a regular visitor at the Public Archives of Canada (today Library and Archives Canada) on Sussex Drive. Curious to see what real archives looked like, Jacques Lacoursière, a friend and historian, offered to lend me a hand. On Mondays, the staff was apprehensive when thay saw us coming. We knew the system: the researchers' room was open day and night; we simply had to ask for the maximum number of documents in advance and place them in cupboards for which we had the key.

An Acadian archivist, Roger Comeau, adopted us. Few people on staff spoke French (except for the night cleaning crew). Roger Comeau initiated us to the research tools and showed us all the collections that had been indexed. In the archives were the Gazette de Québec, military papers, permit applications, bonds of leaving, and lists of oaths taken. We learned, among other things, that in theory people needed "passports" to circulate from one jurisdiction to another, and also to leave the Province of Quebec, whose borders were moved three times between 1763 and 1791. In the latter case, applicants had to prove that they were not leaving bad debts behind.

This copy of the beautiful brochure published by the Jewish community was lent to me by René Hart. Under his full name, James René Hart, he had written, in his best handwriting, the family motto, "Schnell Fussen (Füssig) und Frey." At least, that's how he had noted it. This brochure had had a full life, giving it a particular charm. All the same, I wanted to have a copy in perfect condition, and I spoke to Janice Rosen, archivist of the Canadian Jewish Congress. She sent me a digitized version of the cover, which I used for the title page of this book. The Hebrew writing between the two pillars is the Ten Commandments, before which a rabbi reads a Torah scroll surrounded by eminent men. Below this tableau is a scene from family life, a man blessing his children before a meal. To the right is a chalice, perhaps Elijah's cup from the Seder ceremony. In the lower right-hand corner is a Star of David, behind which is a rabbi blowing a shofar. On either side of the title at the top are menorahs.

The Province of Quebec was not a prison, but who entered and left was controlled—as I say, in theory.

We were particularly interested in the oaths. From our history courses, we knew about the odious Test Oath and, although we were looking for Jewish names, we also wanted to prove false that no Canadien had taken this oath. Mr. Comeau had explained to us the nature of various oaths set out in the royal instructions of 7 September 1763 to Governor James Murray: the Test Oath, which denied the mystery of the Eucharist; an oath of allegiance or loyalty to the king coupled with an oath of abjuration of the branch of the Stuarts who were pretenders to the throne; and an oath confirming the supremacy of the king or repudiating papal authority.

Immediately after the Treaty of Paris was signed, Canadiens had to accept the authority of the British crown and deny the claims of the descendants of James II; it was more difficult for them to accept repudiation of the pope and thus be totally exempted from taking the Test Oath, an old British oath that was aimed at excluding Catholics from public office. This oath targeted transubstantiation and required repudiation of worship of the Virgin and the saints. The texts of the oaths were very clear. For those who didn't know the meaning of the word "transubstantiation," an explanation was given in the oath: "real presence of the body of Jesus Christ at the Holy Communion"—that is, according to the oath, "the elements of the bread and wine" were not transformed, at the moment of their blessing, into the body and blood of Christ.

Our professors had been right, it seems. We found no evidence of a Canadien taking the Test Oath before it was suppressed by the Quebec Act of 1774.

But our main interest was the Harts, and Jews in general. Although they were few in number, they seemed to be extremely active and mobile: we found inn licenses, bonds of leaving, sheriff's sales, and more. We were warned by our Jewish colleagues not to identify Jews only by family names. We also learned not to trust biblical first names, which were widespread among some groups of Protestants, as were certain family names, such as Abraham, David, Jacob, and Hart. Nevertheless, our file grew in size and we began to gain an idea of the Jewish presence in Quebec.

One evening, we found a beautiful document titled "Oath of Allegiance." An archivist had written on the back, "State Oaths for Persons of the Jewish Persuasion." Evidently, one or two words in the oath had been erased and replaced by "a Jew." The word "Jew" (or "juif") was rarely seen in documents of the time, and here it was on an official document. We knew the usual wording of the oaths that ended "upon the true faith of a Christian." "Jew" had been substituted for "Christian."

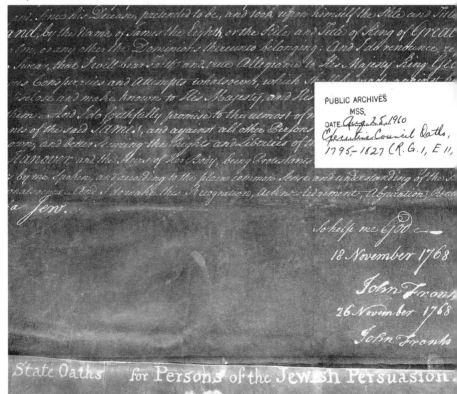

Early the next morning, we went to the copy centre to ask for a photostat[1] of the entire document and also an enlargement of the part that had been changed. On the back, the clerk wrote "Public archives mss" and recorded the date and identification of the document: "Aug. 25, 1960. Executive Council Oaths, 1764–1792, 1795–1827."[2] The document itself ended with the words, "So help me God, 18 November 1769, John Franks. 26 November 1768."

It was only on 15 December 2009 that I discovered why Franks had taken this oath. The Baby collection at the Université de Montréal conserves two documents concerning Franks's commission signed by George Allsopp.

This photostat is from 1960.

The one of 26 November 1768 notes, "John Franks overseer of the chimnies for the town of Montreal personally appeared before me this day and being of the Jewish Religion and Sworn on the Pentateuch or five Books of Moses; took and Subscribes the Oaths of Office, allegiance, Supremacy and abjuration, according to Act of Parliament." John Franks had also signed the document, committing "to the best of my abilities" to act as overseer of chimneys. The other document, also signed by Allsopp, is longer and more explicit and was produced "by his Excellency command," his Excellency being Guy Carleton.

David Rome Points the Way

In 1960, I took what seemed like an intensive course from David Rome, director of the Jewish Public Library in Montreal, and later the archivist and historian for the Canadian Jewish Congress. He was a man of great generosity, unshakable serenity, and considerable scholarship. I never knew, or I have forgotten, when he arrived in Montreal, but he quickly learned English and made great efforts to talk to me in French. He was passionate about history and wanted to understand French Canadian sensibilities.

When I proudly showed him the photostats that I had brought back from Ottawa, he was deeply moved. He explained to me that Jews in Canada, over the years, had seen the restrictions, to which they had been subjected in England, fall one after another. After the conquest of Canada, Jews were tolerated as British subjects but did not have access to certain offices due to an oath that included the words "upon the true faith of a Christian."

I don't remember whether Rome and I discussed the Plantation Act of 1740, the goal of which was to encourage the naturalization of people, other than Anglicans, who settled in the British colonies. Section 3 of the statute was aimed at "any person professing the Jewish Religion." What was important to Rome and me was that a Jew had succeeded, only five years after the signature of the Treaty of Paris, at having the wording of the oath changed with the approval of the governor, or at least his secretary. Rome also had several notes about John Franks, resident of Quebec City, who had been appointed overseer of chimneys in Montreal.

Rome and I went over the intriguing question of whether Aaron Hart deserved the title of the first Jew to settle in Canada (a subject that I have addressed in chapter 1 of this book). To summarize, in 1760, Aaron had left

New York to meet up with Amherst's army as it marched toward Montreal. He had met Frederick Haldimand, who became, in a way, his protector. Present at the surrender of Montreal in the summer of 1760, Aaron decided to try his luck in Trois-Rivières, where Haldimand was stationed for a short time before becoming governor general of Canada. Traditionally, therefore, authors consider Hart to have been the first Jew in Canada.

But Samuel Jacobs was already in Fort Cumberland, New Brunswick, in 1758. The following year, he was operating a brewery in Louisbourg. Could it be said that he was in Canada?[3] In any case, Jacobs was looking for new opportunities. The owner of a schooner, he decided to follow the invading fleet, led by Admiral Saunders, up the St. Lawrence River. After the surrender of Quebec, in September 1759, James Murray, who was put in charge of the town, requisitioned Jacobs's small ship. Jacobs turned this bad luck into good luck, multiplying his business initiatives. He quickly formed a commercial relationship with Aaron Hart, as well as one with Eleazar Levy, another one of the first Jews to settle in the "Province of Quebec." In short, Jacobs had no doubt arrived in North America before Hart. Rome reminded me that he had married a non-Jew and never rose to Hart's stature. Although Hart wasn't the first, he was the most important—in a way, the father of Canadian Jewry. We agreed that the exercise of identifying the first was fruitless; for instance, Levy appears in the documents at the same time as Jacobs and Hart. And they were all in contact with each other as of 1761—a fact that intrigued us. Had they known each other from before they arrived in North America?

We also examined the petitions that Jews signed in support of the British. In 1764, Levy signed a petition addressed to the king in which the "old British subjects" who had moved to the new colony denounced the "flagrant partiality" of the governor and demanded the "establishment of a House of Representatives." As a Jew, Levy considered himself an old British subject. And the Canadiens, who had been there for several generations, were "new" subjects. Furthermore, these "old" subjects, of whom there were only a few hundred, among more than 65,000 Canadiens, wanted a House of Assembly in which only they would sit. After all, had the British not conquered the country? Without fear of ridicule, they envisaged that the "new subjects" could be authorized to "elect Protestants without having to take oaths that their conscience would not allow them to take."[4]

Over the years, this type of petition evolved, gradually making room for the "new subjects"—the Canadiens. The position of the petitioners became more accommodating, envisaging not only the right of "new" subjects to vote, but also eligibility of both "new" and "old" subjects to run for office. At that point, a majority of Canadiens, with Pierre du Calvet leading them, also began to demand an elected House of Assembly.[5]

Creation of the Shearith Israel Congregation in 1768

Although their population was tiny, there were enough Jews to organize community life—at least in Montreal. On 30 December 1768, a minyan, a quorum of ten men, met to pray and plan a congregation that they named Shearith Israel, much later to become the Spanish and Portuguese Congregation. This choice of name was explained less by the origins of the first members than by the influence of New York and London.[6]

In the young, small community, there was much to do. In 1775, Lazarus David, a wealthy merchant, purchased a plot of land, near what was later Dominion Square, for a cemetery.[7] In October of the following year, his remains were buried there. He and his wife, Phoebe Samuel, were the parents of David, Samuel (husband of Aaron Hart's daughter Sarah), and Moses (who married another of Aaron Hart's daughters, Charlotte), Abigail (who married Andrew Hays), and Frances (who married Myer Michaels).

In 1777, Lazarus David's heirs made the gesture of offering a plot of land on Saint-Jacques for the erection of the first synagogue in Montreal, which was funded by a subscription campaign conducted by David Franks and Ezekiel Solomons. The following year, Jacob Raphael Cohen was engaged as the rabbi. Forced to bring lawsuits to get paid by the minyan, he won his case in 1782 but decided to leave Montreal, leaving behind him a divided community. He was replaced by Hazan de Lara, who served until 1810. Subsequently, the synagogue remained without a rabbi for thirty years. Ceremonies were organized by the members of the congregation, who shared the rabbinical functions. Jews from outside of Montreal occasionally participated; among the members were Barnet Lyons and Heineman Phineas, of Petite-Rivière-du-Loup (Louiseville), and Hyam Myers and John Franks, of Quebec.

In short, Jews in the Province of Quebec faced no legal or other external barriers.[8] Their greatest problem was their small numbers. Marriages outside the religion were therefore tolerated. The most famous case was that of Ezekiel Solomons, who married Elizabeth (Louise) Dubois at the Anglican church in Montreal in 1769. Their children were baptized. One of them

This photocopy of the minutes from the Shearith Israel synagogue is taken from the *Canadian Jewish Archives* (vol. 1, no. 4, March, 1959), which Louis Rosenberg proudly gave me. It shows that an election was held at David Franks's house to choose a *parnass* and a *gabay*. Levy Solomons and Uriah Judah were elected. Then, Ezekiel Solomons, and Levy Michaels were designated *Hatan Torah* and *Hatan Bereshith*. Samuel Judah was fined £3, Halifax currency, for having refused the position of *parnass*, while Isaac Judah, Myer Michaels, and Andrew Hays had to pay fines of £2 each for having refused the position of *hatan*.

was nevertheless buried in the Jewish cemetery, it having been agreed that this was not a precedent. Ezekiel Solomons was a respected member of the community, within which he held various positions. According to research conducted by Sheldon J. Godfrey and Judith C. Godfrey,[9] at the time the Montreal Jewish community included six single members, seven men married to Jewish women, six married to non-Jewish women, and four whose marital status is unknown; status is not always easy to establish due to the lack of appropriate registers.[10]

In Trois-Rivières, Aaron Hart and Dorothea Judah maintained close relations with the David and Joseph families and supported a small local community that respected the traditions. This was where, in the 1820s, a reaction began to the religious half-heartedness that had overtaken the Jewish community (see chapter 11). With his electoral victories in 1807 and 1808, Ezekiel Hart had brought the Jewish question into the news. The

War of 1812 then relegated it to the background, but it was only a matter of time before it resurfaced.

Benjamin Hart's Crusade Leads to the 1831 Statute

In 1824, the death of David David, the owner of the land on which the synagogue had been built, led the community to look for a new site. Benjamin Hart, Aaron's third son, took the initiative. To start with, he opened the doors of his Montreal home as a venue for religious ceremonies. Then, he decided to start a crusade. In a long document dated 24 July 1826 (20 Tammuz 5586), he attacked, denouncing "the neglected state of the old synagogue, the Sepulchre, Manuscripts of the Pentateuch, Deeds and Registers, belonging to the Israelites[11] of this Province."[12] In barely couched terms, he accused the David heirs of having transformed the synagogue into a "common store, or receptacle for all pollution, and in the hands of strangers, to the great disgrace of our Holy Religion." His eighteen-point manifesto invited "all the Israelites of this Province . . . to become members of this Congregation under the name of the 'Kahal Kadosh Shearith Israel' [Holy Congregation of Shearith Israel] of Montreal." He proposed a framework for operations and listed eligibility conditions. In conclusion, he invited the community to a meeting on 20 August. Each member would have to pay his annual subscription and at the same time could propose amendments to the regulations that Benjamin was "most humbly" proposing. This printed document marking a new beginning was extremely important to the history of the Canadian Jewish community.

It seems that no minutes were kept of the meeting on 20 August. But concrete proposals were made. A new wall was to be erected around the cemetery: "I will contribute to build the Walls under the tenor of the Act a Bill can be brought before Parliament," Benjamin wrote in a personal memo.[13] The Jewish community had to be able to act as a legal entity.

Benjamin Hart's true character is all over this document, which I would call a manifesto. He skips from subject to subject without a great deal of logic, but his tone is authoritarian or litigious. Finally, he invites his fellow Jews to his office on Sunday, 20 August 1826. He addresses all "Israelites" in the province, but only residents of the city of Montreal are eligible for the position of president or secretary. He insists on receiving payment of the annual subscription but declares himself ready to receive amendments or improvements to the regulations "now most humbly submitted to your consideration."

TO THE ISRAELITES OF THE PROVINCE OF LOWER-CANADA.

GENTLEMEN,

You are all aware of the neglected state of the old Synagogue, the Sepulchre Manuscripts of the Pentateuch Deeds and Registers, belonging to the Israelites of this Province.

A correct understanding of Divine Worship is not only essential to the happiness of every human Being and a duty to the Almighty disposer of events, but also tends to enlarge the mind and improve understanding. With this view, I beg leave to submit to your consideration the present state of the prosperity of the Congregation of this city. The Old Synagogue in possession of the Executors of the late DAVID DAVID, Esqr. is now a common store, or receptacle for all pollution, and in the hands of strangers, to the great disgrace of our Holy Religion. The Sepulcre is abandoned and neglected, and the remains of those committed to the silent tomb disinterred by opening new graves, the fences are in extreme bad order, and insufficient, all of which are contrary to the principles of Judaism, One of the Manuscripts received from the late Mr. DAVID, then acting President of this Congregation, remains in good order in my possession, ready at any time to be delivered up, when a proper place can be found to receive it. The other two, are held and detained by the Executors of the late Mr. DAVID, neglected and suffered to decay and become useless, thereby receiving no part of that care and attention which all Israelites are bound to pay to these sacred writings. The Deeds, Registers and other valuable papers, the property of this Congregation are in like manner held as above. To remedy these grievances and prevent them in future, I humbly beg leave to propose :

1st.—That all the Israelites of this Province shall be solicited to become members of this Congregation under the name and stile of the "KAHAL KADOSH SHEARITH ISRAEL" of Montreal, and all males over the age of Twenty One, have the right to vote personally or by Power of Attorney, which power shall be delivered to the Secretary, and remain on record.

2d.—That a Meeting shall take place on the first *Sunday* of September of each and every year in this city, for the purpose of Electing by a plurality of votes a President, a Treasurer and a Secretary, who shall govern the said Congregation, make Rules, Regulations and Bye-Laws, demand possesssion of the Old Synagogue Manuscripts, Deeds, Registers and other papers, the property of this Congregation, keep in repair the fences around the Sepulchre, and mark out the said ground in rows, to prevent sacrilege.

3rd.—That the President and Secretary so chosen, must be residents of the city of Montreal.

4th.—That the Treasurer may appoint a Deputy or Deputies to receive subscriptions, and solicit donations for the support of this Congregation.

5th.—That hereafter at any period a General Meeting shall have the right of adding Trustees not exceeding Four, to be named from the body of Members.

6th.—That all Rules, Regulations and Bye-Laws so made, must be approved by a General Meeting, to be called at any period by the President, with full fifteen days notice to each and every Member.

7th.—That all monies received shall be applied to the purpose of keeping in good order the fences around the Sepulchre, relieving poor and unfortunate Israelites, and hereafter erecting a new Synagogue, and a Dwelling House for a Reader.

8th.—That a regular account shall be kept by the Treasurer, of all monies received and paid, and yearly submitted at the General Meeting, and afterwards entered into the Register by the Secretary.

9th.—That the Treasurer shall be held to pay out no monies, except on receiving a written order signed by the President and Secretary, and all monies placed out at Interest by the said Treasurer shall be on his own responsibility, except he has the consent of the said President and Secretary in writing.

10th.—That it shall be the duty of the Treasurer in the month of August of each and every year, to solicit subscriptions and donations from all males over and under the age of Twenty-One, and females to support and in aid of the Funds of this Congregation.

11th.—That all males over the age of Twenty-One, shall in all the month of August of each and every year, pay over into the hands of the Treasurer, an annual subscription of not less than the sum of Five Dollars, for the purposes named in the 7th article.

12th.—That all Israelites residing in this Province who do not pay the said subscription, or declare in writing to the President or Treasurer, that their means will not allow them so to do, shall not be considered members of this Congregation.

13th.—That a Register shall be kept by the Secretary, containing the Rules, Regulations and Bye-laws, approved and agreed to by the General Meetings subscribed to by the names of all the members in person, or by Power of Attorney.

14th.—That all Israelites who neglect or refuse to sign the said Register, will not be considered Members of this Congregation.

15th.—That all Israelites who have in their possession property belonging to the late Synagogue or this Congregation, shall deliver over the same to the Secretary.

16.—That all Israelites who shall refuse, or not comply with the above 12th, 14th and 15th articles, oppose the establishment of a Congregation in this city by any ways or means, shall not be considered a member of this Congregation entitled to a Grave in the Burial Ground, the right of Burial, or receive any religious attention to which all members are entitled .

17.—That a Copy of all the Rules, Regulations and Bye-Laws, shall be hereafter printed, and a Copy delivered to each member.

18.—That the first annual meeting for the year ensuing, for the purpose mentioned in the 2d article, shall take place at my office, in this city, on *Sunday 20* of August next, at Eleven o'clock in the forenoon ; when I sincerely trust all Isralites in this Province well wishers to this undertaking, will attend in person, or by Power of Attorney, and pay over their first annual subscription, at the same time submit such alterations and improvements to the rules now most humbly submitted to your consideration,

By Your Obedient Servant,

BENJAMIN HART.

Montreal, 20 Tamus, 5586,
    24th July, 1826.

The absence of registers was also a problem. The births of girls were noted only in family papers; those of boys were sometimes recorded in the journals kept by rabbis. Marriages generally gave rise to contracts sent out to various notaries, who were also responsible for inventories after death.

In Lower Canada, Anglicanism was the official religion, and Anglican religious authorities were very jealous of their prerogatives. Catholics were tolerated; other religions did not exist. On 4 December 1828, "a petition by certain Israelites, of the district of Montreal," was presented to the House of Assembly. After giving a long background to their situation, "the Petitioners professing the Judaic Faith . . . settled in this province . . . for three generations . . . demand that the Parliament pass a law to award the Petitioners and all those of their beliefs . . . the advantage of having public registers in which to register births, marriages, and deaths, and to authorize them to possess, through trustee or otherwise, a plot of land to serve as a burial place and to erect a house of worship and a building for a minister of their religion, all under such rules and conditions, and in the manner that the Parliament of this province, in its great wisdom, will judge agreeable."[14]

The Parti canadien, which had once blocked Ezekiel Hart from taking his seat as an elected representative, immediately showed its true colours. Previously, Hart's religion had served as a pretext to eject a member favourable to the Tory Party. This time, the petition presented by a Jewish group contained demands similar to those formulated by members of "dissident" churches, including Protestants known as Wesleyan Methodists. "It was the House of Assembly," wrote Siméon Pagnuelo, "in which the French and Catholic element was all-powerful, that adopted the first bills in favour of the dissidents, and there are traces of this until 1825. But, for four years— that is, until 1829—it had to withdraw the bills given the ill will of the Legislative Council and the opposition of the Anglican Church."[15] When Louis-Joseph Papineau "took up the torch for the Presbyterians, Methodists, and Jews in the name of religious liberty," wrote the historian Fernand Ouellet, "it was clear that his first object was to undermine the claims of the Church of England."[16]

In reality, the Legislative Council had introduced so many restrictions that the Methodists' bill, introduced first in 1825, no longer made sense and was abandoned. The Israelites' petition dated 4 December 1828 raised the question again. On 13 December, a bill "to extend certain privileges to persons professing Judaism and to obviate certain inconveniences to which

10 C. 75. Anno nono et decimo Georgii IV. A. D. 1829.

CAP. LXXV.

An Act to extend certain Privileges therein mentioned to Persons professing the Jewish Religion and for the obviating certain inconveniences to which others of His Majesty's Subjects might otherwise be exposed.

14th March, 1829. Presented for His Majesty's Assent and reserved "for the signification of His Majesty's pleasure thereon."

1st November, 1830. Assented to by His Majesty in His Council.

18th January 1831. The Royal Assent signified by the Proclamation of His Excellency the Administrator of the Government.

Preamble.

WHEREAS serious inconveniences are experienced by persons professing the Jewish Religion, being British Subjects resident in this Province, from their disability under the existing Laws to have and keep authentic Registers of the Births, Marriages and Burials, occurring among them, which disability may injuriously affect the interests of others of His Majesty's Subjects throughout the Province, and particularly those of such persons as may derive their titles to real property from persons so professing the Jewish Religion; and whereas it is expedient that there should be in each of the Districts of this Province, fit and proper places of Worship and of Burial, for the use of such persons:—Be it therefore enacted by the King's Most Excellent Majesty, by and with the advice and consent of the Legislative Council and Assembly of the Province of Lower-Canada, constituted and assembled by virtue of and under the authority of an Act passed in the Parliament of Great Britain, intituled, "An Act "to repeal certain parts of an Act passed in the fourteenth year of His Majesty's "Reign, intituled, "*An Act for making more effectual provision for the Government of the Province of Quebec in North America,*" and to make further "provision for the Government of the said Province;" And it is hereby enacted by the authority of the same, that the Prothonotaries of the Courts of King's Bench for the Districts of Quebec, Montreal and Three-Rivers, respectively, shall, immediately after the passing of this Act, open and keep, in each of the said Districts, a Register to remain of record, wherein any person residing in the District in which such Register shall be kept, being a British Subject, professing the Jewish Religion, and above the age of twenty-one years, may inscribe his name, age, addition and place of residence, after oath by him made before the said Prothonotaries or any of them that he believes himself to be of the full age of

Prothonotaries to keep a Register of all British Subjects professing the Jewish Religion, resident in the Province, and above 21 years of age.

12 C. 75. Anno nono et decimo Georgii IV. A. D. 1829.

of twenty-one years, and that he is a British Subject, professing the Jewish Faith.

When 15 persons are enregistered the Judge of the District to call a meeting.

II. And be it further enacted by the authority aforesaid, that when and so soon as fifteen persons shall have been so enregistered, it shall and may be lawful for any Justice of the Court of King's Bench, or Judge of the Provincial Court as the case may be upon Petition to that effect to him made by seven persons so enregistered in his District, and such Justice is hereby required upon such Petition to convene a public meeting of all persons so enregistered within his District, to be held in the Chief City or Town thereof, and at such place therein and at such time as the said Justice shall deem it adviseable to appoint, and to name some Justice of the Peace for the said District to preside at such meeting and to make his return of the proceedings thereat to the Prothonotary of the Court of King's Bench for the said District, or Prothonotary of such Provincial Court as the case may be; Provided always that the day on which such meeting shall be held, shall not be more than sixty nor less than thirty days after the time at which the said Petition shall have been presented: and that due notice of such meeting shall be given by inserting such notice during two weeks in such public Newspaper as the said Justices may appoint, or if no Newspaper be published in his District in such manner as the said Justices shall order.

Proviso.

Trustees to be elected at such meeting by a majority of votes.

III. And be it further enacted by the authority aforesaid, that at such meeting it shall be lawful for the persons so enregistered in the District, in which such meeting shall be held, and then and there present, to elect by a majority of their votes five persons from among such persons as shall have been so enregistered in the same district as themselves, to be Trustees for the purposes hereinafer mentioned, which persons shall be returned as such Trustees by the Justice of the Peace presiding at such meeting in his official return of the proceedings had at such meeting as before directed.

Trustees to elect Chairman, and a Secretary and Treasurer.

IV. And be it further enacted by the authority aforesaid, that when the said number of Trustees shall have been so elected as aforesaid, they shall by a majority of their votes elect a Chairman from among themselves, and shall in like manner elect a Secretary and Treasurer.

Prothonotary to record such meeting and the names of those elected.

V. And be it further enacted by the authority aforesaid, that when and so soon as such Election and Return shall have been so made, the Prothonotary shall make an entry in the Register by him kept as aforesaid, setting forth that such Election was made in pursuance of this Act, and the time and place thereof, together with the names, additions and places of residence of the Trustees so elected; and that when and so often as any of the said Trustees shall die, leave the District

14 C. 75. Anno nono et decimo Georgii IV. A. D. 1829.

If Trustees die remove, or resign, others to be elected in their places.

District or resign such trust, the election of so many others as may be required to complete the said number of five shall be proceeded to and recorded in the manner herein before provided, save and except that at such election the Chairman or the oldest of the Trustees shall preside and shall make his return of the proceedings at such election in the manner herein before prescribed, Provided that no Trustee shall remain in office longer than five years.

Proviso.

Trustees to hold Land to the extent of 5 arpents and to appropriate part thereof as a Burial Ground and to build a House for a Minister of the Jewish Religion thereon.

VI. And be it further enacted by the authority aforesaid, that it shall be lawful for the said Trustees so elected and returned as aforesaid, to purchase and hold or to acquire have and hold by devise donation or otherwise, for the purposes hereinafter set forth, in any part of the District, for which they shall have been so elected and returned, a Lot or Lots of Ground not exceeding in the whole the quantity of five Arpents in superficial content, and to appropriate any part of the said Lot or Lots as a Burial Ground, and to erect on any part of the same a Synagogue or place of Worship, and a House for the residence of a Minister of the Jewish Religion.

Ministers of the Jewish Religion to keep Registers in duplicate.

VII. And be it further enacted by the authority aforesaid, that from and after the passing of this Act, every minister of the Jewish Religion acting as such within the Province, being previously licenced by the Governor, Lieutenant Governor, or person administering the Government for the time being, shall keep a Register in duplicate of all Marriages and Burials performed by him, and of all Births which he may be required to record in such Register by any person professing the Jewish Religion, and that all the Provisions of a certain Act passed in the thirty-fifth year of the reign of His late Majesty King *George* the Third, chapter four, intituled, "An Act to establish the form of Registers of Baptisms, Marriages and Burials, and to conform and make valid in Law the Register of the Protestant Congregation of Christ Church, Montreal, and others which may have been informally kept, and to afford the means of remedying Omissions in former Registers," shall be and the same are hereby extended to all Registers hereafter to be kept by virtue of this Act. Provided, that before any Minister of the Jewish Religion shall be admitted to keep the Register as afore mentioned, he shall be required to present a Petition to the Governor, Lieutenant Governor or person administering the Government for the time being, subscribed by the Chairman and Trustees of the District for which he is to act, setting forth his name and addition and praying to be licensed to keep a Register for the District therein mentioned, and it shall and may be lawful to and for the Governor, Lieutenant Governor or person administering the Government for the time being to grant the prayer of the Petition if he shall see fit, and to issue his Licence under his hand and seal to the said Petitioner, to have and keep Registers for the purposes aforesaid, any law usage or custom to the contrary notwithstanding.

Provisions of Geo. 3, chap. 4, extended to Registers so kept.

Provided they have obtained a licence from the Governor, &c.

16 C. 75. Anno nono et decimo Georgii IV. A. D. 1829.

Provisions of the said Act, respecting informal Registers and Omissions extended to Registers kept by Ministers of the Jewish Religion.

VIII. And be it further enacted by the authority aforesaid, that all provisions of the said last mentioned Act, concerning such Registers as may have been informally kept, as well as those concerning the Omission of any matter which ought to have been recorded in any such Register, shall be and the same are hereby extended to such Registers as may heretofore have been kept by any Minister of the Jewish Religion, officiating in this Province.

After the election of the Trustees the birth or death of children to be registered

IX. And be it further enacted by the authority aforesaid, that all persons of the Jewish Religion, may within three months next after the election of the said Trustees, cause the birth of their children, or their death to be enregistered with the same effect to all intents and purposes, as if the same had been done at their birth or death.

Such Registers and Extracts from them declared valid in Law.

X. And be it further enacted by the authority aforesaid, that all Registers which shall hereafter be kept by any Minister of the Jewish Religion in this Province, according to the Provisions of the Act last above mentioned, as well as all certified copies of the entries made therein or in the Registers kept by any Minister of the said Religion, officiating in this Province, before the passing of this Act, or any document legally establishing the omission of any entry which ought to have been made in such Registers, shall to all intents and purposes have the same legal effect, as the Register or extract (*extrait*) of any Register kept by any Priest or Rector of the Roman Catholic Church, or by any Minister of the Protestant Church in this Province, in pursuance of the said last mentioned Act; Provided always that the Regulations and Requirements of the said Act shall in all respects have been complied with.

Proviso.

Ministers of the Jewish Religion or other persons not complying with the provisions of the said Act, liable to all the penalties, &c. imposed by the said Act.

XI. Provided always and be it further enacted by the authority aforesaid, that all Ministers of the Jewish Religion, obtaining and keeping Registers by virtue hereof, shall be governed by the Provisions of the Act last above mertioned, and that they or any other person who shall in any wise neglect or refuse to comply with the requirements of the said Act, shall be liable to the same pains and penalties as are therein in like cases provided, and that any penalties so incurred shall be recoverable, paid, applied and accounted for in the same manner as the penalties by the said Act imposed are thereby directed to be recovered, paid, applied and accounted for.

Public Act.

XII. And be it further enacted by the authority aforesaid that this Act shall be deemed and taken to be a Public Act, and as such shall be judicially noticed by all Judges, Justices and Courts in this Province without being specially pleaded.

CAP

A law is rarely inspiring reading, but I felt that this one should be reproduced in its entirety. It is drawn from the statutes of 1829, which is a bit surprising given the dates of the assent and enactment. It was printed once assent was received.

Register to remain of *Record* in the *Prothonotaries Office* for the *District* of *Montreal* wherein persons residing in the *said District* being *British subjects* and *professing* the *Jewish Religion* being above the age of twenty one *Years*, may under and by *Virtue* of the *Provincial Statute* 9 & 10 George *IV* chapter 75 inscribe their names, ages, additions and *places* of residence.

(1829)

Monk & Monrogh

Oath to be taken in conformity with the *said Statute*.

I *A.B.* do swear that I believe myself to be of the *full age* of twenty one years and that I am a *British subject professing* the *Jewish faith*,—

1	Henry Joseph Senior	55 years	Merchant	Berthier
2	Alex. Hart	48 years	Gentleman	Montreal
3	Benjamin Hart	51 years	Merchant	ditto
4	Israel Valentine	48 years	Gentleman	Montreal
5	M. H. Cays	32 years	Gentleman	Do
6	H. Solomon	42 "	Furrier	Do
7	M. Lewis	28 "	Do	Do
8	Samuel Davis	40 "	Do	Do
9	H. Hart	62 .	Merchant	Do
10	Esdaile P. Cohen	32 .	Merchant	Do
11	Jacob Jacobs	33	Merchant	Montreal
12	Aaron Aaron	39	Montreal	Merch
13	Saml. Joseph	28	Merchant	Berthier
14	S. David	21 "	Student at Law	Montreal
15	S. B. Hart	21 and over	Advocate	
16	A. Hart Jr.	95	Phi...	

This is the register that I like to think I brought to the attention of Jean-Jacques Lefebvre. I must admit that I was being a bit malicious. Mr. Lefebvre impressed me; it was always intimidating to look at new deposits in the archives. Each time, the historian learns a good lesson in humility. Archivists know everything!

other subjects of His Majesty might otherwise be exposed" was brought to the attention of the members, then the legislative councillors. Things moved along briskly and the bill was quickly presented to the governor, who thought it appropriate to submit it for the king's approval. Royal assent was refused.[17] On 26 January 1830, the solicitor general received permission from the House to reintroduce the bill.[18] On 12 March, it was again tabled in the Legislative Council with a proposed last-ditch amendment.[19] The House took cognizance. On 17 March 1830, Jonathan Sewell, as Speaker of the Legislative Council, recommended that Governor James Kempt send the amended bill to London. There was disagreement among the members when they were informed of this. A back-and-forth between the House and the Council ended on 26 March, when the governor settled the matter by once again deciding to reserve the bill for royal assent. On 12 May 1830, a letter was sent to the intention of Sir George Murray, Secretary to the Colonies. On 30 October 1830, Sir George informed the new governor, Matthew Lord Aylmer, that "the Act" was under study and would likely be adopted. On 1 November 1830, His Majesty in council accepted the bill written in March 1829. "The Bill for the relief of persons professing the Jewish faith has received His Majesty's Assent," Murray wrote to Aylmer on 3 November, "because, although that class of persons is probably not numerous in the province, there is no sufficient reason why their religion should deprive them of any convenience which they can enjoy without detriment to the other inhabitants of Lower Canada."[20]

On 18 January 1831, His Excellency Matthew Lord Aylmer solemnly proclaimed the new statute. Jews could, under regulations and conditions to be formulated, hold their registers in which to record births, marriages, and deaths, and they were also authorized to form corporations to own "a plot of land to serve as a burial ground and to erect a house of worship and a building for a minister of their religion."

In the 1831 census, published as an appendix to the Journals of the House of Assembly (1831–32), Quebec's population included 403,000 Catholics, 34,000 Anglicans, 15,000 members of the Church of Scotland, 7,000 Methodists, and 107 Jews, most of whom lived in Montreal (85) and the Trois-Rivières region (19). The district of Quebec City accounted for the other three.

Equal Rights and Privileges for Jews under the 1832 Statute

At the same time that this important steppingstone for a small community of barely more than one hundred was achieved, other members of the Hart family set about to clarify the rights of Jews in Lower Canada. At the time, eligibility for various functions was linked to the taking of a vow prescribed by law. Ezekiel's nightmare had never ceased to haunt the family, especially his sons. The oldest, Samuel Bécancour, decided to take up the torch of this cause. After being approached for a magistrate's position, he noticed that his name had been withdrawn from the list of candidates under the pretext that "a person professing the Jewish religion could not take the qualification oath."[21]

A prosperous merchant, seigneur emeritus, and courageous military officer, Samuel Bécancour Hart was humiliated when the bright prospect of a magistrate's commission was withdrawn. Less than three weeks after

82   C. 56-57.   Anno Primo Gulielmi IV.   A. D. 1831.

Public Act.   VIII. And be it further enacted by the authority aforesaid, that this Act shall be taken and deemed to be a public Act, and as such shall be judicially taken notice of by all Judges, Justices of the Peace, and all others whom it shall concern without being specially pleaded.

CAP. LVII.

An Act to declare persons professing the Jewish Religion entitled to all the rights and privileges of the other subjects of His Majesty in this Province.

31st March, 1831.—Presented for His Majesty's Assent and reserved "for the 'signification of His Majesty's pleasure thereon."
12th April, 1832,—Assented to by His Majesty in His Council.
5th June, 1832,—The Royal Assent signified by the proclamation of His Excellency the Governor in Chief.

Preamble.   WHEREAS doubts have arisen whether persons professing the Jewish Religion are by law entitled to many of the privileges enjoyed by the other subjects of His Majesty within this Province: Be it therefore declared and enacted by the King's Most Excellent Majesty, by and with the advice and consent of the Legislative Council and Assembly of the Province of Lower Canada, constituted and assembled by virtue of and under the authority of an Act passed in the Parliament of Great Britain, intituled, "An Act to repeal certain parts of an Act passed in "the fourteenth year of His Majesty's Reign, intituled, "An Act for making "more effectual provision for the Government of the Province of Quebec, in North "America," and to make further provision for the Government of the said "Province of Quebec in North America;" And it is hereby declared and enacted by the authority aforesaid, that all persons professing the Jewish Religion

Persons professing the Jewish Religion to be entitled to all the civil rights of British Subjects.   being natural born British subjects inhabiting and residing in this Province, are entitled and shall be deemed, adjudged and taken to be entitled to the full rights and privileges of the other subjects of His Majesty, his Heirs or Successors, to all intents, constructions and purposes whatsoever. and capable of taking, having or enjoying any office or place of trust whatsoever, within this Province.

A legal document that removes all doubt.

Aylmer's proclamation was made extending certain privileges to Jews in January 1831, he tabled his own petition in the House: "That the Petitioner is a native of the City of Trois-Rivières; that he professes the Jewish religion, and that he owns considerable Real Estate in this Province; that he is a descendant of Aaron Hart, Esquire, born a British Subject, who came from England to this Province at the time of the Conquest of Canada, with the arms of Great Britain." After noting the freedom that Jews enjoyed in the province, Samuel Bécancour complained about "certain recent acts by the executive Government of this Province, by which, he and all those professing the Jewish religion are excluded from Offices in a very public and mortifying manner, and that the Petitioner cannot support this in silence without losing all right to his self-esteem and the good opinion of his Fellow Citizens, particularly his brothers of the Jewish faith." Then he recounted the facts and demanded that "he and his brothers be relieved of all incapacity."

Samuel Bécancour did not take this step alone. His brothers—Aaron Ezekiel, a young lawyer, and Adolphus Mordecai, a future lawyer—supported him. He also had the support of John Neilson in the House and Denis-Benjamin Viger in the Legislative Council, both of whom were very close to Louis-Joseph Papineau, the leader of the House.

Louis-Joseph Papineau Supports Samuel Bécancour Hart

On 16 March, the House passed in first reading a bill according Jews "all the rights and privileges of other subjects of His Majesty in this Province." Second reading came two days later; third reading, a day after that. There was no debate.

On 21 and 22 March, the bill went through first and second reading in the Legislative Council. On the 28th, a committee of the Council accepted it without amendment and recommended its passage in the next session. On the 29th, the House was informed that the bill had been passed without amendment by the Council. In spite of all of this, the governor judged it prudent to reserve the bill for royal approval, which was granted on 12 April 1832. Such rapidity—and unanimity—is almost suspect! In fact, it seems that this bill was simply recognizing a legal situation that already existed, which Sheldon Godfrey and Judith Godfrey call the Declaratory Act.[22]

Of course, experts interpret the 1832 legislation in different ways. Politicians do, too. Almost a century and a half later, after the victory of

Here is an example of the good relationship between Papineau and the Judahs and Harts. In a letter dated 23 February 1835, he gives a humorous account of his stay in Trois-Rivières. René-Joseph Kimber, who had just moved to a new home, had a house-warming party. Papineau writes that the ladies stayed until two in the morning; the men, until "just after three." "The ladies were those of the house and Mrs. Judah, two Misses Hart, and two Misses Lozeau. . . . Kimber was proud of having gotten several of the Messrs Hart and Mr. Judah Senior so drunk that they did not remember, the next day, how they had left." Papineau himself had avoided the Madeira and the Porto and "limited [himself] to a bit of good Bordeaux." David Rome has often emphasized the good relations between Papineau and some of the Harts. It was a small social group. Papineau was close friends with Henry Judah. In 1845, he travelled to Italy with Judah and his wife. One of Kimber's daughters married one of the Judah sons. The Harts mentioned in Papineau's account are no doubt Ezekiel, one or two of his sons, and two of his daughters. Ezekiel had four sons and three daughters (RAPQ, 1953–55: 353).

the indépendantiste Parti Québécois in provincial elections in 1976, emotions ran high in the Jewish community, and some even talked of an exodus from the province. Premier René Lévesque never missed an opportunity to build bridges to the Jewish community. Since the laws of 1831 and 1832 had been signed by Papineau and attributed to the Parti Patriote, Lévesque created a commemorative day on 1 June 1982 and declared how proud he was of the action taken by the Patriotes. The Canadian Jewish Congress, under president Irwin Cotler (who had reacted extremely after the election in 1976), did not have to be asked to participate in the event. The Congress even published a small brochure titled Tribute to Freedom with an enthusiastic essay written by Peter Samuel Golick.

Godfrey and Godfrey note that the question of the oath had in fact been settled by the British Plantation Act of 1740. In 1768, John Franks had used this statute to have "Christian" replaced by "Jew" in the wording of the oath that he took. According to this interpretation, Ezekiel Hart should have been able to take his seat in the House in 1808. The Canadien members and a few English members had kept him from doing so but for other reasons.

In 1831 and 1832, the Canadien majority made clear amends for its partisan gesture of 1808–09. The historian Irving Abella maintains that, in 1832, "With the possible exception of Jamaica, Canada became the first colony in the British Empire to emancipate its Jews. . . . The act was almost revolutionary in its implications, a milestone in the battle for civil rights."[23]

Father and Son

It is very possible that the 1832 legislation did not create any new rights for Jews in Lower Canada, but Jews perceived it as a great victory. Benjamin Hart, Moses Judah Hays, and Samuel Bécancour Hart were convinced that they could finally be sworn in as justices of the peace.

Aaron Philip, Benjamin's oldest son, saw things differently. Having recently passed the bar and no doubt in competition with his cousins, who were behind the two pieces of legislation, he expressed reservations about the scope of the 1832 statute and strongly advised his father against accepting a magistrate's commission in this legal context. He alleged certain ambiguities in the oath of abjuration. Given the doubts raised publicly by Aaron Philip on the scope of the 1831 and 1832 statutes, the question of Jews' rights was brought to the attention of the House of Assembly, which passed it on to a parliamentary committee chaired by Dr. René-Joseph Kimber and composed of Louis-Théodore Besserer, Frédéric-Auguste Quesnel, Pierre Bureau, and Jean-François-Joseph Duval. These five men were mandated to give an opinion on the debate that had subsisted since the election of Ezekiel Hart. Aaron Ezekiel, Aaron Philip's cousin, was called to testify. He was well prepared. He observed that a 1724 British statute already provided Jews with equal rights, which were detailed or confirmed by the 1740 statute. It was necessary, in his opinion, to avoid restricting its scope to the obtaining of naturalization. The problem raised by a "young man, admitted to practise law barely two years ago, and who is far from famous for the correctness of his decisions, or for the solidity of his judgment," was deemed to be without foundation. Without naming him, Aaron Ezekiel accused Aaron Philip "of having poorly understood and poorly interpreted" the 1740 statute. His error, in Aaron Ezekiel's view, was to have based his argument on the title of the statute and neglected to read the text to the end.

In less than three weeks, the members of the committee sent to the House their report, in which they concluded that Jews had the right to amend the oath of abjuration by omitting the words "upon the true faith of a Christian" when necessary. This provision, they emphasized, was included in the Plantation Act of 1740, the objective of which was to encourage Jews to settle in the colonies, where British citizenship would be granted to them quickly. Some claimed that the wording of the oath could be changed only for a naturalization; others, that this statute "would allow that amendment to be made whenever a Jew was appointed or elected to any office and required to take the state oaths."[24] The Kimber committee, no doubt under the influence of Duval, who was a lawyer, opted for a liberal interpretation of section 3 of the Plantation Act.

In other words, the law passed on 12 April 1832 "was merely a declaratory act passed to remove doubts and did not add anything to the rights of Jews which already existed," Godfrey and Godfrey continued, and "no further amendments were necessary to any legislation regarding oaths because Jews in Lower Canada suffered no disabilities." On 28 February 1834, the House accepted the Kimber report. Young Aaron Philip Hart's efforts had come to naught. Had he chosen to contest the point of view of his cousins Samuel Bécancour, Aaron Ezekiel, and Adolphus Mordecai in order to reduce the impact of their successful campaign in favour of the recent laws concerning Jews? Aaron Philip was, on this point, so convinced and convincing that he had persuaded his father, Benjamin, and a friend, Moses Judah Hays, to refuse appointments as justices of the peace. And heaven knows, Benjamin had coveted an appointment for a long time.

Finally, on 13 April 1837, Benjamin Hart and Moses Judah Hays were appointed justices of the peace in the district of Montreal. For Hart, this was not simply an honorific title. As a magistrate, he became deeply involved in the fight pitting the government and the army against the Patriote rebels. Although the Canadiens had several times defended the Jews, particularly against Lord Dalhousie, and of course by voting in statutes in preceding years, Benjamin decided to align himself with the side in power. In 1837–38, the Hart clan parted ways politically. Adolphus Mordecai and Ira Craig participated in anti-government meetings, and were soon joined by Samuel Bécancour.

Despite his age—he was turning sixty—Justice Benjamin Hart was very active; he gathered depositions that incriminated rebels and closely collaborated with the chief of police, Pierre-Édouard Leclère. His zeal did not go unnoticed. Edmund Bailey O'Callaghan, a Patriote and editor of *The Vindicator*, called him "the harshest of magistrates" and accused him of being responsible for many cases of persecution.[25] Things escalated. There were rumours of a plot to kill Hart, and a police report of a plot to kill all the Jews in Montreal for good measure.[26] After all, did they not all support repression?

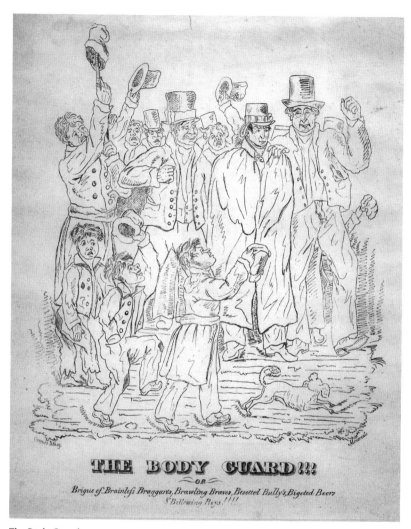

The Body Guard

Historian Brian Young was interested in this cartoon published by a lithographer named Greene. Many had come to see Papineau as a threat to the English of Montreal, which is a risky shortcut. Papineau was defending not the French against the English, but the power of the elected members against an oligarchic regime. It is admitted today that the rebellions resulted from a political problem rather than an ethnic confrontation. The cartoon was accompanied by insults addressed to French Canadians; the subtitle was "Brigue of Brainless Braggarts, Brawling Bravos, Besotted Bullies, Bigoted Boors & Bellowing Boys!!!!" For thirty years, opposition newspapers had been publishing the salaries paid to friends of the government, who defended their privileges.

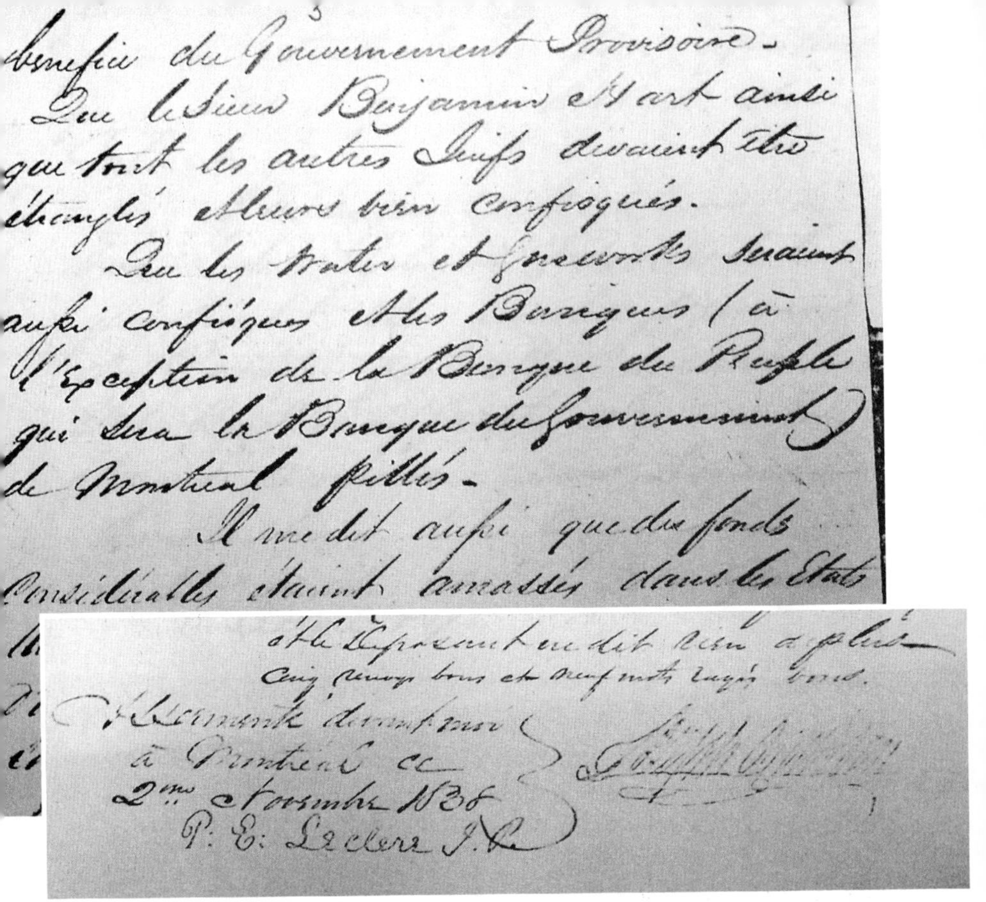

Handwritten deposition (French):

… bénéfice du Gouvernement Provisoire –

Que le Sieur Benjamin Hart ainsi que tout les autres Juifs devaient être étranglés et leurs biens confisqués.

Que les Water et Gasworks seraient aussi confisqués et les Banques (à l'exception de la Banque du Peuple qui sera la Banque du Gouvernement) de Montréal pillés –

Il me dit aussi que des fonds considérables étaient amassés dans les États …

… et le Déposant ne dit rien de plus

Cinq cent trois mots et neuf mots rayés nuls.

à Montréal ce
2me Novembre 1838
P. E. Leclère J.P.

According to Leclère, who as police chief had agents infiltrated everywhere, Joseph Bourdon, bourgeois of the city of Montreal, reports at length on the activity of the Frères Chasseurs. He admits having taken an oath but adds, "Do not tell anyone." After a long description of the conspirators' plans, he writes, "May Mr. Benjamin Hart and all the other Jews be strangled and their goods confiscated . . . and the Banks (with the exception of the Bank of the People, which will be the Bank of the Government) of Montreal pillaged."

"He also tells me," adds Leclère, "that considerable funds had been amassed in the United States" (P 1060400, Province of Lower Canada, District of Montreal). (See Ivanhoe Caron, *Une Société secrète dans le Bas-Canada en 1838: l'Association des Frères Chasseurs,* meeting of May 1926, Transactions of the Royal Society of Canada, third series, vol. 20, 1926: 17–23). According to Caron, "Frédérick Glackmeyer told the same stories to Joseph Bertrand, of Montreal." Bourdon, who signed his eight-page deposition, took the oath in Montreal on 2 November 1838 "before me," notes "P. E. Leclère I.P.," who wrote out Bourdon's statements in his best hand. An addendum gives the latest information on the movements of Beausoleil, Lemaître, Rochon, and Levesque, who were going to establish a camp in Chambly. A general attack, planned in Châteauguay, was imminent. As I have studied this period in detail, I can add that Leclère was particularly well informed and could even count on the superior of the Sulpicians, Father Quiblier, who knew how to wisely use secrets divulged during the sacrament of confession.

Benjamin's son Aaron Philip no doubt felt that his father was going too far and that the authorities were also past the realm of decency. He decided to defend Patriotes accused of treason and liable for the death penalty. One Patriote, Joseph Narcisse Cardinal, himself an accused, attempted to organize a defence for several Patriotes to be tried in a military court. Their lawyers, Pierre Moreau and Lewis Thomas Drummond, did their best to assist them. Revolted by the spectacle of such a trial, Aaron Philip joined them. After hours of pleading before a military court that was impassive and inflexible, the three lawyers eventually threw up their hands: nothing could be done.

All the same, on the eve of the execution, Drummond and Hart made a final appeal to Governor Sir John Colborne. After contesting the jurisdiction of the court, the statute that had created it, and the procedures that had been followed, they concluded, "We hope, in this light, to succeed in convincing Your Excellency of the accuracy of the proposals that we have developed and to establish, beyond all doubt, that the procedures followed with regard to the prisoners were illegal, unconstitutional, and unjust."[27]

"Illegal, unconstitutional, and unjust." Drummond and Aaron Philip had gone as far as they could. Benjamin Hart did not intervene. He no doubt admired his son's eloquence and boldness, but he told himself that he had served His Majesty well.

In November 1837, Benjamin Hart and Moses Judah Hays were on a special committee of justices of the peace chaired by Pierre de Rocheblave. Benjamin was one of those who demanded the proclamation of martial law. He was aware of all the petitions and very active in the Constitutional Association,[28] a group of merchants who were fighting the Parti Patriote. A special council had been formed to replace the House of Assembly. He applied for a seat on it. He mentioned his enthusiasm, his merits, and his importance as a businessman, and he continued to address reports to the authorities highlighting his role and the risks that he had taken. "By my firmness as a magistrate, peace and security was restored in the city," he wrote in July 1840 to Lord John Russell, Secretary in the Colonies. He had regularly marched at the head of his regiment and had not hesitated to confront the rebels.[29] This was believable; it fit his temperament.

Benjamin awaited his reward; he was ignored.[30] He became embittered. Then, the economic crisis dealt him a fatal blow, and he was forced to turn for financial support to his son Theodore. He filed his financial statements, and his wife instigated a lawsuit against him to hold him to their marriage

This well-known drawing is sometimes attributed to Jean-Joseph Girouard. It may represent the executions of 18 January or 15 February 1839; on each of these dates, five Patriotes were hanged on a scaffold built before the Pied-du-Courant prison, still standing at the corner of De Lorimier and Notre-Dame. . In January, those hanged were Joseph-Jacques Robert, François-Xavier Hamelin, Pierre-Théophile Decoigne, and the Sanguinet brothers Ambroise and Charles. In February, along with the famous Chevalier de Lorimier, the victims were Amable Daunais, Charles Hindenlang, Pierre-Remi Narbonne, and François Nicolas. On 21 December of the preceding year, Joseph-Narcisse Cardinal and Joseph Duquette had been hanged despite the appeals made by lawyers Pierre Moreau, Lewis Thomas Drummond, and Aaron Philip Hart. Hart particularly distinguished himself with a three-hour speech followed by a heated four-hour exchange with the solicitor general. The court first recognized the disproportion between the crime of high treason and the corresponding penalty. It sentenced four of the accused to death and recommended that the Executive grant them clemency. It proposed deportation for six others, and rendered a verdict of not guilty for the last two. Merciless, Governor Colborne ordered that the judgment be reviewed. The court had no choice but to declare all twelve defendants guilty of high treason. Clemency remained a possibility, especially given the very doubtful jurisdiction of the court. It was the readers of the newspaper *The Herald* and the members of the Doric Club who had the last word.

contract. The statute providing compensation for victims of repression during the 1837-38 rebellion triggered his revolt. He no longer believed in the British or in Canada, and he was among the authors of an annexationist manifesto that called for economic and political union with the United States.[31] "Benjamin Hart, Esq, opens meeting," wrote Raymond Arthur Davies in his booklet Printed Jewish Canadiana 1685–1900, "and appears as one of the leading spirits in movement and meeting in favour of a peaceable separation of Canada from Great Britain, and of Annexation to the Unites States."[32] Davies added that some four hundred people signed the Annexation Manifesto, including Samuel Goodman, William Benjamin Moses Davies, and Theodore Hart. The painter Cornelius Krieghoff, no doubt a bit nostalgic for life in New York, was also among the signatories, according to Davies, who was unable to track down a copy of the first edition of the manifesto.

Benjamin Hart had gone too far. He lost his rank of lieutenant-colonel and was relieved of his magistrate's position. He took refuge in New York, where his son, Arthur Wellington, tried to take care of him in his old age. He died in a Broadway hotel in 1855.

In Montreal, the wave of Ashkenazi immigration that Benjamin had feared was beginning to subsume what remained of the Jewish pioneers of the second half of the eighteenth century. In his 1826 manifesto, he had denounced those who had transformed the synagogue into "an ordinary building, or a receptacle for all forms of contamination, placed in the hands of foreigners, to the great shame of our holy religion." These foreigners gradually took shape in his writings and denunciations. They began to haunt him in 1833–34. These "bad characters" had a name: they were "Deutsch, German." Paradoxically, Benjamin was himself of German ancestry. That will be the subject of the final chapter of this book.

Benjamin Hart

Ambitious and aggressive, Benjamin Hart (1779–1855) was born in Trois-Rivières. He was the third of Aaron and Dorothea's sons to reach adulthood. His rank in the family had an effect on him, and he tended to team up with his younger brother, Alexander. Everything seemed complicated for him. He wanted a position in the militia and had to confront one of his fellow citizens, Thomas Coffin. He rallied a number of prominent figures to his cause. He also wanted to become a justice of the peace, and this position eluded him for a number of years. He restarted the Sephardic congregation in Montreal and fought off the first German Ashkenazi immigrants in the mid-nineteenth century. He was a zealous magistrate during the rebellions and never reaped the rewards he sought. He was against the Rebellion Losses Bill and free trade imposed by Westminster. Discouraged, if not disgusted, he signed a manifesto in favour of the annexation of Canada to the United States, where he spent the last part of his life.

CHAPTER 7

Moses Hart: Morality and Religion

THE SO-CALLED RIGHT TO PRIVACY is the historian's nightmare—especially mine! Proponents of this right would do well to skip the first part of this chapter, which exposes Moses Hart as—well, as Moses Hart.

Several times in these pages I have quoted Aaron's 1796 letter to Moses, advising him not to enter politics: "You will be opposed as a Jew. That will be more disgrace than the honor will give you as to any Jew." Aaron knew about, and likely as a child had direct experience of, the prejudices that Jews encountered all over the world. The members of his family had been sheltered from anti-Semitism up to then, and he felt that it was his duty to warn them. In short, it's as if he was telling them, "Everything is fine here. Don't force the issue."

But Aaron had other reasons to rein in his oldest son's ambitions. "I should in one Kind be glade you wase elected a member of the House," he wrote. "But Consider the expense of Quebec." He used his best arguments. "It's better to remain an honest merchant than to be known throughout the country." He spoke of the big profits to be made with potash, as prices were on the rise. Finally, he revealed his greatest wish: "All I want is to see you happyer than I see you now, and in a good way to live a life of a man of good character and respected."

A First Marriage Fails

Aaron feared that Moses was completely out of control. He hoped that marriage would calm him down and that his niece, Sarah Judah, might be up to the job. I have already described the circumstances of the marriage and

Portrait of Moses Hart attributed to L. C. de Heer, 1789 (Musée du Château Ramezay, 998.1891). Louis-Chrétien de Heer rarely signed his paintings. French by birth, he came to North America with "mercenary" troops from Brunswick. In 1789, he left Quebec for Montreal hoping to expand his clientele. He advertised his services in the *Montreal Gazette,* offering "good work at a low price." Moses Hart was born in December 1768. In this portrait, he was therefore twenty-one years old. He was ready to be portrayed for posterity!

separation of Sarah and Moses. But I began to have some doubt about Moses's culpability in the matter when I found two affidavits, one from November 1807 and the other from September 1808, signed by employees of Moses Hart, claiming that their employer's wife had had relations with his brother, Alexander Hart, and a certain Lieutenant Wilson. The latter, it was claimed, "put his hands on the breast of the wife of the said Moses Hart." On 23 March 1814, in another affidavit, Moses Hart denounced his wife's behaviour, and on 9 May 1814, notary J. M. C. Duvernay served her with a handwritten note from him bearing his application for separation.[1]

Sarah Judah's reply, of course, was not long in coming. "For seven or eight years," read the minutes reporting her version, "the defendant, forgetting his duties as a husband, abandoned himself to debauchery with women of poor reputation and even kept them at his home—that is, in the home of the complainant with the defendant—to the shame of the complainant and the scandal of her family. Whereas the complainant, notwithstanding these disturbances by said defendant, had for him all the tenderness and deference that an attached wife owes to her husband, for his part he had with regard to the complainant harshness and poor treatment. . . . Continually treated with abuse and infamy in front of strangers, in front of the domestics and servants, and in front of their common children; among other insults, said defendant accusing the complainant of being a bad woman, of having criminal commerce with different men, of having communicated venereal diseases to him the defendant."

Her charge concluded, "That, whereas the defendant enjoys one of the most brilliant fortunes in the Province," to which she had largely contributed, he was depriving her of all means of subsistence. In other words, he was stingy!

Moses struck back. On 15 March 1816, before Judge James Kerr, he recounted the relations that Sarah Judah was reputed to have had with his brother Alexander. "And this deponent swears that the said Sarah Judah one night strongly solicited him to take her somewhere that she might satisfy her lust, adding she preferred tall men."[2] After many long hours of testimony, the court granted Sarah separation of body and property, as well as "formal clothing, everyday clothing, and linens for her use." As for alimony, the court ordered that an assessment of Moses's finances be conducted so that a "reasonable" accommodation could be made. Sarah was asking for annual alimony of £300.

Moses and Sarah had three children. Their daughter, Louisa Howard, was always unhappy and Moses kept her from marrying, feeling that she was mentally weak. One son, Orobio, died at age twenty, in January 1825, in a road accident.[3] The other son, Areli Blake, found himself having to set down roots in Italy. He had ended a long "educational" tour of Europe in Florence,[4] where, posing as Aurèle Blackhart, a "Catholic gentleman, born in the town of Trois-Rivières, in America, Quebec diocese," he married Rosalinda Fiacchi on 18 May 1831. When Moses caught wind of this, he relayed orders, through a series of bankers in different countries, to cut off Areli's allowance. Areli returned home. On 18 May 1838, Canon Franceschi Tiaccini asked Monseignor Signay to trace the family of this "Aurèle Blackhart" through international—Catholic and banking—networks. Finally, Moses purchased peace. "How much for a divorce?" he wrote to his Italian daughter-in-law. "Keep in mind that I'm a poor man. I feel for your misfortune. I was once influent, but am now melancholy and miserable. I have met lately with such severe losses that I am nearly reduced to ruin. . . . Please let me know how much you will take for all your claims under your marriage contract." Even before the case was completely settled (it lasted from 1829 to 1838), Areli married Julia Seaton, a young woman from a good family, who was the final heir to the strategic Sainte-Marguerite seigneury.[5]

Affairs and Affairs

Even during his marriage, contracted in 1799, Moses had various affairs, the most important one to my knowledge being with Mary Cline, with whom he had a son, Alexander Thomas, born on or around 4 May 1804. Alexander Thomas was Moses's favourite. In his holograph will of 1837, Moses identified him as "my adopted son Alexander Thomas Hart, Mariner, who is in my employ and son of the late Mary Cline" (William Burn's registry). The date of birth (1804) confused Anne Joseph, who thought that Alexander Thomas was the child of Sarah and Moses.[6] I have looked high and low for information about Mary Cline to no avail; perhaps I did not read her name correctly.

The affection that Moses had for this boy, who he may have actually adopted, was significant. The child was no doubt brilliant and the mother attractive. It is unlikely that she was Jewish, and so Alexander Thomas wasn't Jewish, but his descendants were through his marriage to her cousin

Miriam Judah. This couple, in my opinion, formed the best of Aaron and Dorothea's lineage; the family branch has been perpetuated to the present day.

Following his separation, finalized in 1816, Moses Hart had a number of women in his life. With some of them he had two children, which seems to indicate that these relationships lasted several years. Mary Racine gave birth to Ezekiel Moses and Moses Ezekiel; Marie Godin, to Abraham and Elizabeth; Margaret Burns, to Sarah Dorothea and Charlotte Mathilde; and Margaret Armstrong, to Orobio Elon and Aaron Moses, who studied together at the academy in Plattsburgh, where their mother may have lived.[7] All of these children were mentioned in one or another of his wills.

One of them particularly caught my attention. Aaron Moses, born in 1823, married Margaret McCarthy at the Protestant church in Rivière-du-Loup (now Louiseville) on 13 December 1842. Since at the time Moses was in a relationship with Mary McCarthy, it is natural to look for a connection between Mary and Margaret. They seem to have been about the same age.*

Mary McCarthy was said to be the widow of Peter Brown, about whom we know nothing except that he was a tailor. To add to the mystery, there was a McCarthy who voted for Ezekiel Hart in 1804. It could not have been Mary, since this person had to have been at least twenty-one years of age and therefore could not have given birth to two children in 1838 and 1840, the years when the two boys that Mary had with Moses were born.

So, to summarize: Moses was involved, in succession, with Sarah Judah, Mary Racine, Marie Godin, Margaret Burns, Margaret Armstrong, and Mary McCarthy. From these six unions, there were thirteen children who reached adult age; a fourteenth child resulted from his affair with Mary Cline while he was married to Sarah Judah. To these, we must add several

---

* Lucien Bellemare, a regular visitor to the BAnQ in Trois-Rivières, has a photocopy of the Protestant register in Louiseville. He confirms that there were no parents' names mentioned in the marriage certificate, which is normal for such Protestant documents. Nor were there any witnesses. So, I turned to the correspondence between Mary McCarthy and relatives and friends in Ireland. I learned that Mary and Margaret were sisters, but they had a difficult relationship. They went two years without speaking to each other! Andrew, their brother in Ireland, tried to reconcile them. Apparently he succeeded, since Aaron Moses was one of Moses's main heirs, along with his two sons, which would not have been possible without the agreement, at the very least, of Mary McCarthy. She apparently had total control over Moses's estate. Mr. Bellemare also told me that the Harts were very important landowners at Rivière-du-Loup (Louiseville) along with the Ursulines, who owned the seigneury that bore the same name (Fonds Hart 0009-J-M-2).

Miriam Judah (1807–87) married Alexander Thomas Hart in 1840 (unidentified photograph, c. 1865). She was the daughter of Catherine Hart and Bernard Judah, and thus Moses's niece. There must have been some blood relationship between Alexander and Miriam, given Miriam's family name, but I was not aware that she was a Hart through her mother. Among the Harts and Judahs, the number of marriages between blood relatives was striking. In Miriam's case, her father was a Judah, her maternal grandmother was a Judah, and if Alexander Thomas had been the legitimate son of Moses, his mother and grandmother would have been closely related Judahs. Moses's infidelity thus introduced a new bloodline. What was the effect on the descendants? Moses Hart himself gave the name of Alexander Thomas's mother in his 1837 will: "I do give and bequeath unto my adopted Son Alexander Thomas Hart, Mariner, who is in my employ, and son of the late Mary Cline the sum . . ." (see p. 268). The term "adopted son" leaves some ambiguity. Moses may not have been the natural father.

Thus, the Jewish nature of Alexander Thomas Hart's descendants was re-established through Miriam Judah. But he had the right to funeral services at the Trois-Rivières cathedral, which took place on 26 April 1852. He was said to have been forty-eight years old, which would indicate to some that he was the son of Sarah Judah and Moses Hart. Moses died on 15 October of that year. He thus had the great sorrow of knowing about the accidental death of his favourite son.

other children that he acknowledged, although I cannot identify their mothers with certainty: William, born in Montreal; Thomas Nathurs, who lived at Saint-Zéphirin de Courval; Suzan, whom he entrusted to Horace Hunt in St. Alban's, Vermont; and Benjamin Moses (likely the son of Anne Galarno [Galarneau]), who was mentioned in his 1847 will.[8] Certain clauses in this will led me to conclude that Abraham and Elizabeth were Marie Godin's children. Marie Godin's name is difficult to read, but Moses treated Abraham and Elizabeth on an equal footing, and below I quote a letter from Marie Godin that leaves little ambiguity about the father of her son Obrem [Abraham], who sends his greetings.

There is little need to add that it is not easy to trace Moses's descendants. I cannot help but think of Aaron, who wanted to build a Hart dynasty in North America! Moses was not able to track down all of his children, and neither can I.

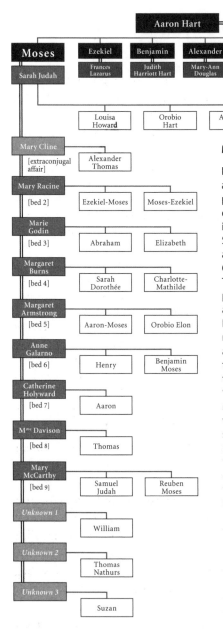

Moses Hart's various unions and descendants

In the vast correspondence over the years, I found a huge number of descendants of the Harts, particularly Moses. Thérèse Perron, who also conducted research on the Hart family, wrote me in June 2003, "There are a number of Harts in St. Anicet, and they all have the same history: the ancestor Louis Hart, married to Josephte Castagnet, who was also one of Moses's children. There are no traces of a marriage that likely took place in 1830, as a child was born in 1831. . . . I have a copy of a letter written by a lawyer, Thomas J. Fitzpatrick of Chateauguay, New York, who has researched the Harts. The letter is dated 1914 and addressed to a Felix Hart in Cazzaville, and he says that Moses Hart died in 1852 and that he had more than 100 children, of whom 4 were legitimate. "Your grandfather was an illegitimate child of Moses Hart's," he wrote, "and he had a brother who died in Boston." To finish, a personal memory springs to mind. In the early 1960s, I received a letter addressed to "Denis Vaugeois, Esq." Oh, my! "Esquire"! I wasn't just some nobody! The letter came from McGill University and was signed "Lawrence Hart." This very dignified gentleman invited me to the professors' club. We had a wide-ranging conversation. I went back to Trois-Rivières truly intrigued. The invitations continued. He realized that I had gathered a great deal of information on his ancestors. He wanted to get to the bottom of his family history. Similarly, people sometimes wrote to the archives of the Séminaire to offer money to Father Tessier if he would help them establish a family relationship with the Harts of Trois-Rivières so that they could claim part of an imaginary inheritance.

Casting His Seed to the Wind

Aside from these relatively enduring relationships, Moses Hart had a considerable number of brief affairs. Raymond Douville examined what he calls the years of Moses's youth.[9] It was evidently a long youth, followed by a midlife crisis and a libidinous old age. He may have been a charming man, but self-assurance and wealth were his main attributes.

There exists a number of pathetic letters from grief-stricken women who begged for assistance for "his child," or sometimes "his children." Douville transcribed one such letter, dated 29 February 1816 (our translation):

My dear sir,

I learned that you will leave for the full year, I hope that you will not forget your dear little children although you have said that they were not yours, you know better than that, for you have always looked upon them as a father who loved them and me as mine as well. I hope that you will not be so cruel as to abandon them as orphans. It is said that they have a father who has so much honour and wealth, I hope that you will give them some recognition as their father. You have always blamed me for being married, but you should assess whether it is better that I married an honest boy who has taken good care of my children than to have stayed as I was. If you want to do something for the children you could give them to us, we would hold a good account for them from which they would benefit. For I have an honest man you have only to inform yourself with my Sieur Salaberi and my Sieur Duchainé and my Sieur Delairie, with all these gentlemen, they can give you his good character. The children send you tender kisses and hope that their father will think of them.[10]

The letter was signed "Ane [Anne] Galarno." By all evidence, this affair lasted some time and made his many stays in the town of Quebec more pleasant.

Everywhere Moses went, he left unhappiness behind. Douville also transcribed a letter from Marie Godin, of Yamachiche, dated 22 April 1836: "Mr. Hart, I am giving you news of myself and your boy, he is very ill, I am asking you to send him shoes and flowers of sulphur and sugar to cure him, and I am alone, I beg you to send me money by mail and I also beg you to send me clothing, he is naked. Please take care to send them quickly." And she added, "Obrem sends you his best wishes."[11]

Obrem was, in fact, Abraham, according to the genealogist Jean Prince. Pierre Abraham Samuel Hart married Arline-Virginie Richer-Laflèche on 12 January 1853. He died at age fifty-two in 1882. The important families of the region did not shun the Harts despite the circumstances of their birth. The Richer-Laflèche family is one example of this; there were many others.

Sometimes, friends of mothers in distress wrote to Moses; sometimes, the letters came from guardians to whom he had entrusted a child. The Hart archives contain a number of such epistles.[12]

The situation was no rosier for children whom Moses placed in various boarding schools. The superior of Collège de Terrebonne, Father Théberge, wrote to him about one of them, "Since he has been at the school you have not sent a penny, any clothing, or paid for his laundry. He suffers due to this. . . . Please send a little money, at least, for the essentials!" The custodial nun of the Ursulines of Trois-Rivières had to write to him regularly to ask for the boarding fees for his daughters Sarah Dorothea and Charlotte, for whom he wanted a good French education. Father F. Martin of Collège Sainte-Marie was categorical about another: "It is my thought that your son should not return to the school. We have had to make some complaints on his conduct, and he does not seem to have profited from these warnings." Writing to Moses from a "Canadien institution" in Varennes, between 1832 and 1835, Amury Girod, the well-known Swiss-born Patriote, had nothing very encouraging to say about his son Ezekiel.[13] All of this to say that Moses simply was not able to take care of all of his children. Often a single father, he was overwhelmed.

In my view, there is no doubt that Moses wanted many, many children. However, he could have done without the ones produced during chance encounters. There were few forms of contraception available at the time. His conquests could choose from among sponges, douches, and diaphragms; the last, though more effective in theory, were difficult to put in and required cooperation between the partners. Abortions were not very accessible.

Furthermore . . .

At age sixty-two, Moses was accused by Marguerite Long, wife of John Fowl, "now a prisoner in the gaol of Three Rivers," of having gone to her home to make indecent propositions. Of course, Moses defended himself with a list of legitimate reasons for having visited her.

Five years later, he was accused of the attempted rape of his niece, Anne Hart. His son, Areli Blake, came to his father's assistance to deny everything. In a draft affidavit, Areli Blake, swearing on the Holy Bible, gives his version.[14] The document seems to have been written by Moses. The explanations are so detailed that they suggest a cover-up.

Finally, in July 1835, Moses had to defend himself from the accusation "of keeping a bawdy and disorderly house." Of course, he was "ready to justify his innocence of such an accusation."[15]

This was much to take in for a small town of three thousand inhabitants. In fact, it was his own brother, Benjamin, who complained about him the loudest. They did not get along very well; they argued over the slightest thing. For years, they had been addressing each other as "Mister" and "Sir."

On 17 November 1829, Benjamin dropped his gloves. This time, he wrote "Dear Moses" and got right to the point: "I was much surprised to hear from Wellington that on visiting our family Burial Ground in Three Rivers he finds you have placed there (removed from some other part) the remains of one of your illegitimate children." This action, he wrote, "defiles that ground for ever—and no Jew can hereafter be placed there. . . . No bastard can be placed in a Jew Burial Ground much less a stranger and one uncircumcised." Benjamin protested that Moses should have more respect for the remains of their own parents and for their children who had died at a young age. Dorothea's death, two years earlier (1827), was still very much on Benjamin's mind. She had been living in Montreal, and he had taken care of the funeral arrangements and had her body transported to Trois-Rivières for burial. "I here Protest," Benjamin emphasized at the end of his letter, "against your dishonorable conduct and demand of you to remove immediately that body to some of your own Private Ground. In doing this I am doing the duty of a Son and a member of the tribe of Israel. I am yr aff br [your affectionate brother] B. Hart."

For several years, Benjamin had been showing a new zeal for the community's affairs. He was concerned about the fate of the Montreal synagogue and its derelict state, which he denounced. Despite his disapproving words, one senses that he was looking for reconciliation with his older brother. The wording of the end of his letter was quite deliberate. For his Montreal projects, he would need the support of everyone, including Moses. Above all, he no longer wanted to hear the jokes that he had been hearing for years about his brother's behaviour. At any rate, in 1835, Moses Hart's name was on the list of those who had contributed to the funding for a new synagogue.

Attacks against the Catholic Church

For unknown reasons, Aaron Hart had never been associated with the activities of the Montreal Jewish community. He was not a member of Shearith Israel and he did not attend the synagogue. Nevertheless, he followed the Jewish calendar and observed the Jewish holidays. He certainly made arrangements for dietary and other rituals. Twice, he had summoned Rabbi Jacob Raphael Cohen to Trois-Rivières. On 22 August 1779, the rabbi circumcised Benjamin, born 10 August. According to the register kept by Rabbi Cohen, he went to Trois-Rivières again to circumcise Alexander (Asher), born 31 January 1782.[16] Aaron's children, following their father's example, remained at a distance from the Montreal group for a long time. Apparently, Benjamin was the first to participate in the congregation in the mid-1820s.

In his way, Moses was very preoccupied with the religious question. Contrary to what one might believe, he had by no means treated the issue as secondary. In fact, he went so far as to develop a new religion. This fact is so important that it is presented separately at the end of this book. However, several interesting documents on religion written by Moses and conserved in the Hart archive deserve attention. They are undated drafts, but certain clues lead me to believe that they extend over a long period.

By all evidence, Moses became interested in religions quite early. Did his personal conduct cause his problems of conscience? Or did being the object of public disapproval incite him to mock the Catholic Church? The latter is possible, although at the same time, he was dealing with the Ursuline nuns and the managers of a number of church councils. As a seigneur, he was involved not only with mills and forges but also with churches.

In any case, in these texts, he expressed himself freely. He was a workaholic, he was intelligent, and he took advantage of his travels to conduct research. The result was surprising.

The Ten Commandments According to Moses Hart

The first document that drew my attention contains forty-six handwritten pages and is titled, "The Ten Commandments of the Roman Catholick church, humbly inscribed to the consideration of the Roman Catholics of Ireland, Canada and the United States."[17] Moses writes an introduction in which he concludes that the Catholic religion is composed of 2/8 cruelty, 2/8 idolatry, 1/8 tyranny by the priests, 1/8 penitence, and 2/8 superstition. He then moves on to his "ten commandments":

- First commandment: Thou shall pay obedience to the pope, as to the Christ.
- Second commandment: Thy Bishops shall not defile themselves with a wife.
- Third commandment: Thy Deacons, and under priests, likewise shall not stain their holy persons with the vile embraces of wife.
- Fourth commandment: Thou shall establish Monk and Fryars.
- Fifth commandment: Thou shall cloister Nuns, or priests in petticoats (?).
- Sixth commandment: Thou shall commit Idolatry.
- Seventh commandment: Thou shall confess thy sins, to the priests, and shall pray in a language, thou do not understand.
- Eighth commandment: Thou shall not eat meat, forty days in Lent.
- Ninth commandment: Thou shall attend Masses and Vespers and Saint holidays.
- Tenth commandment: Thou shall establish an Inquisition to glut the cruelty of the clergy.

Each commandment is followed by historical commentary on popes and other important figures in the history of the Catholic Church. I did some fact checking and found that there was always a foundation or a legend to support his remarks. For instance, he correctly cites Leo I in 460, Felix III in 490, and so on. Of course, it was usually affairs of morals that drew his attention. This document has been transcribed and can be consulted at www.septentrion.qc.ca.

The Jews Accused of Christ's Murder

The second document is titled "The Jews vindicated from the oppressions cast upon them of having conspired the death of Christ; an admonition to the Jews to avoid the precipice of Christianity."[18] It consists of forty-two pages of crossings out and hesitations. Moses denounces the "accusations which has [*sic*] caused rivers of Jewish blood to flow, by the sects demonstrating themselves Christians." He notes, "The sword of persecution have drove [the Jews] from one country to another," and later he describes them as "abused, scoffed and stripped of their inherent birthrights in almost every country, scarcely meeting with a resting place to lay down their weary heads."

He conducts a comparative study of the four gospels and an analysis of the Pentateuch, the cornerstone of Christianity of which the Talmud makes much mention. He recalls that these five books have been falsely attributed to Moses, since they were compiled from a fragile oral tradition that was perpetuated among Jews in captivity.

The history of the Virgin Mary was of particular interest to Moses. In his view, the intervention of the Holy Spirit served to conceal the immorality of two women: Mary and Elizabeth. He was surprised at the reaction of St. Joseph upon learning of Mary's maternity. "A strange composition this Holy Ghost," he remarks.

Various Drafts and Research Notes

The third document is part of a longer text. The first twenty pages are missing, which makes it difficult to understand the story to which he refers. The surviving part starts, "The story was probably invented to frighten children."[19] According to Moses, Jews could not have crucified Jesus. "St. Matthew is supposed to have been an eye witness to the transactions he wrote about," he writes, "but he could not have been an eye witness to anything relating to Christ. His book and other books must have been wrote ages after Christ." Eleven pages of this document are illegible or incomprehensible.

The fourth document[20] is composed of research notes on various subjects. Under the name of Alexander I is written, "Holy water mixed with salt 132 years to be used in church to keep out demony." Moses discusses the cruelties of the Church, blasphemy, rapes, crusades, and other matters.

Four other documents, each two or three pages long,[21] refer to a Trois-Rivières court case concerning Nathaniel Levitt, an American possibly of Jewish origin, who "was indicted, tried and condemned, for having at the house of his father in law, thrown an English Bible, into the fire, saying it was a book of lies, and word of the devil." These were notes of protest written between 13 and 20 September 1821. Moses wrote a number of drafts of open letters, one of which is called "Justice and Mercy." He appeared to be truly disturbed by the Levitt affair. It was quite an unusual trial, and he felt it was an opportunity not to be missed (see chapter 9).

Thus, Moses let off steam in writings that remained private. He might have attacked the local clergy, the religious practice of his fellow citizens, the prejudices of the elites or the common people. He might have sought to flush out manifestations of anti-Semitism. Although he ran for public office a number of times (see chapter 9), he never blamed his defeats on prejudices against Jews.

In fact, his problems were of another order. There is little doubt that he was obsessed by sex and by the history of religions. He was also an active and ambitious entrepreneur and a powerful landowner. He had a hand in many fields and ideas for reform in all of them. Moreover, in keeping with his rather megalomaniac nature, he founded his own religion.

A New Religion: A Master Stroke or a Waste of Time?

Moses Hart's master stroke was to propose a new religion.[22] The first time that I looked at his short treatise titled *General Universal Religion*, I was not surprised to find a text in which the author settled scores with society, various religions, and other entities. All the same, his decision to have his work printed, especially in New York, garnered my respect. This may have been the first work published by a native of Trois-Rivières. Pierre Boucher's *Une histoire véritable et naturelle* must be disqualified because he was French by birth. The notary Jean-Baptiste Badeaux wrote *Le Journal des opérations de l'armée américaine lors de l'invasion du Canada en 1775–1776*; however, he was from Quebec City and his work was published only in 1870.[23] In any case, before even looking at the content, I had various questions arising out of my activities as a publisher about items such as the print run, the cost, and the nature of the contract with the printer.

The Hart archive contains answers to all of these questions. Printed by Van Winckle and Wiley in 1815, the sixty-page booklet had cost $68.75 for a print run of 500. Three years later, a new print run of 250 was stalled for some time at the printer, and Moses changed the work's title to *Modern Religion*. In 1824, the author made a few changes and had a new, slightly revised edition printed by Johnstone and Van Norden.

In his short preface, the author notes the existence of countless religious controversies and observes that, to his knowledge, no one has tried to resolve this discord by bringing the religions together under a single banner—or, at any rate, no one has succeeded in doing so. "How truly distressing to mankind have been their various religious tenets," he wrote sadly. "Alas, how many millions of people have fallen victims to religious intolerance, bigotry, and tyranny! How often has religious imagination been wrought up to such a pitch, as to hurry one sect to imbue its hands in the innocent blood of another."

"In these few sheets," he adds, "it is far distant from my intention to give offence; hence I shall avoid making any remark on any particular sect."

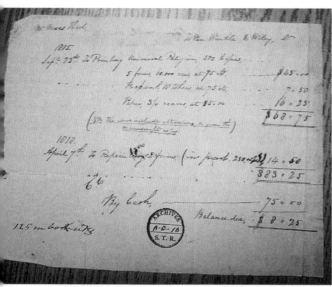

Although some doubt may remain about the true author of *General Universal Religion* and *Modern Religion,* it is well established that Moses Hart ordered and paid for the printing of these pamphlets. Through the invoices conserved, we know that there were three editions, dated 1815, 1818, and 1824. The first two were printed by Van Winkle & Wiley of New York.

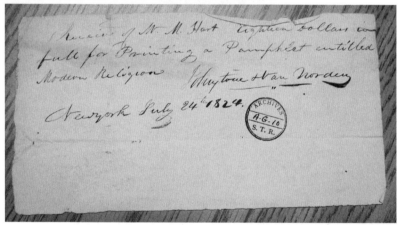

This receipt issued to M. Hart is dated 24 July 1824. I was not able to find a complete copy of the "Pamphlet entitled *Modern Religion*" printed by Johnston & Van Norden.

And he ends the preface, "I do not hesitate to implore the candour of the good people of this enlightened age."

In the introduction, Moses marvels at the perfection of the human body, especially the eye. "We are filled with wonder at the stupendous grandeur of an invisible Creator, although his appearance strikes us everywhere." This is a new Moses Hart: humanist, poet, visionary, and with an analytic, methodical, and organized mind. This is a Moses Hart thinking profoundly: Was there not a Creator behind everything? Did everything not have a beginning and an end?

He then discusses outer space, in which, he posits, there are other planets, some bigger than Earth, also harbouring life; he wonders at the movement of the universe, the beauty and harmony of creation, the faculty of reason. He rejects the idea of eternal punishment—the existence of afterlife chastisements—which seemed to him contrary to the idea that we have of the beneficent Creator. Jews do not believe in hell; Moses agreed with them—perhaps a vestige of his Jewish education or the influence of his parents.

In the 1818 edition (p. 60), Moses included in an appendix some information on his religious upbringing, his culture, his objectives, and the foundations of the religion that he was proposing. A native of Lower Canada, he had received a Jewish education. During his studies, he had analyzed the original versions of the New and Old Testaments, and he had written commentaries on the gospels. He presumed that the early Jews were deists, and he intended to propose his religion to Jews and deists.

Over the years, I returned several times to the various editions of *General Universal Religion* published by Moses Hart. In 1966, before the members of the Canadian Catholic Historical Association, I gave a speech titled "Les positions religieuses de Moses Hart," which was published in the association's journal.[24] I speculated about what might have shaped his views on religion and whether these had any impact. I am not much further along in this speculation today. The documents conserved in the Hart archive show the efforts made to distribute his booklets and the little success obtained. Might he have had a discreet influence on some reformers? Jacob Rader Marcus, an American rabbi and scholar, became interested in the proposed new religion, which, in his view, had received little attention.[25] "Perhaps," Marcus writes, "the 'timing' was bad. Deism was dead, had been dead for almost a generation . . . but did Hart realize it? This work—if it has any importance—is significant as evidence of penetrating influence of deism, eighteenth century liberalism, and the French Revolution in the life of an individual Jew who lived in a quiet Canadian town."

"The whole atmosphere of Hart's religion," Marcus continues, "was akin to that of the French cults of Reason and of the Supreme Being. . . . There was no burning fire of fervor or mystic faith in the author of Modern Religion. He was spiritually cold; he was superficially intellectualistic. There was no deep philosophic insight in him or his ritual. He was a typical eighteenth century deist, not a prophet."[26] Marcus concludes, emphatically, "But let there be no mistake: he was no unsung precursor of the American Reform Movement in Judaism. . . . They were not revolutionists; they were not assimilationists. Hart was."[27]

Marcus tried to identify the authors who might have inspired Moses. It was difficult for me to follow his explanations and hypotheses, as I am not familiar with the deists John Toland and Elihu Palmer, to whom he refers. However, the reference to Thomas Paine drew my attention; my publishing house, Septentrion, has republished two of Paine's works in French. Moses also refers to Paine in his correspondence. But I wanted more than influences. This religious treatise struck me as so different from what I had come to expect from its author that I thought it might have been plagiarized. For years, I researched this possibility. I questioned theologians and nagged a Jewish friend, Alti Rodal, a religious scholar, who had followed my work from the beginning. Nothing.

Then, comparing the 1815 and 1818 editions, my eye was drawn, once again, to a reference to the "learned Dupuis," author of "Origines de tous les cultes," on page 60 of *Modern Religion*. The comment was ambiguous, the title incorrectly transcribed, as often happens for foreign languages.

Out of curiosity, I did a Web search on Charles François Dupuis. The second item on the list of search results mentioned the name Claude Rétat, a researcher at CNRS de Lyon responsible for a Web site on Dupuis, author of *Origine de tous les cultes ou religion universelle*, published in 1795. Of course, part of the title, "Religion universelle," made my heart pound. Perhaps Hart had simply omitted the second part of Dupuis's title in his reference! I immediately sent a Mr. Claude Rétat an e-mail. Ms. Claude Rétat answered quickly, saying that she was available to examine the work by Moses Hart. I inundated her with documents and, throwing caution to the winds, I found an excuse to go and meet her in France.

Rétat did not find any trace of plagiarism—at least, not of Dupuis's work. As I was writing this chapter, I re-examined the copies that have managed to escape the grasp of collectors. Suddenly, something struck me: Moses Hart's name does not appear. On the title page of the 1815 edition, there is no author's name. In the 1818 edition (which may have been printed in 1818 or 1824), the title page of the copy conserved in the archives is missing. The preface is signed "The Author," and the last page begins, "The subscriber, a native of L. Canada, respectfully submits to the consideration

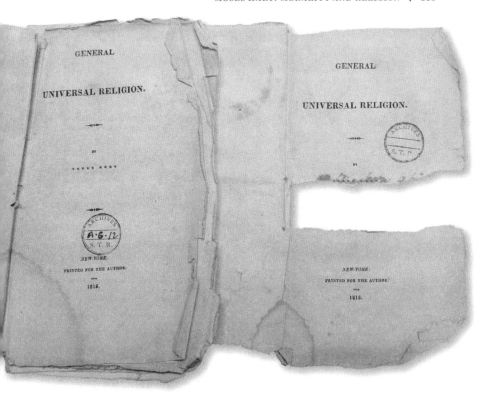

The photograph shows the torn-out part, just under the asterisks suggesting the letters MOSES HART. Someone wrote a name on the asterisks and a comment underneath. Was it Moses Hart himself who tore out a comment questioning his authorship? The mystery thickens when we examine the last page of a subsequent edition (1818 or 1824), in which the title has become "Modern Religion." I have not found a complete copy of either of these new editions; we know that they exist through receipts conserved (see p. 178). Both pages reproduced on page 182 are photocopies of single pages.

of the Jews and Deists . . ." At the bottom of the page, where there would usually be a signature, is a stain that conceals whatever was beneath. This is a loose page that belongs to either the 1818 or the 1824 edition; there is no way of knowing.

Once again I turned to the Internet. I found a copy of *Modern Religion*— "New York, printed for the author, 1818, 58 pages"—in the catalogue of the National Library of Australia. However, the copy in the Archives du Séminaire de Trois-Rivières is sixty pages long and the date on the first page, 1818, is handwritten. This Web search also uncovered a long article

CONTINUATION OF THE FESTIVALS,

VIDE PAGE 21.

1 *Signifies Spring, or First Moon ; 5, Harvest ; and 9, Winter Festival, being the first Wednesday of the Moons.*

1 - - -	6 May, 1824.	1 - - -	2 May, 1832.
5 - - -	25 August.	5 - - -	29 August.
9 - - -	22 December.	9 - - -	26 December.
1 - - -	20 April, 1825.	1 - - -	24 April, 1833.
5 - - -	17 August.	5 - - -	21 August.
9 - - -	14 December.	9 - - -	18 December.
1 - - -	10 May, 1826.	1 - - -	14 May, 1834.
5 - - -	6 September	5 - - -	10 September.
9 - - -	3 January, 1827.	9 - - -	7 January, 1835.
1 - - -	2 May.	1 - - -	6 May.
5 - - -	29 August.	5 - - -	26 August.
9 - - -	19 December.	9 - - -	23 December.
1 - - -	16 April, 1828.	1 - - -	20 April, 1836.
5 - - -	13 August.	5 - - -	17 August.
9 - - -	10 December.	9 - - -	14 December.
1 - - -	6 May, 1829.	1 - - -	10 May, 1837.
5 - - -	2 September.	5 - - -	6 September.
9 - - -	30 December.	9 - - -	3 January, 1838.
1 - - -	28 April, 1830.	1 - - -	2 May.
5 - - -	25 August.	5 - - -	22 August.
9 - - -	22 December.	9 - - -	19 December.
1 - - -	20 April, 1831.	1 - - -	17 April, 1839.
5 - - -	10 August.	5 - - -	14 August.
9 - - -	7 December.	9 - - -	11 December.
		1 - - -	6 May, 1840.
		5 - - -	2 September

OMISSIONS AND ERRORS TO MODERN OR NATURAL RELIGION.

7th page, line 15, omit, *ought there to be,* and read, *has he.*
12th and 54th pages, females are to omit the word *rape.*
30th page, 19th line ⎱ omit *rape and bestiality.*
31st page, 8th line ⎰
43d page, 9th line, 45th page, 16th line, 46th page, 16th line, for *has* read *hath.*
54th page, instead of the 1st and 2d lines, read, *the right hand may be held up, and sworn, in the name of the Almighty Creator.*

[59]

THIS subscriber, a native of L. Canada, respectfully submits to the consideration of the JEWS and DEISTS, the propriety of establishing a *Ceremonial Religion,* founded on natural principles.

He begs leave to enlarge on his prior intentions, in stating that he had received a Jewish Education, and was prompted to turn his early studies in tracing the original compilers of the Old and New Testaments.

The five Books ascribed to Moses, were not wrote by him, but by Esdras; in the time of Cyrus.

It was then said that Moses had wrote thirteen of his Books, one of which he deposited in the Ark, and the remainder distributed among the Tribes of Israel ; and from the captivities of the Jews, every vestige of these Books had long disappeared.

Esdras then states, that he assembled the Jews, and from the various accounts they had received, by oral tradition, respecting the writings of Moses, he composed the present pentateuch, in Hebrew ; vide the Talmud.

Hence we may presume, that the Jews were originally a species of Deists.

We have not any guide to lead us to a knowledge of any of the authors of the remainder of the Old Testament.

St. Matthew, St. Mark, St. Luke, and St. John, the four principal founders of the New Testament, do not give us the slightest hint of themselves. We are ignorant whether they wrote by inspiration, hearsay, or ocular demonstration : at what period they flourished, of what country they were, or even the language they wrote in.

The learned Dupuis, in his *Origine des tous les Cultes,* gives a far different account of the origin of the Christian Mission.

This Book, which he now offers for perusal, may be seen at

it contains a weekly day of rest, and three holidays ; the prayers are brief, and avoid a repetition ; the ceremony is moral, poetical, and musical ; the two latter parts are optional, and not yet completed : it contains no flattering miracles, to gratify the ear of the credulous ; nor yet does it presume to lower the exalted dignity of the Creator, by familiar intercourse, to please the creature, as is inculcated in the Testaments ; and which has been the means of their gigantic promulgation among mankind.

[60]

The list of omissions or errors given on page 59 offers a clue that enables us to associate these two pages with the corresponding edition, of 1818 or 1824. Since festivities and ceremonies are a large part of the treatise, the author felt that it would be convenient to present them in a table. On the following page, he decides to introduce himself—to satisfy the curiosity of his followers. Designating himself as the "subscriber," he says that he was born in Lower Canada and indicates that he has received a Jewish education. This time, the signature has been blacked out; it is completely obscured. I have done my best to see what it covers, but unsuccessfully. The absence of signature, the use of asterisks, the tearing out of part of a page, and this blacking out are not coincidental. There's something fishy here. Moses Hart had ordered the print runs. He had paid for them. He had distributed the pamphlet and made himself the propagandist for a new religion, but had he written this treatise? He may have plagiarized an author whose identity is lost. I suspected Dupuis, but he turned out not to be the one. There is still the hypothesis of an anonymous writer paid by Moses Hart.

The "subscriber's" statements, however, are clearly inspired by Moses's ideas; we find them written by him in a document titled "The Jews vindicated from the oppressions cast upon them of having conspired the death of Christ: An admonition to the Jews to avoid the precipice of Christianity" (see p. 175).

published in volume 4 of *The Republican* written by "A Citizen of the World, R[ichard]. Carlile, Dorchester Gaol, dec., 1820." He pokes fun at Moses Hart and his "religious code."

The Bibliothèque Jean-Charles Bonenfant at Université Laval has a copy of *General Universal Religion* on microfiche made from the copy of the original edition at Library and Archives Canada, with the note "Author's name erased from t.p. [title page]. Work attributed to Moses Hart." On the title page of the 1815 edition, where the author's name should be, I found, "By XXXXX XXXX" (the number of Xs matching the number of letters in his first and last names). Strangely, Moses paid the bills, distributed and promoted the work, but hid his authorship of it.

In the end, what did Moses Hart's religion consist of? Hervé Biron describes it as "a vague religious system and prayers for all life circumstances." Much of it was naïve, and some of it was ridiculous. The prescribed oath was accompanied by ten commandments full of pious wishes and good intentions.

Although the work is not signed, it bears the hallmarks of Moses Hart. In the 1815 edition, he invents "second-degree marriages" and "half-marriages." These, of course, were made to measure for his lifestyle: "If the parties have already cohabited together, and have any child or children living, of such cohabitation, the names of such child or children shall be inserted in the certificates, and shall be eligible to the rights of this half marriage. By this half marriage the parties may at any time separate, or formally marry, or marry indifferent persons." Later, he specifies, "They [the child or children] are not to be deemed bastards." This short section on half-marriages does not appear in the 1824 edition.

Moses Hart may not have plagiarized from another work, but he had the means to hire a ghost-writer. That is my final hypothesis. Readers can make up their own minds by reading the reproduction at www.septentrion. qc.ca. Moses Hart's proposed religion was, above all, a ceremonial. Its author was neither a mystic nor a hoaxer; he was either a tormented human being or, according to my colleague Gaston Deschênes, a masterful charlatan attempting to cloak his own moral turpitude.

CHAPTER 8

Moses Hart in Business

OR MOSES HART, business seemed to be a springboard to power and respectability. I write "seemed" because I am not completely certain. He was a very complex man, and he took an interest in a wide variety of activities. He was involved in shipping, he ran a brewery, he founded a bank; he exported fur and wood and operated seigneuries; he coveted the Jesuits' properties and wanted to exploit the Shawinigan waterfalls; he was even accused of running a bawdy house. There was only one business that he did not get involved in, iron, even though Trois-Rivières was surrounded by ironworks. The Saint-Maurice ironworks was owned by another giant of industry, Mathew Bell. Moses Hart was born in 1768; Mathew Bell, in 1769. The former died in 1852; the latter, in 1849. Apparently, they avoided each other throughout their lives.

Moses Hart could be labelled as much a wheeler-dealer as a businessman. He tried his hand at almost everything, but never became deeply involved in anything. He was full of ideas, but he always encountered obstacles, which he attacked head-on rather than seeking a way around. Although he ranted and railed about injustice, this didn't keep him from exploiting people and the "system." He was bursting with ideas for reforms—reforms, of course, that would serve his interests. Sometimes, he was also intrepid; he showed this side of his character in the shipping business, in which the challenges were considerable.

Shipping

In late August 1809, Moses Hart glimpsed on the river, in front of Trois-Rivières, the first Canadian steamship. It belonged to the Molsons, his rivals in the brewery business. He quickly decided that, the following

---

Had Moses Hart guessed the potential of the Shawinigan falls? In any cases, he was interested in them, and he tried to get them included within the borders of his seigneuries. On 26 May 1832, the governor's secretary demanded that he produce land deeds to support this claim (ASTR, Fonds Hart, 0009-K-f).

summer, he would build a vessel (to be dubbed, of course, the *Hart*) to compete with the *P.S. Accommodation*.

Moses had attempted to dip his toe into the shipping waters a number of years before. In 1796, when he was living in William Henry (Sorel), he undertook to purchase a brigantine from John Polley, a shipbuilder. According to the papers conserved in the Hart archive,[1] there was a financial disagreement and Polley threatened to leave the shipyard repeatedly. In fact, I am not certain that the small double-masted sailing ship was ever completed. This early experience was typical of Moses Hart's business style: demands, threats, lawsuits.

In the summer of 1810, the *Accommodation* had no competitors, but the small steamer was getting long in the tooth. The Molsons replaced it in 1812 with the *P.S. Swiftsure*. Two years later, the *P.S. Malsham* joined the fleet. The owners took advantage of the Anglo-American war to pay off their investment. It might aptly be said that Moses Hart had missed the boat. In fact, rounding the buoy before him were also Thomas Torrance (*P.S. Car of Commerce*) and Black & Goudie of Quebec City (the *P.S. Lauzon* and the *P.S. Québec*). The Molsons added to their fleet again in 1817 and 1818 with the *P.S. Lady Sherbrooke* and the *P.S. New Swiftsure*. Competition was fierce, and the Molsons were in the lead.

Moses Hart had dropped out of the race for the moment; he likely had neither the time nor the money. To get back into the game, he needed assistance, and it was to come from his nephew, Ira Craig, and his son, Alexander Thomas. In 1832, Moses took an interest in the *Lady Aylmer* (built by James Jeffery in 1831). John Miller offered him a one-third share for £1,000 payable in three instalments. A series of transactions ensued involving William Price, John Class, William Philips, Francis Bell, and Miller. In May 1833, Moses ceded half of the *Lady Aylmer* to Alexander Thomas. The steamer sailed between Montreal, Sorel, Berthier, Port Saint-François, Trois-Rivières, Batiscan, Portneuf, and Quebec City and also specialized in towing timber rafts. The Harts thought of using it as a ferry between Trois-Rivières and the south shore of the St. Lawrence to serve Nicolet and Yamaska. Typical of transactions in which Moses was involved, the *Lady Aylmer* was a pawn in various ploys. Miller's shares were put up for auction and it was agreed that Alexander Thomas would try to drive up the price. Finally, in August 1835, the Harts decided to sell the ship. I don't know what happened to it or to the litigants' various claims. But I do know that Édouard Defoy, the captain of the *Lady Aylmer*, claimed his

Timber raft on the Ottawa River facing Hull (Collection Arthur Robidoux). *L'Ère des cageux*, brochure published by the Société patrimoine et histoire de l'île Bizard, 2004, edited by Roger Labastrou and Éliane Labastrou.

Towing timber rafts

The transportation of tree trunks bound together into rafts was an old practice used in France. Intendant Jean Talon apparently had the idea of tying together pine logs, which floated naturally, and oak logs, which were heavier and tended to sink. In the early nineteenth century, as the lumber industry was expanding, large cages of hewn logs appeared. They consisted of frames made of pine logs that served as a floating base, and oak logs were placed on top of them. On the Ottawa, Philemon Wright was an extremely active pioneer in the early 1800s. According to Léon A. Robidoux (*Les Cageux*, L'Aurore, 1974) and Le Vieux Prince (nickname of Aimé Guérin—published, as might be expected, at Guérin [1988]), in 1823 alone, 300 timber rafts were floated from Hull to Quebec. Other rafts came from Kingston. Their path was strewn with many rapids as far as Lac Saint-Louis (175 miles in three days). The rafts were detached from the frames to get by the Lachine Rapids, then reassembled and pulled by tugboats to Quebec. See Rodolphe Girard, *Marie Calumet* (1904) and the permanent exhibition on the Promenade Champlain in Quebec City and the site of the Musée du parc des Ancres in Pointe-des-Cascades.

due from Moses Hart as Ira Craig's boss. Moses responded that Ira Craig was an employee of Alexander Thomas, whereas Defoy had been hired by Miller, whose property was also seized.

There are dozens of stories about Moses's difficulties with making payments. And then there were the difficulties with insurance companies; damaged, lost, and stolen merchandise; and other problems. The Hart archive mentions some fifty ships, most of which belonged to the Molsons or to Torrance. Thus, although they did not always own ships, the Harts were major customers of the shipping companies. They traded in wood and potash with merchants in Montreal and Quebec City, and also with dealers in Europe. Their goods were regularly shipped on the *Everetta* (or *Eweretta*), chartered by Henry Joseph of Berthier, one of Moses's cousins. Moses avoided the agents in Montreal, Quebec City, New York, and Halifax, and maintained the direct links established by relatives such as his uncle, George Joel, and his cousin, Judah Joseph.[2] He exported mainly potash and grains and imported everything that he could make a profit selling in his general store in Trois-Rivières.

There are many more stories about ships. For instance, in 1824, Moses attempted to purchase the *Telegraph*. John Molson told him that the amount he had proposed was ridiculous.[3] When Moses attempted to purchase a brig, the *Merope,* his son Areli Blake, at the time a law student, represented him. The plan was to send the small ship to Buenos Aires. Areli and the captain, William Lampron, did not get along.[4] The project was cancelled, and the *Merope* later ran aground in front of Quebec City.

The *Toronto* was apparently built in Trois-Rivières around 1834 or 1835. It was sold at auction on 22 May 1841 for £2,500.[5] The *Hart*, which may also have been built in Trois-Rivières, in 1839, by Olivier Cloutier, had a longer career.[6] The files for the years 1841 and 1842 are quite complete and record numerous towing contracts. The *Hart* (45 horsepower) was sold at auction on 27 March 1845 at the Saint-Antoine de Tilly dock. Apparently, it was replaced by another steamer of the same name. It was on board a steamer of this name that Moses's favourite son, Alexander Thomas, had a fatal fall in 1852. In their annals, the Ursulines briefly described this accident: "He was on board the *Hart*, a steamer that travelled between Quebec and Montreal: the vessel was at the town dock at the time. While strolling on the deck, Mr. Hart fell into the bottom of the hold. He died at the Ursuline Nuns' Hospital. His body is in repose at the Saint-Louis cemetery, on the land of his brother, Mr. Ezekiel Hart. The wife of Mr. Alexander Hart, née

Judah, was Jewish. As a widow, she went to live in her seigneury of Saint-Zéphirin de Courval."[7]

Moses Hart ultimately gave up on the shipping business, after many difficulties. It is obvious that he understood the importance of this economic activity, but he would have had to concentrate on it personally from the 1810s on. He had let Molson and Torrance families gain an insurmountable lead. In the end, even the Torrance family would give way to the Molsons.

Brewing Beer

Aaron had pushed for the creation of a brewery as a way to get his sons to work together in an enterprise that was profitable and, it might be said, risk-free. On 2 December 1796, Moses, Ezekiel, and Benjamin formed a company "to build a Brew and Malt House for the purpose of carrying on the business of brewing Ale or Beer . . . and likewise to erect a manufactory of Pot and perlash . . . and also a Bake House for the Baking of Bread and Biscuit."[8] The three brothers were equal partners; the enterprise was financed by Aaron. The agreement was to last for six years, and the written consent of all three partners was necessary to change it.

Since Moses lived in William Henry (Sorel), Ezekiel took the lead on the project. He purchased plans for a brewery and beer recipes, as well as a lot, on Rue Haut-Boc, on which "hops for brewing were cultivated and flourished." He had little difficulty persuading Jean-Baptiste Corbin to sell him this lot, 60 feet in frontage by 120 feet in depth, for £250.

A lot near the river then had to be acquired to provide water supply and facilitate transportation of the products. Pierre-Ignace d'Aillebout had the ideal site situated facing the Ursulines monastery. The nuns were aware of the Harts' plan, and they were not eager to have a brewery under their windows. D'Aillebout knew this. However, Aaron had been among the religious community's generous benefactors. Aware of the nuns' power—the only power to have survived in the region after the conquest—he had done them many favours, even lending them £8,000, at a five percent interest rate for the first £4,000, then interest-free for the remaining £4,000. He had also sent his daughters to them for schooling, which made them happy. Ezekiel knew and understood his father's dilemma. He was also the kind of person who wanted to keep both sides happy.

Moses had a completely different temperament. And when he landed in Trois-Rivières, things began to get moving. Cunning, to say the least,

Moses asked d'Aillebout to show him the documents proving his titles of possession. D'Aillebout had acquired part of the land Moses wanted on 4 May 1783 during a transaction with the nuns. Of course, everything was in order; the nuns already had the Harts' proposal in hand. D'Aillebout had been ambushed; the notary had prepared the paperwork and all that was left was for him to sign on the dotted line.

Moses had gone to the monastery with the Harts' proposal and with the notary hot on his heels. The superior, Sister Marguerite le Cavelier de Ste-Ursule, had consulted the members of the council that included sisters Marie-Magdelaine LaPalme de Saint-Henry, Jeanne Lévesque de Saint-Joseph, and Marguerite Chevrefils de Saint-François-Xavier. Intuitively, they were on the defensive.[9]

The community's status placed it under the authority of the vicar general of the district of Trois-Rivières, Father François Noiseux, who acted as the

In 1797, under the watchful eye of Aaron Hart, his three sons, Moses, Ezekiel, and Benjamin, started up a brewery. The father was trying to initiate his sons to the world of business, if possible through a partnership. For this purpose, he created Hart's and Sons. After his death, family members began to quarrel. On his 1815 map, Bouchette indicates the site of two breweries, noting that the one located near de la Commune, to the east, belonged to Ezekiel Hart.

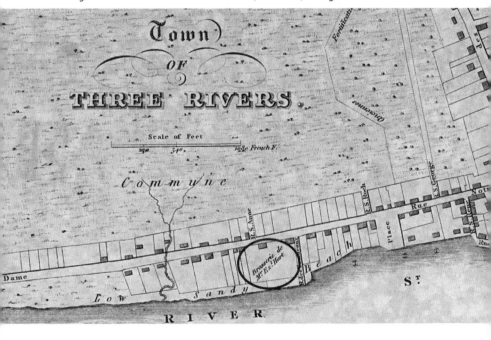

Ursulines' superior. One might imagine the conversations: Canadiens liked beer and were already making home brew. The nuns remembered watching their mothers make it. They also remembered that men took refuge in drink, and women in prayer—the former found comfort in liquor, the latter in rosaries. They questioned Father Noiseux on beer production by the Recollets, the Jesuits, and, it was said, at the seminary in Quebec City. Was it true that the Grey Nuns made it in Montreal? They, too, were businesswomen. They ran a school and a hospital; they had farmland in production, and they even operated a seigneury near Louiseville (Rivière-du-Loup). If it was a good idea for the Harts, why not for themselves? Father Noiseux felt obliged to mention that, in fact, wealthier Canadiens opted for wine; port and sherry were highly appreciated and rum was so popular that two distilleries had begun to produce it in Quebec City.[10]

Aaron Hart was well aware of all of this. His friend Samuel Jacobs had told him about his experiences in Nova Scotia, and then in Quebec. Rum production depended on the importation of molasses, with all of the difficulties that involved. Aaron preferred importing the finished product, but one day, who knew? Perhaps his sons would be interested in distilling.

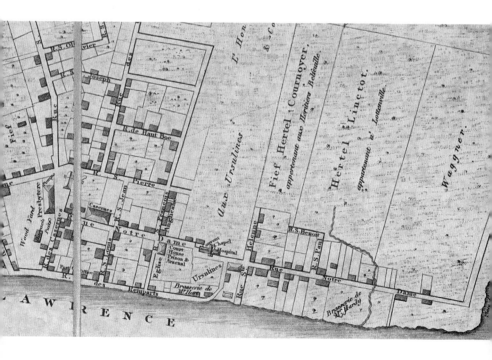

The nuns knew Aaron Hart well as a merchant, and they told themselves that he must know what he was doing. His oldest son's lack of manners surprised and displeased them. Aaron may have been obsequious, but Moses was boastful and easily moved to impatience. If seduction didn't work, he got anxious. The nuns had seen others like him. However, they liked the Hart family. Father Noiseux had emphasized the Harts' merits: they worked hard; the mother had done nothing to hold the family back; they were practically good Christians. In fact, they should not be treated as foreigners and no prejudice should be shown toward them.

The nuns had planned to "build a lime furnace on the designated site." In the document prepared by the notary, after acknowledging the sale agreed to by d'Aillebout, they declared that they "have voluntarily renounced and renounce now and forever all rights" in this regard. In return, the Harts ceded the part of the lot with twenty-six feet of frontage on Rue de l'Hôpital and extending to the paupers' cemetery. Moses had won. The nuns had given in.

Benjamin went to Montreal to purchase the necessary equipment. Raymond Douville has reconstructed the list: "pumps, vats, cauldron with a capacity of eight hundred gallons, a still, and a hundred-and-twenty-gallon worm."[11]

Moses and Ezekiel decided to purchase their wood in Village des Forges. They paid Jean-Baptiste Choret with a few *piastres* and a barrel of rum. Two more barrels went to Joseph Richard, Gervais Parenteau, and Joseph Doucet, who transported the wood to the site of the brewery; they also shared several hundred pounds cash to ensure family peace, as the rum might have had the opposite effect.

The Harts knew how to negotiate, but they were not good at manual labour. They needed arms, strong arms, for construction. A certain Gibbard and his two sons were to build the malt-curing barn. Moses hired an expert, John Brown, to supervise the project. Despite this precaution, the work was poorly done. The first tests showed that the malt oven could not withstand high temperatures. Moses fired the Gibbards and refused to pay them. Brown hired other workers to modify the facilities.

Brickmason Dominique Gougé was hired to build the brewery "from this date until the 30th day of next April [1797] for two shillings, Halifax currency, per day." The contract prepared by the M. and E. Hart Company set out that Gougé would have to "work at night when necessary, without other recompense."

When the time came to build the potash factory, the Harts hired Baptiste Dubois de Bécancour,[12] who "guarantee[d] to make good potash." They paid him "eighteen Spanish dollars a month," the contract read, "and, if they are not satisfied with him at any time, to pay him and dismiss him."[13]

The Harts did not like to wait for customers. The kegs of beer were loaded onto barges and sent to the south shore, from Bécancour to Nicolet, and the north shore, from Berthier to Sainte-Anne de la Pérade. The Harts also issued coupons that could be used for beer purchases—a time-honoured marketing ploy.

The brewery went into operation at about the same time as Aaron Hart died. The settlement of the estate divided the family. Benjamin slammed the door behind him, and Ezekiel followed soon after. He sold his shares in the brewery to Moses for £338 6s8d. The contract gives a detailed description of the facilities: "A stone brewery and a potashery, with all the pumps, vats, barrels, three potash boilers, and a copper boiler of about 120 gallons capacity . . . one shed for brewers' grains," the malt factory, and the land on Rue Haut-Boc where the hops was grown.[14]

It is not clear whether the brewery was profitable. In the brewery file,[15] I found a proposal from William Dow dated 16 September 1820. Dow had arrived from Scotland and wanted to establish a brewery.[16] Although Moses Hart's beer was not outselling the Molsons' beer, it was nevertheless known in Montreal. Dow's proposal was turned down. He went on to make a name for himself in the brewery business. The Dow Breweries did very well until the unfortunate incident in the 1960s when too much cobalt was added to the hops in order to enhance the head on the beer.

Moses Hart let go of the brewery during the 1830s. The coupon system had prepared him to take another direction.

Banking, The Hart's Bank

During the military occupation in the early 1760s, Aaron Hart had been the paymaster for the British troops. He had then become the main supplier to the army and the administration, both of which paid in hard cash. If he didn't know much about the various types of currency in circulation when he arrived in Trois-Rivières, he quickly learned to assess their value and became an expert in currency exchange. Naturally, he became a money-lender. Although the loans were generally for small amounts, they were all duly registered before the notary. The interest rates were reasonable, but the due dates were set in stone.

Moses got involved in many ventures but in this area he was inspired by his father. He managed a sort of credit union. His trips to the United States had put him into contact with bankers, and he had discovered the stock market. The insurance sector intrigued him. As always, he was on the lookout for new opportunities.

In 1817, the Bank of Montreal was founded. The developers found only twelve subscribers outside of the city, including two in Trois-Rivières: Moses and Ezekiel Hart. Four times the following year, Moses purchased additional shares, worth a total of £480, which were added to those he had purchased for £150 the previous year. He now held 124 shares. He continued to purchase shares: for at least £520 in 1819 and 1820, and I have found more sets of shares acquired between 1818 and 1830. David David, the brother of Samuel and Moses David—who were married to Aaron's daughters Sarah

This bill of exchange with a value of half an *écu* is associated with Hart's Bank. It is dated October 1837 and was issued at Trois-Rivières. It had a more reasonable value than did the bank notes issued by the Harts the following year. This note had to be personalized and might be numbered. It is nicely designed and contains much information. It specifies that the half-*écu* is worth 60 cents, an amount that a Canadien *habitant* such as the one pictured at the right might use. This value is repeated in English currency (2s.6d, or two shillings and sixpence—pence indicated by the letter "d," or denier) and in French currency (3 francs). The old French *livre* (pound, penny, denier) was swept away by the revolutionary whirlwind in France and replaced by the franc, the first coins of which were issued by Napoleon. One *écu* was worth 6 francs; a half-*écu*, 3 francs. The shilling was worth 24 French *sous*; a penny, 2 *sous*, since it took 12 pence to make a shilling (2 x 24 + 6 x 2 = 60 *sous*). The text on the note is bilingual.

Notes from Hart's bank are very rare. Here are three that are quite similar and with English text only, except to indicate the value. The five-dollar (or five-*piastre*) bill was worth, according to Denis Lacasse, one English pound—a large sum, as a labourer earned about 40 cents a day. This was therefore a note of guarantee for exchange between banks. The three-dollar and five-dollar bills were very similar, with a goddess on the left and a steamship on the right. In the centre is a lovely sleigh driven by a French Canadian, with a gentleman as passenger. Each bill was payable on demand and was personalized. I found it interesting to note the different kinds of numbers used: "1," "un," "one," and the Roman numeral I; the three-dollar bill is the same. The five-*piastre* bill uses "V" and "IIIII" as Roman numerals. If these bills were ever in circulation, they were apparently bought back by the Harts, since their bank had not received a permit.

and Charlotte, respectively—was also among the shareholders. In February 1818, David David became a director of the bank. The presence of a Jew on the board of directors did not keep the charter application from moving through the various legislative steps. The incorporation act was passed in 1821 and received royal assent in May 1822.[17]

The Bank of Montreal began to face competition in 1818 when the Bank of Canada was founded.[18] On 18 June, Moses Hart acquired twenty shares for a total cost of £100. Two months later, he acquired twenty more shares, this time paying £150. Moses was thrilled at the increased value of his shares. By February 1819, the early excitement had faded; at this point, he was able to acquire twenty more shares for £50. In 1820, 1821, and 1823, he purchased, respectively, fifteen, thirty, and forty-five new shares.

When the Bank of Quebec was founded in 1818, the two Hart brothers were again among its shareholders. The seminary archives conserve numerous notes exchanged between Moses Hart and Noah Freer, the executive director of the bank, between 1824 and 1847.[19] In 1824 alone, Freer offered Moss three blocks of shares for a total value of £950.

In 1833, the City Bank opened a subscription register in Montreal. Moses was among the shareholders and gave this bank part of his business, at least from 1835 to 1840.

The financial sector was in a frenzy. In 1835, Louis-Michel Viger and Jacob De Witt founded the People's Bank; in January of the following year, the memorandum of association was signed by nine French-Canadian businessmen.[20] The new bank's customers included Moses Hart, who was setting aside his political opinions. All of this banking effervescence was a bad sign. There was a financial crisis in the United States in 1837, and a good number of banks stopped making payments in cash; the Canadian banks followed. Given the shortage of hard cash, large merchants reacted by issuing their own money.

In 1837, the Thomas and William Molson company issued "Molson's Bank" paper money. After shipping and beer production, a new field of competition opened between the Molsons and the Harts. The score was two to zero for the Molsons. Moses Hart didn't hesitate. The time was now or never to realize an old family dream. He had "Hart's Bank" paper money printed.[21] (The bank notes have disappeared from the Hart archive, no doubt into collectors' hands.) On 9 May 1839, Moses applied for a license to operate "a private bank, called Hart's Bank, established the [preceding] year for the benefit of the town's [citizens]." He specified in his application that there were already bank notes in circulation and gave a brief overview of his financial situation, assessing his real-estate properties at £15,000 and his accounts receivable also at £15,000.

Moses's application came at a bad time. A few weeks before, the Bank of Montreal and the Board of Trade had asked the Special Council (as activity in the House was suspended because of the rebellion) to ban circu-

Moses Hart was present and active in almost every possible sector; he let no business opportunity pass him by. Why was he not interested in the Forges Saint-Maurice? I really don't know, unless it was that he always avoided confronting, or even dealing with, Matthew Bell, the owner of the ironworks and another industrial giant from Trois-Rivières.

lation of private money. A statute to this effect was proclaimed and came into effect on 1 June 1839. To add to the pressure, the chartered banks decided not to accept private money and closed the accounts of those who did not cooperate, such as the Molsons. The Molsons were forced to give in. They were to bounce back in the banking sector when a new statute authorizing private banks was passed in 1850. Although running a bank was a difficult and risky operation, brothers John and William Molson now applied for chartered bank status, which was granted in 1855.

By this time, it was too late for the Harts. In 1850, Ezekiel was dead. Benjamin, who had moved to Montreal, had gone bankrupt and, furthermore, had just signed a manifesto proposing annexation to the United States. Moses was suffering from palsy and could no longer sign his name.

A number of factors had played in favour of the Molsons. The first member of the family to arrive in Canada, John, was born in 1763; when he set foot on North American soil, in 1782, he was not yet thirty. His will contained very restrictive directions for his three sons: they were given five years to establish the terms of a reconciliation and two more to complete it. On the personal and financial fronts, the second generation of Molsons did better than their Hart counterparts, but the Harts of the second and, especially, the third generation had a major impact on the history of the Jewish community and, thus on the history of Quebec (see chapter 6).

Province of Lower-Canada, } A T His Majesty's Court of King's Bench for the Distri_
District of _Three Rivers_ to wit: of _Three Rivers_ begun and holden at the Cou_
all crimes and criminal offences on _Thursday_ the _thirteenth_ day of _September_
in the year of our Lord one thousand eight hundred and _twenty one_ and in the _second_ ye_
of the reign of our Sovereign Lord GEORGE the Fourth by the Grace of God of the United Kingdom _
Great-Britain and Ireland King, defender of the Faith, before the Honourable _Jonathan Sewell Chief
Justice of the Province of Lower Canada the Honourable James Kerr one
of the Justices of the Court of King's Bench for the district of Quebec The
Honourable _____ one of the Justices of the Court of Kings
Bench for the District of Montreal and the Honourable Pierre Bed_
_ Provincial Judge for the district of Three Rivers_

Three Rivers to wit: **The Jurors** for our Lord the King, upon their Oath present, That _Nathaniel
Leavitt late of the township of Shipton in the County of Buckinge
ham in the District of Three Rivers labourer contriving and intendin
to scandalize and vilify the true and christian religion as received
publicly professed within this Province of Lower Canada and
wickedly and profanely intending to bring the holy Scriptures and
Christian religion into disbelief and contempt among all the liege
subjects of our said Lord the King did heretofore with on the twelf_
day of April in the second Year of the reign of our Sovereign Lord
George the Fourth by the Grace of God of the United Kingdom of Great
Britain and Ireland King Defender of the Faith at the township
aforesaid in the County and district aforesaid with force and arms
and **irreverently** in the presence and sight of divers liege subjects
our said Lord the King did throw a holy bible containing
scriptures of Almighty God which he the said Nathan_
iel Leavitt in his right hand then and there had and held
into and upon a certain fire there being with intent then a_
there to burn and consume the same and then and there
unlawfully wickedly and blasphemously in the presence and
hearing of divers liege subjects of our said Lord the King d_
call the scriptures of Almighty God the word of the Prince
the great dishonor of Almighty God in contempt and to the
great scandal of the Christian Religion to the evil example
of all others and against the Peace of our said Lord the King his
Crown and Dignity

And the Jurors aforesaid upon their oath aforesai_
do further present that the said Nathaniel Leavitt after_
wards to wit on the day and year aforesaid in the township
aforesaid in the County and district aforesaid contriving and
intending as aforesaid with force and arms unlawfully wicked_
and irreverently in the presence of divers liege subjects as afore_
said did throw a certain other holy bible containing the
scriptures of Almighty God into and upon a certain othe_
fire then and there being with intent then and there to bu_
and consume the same and did thereby then and there

CHAPTER 9

Moses Hart: Reformist or Agitator?

BEFORE WRITING THIS CHAPTER, in which I present Moses Hart the man of ideas, reforms, and plans, I returned to my databank to refresh my memory on his attitude toward justice and what we would call the public arena today. I had accumulated an enormous amount of material over the years, and I came to the realization that it leaves a very poor impression. Moses was constantly involved in trials. His suppliers had to threaten him with lawsuits in order to get paid, and they regularly proceeded to trial. He did not want to pay, no matter who was making the claim.

In 1843, for instance, Moses received a notice of action from Ira Craig Hart, his nephew, who had been an exceptional partner to him in the shipping business. Ira Craig was committed, perceptive, and attentive. He was claiming £2,050 from his uncle, who was seventy-five years old. This was a large sum! It seems that the claim coincided with the death of Ezekiel, Ira Craig's father, who had apparently managed some of the shipping activities and neglected certain payments. I was not able to establish whether it was justified, but Moses's response was scathing: "I owe you nothing!"[1]

Hooked on the Justice System

There were several court cases in which Moses was involved for almost his entire adult life. Two concerned the Courval seigneury, which he intended to bequeath to his natural, and favourite, son, Alexander Thomas. In the end, Alexander Thomas's widow, Miriam Judah, was to inherit this property.

The first of these cases was against the notary Joseph Badeaux. The Hart archive contains 293 documents on this case, ranging from the concession

This parchment and its content are particularly impressive. It has everything: the names of the judges (Perrault of Montreal and Bédard of Trois-Rivières), the circumstances of the offence, the charge, the arrest, the court appearance, and more.

of the property to the Cressé de Nicolet family in 1754, to its being caught up in the estate of Louis Poulin de Courval, who was in debt to Aaron Hart in 1800, to the interminable procedural war of which Moses was ultimately the winner.[2] The second case was against K. C. Chandler, owner of most of the Nicolet seigneury. The property of Isle à la Fourche, neighbouring the Courval seigneury, was the source of the conflict.[3] According to a ruling by the Court of Appeal on 16 November 1833, Moses was required to move the Courval mill, which had been built on the neighbour's land. On 3 September 1836, in a deposition made at the court, Chandler accused Moses of not having restored the site. Chandler stated that he could not use the land, on which there was still a "log house," a stable, and a sawmill, as well as a dam on the nearby river. From the Court of King's Bench, before which Chandler had proposed "an amicable arrangement" (7 December 1833), the case went to the court of appeal, and then to the Privy Council in London.[4]

These are just a couple of examples from among dozens. The archivist Rénald Lessard made a quick list of cases registered between 1809 and 1900 under the name Hart at the Superior Court and the Court of King's Bench (civil) in the Quebec City district. Under Alexander's name were 10 cases; under Benjamin's, 16; under Ezekiel's, 28; under Ira Craig's, 73; and under Moses's, 213. With archivist Sophie Morel and a colleague, Anthony Deshaies, I glanced at a few registers for the Trois-Rivières district. The picture was similar: pages with the names beginning with A, B, C, D, and so on, were full, but with the names of various people. The "H" page was filled with one family name: Hart (see appendix 3).

A False Lead… Leads to a Brothel

Before getting to the meat of my subject—Moses Hart's attitude toward justice—I wanted to delve into two questions. First, did Moses really operate a bawdy house? Second, why did he react so strongly to the conviction of a certain Nathaniel Levitt for blasphemy and profanation?

I asked Anthony Deshaies to help me research the Levitt case. He rolled up his sleeves and began to explore. Was this type of trial heard in civil or criminal court? I am no expert on legal matters, and the archivists provided much-appreciated assistance.

As far as I remembered, the Levitt case was heard in 1825 or 1827 but I was not certain of the date. Anthony and I spent the morning going through the contents of the boxes brought to us by Maryse Dompierre at the BAnQ in Trois-Rivières. Looking resigned, she told us that things were a bit disorganized. The depositions were grouped by year; they were neither inventoried nor sorted. The documents were folded and dusty, and some were barely legible. We began our task. Every once in a while, we found a deposition concerning the Harts, but nothing exciting. Nevertheless, I encouraged Anthony, telling him that legal papers usually held treasures. Over lunch, I told him that my biography of Sigismond Mohr had been at a dead end until I followed the archivist's advice and dived into some legal papers that had just been deposited at the BAnQ. I then discovered one of the most interesting figures I have ever met. He is introduced in chapter 11.

In the afternoon, back at the archives, Anthony suddenly looked at me, smiling. He had in his hands an affidavit by Manuel Hurado,[5] recorded by René Kimber and dated 10 March 1827. "A retailer in the city of Trois-Rivières, Manuel Hurado *dit* Firmin . . . deposes and says that for some time" a house situated near the hay market "has been inhabited by girls or women who appear to be living a loose, disorderly, and scandalous life and that harms public morals and this deponent has every reason to believe and firmly believes that said house is a bordello and that the girls or women living there are sustained and supported by those named Moses Hart and Areli B. Hart his son." Hurado described the delivery of a load of wood, an exchange of words with Areli, and the behaviour of Moses, who was absent at the time, but who had come that morning to threaten his life.[6]

Also on 10 March, Alexis Morrissette, cabinetmaker, reported that "a girl whose name he did not know" had come to ask for "the assistance of the constables because there were people at her house assaulting Mr. Areli Hart and wanting to kill him, at the same time shouting and making a horrible noise that would disturb the public peace." The word "public" is crossed out. The deponent felt it important to add that "said girl by all appearances leads an idle, scandalous, unbalanced, disorderly, and disorganized life." Morrissette added that there were other girls or women with her "supported and sustained in vice by Moses Hart and Areli B. Hart, his son."[7]

The following 5 December, a new affidavit was deposited by Emanuel Firmin. This was apparently the same person as Manuel Hurado. He accused Moses Hart of having assaulted and hit him that very morning. He demanded that his assailant "be apprehended for processing under the law."

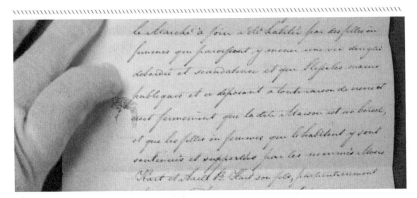

"[A house situated near] the hay market has been inhabited by girls or women who appear to be living a loose, disorderly, and scandalous life and that harms public morals and this deponent has every reason to believe and firmly believes that said house is a bordello and that the girls or women living there are sustained and supported by those named Moses Hart and Areli B. Hart his son, in particular." 10 March 1827.

"Alexis Morrissette, cabinetmaker, living in the town of Trois-Rivières, after having been duly sworn in, deplores and says that yesterday in the evening between eight and nine o'clock, a girl# (#or woman) whose name this deponent does not know, came to the house of said deponent asking for the assistance of the constables because there were people at her house assaulting Mr. Areli Hart and wanting to kill him, at the same time shouting and making a horrible noise that would disturb the public peace and cause a public scandal; and this deponent has every reason to believe that said girl by all appearances leads an idle, scandalous, unbalanced, disorderly, and disorganized life and by her poor conduct has disturbed the public peace of the neighbourhood or even this deponent in this town, on the hay market, for some time; and that the other girls in the same house, with her, who seemed to lead the same type of life and by their scandalous behaviour harm public morals, and that it appears to this deponent said girls or women are sustained and supported in vice by Moses Hart and Areli B. Hart his son, who are there continually and have brought them there."

We completed our examination of the box the contents of which ended in the year 1827. During a break, I looked at my files. According to the notes of Moses Hart,[8] Levitt had been convicted in September 1821. Moses and his son had played a trick on us; we had been exploring the years 1825 to 1827 in error. I asked Anthony to check whether a trial had really occurred in that year. Quickly, he confirmed that a verdict of not guilty had been made on 21 October 1835.[9] Had the bawdy house been in operation for a decade? I had neither the time nor the desire to examine the depositions for 1828 and the ensuing years. Also, Areli left for Europe in July 1829 and returned around 1832. This is a question that remains open to future research.

Levitt Pilloried[10]

The next day, I was alone at the archives, determined to shed light on the Levitt affair. The archivist, Sophie Morel, brought me the trial records for the Court of King's Bench for 1821. These documents are on parchment: they look beautiful, but the ink is very pale. As is usual for court documents, they are folded and on one side one can, or should be able to, read the nature of the case. The basics are usually there, including the verdict.

I was more or less resigned to finding nothing when I finally laid my hands on the document I had been looking for. I was thrilled—and a second later I was a bit disappointed. There was little information on the individual or on the place where the "crime" had been committed. Nathaniel Levitt was said to be from the township of Shipton, where Moses Hart owned properties. It remains to be verified whether they knew each other.

The offence was described as follows: on 12 April 1821, Levitt had deliberately set out to scandalize witnesses of the Christian religion by making irreverent statements "with force and arms" and, in the presence of eight Christians, "throw[ing] a holy bible containing the scriptures of Almighty God which he the said Nathaniel Leavitt in his right hand then and there had and held into and upon a certain fire there being with intent then and there to burn and consume the same and then and there unlawfully wickedly and blasphemously in the presence and hearing." Very poetic!

On the back of the document are written the names of the members of the grand jury:[11] Wagner, Badeaux, Antrobus, Robin, Dumoulin, Montour, Lozeau, Dionne, Duchenay, Kimber, and perhaps David Frank, if I read correctly. Morel insisted that the verdict was usually written somewhere. Indeed, slid into all of this information, between two

A pillory. Château de Murol. Puy de Dôme.

large braces, were the words "Verdict/Guilty." She then brought me the register of court hearings for 1821 and explained how to use it. I was surprised at the clarity of the register and the wealth of information that it contains. On page 154 (13 September), the prisoner—who apparently had been incarcerated since April—appeared in court to plead not guilty. Page 166 contains the testimony of three witnesses, Steymen Mathews, George Mathews, and William Dandon. The jury made its ruling immediately: guilty. Finally, on page 171 (15 September), the sentence: one year in prison and "on Thursday 20th day of September, instant to be set and upon the Pillory in front of the Gaol for the space of one Hour." I had forgotten that pillories existed in Quebec! The magistrates added that when Levitt left jail he would have to stand in the pillory again for one hour, exposed to the insults of passersby. Furthermore, to guarantee his good behaviour, he would have to deposit a bond of £100 for a period of five years.

Moses Hart quickly became interested in the Levitt affair. He believed that the defendant was American. I believe that Levitt was Jewish; the name suggests it, but nothing in the documents I consulted confirms it.

For Moses, the question of whether Levitt was Jewish was apparently of no interest. It was the charge of blasphemy that revolted him. He drafted a number of letters, no doubt intended for the newspapers, though it is not clear whether they were sent. He denounced what seemed to him to be the symptoms of an inquisition gaining strength in Canada: "Any printing, publishing, leading to scandalizing the Christian religion, the holy scriptures of Jesus Christ will come under the laws of blasphemy." To his knowledge, Nathaniel Levitt was the first person in Canada to be convicted under a law regarding blasphemy, an obsolete statute not applied in Quebec.[12] Moses said that he was a follower of a new religion based "on a firm belief in the Great Creator and his providence." Was it his intention to exploit the Levitt trial to promote his pamphlet, *Modern Religion*? In any case, he adopted a more severe tone than in his treatise: "Law hatched by bigotry to link church and state together, to render an established cruel predominant to banish the investigation of Natural truth to shackle the mind." He added, "Does morality become tainted from the expansion of freedom in religious discussion, or is the state to be shaken or convulsed by extension of religious opinions?"[13] Finally, he asked the legislature to deal seriously with the issue of religious offences.

On 23 August 2010, the staff at the BAnQ in Trois-Rivières found three depositions concerning the Levitt case. On 16 May 1821, before police officer Daniel Thomas, George Mathews denounced "Nathaniel Levit of Shifton in a blusphemans [this misspelling suggests how rare such a charge was] and impious manner called the Holy Bible the word of the Devil and threw the holy bible into the fire by force and violence attempting thereby to consume and totally distroy [*sic*] it," accompanied by mockeries and derisive statements. Then, the deranged man forced his way "by force and violence" into the residence of Heman Mathews, George's father. He then violently attacked the deponent. This crime took place in April.

In a deposition also made on 16 May, Heman Mathews corroborated the account of his son George, a minor, and confirmed that he was assaulted. He feared for the safety of his wife and children.

There was a surprise in store for me. In a letter from police officer Daniel Thomas, dated in Melbourne on 28 August 1821, to the Honourable Thomas Coffin, Officer Thomas related that a police officer called Captain Lawrence had brought before him "Nathaniel Leavitt," who had escaped from the guards the previous May, as well as an arrest warrant. Levitt had apparently left the region and then returned to lurk in the nearby woods with the intention of following up on his threats of vengeance. Officer Thomas, feeling that he was not authorized to issue another arrest warrant, gave "a sort of certificate" to Captain Lawrence "to justify him in bringing him [Levitt] before you." He added, "This Leavitt is a dangerous fellow in Society & ought to be kept where he can be safe."

After that, this bizarre individual slipped below the radar. It is likely that the violence and threats were much more at issue than was the blasphemy. People in ordinary society of the time were thick-skinned. Swearing and blasphemy were part of daily life.[14] A Bible thrown into a fire in a moment of anger did not lead to prison. Levitt remains an enigma, or else the religious practices of the English-speaking people in the townships are a mystery.

Moses Hart: A Reformer Inhabited by the Demon of Politics

Moses Hart had ideas about everything—and, in his view, everything was going badly. He was not resigned to calmly watching the general decline. He had started at the beginning: proposing a new religion. In 1815, he published the pamphlet discussed in chapter 7, which he distributed through his businesses—accompanied by invoices for this "merchandise." The responses were, perhaps, predictable: "We have received five more copies of your pamphlet. Don't send any more; we still have some from the last shipment!" or "I am returning the copies of your pamphlet, which we did not order."

He also sent copies to experts to solicit their commentaries. Either he received few comments, or he quickly circulated those that he did receive. The only one that has survived is signed J. Mountain. Moses Hart's neighbour in Trois-Rivières was Jehoshaphat Mountain, the brother of the Anglican bishop of Quebec City, Jacob Mountain, who probably wrote the letter. "I return you your book with thanks for your civility in sending it for my inspection," Mountain wrote. "The prayers are, I think, pious addresses to the divine Being, but they are deficient . . ." However, this correspondent did not want to go into detail on a subject that "inevitably provokes disputes."

Moses's treatise was in fact not very provocative except, perhaps, for his notion of half-marriage, which he withdrew from the 1824 edition. Considering, no doubt, that he had done his part to ensure the redemption of his people, he came back down to earth.

Then, before planting himself squarely in Lower Canada, Moses took a mental detour to England. In the spring of 1826, he sent a long letter to Lord Bathurst, Secretary to the Colonies,[15] which is worth quoting in its entirety.

Three Rivers in Lower Canada.
June 10th, 1826.

My Lord,

I beg leave to inform your LordShip that I am a native of this place, 57 years old, that I am the oldest English Canadian in Canada and the richest man in the District of Three Rivers. I mention these circumstances to add that I consider myself well versed in the concerns of this province, and enabled thereby to convey information to your LordShip, when it should be your wish. The abuses existing here are numerous. Education is almost prostrated and neglected. We have parishes on the St. Lawrence of 200 to 300 families, among whom only 4 or 5 can write their names.

2—We have a wretched Code of Civil justice, made up of a medley of the worst parts of the french edicts, *coutume de paris*, and a host of contradictory commentaries; and that resting on the arbitrary and uncontrolled decision

Judges, and addled with enormous Law fees; established as it occasionally pleases the Judges.

3—We must to safety or secure title in the purchase of lands.

4—Several places of profit is here heaped on the same man and that man most often deficient in talent. Our little House of Assembly consist of 50 members, attended by about 30 who have not only usurped the title but the priviledges of parliament, are about 4/5 French canadians, and led by lawyers, have on occasions evinced strong symptoms of illiberality, and mischief, inimical to change and english customs, and instead of bettering the system have in many instances, rendered it more insupportable.

The Legislature Council is not entitled to much praise, and both require a remedy which can only be effected by a union of Upper and Lower Canada, of the present members subject to augment their number, to be assembled at Montreal until altered, a restriction of taking the name or priviledges of parliament religious opinion to be for ever free and equal, and no Judge to vote in either house, and in 5 years the english civil laws, to take effect throughout Canada.

There are about 50,000 English Canadians in Lower Canada, whose rights are prostrated, they are yoked to foreign Laws and customs, on a British province; laws which they detest are deprived of full Jury trials in civil suits, registration offices, and bankrupts Laws.

It is to the Imperial parliament, who ought to remedy the errors committed in establishing the French Laws in 1774, and subsequently dividing the Province.* A union of the two provinces and the establishment of English civil Laws, I am positive in asserting is the wish of a numerous body of french Canadians, and in many parishes a numerous majority for, and numbers have repented signing against the Union.

The province was divided without consulting the people and the union, a measure of the highest necessary importance, ought not to be delayed.

If it is your LordShip's wish, I will frame the Bill for a union. The tenure bill which part the Imperial parliament last year, is an excellent bill, except that part of it which authorises an escheat office, ought to be suffered to go into operation. The men in power would convest it into an engine of injustice, by taking away land from the honest purchasers, to bestow it on favorites. We do not want escheat commission to force settlements in the woods, it would retard it.

---

* Moses is well informed and knows the Quebec Act under which the British made concessions to the Canadiens in order to ensure their loyalty against the American rebels. The 1774 Constitution appealed to the Catholic clergy and the seigneurial class, but not to the English merchants in the Province of Quebec. Nonetheless, all were happy to see the much extended borders, which in turn were perceived as an "intolerable" provocation by the Thirteen Colonies.

I can refer your LordShip for my character, to any person from this province, and actuated with a desire of being useful, permit me to sollicit that your LordShip will please order me to be nominated a legislative or executive councillor of Lower Canada, with every respect,

I am your LordShip ob. servant,

Moses Hart.

In the spring of 1827, Moses Hart received the following response from J. Monton, Lord Bathurst's secretary: "Sir, I was designated by Lord Bathurst to acknowledge the receipt of your letter of the 24 Oct. last, and to acquaint that you should address yourself to the Lords Commissioners of the Treasury, as His LordShip is altogether ignorant of the circumstances stated in your letter, and the subject is in no way connected with his LordShip's Department." This response to the letter received on 24 October was dated 31 December, the secretary thus had cleared of his desk for the New Year's Day holiday.

Moses was well aware that Lord Bathurst was mocking him. In London, the most hotly argued issue regarding Canada was probably the plan to unite the two Upper and Lower Canada, which had been created in 1791. It was a debate that went back to the era of Craig, Sewell, and Ryland. It had indirectly kept Moses's brother, Ezekiel, from occupying his seat as a member of the House of Assembly.

While he was at it, Moses decided to write the king directly. He was well aware of the many scandals in the royal family (just as he kept an ear to the ground for juicy tidbits about the popes, past and present). His letter was dated 30 November 1830. William IV was about to succeed George IV. Moses decided to speak his mind. He knew that His Majesty suffered from gout. He knew a cure—which he would be happy to divulge if the king were to express his interest . . .[16]

Although he was about to turn sixty, Moses's sex drive had not abated. He continued to father children and have affairs. Things reached a peak in 1835, with his trials for running a bawdy house, for having abused Mary Catherine O'Connor and having her thrown in jail,[17] and for taking advantage of the imprisonment of J. Davison to court his wife.[18] The testimony in these cases was lurid.

The political situation in the 1830s was difficult. Two cholera epidemics (1832, 1834) had created social tension. The Parti canadien was issuing ultimatums, and a number of Britons believed that a rebellion was desirable or should even be provoked so that military repression could be justified.

Moses Hart, his personal crisis now over, asked the population to remain calm; he pleaded with people not to revolt.[19] His union with Mary McCarthy was followed by the union of the two Canadas under the Act of Union in 1840. Moses once again saw an opening. He was expecting a great deal from the new political regime. He hoped to receive the licence he had been seeking to found the Hart's Bank.

Moses celebrated the Act of Union along with his seventy-second birthday—a good time to take stock of all the reforms that he had drafted over the years. He held the seigneurial system partly responsible for the rebellions, or at least for the Parti Patriote's Ninety-Two Resolutions, a political manifesto expressing discontent with British rule. Moses had wanted to reform the prison system, reduce legal costs, abolish recourse to London, introduce free education, establish a system for registering mortgages and land deeds, adopt a law for bankruptcies, reduce the use of the death penalty, and more.[20] These proposals had been worked out to various degrees of detail. He had even written notes for a new legal code and a review of the judicial system[21] and a plan for prisons, including a description of the sites and personnel and a draft budget.[22]

Moses hoped that the Act of Union would eliminate the French laws. "Our civil laws," he wrote in a draft letter to the newspapers, "are the corrupt, old, unintelligible civil laws of despotic France branched out in a labyrinth of stupidity, contradiction and non sense, and some of our Judges decide by haste, passion, supposition, generally on the wrong side." This hope, however, went unrealized. At least, he had the consolation of seeing that the French language would have no legal status.[23]

He had to strike while the iron was hot. He wrote to Lord Sydenham, Sir Charles Bagot, House member Louis-Hippolyte La Fontaine, and Lord Metcalfe. In a letter dated 6 December 1843, he wrote to Metcalfe, "I am the oldest English Canadian in Canada[24] and the largest landholder in this district and am well versed in its affairs. . . . I think I would be of service to him and the Country if called to the Legislative or Executive Council." A year before, on 2 October 1842, he had made a similar proposal to La Fontaine after congratulating him, in English, on his political successes.[25] He didn't understand La Fontaine's approach: La Fontaine had decided to play the game, but he had not given up his principles or convictions. Moses also was not aware of La Fontaine's famous speech of the previous 13 September in which he spoke in French despite the loss of status under the Act of Union.[26]

Louis Hippolyte LaFontaine (1807–64). Both a very fervent patriot and a man of compromise.

At any rate, most of his letters went unanswered. The appointments solicited were not made. No matter. His remaining source of hope was the House of Assembly. He had offered his services to the electorate in William Henry in 1796, in Trois-Rivières in 1809, in Saint-Maurice in 1819, and in the Upper Town of Quebec City in 1820. And he was not done yet: in November 1844, at seventy-six years of age, he was a candidate in Nicolet and in Trois-Rivières. He was defeated and obstinately contested the result. He sent a petition about it to both Houses.

A Bellicose Nephew... At the Right School

At the very least, Moses Hart was setting a poor example for his family up to the end of his life, even if they were combative by nature to begin with. The third generation of Harts included a number of lawyers. Two of Ezekiel's sons went into law: Aaron Ezekiel, the first Quebec Jew to become a lawyer, and Adolphus Mordecai.

Adolphus Mordecai (1814–79) was the youngest of seven children. He was born in 1814 and admitted to the bar in 1836. David Rome wrote the article about him in the *Canadian Dictionary of Biography*. A passage in this article piqued my curiosity. Even before completing his clerkship with Charles Richard Ogden, the young lawyer had brought a complaint before the House of Assembly "against the actions of Justice Edward Bowen." At first set aside, the complaint later resulted in an inquiry, and on 10 March 1836 the grievance committee found Bowen guilty.

Ready for a fight, Adolphus Mordecai sparked the hostilities, in November 1835, in an article signed "Justicia" in *The Vindicator,* a newspaper edited by Edward Bailey O'Callaghan, a close friend of Louis-Joseph Papineau's. Adolphus Mordecai denounced aspects of the legal system, homed in on Justice Bowen, and accused him of nepotism. He sent various articles along the same lines to the *Mercury* and the *Quebec Gazette.* A letter of 2 December 1835 provoked a reply from Justice Bowen in the *Mercury* of 7 December 1835, in which he defended himself and concluded that a web of lies had been woven. The pseudonym "Justicia," he stated (quoting Virgil in the *Aeneid,* Book 1) was wrongly used, *"propter iram memorem crudelis Junonis* [sic]."

Justice Bowen conducted his own inquiry: "I was determined to discover the author of so base and cowardly an attempt." Sarcastically, he stated that it would be "an injustice to permit the public longer to remain in ignorance of its champion" and uncovered his identity: "Adolphus Mordecai Hart, of Quebec, Student at Law." This revelation was published in *The Vindicator* on 8 January 1836, as was a reply from Hart. That his name was known, he wrote, gave him the freedom to target his attacks, made "under an honest conviction." "I have asserted nothing but what I am ready to prove is true and correct," he added.

Thus, through petitions by Hart and then Bowen, the affair was brought to the attention of the House. Expert jurists faced off. Finally, a House committee heard the testimony of Aaron Ezekiel Hart and Henry Judah (also a friend of Papineau's).[27]

Aaron Ezekiel called Justice Bowen's behaviour "arbitrary and domineering" and claimed that he gave "frequent personal reflections" during trials. "I may enumerate myself as one of those against whom he has evinced much passion and prejudice," he noted. His distant cousin, Henry Judah, testified similarly: "He is frequently in the habit of interrupting the Gentlemen of the Bar, not always in the most gentlemanly style." Judah, himself a gentleman, was not vindictive, but he nevertheless pointed out that during a recent trial, Justice Bowen "has frequently by his petulant interruptions and rude personal remarks hindered me from performing my duty, and deprived the party whom I represented from being fully and impartially heard." Asked to recall an appearance by Justice Vallières de Saint-Réal, Judah emphasized that the two other magistrates were "cool and dispassionate" in their treatment of the witness, whereas Justice Bowen demonstrated "a degree of bitterness in the personal allusions to the prejudice of Mr Justice Vallières de Saint-Réal." There was an extremely partisan background to this affair. Bowen was

Edward Bowen (1780–1866), a controversial judge with an ebullient character, a champion of favouritism. All this does not totally explain the Harts' attacks. Bowen's role in 1807 should be examined more closely.

a loyal Tory, highly placed in the party structure and in control of political favouritism. In a way, Adolphus Mordecai's attacks gave the majority of the House an opportunity to take a bit of revenge.

The House was preparing for final deliberations, possibly leading to an indictment, when it was suspended by Governor Gosford. It was August 1837. The House of Assembly of Lower Canada had sat for the last time. Bowen was saved by the bell—or, rather, by the rebellion, which triggered a series of arrests. Among the magistrates who went zealously about their job was Benjamin Hart.

David Rome took a longer look at the Hart vs. Bowen episode.[28] With his usual wisdom, he sized things up. In one corner was a magistrate who could be tyrannical and rude. In the other corner was a young and skilful lawyer who was determined, even pugnacious. Although his case was relatively weak, the student had brought his adversary, a magistrate with sixteen children, to the verge of disgrace and ruin.

Above all, this unusual episode, Rome wrote, "speaks eloquently of the ease of the Jewish citizenry and of its several lawmen in the highly structured legal society. The fact that a Jewish lad could institute the proceedings so early in Canadian emancipation, indeed in the liberation history of the Jewish people, is remarkable."[29] I have no doubt that Adolphus Mordecai would agree with Rome's comments.

But did Adolphus Mordecai also have a personal agenda? Who was Bowen to him? To the Harts? It did not take me long to find out that he had been on the bench with justices Kerr and Bédard at the time of the separation of Sarah Judah and Moses Hart. In his provocative style, Bowen had made statements and taken attitudes that had shocked the family. Adolphus Mordecai was still in diapers at the time, but he had been told about it. No doubt he had also been told that this very Bowen had written, in April 1807, the oath that members of the House had to take[30]—the oath that had kept his father from taking his seat in the House.

Over the years, Bowen had become no less arrogant—even disdainful—in the view of the Harts. Adolphus Mordecai had him in his sights. When he finished his clerkship, he attacked, under the cover of anonymity, the powerful judge who advertised his fierce opposition to the Parti Patriote, which had corrected its position of 1807–08 regarding his father by voting in the statutes favourable to Jews tabled from 1830 to 1832.

Beginning and End of a Dynasty

Indirectly, Moses Hart summed up his tangles with the legal system in a very special petition that he sent to the House of Assembly.[31] He had decided to put the judiciary on trial through the rulings made by Justice Dominique Mondelet, most of which were "striking examples of partisanship, insults to good sense, and contradiction." He asked for them to be reviewed. At this time, he was in decline and his mind had begun to wander.

Moses had rather vague reasons for hammering away at Mondelet, the successor to Vallières de Saint-Réal, who had been suspended because of his sympathy for the Patriotes. Mondelet was simply in the wrong place at the wrong time. In a two-page draft, Hart accused him of making rulings "against the law and fairness."[32]

The petition that Aaron Moses Hart delivered to the House began, "The said Moses Hart has two legitimate children who are foolish, and eight illegitimate children including . . . Aaron Moses Hart, the natural son of Moses Hart." The name is ironic, for Aaron's dreams had rested mainly on his own oldest son, Moses.

Moses Hart's Estate

Moses Hart died on 15 October 1852. He had been living with Mary McCarthy for fifteen years. They had two sons: Samuel Judah, born on 22 October 1838, and Reuben Moses, born on 29 October 1840.

Writing Moses Hart's biography for the *Dictionary of Canadian Biography*, I hypothesized that Mary McCarthy had been with Moses since 1825 or 1826. This was completely wrong. Between 1825 and 1837, Moses had at least nine children. Three of these children were born to unknown mothers; six others were born to Marie Godin (Abraham and Elizabeth), Margaret Burns (Sarah Dorothea and Charlotte Mathilde), and Margaret Armstrong (Orobio and Aaron Moses). And so I am now correcting what was no doubt the greatest factual error in the *Dictionary of Canadian Biography*, a remarkable work edited with devotion and skill by the late Jean Hamelin and Ramsay Cook. The copy editors exercised their usual zeal, but who could have suspected such activity or fecundity? My excuse is that I had forsaken historical research for politics. In 1976, I followed in Ezekiel Hart's footsteps as a member of the Quebec National Assembly for Trois-Rivières.

At an unspecified date, the seminary archives received several new documents concerning the Harts, including "the inventory of the estate of the late Moses Hart began on 19 October 1854. No. 4925. Donation by the Ursulines Trois-Rivières." The document now bears the archive number 0009-J-0-1. In the directory that I have always used, which dates from May 1950 (p. 43), this document is not mentioned. Yet, this inventory, which is now in my possession, does mention Moses's last will and testament, dated 1 April 1847, which is conserved at the office of the prothonotary of Trois-Rivières, and which I found "in the study of lawyer V. Guillet."

To truly understand this will, it is essential to consult a holograph will written by Moses Hart in 1837, which is today in the court registry of notary William Burn. This will has not yet revealed all of its secrets. To decipher it requires multiple keys. My bunch of keys has grown since I began to write this book. In the 1837 will, Moses directly admits his paternity of Anne Galarno's sons: "Henry and Benjamin, the sons of late Anne Galarno." These two names complete a short list presented in paragraph eight of the will and are followed by, "All of whom are well known to my Executors, the sum of thirty pounds currency to each of them."

To add to the confusion, the eighth paragraph also mentions "Elizabeth, daughter of Marie [illegible] . . . a minor, and unto my adopted sons Moses the son of Mary Racine, Aaron the son of Catherine Holyward, and Thomas the son of Mrs Davison." Furthermore, not all of the heirs grouped by mother are in paragraph 8. In paragraph 7, for instance, Moses makes a bequest to his "adopted son, Ezekiel M. Hart, son of Mary Racine." In other words, the 1837 and 1847 wills complement each other but leave large areas in shadow.[33] I have already noted that Moses seems to have written the 1837 will after confessing his past to Mary McCarthy.

Compilation of Moses's inventory after death started on 19 October 1854. It began with an introduction of the heirs. Two years had passed since Moses had died. His will accorded to Mary McCarthy "the use for two years only of the site and the two-storey stone house and outbuildings built upon it, situated on Rue Notre-Dame, where he currently lives, with as well the use for the same period of all the household furniture . . . for after said use to return to the mass of his assets that compose the universal bequest hereunder mentioned." During this period, Mary McCarthy seems to have acquired the shares left to four heirs: from Elizabeth by a deed of conveyance dated 16 May 1853; from Abraham by a deed dated 17 May 1853;

Whereas William Benjamin, the treasurer of the Montreal synagogue, proposed that Mary McCarthy pay for an *escoba* (prayer) to the memory of Moses Hart, the gravestone manufacturer, W. Cunningham, was in correspondence (27 October 1853) with her to finalize the text of the inscription to be placed on the stone. It seems that the draft written by Rabbi De Sola was lost and he was ready to write a new one if she was in agreement.

and from Sarah and Charlotte by a deed dated 1 June 1853. Furthermore, Thomas was officially named curator for Orobio M. Hart, one of the natural sons of the late Moses Hart, and Mary McCarthy represented Areli, who was absent from the town. The inheritance was divided into fourteen shares allocated to nine people. Mary McCarthy's two sons and Margaret Burns's two daughters had two shares each. These four people, who together held more than half of the estate, were baptized either at birth or on the eve of their marriage. Moses knew this. The other heirs had one share each: Elizabeth, Abraham, Thomas for Orobio, Areli, and Mary McCarthy. Although Mary had only one fourteenth of the estate, her influence on the last wishes of the deceased was enormous—her substantial revenge on those in Moses's family who had done everything possible to block their marriage (see chapter 10).

One detail struck me in passing: in his will, Moses Hart always wrote "Mary McCarthy, alias Brown, widow of Peter Brown." He wanted to marry her, but he was kept from doing so. Was he expressing some frustration? Or did the notaries take the initiative to constantly mention the civil status of his "widow"?[34]

On the morning of 19 October 1854, the notaries followed Mary McCarthy into the west front room. In the afternoon, they moved into the large room on the north side, then the large southwest room, and so on.

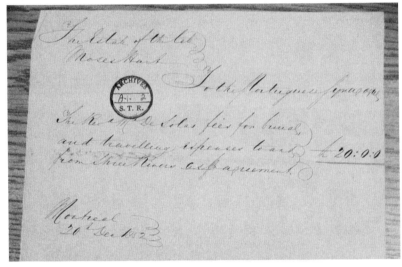

Moses Hart kept every scrap of paper. Mary McCarthy apparently inherited this habit. In the papers relating to the funeral of her "spouse," we find the invoice sent by treasurer William Benjamin and the letters of claim by the rabbi, Abraham de Sola. The invoice of 20 December 1852 specifies £20 "for burial and travelling expenses . . . as agreement."

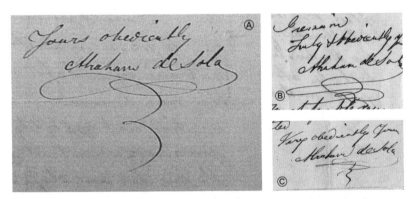

The rabbi's claims stretched from 25 November 1852 (A) to 13 November 1853 (C), if not longer. Cunningham's intervention (p. 215) no doubt reminded her that his account was still in arrears.

Montreal 20 Dec 1852

Mrs McCarthy

Madam I beg to enclose copies of
a/c for fees due the Revd Mr DeSola for the
burial of the late Mr Moses Hart as agreed
between yourself and Mr De S. you will be
good enough to remit the amt at your convenience

I remain

Your Mo. Obgt Servant

Wm Benjamin
Treasurer

P.S. Mr Harts father and many of his family have
after their death a perpetual "Escoba" ~~amount~~ for
the rest of their souls always said in the Synagogue
which if you think necessary the fee will be $100.

On 20 December 1852, William Benjamin, treasurer of the synagogue, sent Mary McCarthy "copies of a/c for the fees due the rev. A. De Sola for the burial of the late Moses Hart as agreed between yourself and Mr. De Sola." In a postscript, he recommended "a perpetual *escoba* [prayer]" for the repose of the soul of the deceased, as had been provided for Moses's father and other family members. To my surprise, there are, among the papers related to the funeral, receipts attesting that Moses Hart had, at various times in his life, maintained ties with the synagogue.

They made a tour of the house and the attic. They then examined the accounts kept by Mary McCarthy: rent, various debts, dividends from the Bank of Quebec and the People's Bank, some interest payments, sometimes a final payment such as the one for a property belonging to Mr. Baptist.

In December, it seems that a problem arose. A meeting was planned for 31 December, then 16 January 1855 (p. 49 of the inventory, according to my pagination). On that day began the assessment of receipts and money from the sale of buildings by Mary McCarthy. Here, a parcel of land had been sold to the Ursuline nuns; there, a house and a lot on Rue de la Montagne in Quebec City had been sold to the Corporation de la ville; and so on, for a total of £1,196 8s10d. The next day, the notaries continued with a list of expenditures made by the "lady executrix": trips to Quebec City by steamboat, cart, postal costs, registration costs, and small invoices, including those from notary William Burn, who had written up a marriage contract for Moses and Mary and then had written a cancellation. This is how I learned about the existence of these two documents, which were subsequently obtained by the Sherbrooke bureau of the Archives nationales.

A list of extremely diverse invoices followed: subscriptions, taxes, repairs to the kitchen, travel expenses for a certain William McDougall, including a trip to New York, and so on. Finally, the notaries addressed the "active and passive debts due at death." There were several large amounts resulting from court rulings. On the evening of 9 October 1856, after a particularly intense day, Mary McCarthy's hand, I could not help but notice, was trembling as she signed her name on the document.[35]

On 16 October, the notaries established total debts due of £7,915 7d, then accumulated rents, for a total of £1,007 19s7d, and arrears of £151 2s2d. After that came the doubtful and bad debts: £12,810 10s1d and £4,315 19s. On this document, Mary McCarthy's signature had not improved.

The inventory ended with two lists. The first was composed of seventy-nine buildings belonging to Moses Hart at the time of his death. These were located in various places: a number in the Eastern Townships, many of them acquired by sheriff's sales; for the others, the date and nature of the transaction were indicated. The second presented the odd bits of stock held.

Finally, among the accounts to be settled, I found the funeral costs. I am not certain that Mary McCarthy settled them with the Montreal synagogue or with Rabbi Abraham de Sola. I found at least four claims addressed to her by the rabbi in the weeks following his visit to Trois-Rivières for the interment.

CHAPTER 10

The Pleasure of an Inquiry: An Open Church

INQUIRIES HAVE ALWAYS FASCINATED ME. My approach as a historian is full of "hows" and "whys." I have come to realize that the best explanations are usually the simplest ones. Great theories and grand concepts are very fashionable, but they are rarely necessary in history. It is my belief that people make history—people with their desires, tastes, and ways of being. I believe in God, but not as a way to explain the fate of peoples. This statement may seem paradoxical for a historian who is interested in the "chosen people," elected by God—the Israelites. Traditional historical accounts made great use of the "hand of God" or the benevolence of fate. Today, the "meaning of history" comes in all flavours. "History makes us," the literary critic Pierre Lepape has written, "but we also make it, and we are thus as much constrained to follow it as free to choose it."[1]

To explain the French adventure in North America, there was in the 1700s a rather silly fashion in France: the beaver hat. To explain England's choice at the time of negotiations for the Treaty of Paris of 1763, one might think of sugar in one's tea; the English were willing to pay a high price for such sugar. During the time of the "great discoveries"—in fact, since time immemorial—Europeans took huge risks to get their hands on spices and silk.

I find it amusing to see on the shelves of American bookstores tomes on the rise and fall of civilizations by authors such as Jared Diamond, Charles Mann, and Mark Kurlansky. When I first saw Kurlansky's book on codfish, I had to smile, especially when I read the subtitle, "A Biography of the Fish that Changed the World." In the book that I wrote with Käthe Roth, *America's Gift, What the World Owes to the Americans and Their First Inhabitants*, I took a great interest in plants that changed the world. In *Mapping a Continent* Raymonde Litalien, Jean-François Palomino, and I examined the devastating effects of epidemics that were much more likely

This lovely stained-glass window belongs to the McCord Museum. It was saved by a collector when the Shomrim Laboker synagogue, located on Rue Sainte-Dominique, was demolished.

explanations than the superiority of some races over others for conquests throughout history. Of course, American bookstores also feature Alexis de Tocqueville's *Democracy in America,* Francis Parkman's *Oregon Trail,* and Stephen E. Ambrose's *Undaunted Courage,* books that explore the great sweeps and dreams of history.

Quebec: A Land of Turbulence and Accommodation

Of course, Moses Hart had not read Jared Diamond's *Why Sex Is Fun,* but that might have been his motto. What fascinated me, however, was not so much his excesses, but the broad view of the society he lived in. Above all, the attitude of the Catholic Church in that society astonished me, and astonishes me still. Where was the well-organized, puritanical society, more Catholic than the pope, and even, in the view of some, intolerant?

Father Jean Panneton superior of the Séminaire de Trois-Rivières, who was preparing to write the history of his institution, asked me for information about Ezekiel Moses Hart, who was one of the founders of the college. In the Séminaire's almanac, he was said to be a "descendant of the illustrious Hart family." It was not a common thing for a member of an important Jewish family to co-found a Catholic college, even though this one began as a business college and all eight founders were laypeople. Father Panneton was anxious to find out more about Ezekiel Moses Hart. There were so many legends about the Harts, including those perpetuated in Raymond Douville's books, which Father Panneton had read. But what he had learned about Ezekiel Moses reassured him a bit: he was presented as a banker, and there was nothing more respectable than a banker!

It turned out that Ezekiel Moses had a brother named Moses Ezekiel. At first I thought that there was only one individual and someone—perhaps Ezekiel Moses himself, having a bit of fun—had inverted the first names, but I found out that there were two highly respected citizens who had married two sisters, Joséphine-Domithilde and Marie-Joséphine Pothier. Of course, I initially thought that there was only one Miss Pothier and a single Hart-Pothier marriage. The registers, however, were clear: both Hart brothers were married at the Catholic cathedral, with exemption from the publication of banns—the public proclamation of a marriage—at two years' interval: Ezekiel Moses in 1848 and Moses Ezekiel in 1850.

The archivist for the diocese of Trois-Rivières, Denise Maltais, explained why an exemption from publication of the banns might have been granted.

Usually, there were "pressing" reasons for exemption from the second and third publications. Someone might declare an obstacle to the marriage due to information obtained in the secrecy of confession or through the practice of his profession (for instance, a doctor or lawyer). Family members and friends were required to make any possible impediments to the marriage known. The existence of a previous marriage or a still-living spouse had to be declared, as did any blood ties that created a too-close consanguinity. The future spouses could request an exemption, for a fee, if publication of the banns might lead to an embarrassing situation; the bishop would judge whether the embarrassment was serious enough. In fact, the history of publication of banns is fascinating. I discovered, for instance, that French President Nicolas Sarkozy and Carla Bruni obtained a similar exemption, out of "concern for discretion." "*Il n'y a pas de souci!*" (nothing to worry about) as the French like to say. Apparently, however, there was in this case. No doubt, I thought, both brothers were concerned about discretion. In fact, the marriage acts showed that both brothers were sons of Moses Hart, "merchant esquire of this town." Like the Virgin Mary—a figure of whom he often made fun—Moses had two sons with no partner! If I understand the marriage certificate, the exemption from publication of all three banns was accorded by Bishop Thomas Cooke with the "consent of the parents"— that is, the parents of the Pothier sisters. Their mother, Josephte Labarre, did not, I noted, sign the marriage certificate. However, the Pothier-Labarre family was apparently open-minded, as there were a Harline Pothier and a Caroline G. Labarre among the witnesses.

Moses Hart, the father of the grooms, said to be sons of adult age, was absent from both weddings. He nevertheless wrote Ezekiel Moses and Moses Ezekiel into his 1847 will. The officiants at the weddings avoided using the terms "legitimate child" and "natural child," which makes me think that a look at the brothers' baptismal certificates would be relevant; the church may have been open, but it was reluctant to marry people of different religions. In these cases, the non-Catholic spouse had to agree that the children would be raised in the Catholic religion. Of course, the baptism of the non-Catholic spouse would have solved the problem.

Curiously, the story of the brothers Ezekiel Moses and Moses Ezekiel had a counterpart in two of Moses's daughters. Margaret Burns succeeded Mary Racine, the presumed mother of Ezekiel Moses and Moses Ezekiel. Margaret and Moses had two daughters, Sarah Dorothea and Charlotte Mathilda. In a show of filial piety, Moses named his first daughter after his first wife, Sarah Judah, and his mother, Dorothea. She was born on 25 October 1829 and baptized on 22 November 1847, two days before she married Nérée-Ludger Désilets. Charlotte Mathilda, who was born in 1831, preceded her sister to the baptismal font, as she was baptized on 20 October 1847, five days before she married Nérée-Ludger's brother, Joseph-Ludger Désilets.[2] Joseph-Ludger was the first lawyer in Trois-Rivières; Nérée-Ludger, practised medicine in Saint-Grégoire. Their wives were to become

René Hart poses in front of the Hart monument situated in Parc Champlain. The monument bears the following inscription: "On the occasion of the bicentennial of the settlement of Jews in Canada, this plaque is dedicated to the city of Trois-Rivières, to recall the friendship and the democratic feelings of its citizens, who, in 1807 and 1808 elected Ezekiel Hart, a citizen of the Jewish religion, a member of the Legislative Assembly of Lower Canada, inspiring the historic decree of 1832 that fully recognized the civil rights of all citizens" (Canadian Jewish Congress).

Aaron ➜ Moses ➜ Ezekiel ➜ Moses ➜ Henry ➜ Ezekiel ➜ Joseph ➜ René. René Hart, son of Joseph Hart and Éva Hamel, who had seven children. Joseph Hart, known as Jos Hart, was prothonotary for the Superior Court. He was the only son of Henry (Ezekiel) Hart and Marie-Louise Brûlé. The death certificate of Henry Ezekiel Hart bore only the signature "Joe Hart," identified as his son. There was no spouse's name. No marriage certificate was found. In his will, Henry Ezekiel entrusted his son to Louise Plante, "homekeeper." Henry Ezekiel was born on 18 December 1848. He was the oldest son of Ezekiel Moses Hart and Joséphine-Domithilde Pothier. He died on 1 April 1907. Henry Ezekiel had four sisters, who married, respectively, men named Ritchie, Kiernan, Barnston, and Rogers. The children of Moses Ezekiel, Ezekiel Moses's brother, had spouses named Harnois, Mailhot, and Loranger. Ezekiel Moses Hart, René Hart's great-grandfather, was one of the natural sons of Moses Hart and Mary Racine. He was named in article 6 of Moses's will registered with notary Burn in January 1837. Curiously, Moses did not mention Moses Ezekiel in this will, although he did in his 1847 will. Ezekiel Moses married in 1848, and Moses Ezekiel married in 1850. In their marriage certificates, they were both identified as adult sons of Moses Hart, identified as a merchant. Of course, the mother's name was not mentioned. Ezekiel Moses and his son, Henry Ezekiel, both very active citizens, were bankers and brokers. Moses Hart was the oldest son of Aaron Hart and Dorothea Judah.

co-seigneuresses, as they inherited the Saint-Grégoire, Godefroy, and Roquetaille fiefs.

When it is summarized this way, the integration into Canadien society of four natural children born to a Jewish father seems simple. However, Ezekiel Moses, Moses Ezekiel, Sarah Dorothea, and Charlotte Mathilda took a very unusual path to entering that society. For help, I turned to a remarkable genealogist, Jean Prince; the archivist of the diocese of Trois-Rivières, Denise Maltais; and one of Aaron Hart's descendants, René Hart, who was particularly interested in knowing more about his own ancestry. "My father didn't want to talk about it," René told me during one of our early meetings. "I found it strange." Together, we managed to uncover the secret of his parents, Joseph Hart and Éva Hamel. Joseph, who died in 1973, had been a prohonotary at the courthouse. "Jos Hart," as he was known, was the only son of Henry Ezekiel Hart and Marie-Louise Brûlé. There was no spouse mentioned on Henry Ezekiel's death certificate, but a "Jos Hart," identified as his son, signed the certificate.

It was the holograph will of Henry Ezekiel Hart, René Hart's grand-father, that gave us the key: a son was born out of wedlock, Jos Hart, René's father. Henry Ezekiel Hart was the son of Ezekiel Moses Hart and Joséphine-Domithilde Pothier. Ezekiel Moses was the co-founder of the seminary, and he and Henry Ezekiel listed their profession as bankers and brokers in the censuses.

The tolerance that I have mentioned several times was not simply that of the church or the Jewish community, but of society as a whole. Since the beginnings of the colony, Canadiens had accepted people of mixed blood; at the time of the British Conquest, mixed marriages were part of daily life, even though in principle the practice of Catholicism raised an obstacle for people of different religions. Some Jews were reluctant to accept this type of union, but they had to face reality. On the one hand, there were few young Jews on the matrimonial market and on the other hand, Catholics and Protestants were not averse to marrying them.

Not only was there little prejudice, I would say there was none at all; the population even remained impervious to the most excessive, provocative, and odious behaviour of someone such as Moses Hart. People were clearly resigned—especially Canadiens, who formed the great majority. It was the result not of openness of spirit but of a sense of passiveness among those who were being dispossessed and dragged into court. Time would take care of things, they seemed to be saying.

But submission lasted only so long. Revolt broke out in 1837.* Among the leaders were a surprising number of physicians. Marcel Rheault and Georges Aubin have written a book about them, *Médecins et patriotes, 1837-1838* (Doctors and Patriotes). I expressed my surprise to Rheault about the numerous doctors involved in the rebellion. "Doctors are close to the people," he replied. "They see their misery, they share their unhappiness; they become indignant. They are educated and capable of denouncing the misery that they see, and of demanding corrective measures."

An Invaluable Holograph Will

One day, René Hart gave me a photocopy of a photocopy of a holograph will[3] written by Moses Hart. It was difficult to read, but I quickly realized that I had a priceless document in my hands! In it, Moses Hart carefully recounted part of his love life. I absolutely had to obtain a better copy of the document. Research led me to the register of notary William Burn, conserved at the Archives nationales du Québec in Sherbrooke. Archivist France Monty immediately sent me a digitized copy of the will. It was marvellous to be able to enlarge the document on screen, increase its contrast, and make even the parts that were in terrible shape much more legible.

On 25 January 1837, Moses Hart had given notaries Dumoulin and Burn "a holograph will and codicil at the bottom of said will, both dated on the fourth day of the month of September last." Following the codicil was "a list of the names and ages of the heirs of M.H." The list included the dates of birth, but not the names of the mothers, although some of them were mentioned in the will itself.

Nevertheless, Moses partially lifted the veil on his many affairs. In the codicil, Orobio Elon was listed as born on 18 October 1823, and in his will

---

* The revolt broke out into the open in 1837, and it was aimed at the oligarchy. Contrary to what many believe, the rebellions were not about nationalism but about government by and for the people. At Louis-Joseph Papineau's side were Edmund-Bailey O'Callaghan, Thomas Storrow Brown, Wolfred Nelson, and Wolfred's brother Robert Nelson. Lower Canada's declaration of independence written by Robert Nelson was surprisingly modern; it included separation of church and state, respect for the Indians, and the use of French and English. The historian Gilles Laporte has noted that in proportion to their numbers, more English than French Canadians rose up against the oligarchy. Of course, similar problems existed in Upper Canada. To quell this popular revolt, the authorities provoked the taking up of arms. This was the only way to reach their goal.

Moses wrote, "My adopted son Orobio Elon Hart, a minor now living with me, and son of Margaret Armstrong."[4] Since I have found no trace of this son,[5] this information was not important to me, but this was not the case for the future co-seigneuresses of Saint-Grégoire, clearly presented as being the daughters of Margaret Burns.[6] Born, it seems, of a common-law union between a Jewish father and an English Protestant (or possibly Catholic[7]) mother, they received an education that prepared them for a "good marriage." The Ursulines' registers probably contain an explanation. Sarah Dorothea and Charlotte Mathilda were not the first Hart girls to be taught by these nuns. Aaron Hart's daughters and several other female descendants also had this privilege[8]—despite the fact that many believe that Catholic schools were closed to non-Catholics.

The Influence of Mary McCarthy, Widow of Peter Brown

Succeeding Margaret Armstrong and Margaret Burns, Mary McCarthy became an important part of Moses Hart's life in January 1837, at the time when he was preparing to write his will. This was no doubt not by chance. Before becoming committed too deeply and planning for the birth of a first child, she wanted Moses to come straight with her.

Their first son, Samuel Judah, was born on or around 22 October 1838. The date of the writing of the holograph will coincides with the time when this first child was conceived. In Mary McCarthy, Moses, who up to then had had a wild love life, may have finally met his match—his mistress in every sense of the word. Or perhaps, all too aware of the reputation of this ebullient businessman's multiple indiscretions, Mary had put her cards on the table. All indications are that she was a woman of strong character. In 1837, he was sixty-nine years old and she was thirty-six. She was said to be the widow of a man named Peter Brown. Nothing is known about him, including the date and place of his death, except that his name was associated with Mary McCarthy's. She had family in Ireland, and several letters addressed to her have survived.[9]

To complicate matters, there was a McCarthy among the electors in Trois-Rivières in 1804 and a Margaret McCarthy who married Aaron Moses Hart. This is the full name of "our" Moses Hart, Aaron's oldest son! The most expert genealogists' heads would spin! Who is this other Aaron Moses? Who was his mother? Unfortunately, there were no Jewish registers kept—and even had they existed, they might not have provided an answer.

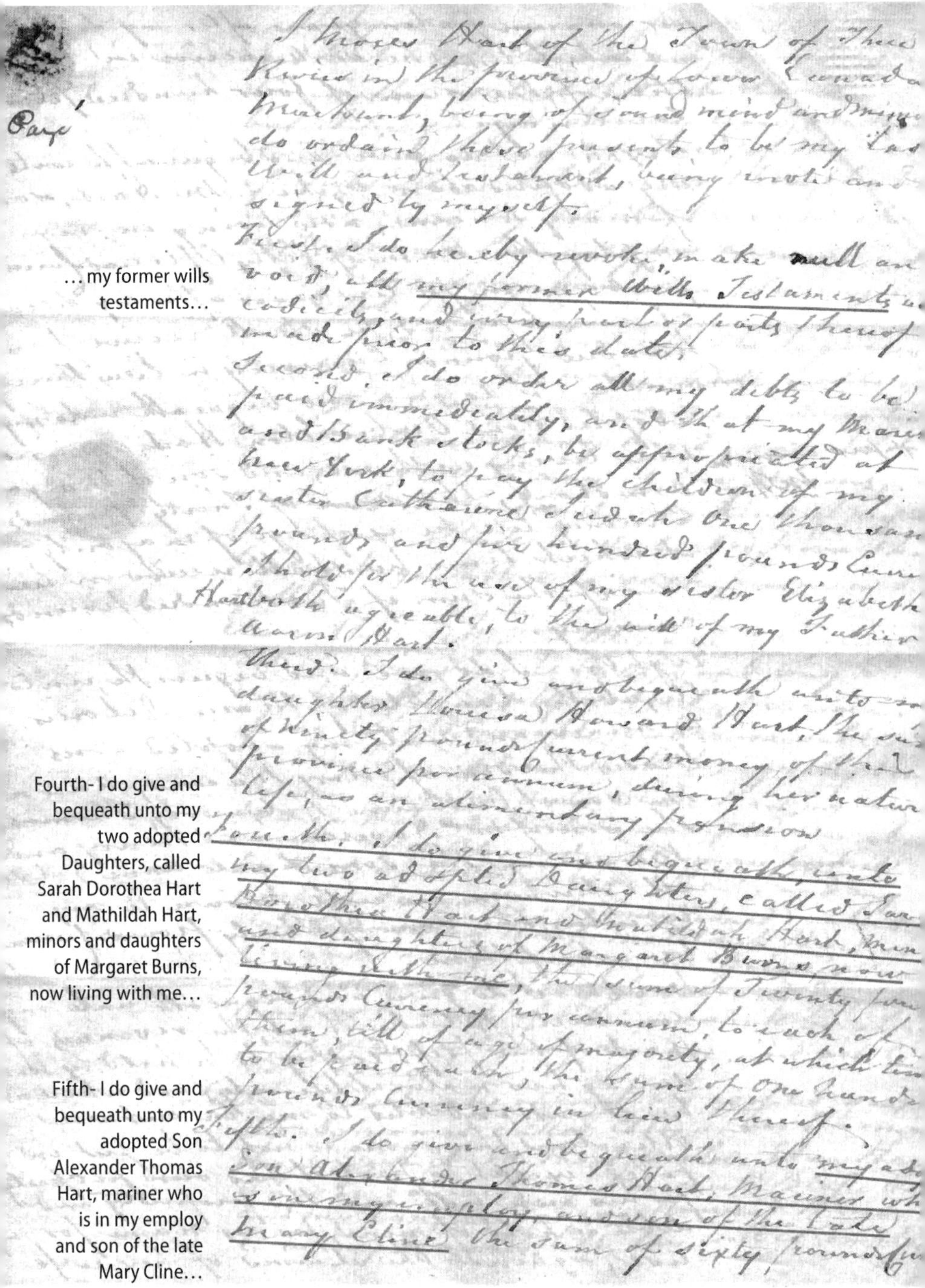

…my former wills
testaments…

Fourth- I do give and
bequeath unto my
two adopted
Daughters, called
Sarah Dorothea Hart
and Mathildah Hart,
minors and daughters
of Margaret Burns,
now living with me…

Fifth- I do give and
bequeath unto my
adopted Son
Alexander Thomas
Hart, mariner who
is in my employ
and son of the late
Mary Cline…

Eleventh- After settling and paying all the forgiving legacies…

… shall be equally divided between my son Areli Blake Hart, my daughter Louisa Howard Hart, my adopted son above named called Alexander Thomas, Ezekiel M. Hart and Orobio Elon Hart, and adopted daughters before mentioned called Sarah Dorothea, Matilda Hart and my sister Catharine Judah and Elizabeth Hart or to such of them and shall be alive four years after my decease, and not to their heirs.

Summary of a Tumultuous Life: A Last Will

In 1847, Moses Hart decided to write a new will and have it notarized.* My copy, carefully typed, comes from the prothonotary of Trois-Rivières, who made a "true certified copy of the minutes of the act found above in the study of V. Guillet, lawyer." This was Moses's last will, made when he was about eighty years old. I used it to dissect the monumental inventory of his property after his death, on 15 October 1852. It gave information about one of his heirs, "Mr. Aaron M. Hart, one of his natural children from whom he received services" and to whom he was particularly generous. Moses did not reveal the mother's name, and the notary did not ask questions. He also listed among his heirs "two children currently living resulting from the marriage of said Aaron M. Hart with the aforementioned Margaret McCarthy."[10] In fact, this couple (Aaron M. and Margaret) had at least seven children. In the cathedral baptism registers, archivist Denise Maltais found Moïse-Orotio (Orobio?) Hart baptized on 16 May 1848 (at the age of three), son of Aaron Moses Hart and Margaret McCarthy. Charles Pézard and Luce Lottinville were the godparents. Another boy, Edmond Henry, born to the same couple, was baptized the same day, at the age of two years.

In the 1847 will, Moses gave only the names of his first wife, Sarah Judah, from whom he had been "divorced"[11]—twice—and his last, Mary McCarthy. There were other natural children among the heirs; some of them, such as Alexander Thomas Hart, have been worthy of particular attention.

The two children whom Moses had with Mary McCarthy were Samuel Judah Hart and Reuben M. Hart, whom he called in his will "natural children who are still minors," for whom "their mother" agreed to act as their "ad hoc guardian" with regard to the shares of the estate intended for them. Moses Hart never took a straight line; for him, everything was complicated.

---

* I am more and more firmly convinced of Mary's veiled influence on Moses. For instance, the will specified that she was allowed to occupy the principal residence for two years following Moses's death, after which it would become part of the general estate. She started the inventory two years after Moses's death and, in the meantime, acquired the shares of several other heirs. She was joint executor with her brother-in-law, Aaron Moses, "from whom," Moses explains, "he received services." Even more strangely, Moses left Aaron Moses a three-storey house on Rue du Platon starting "on the day of his death." As to Moses's legitimate son, Areli Blake, he was not mentioned in the will, but, in compliance with Aaron's last wishes, as the oldest son of a legitimate marriage he inherited the Sainte-Marguerite seigneurie and the Marquisat du Sablé. Grandfather was a good provider.

Reuben

The last son of Moses Hart and Mary McCarthy, Reuben Moses Hart was born in 1840 and baptized in the Trois-Rivières cathedral. With his brother, Samuel Judah, he was among Moses Hart's heirs, but Moses specified in his will that they would inherit as Reuben Moses and Samuel Judah rather than Pierre and André, their baptismal names. Given his elegant attire, everything indicates that Reuben Moses took advantage of his heritage, both financial and genetic. His parents were exceptionally determined and ambitious people. His father died in 1852 and his mother in 1861. This photograph by William Notman is dated 1862 (McCord Museum, L-5091.1). Since there are no photographs of Moses and Mary, it is particularly moving for me to have an idea of what they might have looked like. Reuben Moses seems to be solidly built, of medium height, and proud. He is handsome and resembles his father, to judge by the painting conserved at the Château Ramezay (see p. 164).

Aaron Moses's and Margaret's sons were identified in the will as Edward, instead of Edmond Henry, and Moses Aaron, instead of Moïse-Orobio. Moses was aware that they had been baptized, and this was his way of protesting. But he was more explicit for Mary McCarthy's boys. He referred openly to their baptisms, named the priests J. Harper and Geo. Lemoine, and listed their Christian names: André Benjamin and Pierre. Thus, "said testator," he wrote, "wishes and intends that said Samuel Judah Hart and Reuben M. Hart take and accept the bequest to them made in the present paragraph and all those that could be made in the present will and that they enjoy and dispose of their income under their said names of Samuel Judah Hart and Reuben M. Hart, notwithstanding the names that were given to them at their baptism, as stated above." Moses took what consolation he could, but Mary McCarthy kept her eyes on the prize, even if the Hart family had blocked her plan to marry Moses, as I shall describe below.

A Mysterious Death Announcement

Moses Hart died on 15 October 1852. He received a Jewish burial. Mary McCarthy survived him until 1861, and she had a Catholic burial. Historians Raymond Douville and Hervé Biron have written that she was interred under the cathedral, although they do not specify where they got this information. I finally realized that they had found a document buried among the tens of thousands of letters, invoices, and various notes conserved at the archives of Séminaire Saint-Joseph de Trois-Rivières.

The Hart archive is exceptionally rich but also extremely complex. To date, many researchers have gleaned bits of information from it, but none has dared to undertake an examination of the whole. It would be a superhuman task. Marcel Trudel has assessed the mass of papers in the archive at some 100,000 pieces.[12] Most of the documents are handwritten, in a rather improvised English; some are lists of merchandise and columns of figures, and others are drafts or copies, written in haste, of various letters. Despite the precautions taken by the authorities, people have made off with bookplates that had been conserved and bank notes from the Hart's Bank. One can imagine how excited and covetous researchers have been when they saw these documents, which I discovered when I began my research.

In this mountain of documents, conserved today in archival folders and boxes—the archive is now classified by the government for its historical value—there are two printed documents that are striking. Both concern Mary McCarthy. One, dated 18 December 1858, attests to her affiliation with the Congrégation de la Sainte-Croix et de la Passion; the other is a death announcement.[13] "You are requested to attend the funeral of the late Mary McCarthy which will take place on Friday the 25th instant," it reads. "The funeral will leave her late residence on Notre-Dame Street at half past eight O'Clock A.M. for the French Cathedral place of interment." This is likely the source of the statements by Douville and Biron, at least in part, for Douville specifies, "She was interred in the Catholic church because, it was said, she had gratified the clergy with the land on which it sat, on condition that she would rest there after her death."[14]

Three Rivers, 24th January 1861.

Sir,

You are requested to attend the funeral of the late Mrs. Mary McCarthy, which will take place on Friday the 25th instant.

The funeral will leave her late residence, Notre Dame Street, at half past eight o'Clock, A. M., for the French Cathedral, place of interment.

his death notice was designed and written by Mary McCarthy. It was part of her last wishes. The details of the nquiry recounted here leave no doubt about this.

The certificate of 18 December 858 is made in the name of Mrs. Moses McCarthy, who was to have he right to the protection of the ongregation of the Holy Cross and he Passion in exchange for her enerosity. She therefore received er "husband's" first name.

ANTHONY OF S. JAMES

SUPERIOR GENERAL OF THE CONGREGATION

Of discalced Clerks of the most Holy Cross & Passion of our Lord J. C.

To our well=beloved in Christ *Mrs Mary McCarthy* health in Our Lord.

We feel ourselves bound in gratitude to make a return, in the best way we can, to those who assist and do good to the Children of our Congregation, by alms and in other ways. Hence, in consideration of the like benefits received from you, we grant you the title of Benefactor of our Retreat of BLESSED PAUL, near Pittsburgh; and most lovingly impart to you a special participation in the sacrifices, prayers, and all other good works, which are performed in the above named retreat, day and night.

Given at *Bless'd Paul's Monastery, this 18th day of December 1858.*

A Church Basement Filled with Cadavers

The first time I saw Douville's note, I was skeptical. It seemed to me that only the members of the high Catholic clergy, or at least very important people, would have the right to such an honour. Always in my memory is the discovery by the historian Gustave Lanctôt, who claimed to have found the skull of Jacques Cartier under the ruins of the Church of Saint-Malo, something that my professor, Guy Frégault, mocked.[15] Was Mary McCarthy buried in the Trois-Rivières cathedral? How could this be verified?

In 1987, the Presses de l'Université Laval published an essay by Serge Gagnon, *Mourir, hier et aujourd'hui*. The circumstances of the death and burial of Louis-Joseph Papineau was of particular interest to me then. He had had a small chapel erected to serve as a funerary vault for the members of his family. Although he was not observant, he had in mind the Guibord affair, a case of exclusion from a Catholic cemetery in 1869. He had hoped for a civil funeral and, as a precaution, had asked that his body rest in the tower of his library if he was not able to join his relatives in the family crypt, a holy site. His fears had proved to be unfounded; Bishop Bourget, who had been intransigent for Guibord, averted his eyes.

A chapter subtitle in Gagnon's book drew my attention: "Basements Full of Cadavers." "As late as the nineteenth century," Gagnon writes, "the parish church occasionally served as a burial site. Notre-Dame, in Quebec

The Trois-Rivières cathedral was the fulfilment of Father Thomas Cooke's great dream. The "French Cathedral," Mary McCarthy's "Place of interment," was inaugurated in 1858. A subscription campaign had been launched in 1854, two years after the diocese was created. In the documents, the old parish church is often designated as the cathedral. In fact, the registers are the same.

City, contained more than nine hundred bodies in the late nineteenth century, 40 percent of whom had died after the Conquest: colonial small aristocrats, members of the bourgeoisie, members of the liberal professions, and craftspeople formed the cohort of laypeople excluded starting in 1877." Later on, Gagnon specifies that to have the right to this honour, one could make "a large donation to the church—for example, a parcel of land that becomes property of the church council" or be a well-known figure or a priest. However, over the years, fees were instituted to both increase the church council's revenues and serve as a dissuasive measure.

Maltais confirmed that bishops, priests, and laypeople had been interred in or under the Trois-Rivières cathedral, but that all the bodies had been moved to a cemetery long ago. Was it possible that a woman named Mary McCarthy, common-law wife of a Jew, had received the honour of such a burial?

Mary McCarthy's Death Notice is Clear

Was Mary McCarthy indeed the common-law spouse of Moses Hart, a Jew? His after-death inventory left no doubt that she was. The notary William Burn had sent the widow a bill for the writing of a marriage contract dated 5 May, which had been cancelled several weeks later. In fact, by notarized act, on 30 July 1847, "they renounce[d] to the intended marriage which was to take place between them" and therefore the marriage contract written the previous 5 May "remains null and of no effect whatever." Had the couple had a quarrel? More likely, there was a serious family disagreement. The day before, 29 July, Adolphus M. Hart, "lawyer of the city of Montreal," son of Ezekiel and nephew of Moses, asked for an "authentic copy of said marriage contract," claiming "that it is necessary for the support of the allegations of a request that your supplicant has in recent days submitted to your honour in order to obtain an interdiction of said Moses Hart." At the beginning of his application, Adolphus M. Hart evoked information heard "from a number of people, and in particular of several of Moses Hart's children."

On the previous 1 April, at the time that he was finalizing his will, Moses had been found to be "sound of body, of memory, judgment, and understanding," by the notaries Lottinville and Guillet. "After the present will had been read and reread to him by one of the said notaries," they concluded, "the other [notary being] present, and he having declared that he had heard and understood and had persisted after reading and rereading," said testator had signed the will. Was there a doubt about Moses's capacities? Five weeks later, Mary McCarthy and Moses were at notary LaBarre's office to prepare a marriage contract. Both of them signed the draft contract and the cancellation of 30 July. Mary's signature was made with a trembling hand, whereas Moses's signature seemed steadier. Moses Hart was still quite active, although at this time he began to wind down his businesses—or, at least, the evidence of his activity has not been preserved. Above all, there was no trace of marriage. He became paralyzed and incapable of signing his name sometime before his death.

In the diocese archives, burial certificates are indexed, and Maltais was quickly able to find Mary McCarthy's. Together we read the handwritten document: "The twenty five January eighteen hundred sixty-one, we, Priest undersigned, have interred in the cathedral church of this city the body of Mrs. Mary McCarthy, deceased in this parish the twenty-eighth of the present month, at the age of about fifty-nine years.[16] Present at the burial were Samuel Hart, Ruben Hart, Sir Denys Genest Labarre, and a number of other relatives and friends." The register was signed by Samuel Hart, Reuben M. Hart, Edm. M. Hart, M. Dennison, Philippe Désilets, Arthur Désilets, Margaret Hart, D. G. Labarre, P. Burn, F. Lottinville, L. J. O. Brunelle, and the priest, Jos. Élie Panneton.

Looking for an Explanation

The announcement was clear, and yet a doubt had remained in my mind. The burial certificate settled the question, yet why was the honour bestowed upon the deceased. It was said of her, at the time, that she was a woman of charitable works. Certain documents suggest this, but did she go so far as to give land from Moses Hart's estate to the episcopal corporation for the construction of a cathedral? Bishop Thomas Cooke had been appointed to lead the new diocese of Trois-Rivières, created in 1852, and he quickly launched the plan to build a cathedral.

I began to look for the name of the owner of the land on which the cathedral and bishop's palace were built. Later, I remembered having in my files the assessment roll for Trois-Rivières for the year 1845 but because of the lack of detail I turned instead to the after-death inventories of Ezekiel and Moses Hart. The cathedral was situated on land that extended behind Champlain Park, city hall, and a large residence on Rue des Forges that

The Harts' house is often designated as a former governor's residence. The photograph above was made into a "stereoscopic" image, a sign of the interest shown in house. In "Miettes d'histoire," an article published in the *Revue canadienne* in 1870, Benjamin Sulte wrote about Ezekiel's three children who were living in this immense residence: Caroline Hart, James Henry Craig Hart, and Adolphus Mordecai ("Mardochée," as Sulte called him) Hart.

In the second half of the nineteenth century, development of the downtown area required constant negotiations with the heirs of the Hart family. Developers were also building new neighbourhoods on land that had had almost always belonged to various members of the family.

belonged to the Harts. René Hardy, co-author with Normand Séguin of *Histoire de la Mauricie*, published by IQRC in 2004, remembered photographs showing that house. "In fact," he told me, "the cathedral was built in the Harts' backyard." I sent a request to the archives department of the city of Trois-Rivières. Archivist Céline Lamy responded quickly. Yet again, I was amazed to receive, via Internet, documents that were digitized and thus much easier to read.

The lots on which the "public square" had been created had been acquired in 1869 from the estate of Ezekiel Hart, represented by Ira Craig Hart, Adolphus Mordecai Hart, and Caroline Hart "for the price set by the arbitrators." This land became Parc Champlain, and a city hall was built on it. I continued to dig into the inventory of Ezekiel's estate, in vain.

Intrigued by the story of the donation of land, archivist Maltais continued her research. She found a carefully kept register of subscriptions made to fund Cooke's projects; the donors' names were listed in alphabetical order. She showed it to me without comment. In February 1854, "Mrs. Mary Brown (widow of Moses Hart)" had given £100 and then three deliveries of wood for a total of £71 16s3d. At the letter H, there was a cross reference to the donation of Mrs. Moses Hart that referred to B for Brown.[17]

Was it possible that this large donation justified her burial in the cathedral? I reviewed the amounts listed. There were few over £100. I found two, for the same amount, in the names of P. B. Dumoulin and Étienne Tapin. After checking quickly, Maltais confirmed that both had been buried in the cathedral. A donation of land was no longer necessary as an explanation. But I wanted to be very certain.

Acquisition of the Land on which the Cathedral Was Built

Denise Maltais was patient and accustomed to my stubbornness. On 21 January 2010, she showed me a note signed by Bishop Thomas of Trois-Rivières: "I the undersigned bishop of Trois-Rivières, president of the episcopal corporation, bequeath and cede to said episcopal corporation all the money that I advanced for the acquisitions of the sites, and notably that acquired from Samuel Hart, Esq., which all together form the land on which the cathedral is placed." It was as if Bishop Cooke himself had zipped my mouth shut.

Cooke's father, like Mary McCarthy's, was Irish by birth. There was no doubt in my mind that they knew each other well, and they probably helped each other out. The Samuel Hart mentioned by the bishop could not be the son of Mary McCarthy, for Samuel Judah Hart, born in 1838, was too young to be the one to whom Cooke was referring. I told Maltais that I was continuing my research, which admittedly was bordering on obsession. Might the bishop have used Samuel's name instead of that of his mother, but leaving out the detested name Judah?

On 28 January, Maltais sent me another digitized document with a short note: "Have a good read." I was once again plunged into examining Ezekiel's property inventory because I was now thinking that "Samuel Hart" could have been Samuel Bécancour Hart, Ezekiel's oldest son. On the second-to-last page of the inventory written in 1843, I found a lot "with its front on Rue Royale and abutting Thomas Launière" measuring "fifty-seven feet of frontage at the front and fifty-nine feet at the back by a hundred and seventy-seven feet in depth in the southwest line and only one hundred and seventy-two in the northeast line." The cathedral is at the corner of Rue Royale and Rue Bonaventure.

I opened the document received by e-mail. It was a certificate of sale for a lot belonging to Samuel Bécancour Hart to "His Eminence Thomas Cooke bishop of Trois-Rivières for him personally and his estate." After a review of the "poll taxes and rents and seigneurial rights" attached to the Niverville fief came the price: "Two hundred and seventy-five pounds in the current exchange of this province that said acquirer seigneur bishop has paid in cash" for a lot the description of which corresponded exactly to that found in the after-death inventory "with a front on Rue Royale." The lot on which the cathedral had been erected came from the estate of Ezekiel Hart and had been acquired from his oldest son, Samuel Bécancour.

Did the Final Word Belong to Those Conquered in 1760?[18]

Aaron Hart's descendants, particularly Moses's and Ezekiel's children and grandchildren, inherited large tracts of property and seigneuries. Being attached to their vast properties, many decided to remain in the region rather than move away and lose everything. Within two generations, the *Canadiens,* who had lost so much of their property to the Harts after the Conquest, ended up integrating the family among the local population.

Exactly one hundred years after Aaron Hart arrived in Trois-Rivières and despite all the care he took to raise his children in the religion of his ancestors, a number of his grandsons were baptized and married in the Catholic Church. The remains of one of his daughters-in-law were even interred in the crypt of the "French cathedral."

My research led me to a considerable number of Moses Hart's children born out of wedlock. Many of them were welcomed into the Catholic Church and baptized as part of its strategy of conversions. During his lifetime, Moses did not disown these children, despite everything that he said and wrote about the Church and its popes, bishops, priests, and followers. Half of the heirs listed in his 1847 will had been baptized. He knew it. For the last two boys that he had with Mary McCarthy, he gave their baptismal names and even named the priests responsible, though he stated that these sons were his heirs under their Jewish names.

One may also wonder if he expressed his final wishes for his own burial. I was surprised to find that his funeral followed the Jewish rites, which, it goes without saying, were very different from the Catholic ones. Among other things, there was no embalming, and the burial took place without delay. The service was conducted by the great rabbi Abraham De Sola, who came to Trois-Rivières from Montreal for the occasion. Was this because of the intervention of Moses's brother Benjamin or another member of his family? Was Mary McCarthy involved? If she was, why did she ignore the rabbi's demands for payment? One thing is certain: Abraham De Sola had heard about Moses Hart, but he refused to judge him.

One day, the mystery of Mary McCarthy will have to be solved. The childless widow of a modest tailor, Peter Brown, she was seduced by the unavoidable Moses Hart, then around seventy years old. She had ambition and character. She knew her man. All of Trois-Rivières knew about him. He was a ladies' man, impenitent, always on a war footing. She was ready and waiting: Moses willingly admitted his seamy past; he confessed, almost voluptuously, to his countless affairs, even committing some of them to paper. He summarized them in the form of a will (1837) in which he recognized a number of his illegitimate children. Moses and Mary made a new start. Together, they had two sons. She had them baptized. Samuel Judah and Reuben Moses became, in the Catholic Church, André Benjamin and Pierre. Moses allowed this to happen, but in his will he left part of his estate to Samuel Judah and Reuben Moses.

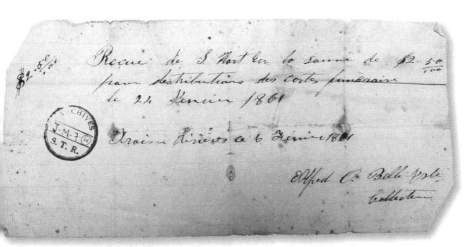

After ten years of cohabitation, the couple decided to get married. The family objected loudly and had the draft marriage contract cancelled. Mary fell back on the writing of a last will. Moses made a new accounting of his life. He tried to put his children in order, and he seemed to ignore his only still-living legitimate child, Areli Blake, who was relegated to the background. He nevertheless left Areli Blake his jewel, the Sainte-Marguerite seigneury. On the other hand, did he have a choice? Remember Aaron's will: "Mr. Moses Hart will be able to take possession of [the Sainte-Marguerite seigneury and the Marquisat du Sablé] in usufruct only for his lifetime, the property and the fiefs and rights attached to it will belong to the oldest son in a legitimate marriage of Mr. Moses Hart, and in the case that said Mr. Moses Hart dies without male child born or to be born in legitimate marriage, said testator wishes and orders that the property of said fiefs and all rights attached to them be bequeathed to the male child born in legitimate marriage of Mr. Ezekiel Hart …"

Mary McCarthy did not want needless arguments. Moses had divided feelings about Areli Blake, who had caused him much worry but whom he sometimes brought in as his partner. They had clearly been partners in the episode of the "house of ill repute."

In the last months of his life, Moses was an invalid. Mary took command. When he died, did she send for the rabbi from Montreal? Or was it the initiative of a family member? Either way, she was in no hurry to settle his account.

Mary McCarthy was to have a Catholic burial. She spent time with her compatriot, Father Cooke. She contributed to the subscription campaign that he launched for construction of a cathedral. She knew that £100 would earn her the honour of being buried in the cathedral—all the more reason to contribute! She was a charitable woman; she belonged to the Order of St. Anthony.

She made sure that an announcement was printed and that everyone would know that she had the right to great honours. She took her revenge on the devout, zealous churchwomen.

The Evanescence of a Great Family and a Founding Community: Sephardim vs. Ashkenazim

BENJAMIN HART WILL BE THE GUIDE for this last chapter. In fact, he served as a guide for the Montreal Sephardic community by helping to revive it in the 1830s. I would like to add a small detail to the rank that Benjamin held among the Hart sons. In the biography of Benjamin Hart in the *Dictionary of Canadian Biography*, author Carman Miller notes that he was Aaron and Dorothea's fourth son; I thus conclude that Miller included among their children Samuel, who may have been born in 1774. I have found no documentation on him, except that he no doubt was present at Ezekiel's wedding (see page 243). Moses, the oldest, was eleven years older than Benjamin; Ezekiel was nine years older. Benjamin absorbed the blows of these older brothers while trying to protect the youngest, Alexander. The three older brothers were forced by circumstances to form a team, at least for several years. Then their marriages made them grow apart. Benjamin and Alexander married wealthy women, which did not protect them from the ups and downs of business.[1]

The McCord Museum has a daguerreotype identified as "Benjamin Hart and his grandson, Gerald Ephraim Hart." The date given is between 1852 and 1855. Benjamin Hart died in New York in February 1855, where he had been living for some time. The child he is holding may be Gerald Ephraim, his grandson—and also the grandson of Ezekiel (see p. 308). Gerald Ephraim Hart, a collector, left important documents and some objects to various archives and museums, including this photograph. Benjamin was a complex character who had a difficult life. The Jewish community in Montreal underwent somewhat of a renaissance in the 1820s and 1830s thanks to his efforts.

Discomfort in Trois-Rivières

Life could not have been easy for Benjamin and Alexander Hart in Trois-Rivières. Moses's behaviour certainly led to disparaging comments and incessant ridicule. Sarah Judah's first application for a separation, in 1807, would have been a subject of gossip. It was ten years before she made her second application and the court ruled in her favour. In the hearings for each application, the couple's domestics were called upon to testify in public. Moses played the bad guy. No doubt he kept up a brave face, but he couldn't help but see the disapproval written on people's faces.

Alexander was the first to leave Trois-Rivières for Montreal; he went to join his mother. Benjamin was less mobile. His family was growing at the rate of about one child a year. He married in 1806; his first child was born in 1807 and his last in 1828: sixteen childbirths in twenty years.[2] We can imagine Benjamin, exhausted from his struggle to feed all these mouths, coming home every evening to a wife who constantly complained about the never-ending scandalous behaviour of her brother-in-law.

Since her arrival in Trois-Rivières, Harriott Judith had had little contact with the people of the town. Trapped by her ever-growing brood, speaking no French, she had a limited social life. Ezekiel's wife, a fellow New Yorker, might have opened a few doors for her, but it is my impression that the two

Presented as another donation by Gerald Ephraim Hart, this daguerreotype is of Harriott Judith Hart, Benjamin's wife. Given their large family, the bequest of his father-in-law's estate was welcome but not sufficient. Benjamin was a jack-of-all-trades, master of none. Almost all of their offspring left Quebec to live in the United States. Their father had often been dogged by misfortune and, in short, was not very happy in Canada (see p. 265).

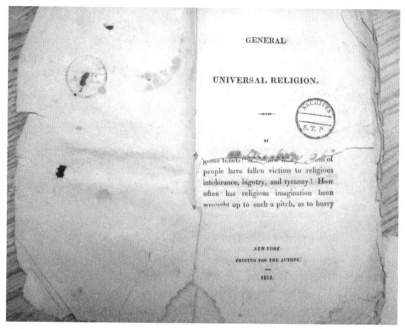

GENERAL

UNIVERSAL RELIGION.

gious tenets! ... ons of
people have fallen victims to religious
intolerance, bigotry, and tyranny! How
often has religious imagination been
wrought up to such a pitch, as to hurry

NEW-YORK:
PRINTED FOR THE AUTHOR.

1815.

The part torn out was not done inadvertently. (See page 181.)

husbands did not see much of each other, or perhaps there was some rivalry between the women.[3]

In the end, Benjamin and his wife realized that nothing was keeping them in Trois-Rivières. The scandal that surrounded the separation of Sarah and Moses and the publishing of the pamphlet on a new religion, which no one read but everyone ridiculed, were no doubt the last straws. Benjamin was very religious. When he read *General Universal Religion,* he must have choked with shame or rage. He was fed up with suffering the sarcasm of those around him; he began to dream that his brother would be stoned in the public square, and he wanted to cast the first stone. And what if it was discovered that Moses had simply plagiarized from a text by an itinerant deist or had paid someone to write the tract for him? Benjamin knew how proud his brother was, and he had noticed that the pamphlet did not name the author. There was no explanation, and he didn't want one. It was simply Moses's folly. If lightning was to strike, he wanted to be far, far away. Even given the size of their family, Harriott Judith was ready to pack up their things.

Benjamin Takes On a New Cause

Around 1817, Benjamin moved to Montreal to seek his fortune. He tried a number of different ventures without great success, it seems. However, the death of his father-in-law in 1825 gave him access to a fortune. He quickly took on a new attitude and decided to become involved in the affairs of the Jewish community in Montreal. The community had become fragile; the synagogue was being poorly maintained and, worse, in 1824 the land that it was sitting on had passed into the hands of the heirs of David David.[4] In 1777, David had donated a site for the erection of a first synagogue, imitating the gesture made by his father, Lazarus David, who had offered, in 1775, a plot of land near today's Dominion Square "to serve in perpetuity as a cemetery for individuals of the Jewish faith who may die in the Montreal district."[5] David David was single; in Benjamin's eyes, his heirs did not appear to have his attachment to or respect for Jewish institutions.

Benjamin Hart decided to make a grand gesture (see p. 148). He sent out a printed invitation "to the Israelites of the Province of Lower Canada"

Detail of Bouchette's 1815 map. The first synagogue was erected in 1777 on Rue Notre-Dame with an entrance via Rue Saint-Jacques on a lot belonging to David David, near the site where the Palais de Justice now stands.

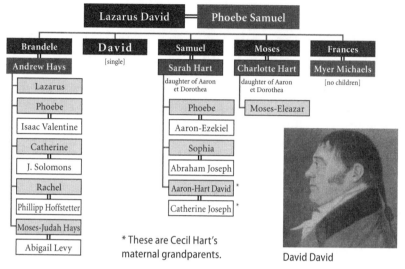

Ties linking the Davids to the Hayses, the Harts, the Michaels, the Valentines, the Solomons, the Hoffsteters and another branch of the Levy family.

Lazarus David = Phoebe Samuel

- **Brandele** — **Andrew Hays**
  - Lazarus
  - Phoebe — Isaac Valentine
  - Catherine — J. Solomons
  - Rachel — Phillipp Hoffstetter
  - Moses-Judah Hays — Abigail Levy
- **David** [single]
- **Samuel** — **Sarah Hart** daughter of Aaron et Dorothea
  - Phoebe
  - Aaron-Ezekiel
  - Sophia
  - Abraham Joseph
  - Aaron-Hart David *
  - Catherine Joseph *
- **Moses** — **Charlotte Hart** daughter of Aaron et Dorothea
  - Moses-Eleazar
- **Frances** — **Myer Michaels** [no children]

* These are Cecil Hart's maternal grandparents.

David David

to a meeting on Sunday, 20 August 1826. I have already written about the indignation that he expressed in this document and the nature of the initiative that he was undertaking. His approach was mainly legalistic. He wanted to gather the forces of his community to re-establish conditions favourable to religious practice in a well-ordered, disciplined way. Although he was an intransigent person, in extremis he was open to suggestions by those who "pay over their first annual subscription." He was aware of the enormousness of the task, which consisted essentially of reorganizing his community and having it be recognized by the government.

At the time, the Jewish community had two main problems, to which it had accommodated itself until then; the first came to the fore with the death of David David. The community now needed the power and the right to organize legally in a corporation, which had to be able to own and manage assets. The second problem concerned the absence of registers, which had to be compensated for with expensive legal documents that were poorly adapted to the laws in effect.

At the meeting of 20 August, Benjamin quickly realized that he had started a political movement that he could not control. The Israelites of Montreal took to the barricades. No doubt to their surprise, they received support from the Parti canadien (soon to be the Parti Patriote) led by Papineau, and the statute that they petitioned for was passed in 1830 (see chapter 6). Benjamin swung into action once again. A register was opened in Montreal. A date was scribbled in at the beginning of the register: 11 September 1832. This date is no doubt wrong. There is no reason that those who had agitated so strongly to obtain this right would have waited almost two years to start the register. The name of Henry Joseph Sr. is the first one registered; Joseph, who was Aaron Hart's nephew and the husband of Rachel Solomons, was a well-known figure, the forebear of a remarkable Jewish family that settled in Berthier and still has descendants in Quebec. As a venerable patriarch, he was given the honour of having the first signature in the register.

Henry Joseph died in June 1832, struck down by cholera.[6] The disease first appeared in Quebec City on 8 June and then spread as quickly as did the news of its appearance. The first cases had been found the previous year at Grosse-Île. A quarantine was instituted, but probably too late to keep the first carriers from leaving the island. Henry Joseph was in Montreal when he heard that his son, Samuel, had been taken ill. He rushed to his side and contracted the disease himself. Samuel died on 15 June, his father, a few days later.[7]

The register was no doubt started soon after royal sanction on 1 November 1830. That said, it is interesting to note the first names that appear after Henry Joseph's: Alexander Hart, Benjamin Hart, Isaac Valentine, M. J. Hays, and H. Solomons.

Henry Joseph, son of Naphtali Joseph and one of Aaron Hart's sisters. He immigrated to the "Province of Quebec" with Aaron's encouragement, as did his brothers, Abraham and Judah Joseph.

Isaac Valentine had lived in Trois-Rivières and apparently became a good friend of Benjamin's. He was the brother-in-law of Moses Judah Hays. These three, supported by Alexander Hart, Henry Solomons, Isaac Aaron,[8] Aaron Philip Hart, and Eleazar David David, decided to take the initiative. There were enough signatories to undertake the steps needed to form a "congregation." On 22 September 1832, they sent a letter to this effect to the chief magistrate of the Court of King's Bench. The next day, George Pyke called a meeting for 15 October to elect five administrators. Augustin Cuvillier, a wealthy businessman who had been appointed a justice of the peace not long before, was designated to chair the meeting, during which Isaac Valentine, Moses Judah Hays, Benjamin Hart, Henry Solomons, and the mysterious Isaac Aaron were elected.

Hart, Valentine, and Hays Plan The New Synagogue

The objective of the new administrators was to provide the community with a synagogue. Since the previous one had been abandoned or demolished, religious services had taken place at Benjamin Hart's residence. Benjamin therefore had another reason to get the project underway. But he was also stubborn.

Benjamin quickly formed an alliance with Moses Judah Hays. Hays was also quite a character, but he was more practical than Benjamin. Having served in a military engineers' corps, he had a keen interest in public projects. He was overflowing with ideas and ambitions. He followed the plans to build an aqueduct closely. In 1832, he purchased the Montreal Water Works for the considerable sum of £15,000.[9] Fifteen years later, after a number of improvements, he sold the company to the city of Montreal for £50,000.

In February 1831, even before he acquired the aqueduct system, Hays submitted to the House of Assembly a plan for a crossing from Montreal to Longueuil. The first step would be to construct a floating bridge leading from the Bonsecours market to a small island southwest of St. Helen's Island; after that, a bridge would be built across the river. The bridge would serve both personal travel and business. It took the members of the House eleven days to reject the project. Work on the Victoria Bridge began twenty-four years later.[10] Hays had been a quarter-century too early.

Benjamin was fascinated by Moses Judah Hays's audacity. By acquiring the aqueduct system, Hays knew that he was acquiring many problems: runoff water from the mountain was not plentiful enough, technical progress required constant reinvestments, expansion of the network called for new piping systems; the pipes had to be replaced by bigger ones, streets would have to be opened, and more. And on top of that, he wanted to build a bridge over the St. Lawrence.

Hays knew the city like the back of his hand. Benjamin trusted him. They formed a team with Valentine. First, they had to raise funds.

Moses-Judah Hays

The Aqueduct

The abundance of small waterways flowing through Montreal necessitated the construction of bridges but at the same time led to the establishment of open-air sewers. Advantages turned into disadvantages, as the small rivers were less and less suitable as sources of drinking water. Solutions included the construction of wells and taking water from the St. Lawrence. Of all the municipal public works, water service was the last one to draw the attention of businessmen, and thus of elected officials. As Dany Fougères (2004, p. 58) notes, it belonged to the world of technical curiosities. The scene portrayed in this watercolour belongs to a world that was disappearing around 1800 when a group of businessmen, led by John Gray, who had made the transition from the fur trade to real estate, obtained a provincial charter (in 1801) to create a company charged with supplying "good, healthy water" to Montrealers. This is the company that Moses Judah Hays bought in 1832.

In 1800, elected officials were taken with a "revolutionary" plan. I cannot resist sharing some excerpts from the memorandum of the developers, who "have recently formed a partnership to supply to the city and suburbs of Montreal water for the use of such inhabitants here . . . that they have obtained from the Gentlemen of the Seminary of Montreal the right to take water from certain springs that give the purest water that are on their land . . . to gather water at high cost and have passed it through pipes put in ditches . . ."

Prominent citizens and businessmen came to the rescue of the petitioners: "That nothing contributes more and is more essentially necessary to the health of man than pure and healthy water . . . That the inhabitants of the city of Montreal from its foundation to the present have had to bring, by hand, from the St. Lawrence all the water for the use of their families, which water in the spring, summer, and autumn is extremely dirty and cloudy due to the city's garbage and sewage." The elected members were enthusiastic; the legislative councillors were slower. The applicants had to return to the hustings in 1801. This time, they specified "that they should be allowed the privilege of taking water across the property of individuals and make use of the springs that might be found there, by paying the owners some reasonable compensation."

The application was extraordinary and ran counter to the right to private property. Expropriation was not permitted on the municipal level; the legislature was cautious and made consent of the landowner a requirement but ignored the obligation to submit plans to the local administration. It must be remembered that the municipality was incorporated only in 1831.

For instance, "it will be permissible for said company . . . to dig, disturb, and move the Land, Fences, Sewers, Drains, or Paving Stones of any Street, Neighbourhood, Market Square, Alley, Hill, Open square, Alley, Yard, Road, Vacant Lot, Footpath, Dock, Bridge, Gate, Gateway, City Ditch, Paddock, Fence, and other Passages and Squares of said City of Montreal and adjacent parts . . . to dig and make trenches, and to put in them Pipes, and to place, fix, and establish Machines to stop the watercourses, fire hydrants . . . as they deem necessary to conduct the water to Houses, Offices, and other buildings" (Fougères 2004, 63–67).

This description in itself is an illustration of the difficulties that awaited the promoters. The company collected its water in a pond situated north of Côte-des-Neiges and routed it by gravity through wooden conduits to two reservoirs. The people on Rue Notre-Dame were among the first to benefit. In summer, the water was scarce; in winter, the pipes froze. Throughout the year, problems piled up. Nevertheless, Moses Judah Hays expanded water service, lighting the way for another peerless entrepreneur, Sigismund Mohr (1827–93), who developed telephone and electrical services in Quebec City late in the century.

\\

On 5 November 1832, Valentine, on behalf of his congregation, wrote to Solomon Herschele, the rabbi responsible for the "Portuguese" Jewish community in London. His message was that there were too few Jews in Montreal to support financially the acquisition of the land necessary and the construction of a new synagogue and a residence for the rabbi; they needed help.[11] Three days later, Valentine drafted two more letters; his colleagues had convinced him to write to Nathan Mayer Rothschild and his brother-in-law, Moses Montefiore, known to be a philanthropist.

Even before they received a reply, Valentine, Hays, and Hart began to make plans. In a letter dated 14 October 1833, Benjamin summarized his very concrete project.[12] He sketched out a plan for the future synagogue, and he assigned the seats and set the price for each. He was obviously aiming for a full synagogue and opened the doors to outsiders, as they "have all told me they prefer our Ceremonies to their own." Benjamin had a very specific goal in mind that pushed him to make this concession. However, he soon changed his mind.

Benjamin also had very definite ideas about the location of the planned synagogue. He wanted a "middle lot. "To Build on a corner," he explained, "you have Two faces to make, each at a cost of £100. The entrance must be on the rear and the shool [shul] much exposed to bad Characters to Break the Window Glasses, etc."[13] To make himself very clear, he added, "On a Middle Lot on the other side, you have but the frontage with a proper entrance, the shool more safe from Bad Characters and Room hereafter to build a House." He foresaw discussions or objections, but "It's full time,

Around 1843, John Murray portrayed Rue Notre-Dame facing east. The towers of the basilica had just been completed. We can see that the passers-by are very elegantly dressed; it was an upscale neighbourhood.

to make Bylaws. We are three, which carries all, and no one can go against the same."

Finally, he was concerned about new arrivals in Canada. "We are perfectly Secure from the Germans, our young ones are numerous. We have now A. P. Hart, C. David, in March we have Mr. David E. Wellington, and in 18 months, Fred Hart & Jacob Joseph, in 3 years, 5 or 6 more young ones. So that we hold the force in our own hands, if only quarrels can be kept out." And, curiously, he added, "No Dutch [Deutsch?] will ever have our Shool for their own, they are themselves ashamed of their Ceremonies." He was quite discouraged, and it is not surprising that he concluded,

"I have a strong wish to retire from the board—but fear to do so—at this moment—I beg you to communicate this to Mr. Hays." It was an appeal for assistance; he wanted Hays to become more involved.

On 23 December 1834, Hays was present at the meeting of administrators. He received the mandate, upon the motion by Benjamin Hart, seconded by Isaac Valentine, to proceed with an exchange of lots, giving up those acquired from François-Antoine Larocque to obtain those owned by J. Quesnel or M. Deschenes.[14]

The Acquisition of Land

The transaction took place on 30 June 1835 before notaries S. S. Martin and P. Lacombe. It is an interesting document. First, it involved important personalities of the time. The land that Hays and his colleagues wanted was in the estate of Gabriel Cotté, a major fur trader. Cotté had been particularly proud of the marriage of one of his daughters, Marie-Catherine-Émilie, to François-Antoine Larocque, a famous *voyageur* who had surprised the American explorers Lewis and Clark by going to meet them among the Mandans of Missouri in the fall of 1804.[15]

The transaction involved Gabriel Cotté's three daughters, confirming that this was their inheritance. Their husbands, Alexis Laframboise, Jules Maurice Quesnel, and François-Antoine Larocque, "authoriz[ed] their respective wives" to proceed with the transaction, although they were present. The representatives of the Jewish congregation were therefore doing business with women. The contract mentioned taxes and rents, and required the purchasers and their heirs to undertake "to preserve uniformity in the line of buildings." That is, they would have to be aligned with the residence of Larocque, who lived on the same street, which places the site in the St. Lawrence borough, between Lagauchetière and Chenneville streets, and bordered at the back by the Protestant cemetery. The price of the lots was £350 cash.[16]

A Subscription Campaign

Benjamin had been waiting for this signal to launch his subscription campaign, which he did in July 1835.[17] Not the type to stand idly by, he raised the hefty sum of £4,033 20s, £3,790 of which came from the community itself. David David's heirs did their part; David himself had left £400 to

There are at least three existing portrayals of this synagogue, including a print by James Duncan made in 1839. I also found a photograph of the building, which became a Presbyterian church in Chinatown. There is still a church on this site, the structure of which may be an adaptation of the synagogue opened in 1838. The Montreal basilica dated from the same era.

On 9 July 1835, Isaac Valentine, Moses Judah Hays, and Benjamin Hart circulated an official document announcing a subscription campaign: "Gentlemen, Resolution having been concurred in by a general meeting of the Israelites of Canada held in this city in January 1835 for the purpose of Establishing a Congregation and for the Erection of a suitable Edifice to be dedicated to the service of God." The signatories explained the terms of the subscription and reminded readers that the Israelite community in Montreal counted no more than fifty members, that work was already well advanced, and that the building would no doubt be completed by the new year.

List of Subscriptions towards the Erection of a Synagogue in Montreal, Lower Canada

	$	
Mrs Frances Michaels, Montreal	1000	
Legacy of the late D David Esq.	400	
The Executors of the late D David Esq. for the site of the old Synagogue	600	
Benjamin Hart Esq. Montreal	200	
Mrs Charlotte David	100	
Moses E David Esq.	100	
Mrs Henry Joseph	120	
Isaac Valentine Esq.	100	
Mrs Phœbe David Valentine	100	
Moses Judah Hays Esq.	100	
Mrs Abby Levy Hays	100	
Eleazar David David Esq.	100	
Aaron Hart David Esq.	100	
Mrs Cathrine Solomons	100	
Mrs Rachel Hoofstetter	50	
Jacob Joseph Esq.	40	
Mr Abraham Joseph	40	
Aaron Philip Hart Esq.	40	
Moses Hart Esq. Three Rivers	40	
Samuel B Hart Esq.	40	
Mr George Benjamin Montreal	20	
Mr Moses E David	20	
Charles E Levey Esq. Quebec	21	
Messrs A. W. Hart & Co. Toronto	40	
Messrs Hart, Brothers Kingston	20	
Mrs Widow Binley	40	
A. Samuels Esq. Miramichi	20	
Eshaile P Cohen Esq. Baltimore	30	
Mrs Frances Hays Cohen	50	
Samuel Hart Esq. London	60	
Moses Montefior Esq.	22	20
$	3833	20
From Moses E David Esq. Montreal for the Honor of placing the Corner Stone	200	
$	4033	20

Subscription campaign to support the construction of a new synagogue. Initiated mainly by Benjamin Hart, who had sharply criticized the heirs of Lazarus David, the campaign was a real success thanks, in fact, to the David family. Leading the campaign was Frances Michaels, the sister of the late David David. She contributed $1,000, which was added to the $400 provided in her brother's will. It is interesting to note the appearance of the dollar sign with two vertical bars (see p. 103). Their nephew, Moses Eleazer David, paid $200, which bought him the honour of laying the first stone. The first synagogue had been built on Rue Notre-Dame around 1777. A few years later, it was moved to Rue Chenneville thanks to this subscription campaign. For some time, I believed that the synagogue on Stanley dated from 1835; however, a report signed by Hays, Hart, and Valentine mentioned the purchase of a lot from a Mrs. Cotté (Côté). This was the site on rue Chenneville.

the community in his will; his sister, Frances, married to Myer Michaels, gave £1,000, and his nephew, Moses Eleazer David, had the honour of laying the first stone.[18] Benjamin was forced to swallow the malicious insinuations made in his address written in 1826. He paid £200, and the Hayses and Valentines also paid £200 each.

Benjamin managed to get £40 from his brother Moses, but nothing from Ezekiel, who had retreated into his shell. I believe that his struggles for equal rights had left scars. The confrontation between Aaron Philip and Ezekiel's sons (see chapter 6) created a deep division in the family. Nor did any of Ezekiel's sons contribute to Benjamin's fund. It may have been that Jews living in Trois-Rivières didn't care about a Montreal synagogue, but there may have been other reasons. More will be said about this at the end of this chapter. Distance alone did not deter Henry Joseph's widow, in Berthier, and her son, Abraham, from doing their part. Contributions came from Quebec City, Kingston, Toronto, and London. Moses Montefiore responded symbolically to the call.

Times were hard for everyone. The 1832 cholera epidemic was followed by another one in 1834. The House of Assembly and the governor were at loggerheads. A single spark would suffice to ignite hostilities: the Tories lit it. Only the taking up of arms by the Patriotes would make it possible to crush them militarily. It was in this extremely tense context that the Montreal Jews completed their project; on 25 August 1838, they proudly inaugurated their new synagogue. For several hours, Benjamin Hart and Moses Judah Hays forgot that they were justices of the peace[19] and gathered in memory of the founders of their community: Aaron Hart, Andrew Hays, Lazarus David, Ezekiel Solomon, Benjamin Lyons, Henry Joseph, and others.

New Jewish Immigrants

Moses Judah Hays was justifiably proud. He had steered the construction and development of the synagogue through the tumult of the street and the community. With a sense of accomplishment, he could return to his own affairs. In the ensuing years, without taking his eye off the congregation's activities, he attacked the problems of his aqueduct company: modifying water-transport conduits, installing a new pump, improving water hook-ups, extending the network, managing the service, and so on.[20] During this time, Benjamin was more concerned with his own advancement; no longer satisfied with his position as a justice of the peace, he highlighted his services rendered in the hope of an appointment. He continued to follow the community's affairs, but he had lost his influence. In July 1840, he resigned as administrator, then changed his mind and returned to his duties. In 1843, he resigned again.[21]

Building a synagogue was one thing, but operating it, recruiting a rabbi, managing the membership, revising the rules, and changing its name when the time came was another.[22] In 1840, the congregation welcomed a new member, David Piza, who agreed to become the rabbi. When he left, six years later, the administrators found an extraordinary man, Abraham De Sola.[23] Very quickly, he asked Moses Judah Hays to come to the assistance of the increasing numbers of totally helpless immigrants. Despite the difficult financial context at the time, Hays had managed to develop some daring projects. He built a large hotel and an adjacent theatre, which he rented to the government in 1849 after the fire at the Parliament.[24] These two buildings were destroyed by flames three years later during a gigantic fire that razed more than a thousand houses, many of which belonged to Hays. Ruined but not defeated, Hays took on a variety of roles. As municipal police chief starting in 1845, he was in a position to observe at first hand the misery of the immigrants. This led him and Rabbi De Sola to intensify their efforts, in particular with the Hebrew Philanthropic Society, "to help the unprecedentedly large number of Jewish immigrants who arrived in Montreal."[25]

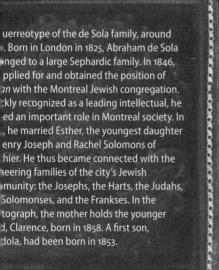

uerreotype of the de Sola family, around
. Born in London in 1825, Abraham de Sola
nged to a large Sephardic family. In 1846,
pplied for and obtained the position of
ın with the Montreal Jewish congregation.
:kly recognized as a leading intellectual, he
ed an important role in Montreal society. In
, he married Esther, the youngest daughter
enry Joseph and Rachel Solomons of
hier. He thus became connected with the
neering families of the city's Jewish
munity: the Josephs, the Harts, the Judahs,
Solomonses, and the Frankses. In the
tograph, the mother holds the younger
d, Clarence, born in 1858. A first son,
Jola, had been born in 1853.

This wood engraving is by John Henry Walker. There is some confusion about who is portrayed carrying the torch. As the Rebellion Losses Bill of 1837–38 had been sanctioned by Lord Elgin, some believed that the artist was portraying him. However, it is in fact LaFontaine, who was often identified by his forelock (see p. 210). LaFontaine had defended the Rebellion Losses Bill, which Walker interpreted metaphorically as having ignited the fuse, but he did not set fire to the Parliament building. Rather, he received serious threats. It is to be noted that by voting in the Rebellion Losses Bill, the parliamentarians of the United Canadas adopted a bill that followed on a similar one voted in Upper Canada before Union.

On 25 April 1849, the Parliament building was sacked and then set ablaze by rioters. Curiously, one version holds the French-speaking Canadiens responsible for the fire at the Parliament building. Gaston Deschênes, in his book *Une capital éphémère. Montréal et les événements tragiques de 1949*, published by Septentrion in 1999, provides much interesting information. Though the "English" had a reputation for being phlegmatic, in this case, some were hysterical. It was in fact the Tory members who fed the agitation that had been growing since February of that year. Those who were mainly responsible were "English," and some were later identified. For instance, Alfred Perry, the fire chief, later boasted about how he set fire to the building. Beyond the question of eventual compensation, a political climate reigned linked to measures favourable to the reformers' demands. The governor himself required a heavy escort to travel. Of course, I tried, unsuccessfully, to establish the role played by Moses Judah Hays in particular on that 25 April. In this painting, an unhappy fireman strains to pull a fire hose that has been cut.

A Schism on the Horizon

Benjamin Hart's path was different. He was both depressed and outraged. He was looking to make trouble, and he made it inside his congregation. He declared war on 19 May 1847.[26] Under the pretext of discussing the regulations, he claimed that there was a threat to both the German and Polish Congregation and his own congregation, which was being contaminated by an insidious invasion. Despite Rabbi De Sola's laudable efforts to "mak[e] the Service Respectable in the Spring," he wrote, "it is now again

Duncan Del.ᵗ   THEATRE ROYAL.   Christie Sculp.ᵗ

The summer of 1852 was particularly hot, and water supply was seriously deficient. The Carré Saint-Louis reservoir was empty, and the authorities took advantage of the drought to clean it. Firefighters had no water to fight fires. Hays had always feared such a situation. He had never hesitated to cut water supply to avoid emptying the reservoirs; he preferred to face the protests. Moses Judah Hays's theatre, burned to the ground in 1852, was replaced by the Theatre Royal built by Jesse Joseph (see p. 250).

"Moses Judah Hays," *Dictionary of Canadian Biography*, vol. 9. This very interesting biography by Carman Miller was extremely useful to me. However, I had difficulties with the date of appointment of Hays as chief of police. Rome gives this date as 1845, as do Godfrey and Godfrey, whereas Miller gives 1854 (no doubt an inversion of the numbers "4" and "5"). Léon Trépanier, the famous popular historian, notes that Hays had the longest mandate ever as Montreal chief of police (*CJA*, no. 20 [1981], p. 255). Hays died in 1861. The aqueduct system was sold to the municipality in 1845, and we know that Hays remained in the company's employment to ease the transition. Finally, Rome cites a report that refers, it seems, to the typhus epidemic of 1847, in which Hays was to play an important part (*CJA*, no. 20 [1981], pp. 255–560).

back to its old Vulgar Stand." Three or four members had been deprived of their right to vote, he claimed, because they did not live in the city, even though they had contributed to construction of the synagogue, and "at the same time you will admit a set of Strangers, who don't belong to us—to destroy our Congregation." He concluded that it would be an insult to the memory of Mrs. Michaels, who had been so generous, to thus place the synagogue in German hands. He predicted the worst.

On 1 June 1847, at the beginning of a meeting intended to examine draft regulations submitted to members on the preceding 13 April, Benjamin put

Abraham de Sola (1825–82) was the rabbi for the Shearith Israel synagogue from 1847 until his death. A cultured and educated man, he was intensely involved in the intellectual life of Montreal society. He wished to reconcile religion and science, and he lectured and wrote a great deal. In 1848, he began to give courses in Hebrew and rabbinical literature at McGill University; he was appointed a professor in 1853. Five years later, McGill University awarded him an honorary doctorate in law. As a rabbi, he was highly respected and appreciated. He constantly supported schools and charities. As part of his work with immigrants, he tried to bring Sephardim and Ashkenazim together by formulating common rites in the hope of encouraging members of the two Jewish traditions to unify.

his cards on the table. He contested the legality of the meeting and called the proposed regulations "repugnant and in direct violation of the Act 9 Vict. thereby placing all powers in the hands of the members." In his view, certain people were out to destroy the congregation—"men who are not Portuguese Jews but German and Polish Jews in violation of the law." He announced that he would bring this affair before the Court of Queen's Bench.

The chair acknowledged Hart's position but declared that the meeting was legal and decided to open discussion of the various proposed regulations. The session was stormy. Benjamin was constantly jumping up to object and demanding that votes be taken. Inevitably, the time came when he contested the right of a participant, a certain Samuel Lyons, to vote, and he demanded the cancellation of the vote taken during the meeting, which he claimed was illegal. Obstinately, he returned to the charge again and again. Finally, he offered a lengthy resolution that began, "B. Hart a Member and part Proprietor of the Montreal Portuguese Synagogue and Congregation—Objects and protests against the Chairman of the Unlawfully Meeting receiving the vote of Samuel Lyons . . . the said Lyons belongs to the German and Polish Jews . . . is not, not ever was a Portuguese Jew, never attended or belonged to a Portuguese Congregation nor acquainted with the form of prayer their Service or their Customs . . ."

The meeting continued. Benjamin, persisting with his interruptions, proposed amendments, many of them seconded by Abraham Joseph. According to the minutes, there were sixteen participants, at the beginning at least: Dr. A. H. David, chair;[27] Myer Solomons, secretary; Benjamin Hart, G. J. Ascher, Goodman Benjamin, M. Samuel David, William Benjamin, Simon Hart, Wolff Wenk, Jesse Joseph, Henry Solomons, Abraham Joseph, Samuel Benjamin, Adolphus Hart, Samuel Lyons, and John Levy. Many of the votes were close. At a given moment, the vote was seven to seven, and the chair "gave the casting vote." Levy and the Benjamins were also particularly vocal.

Three days later, at the request of Benjamin Hart, two notaries, John Helder Isaacson and E. Guy, went to the office of Dr. Aaron Hart David to explain their client's grievances. The gist was that "German and Polish Jews hav[e] no knowledge of the Portuguese language, prayers, customs,

These two illustrations are taken from *1847. Grosse-Île au fil des jours* by André Charbonneau and André Sévigny (Parcs Canada, 1997). In the top illustration, artist Bernard Duchesne portrays what he called "the waiting line of ships in quarantine at Grosse-Île." The bottom illustration is of "the hospital area of Grosse-Île before the construction of new shelters in 1847."

According to the emigration agent, Alexander C. Buchanan, a total of 98,649 people left for Quebec in 1847. Six out of seven immigrants were from Ireland. About eighteen percent (17,477) of the emigrants died during their voyage—on the ship, during quarantine, or on the island. Charbonneau and Sévigny add, "The Grosse-Île quarantine station was the site of extraordinary humanitarian action."

"Soon after the sale of the waterworks, [Moses Judah Hays] had opened an elegant hotel and theatre on his valuable property in Dalhousie Square," writes Carman Miller (DCB, vol. 9, 418–19). The "four-storey stone structure with a theatre in the back was administered by George F. Pope, the former manager of Donegana Hotel. Winter entertainment featured a German orchestra and Viennese dances."

After the burning of the Parliament building, of which he appears to have been a powerless observer, Moses Judah Hays rented his theatre to the authorities "for a six-month period for the price of £125 per month." Three years later, he was himself the victim of a terrible fire. His hotel and theatre situated on Dalhousie Square were swallowed in flames. The Saint-Denis street district was totally razed. James Duncan made both an extremely striking painting of the fire at Dalhousie Square showing the general confusion and a very restrained print portraying "the ruins of the great fire in Montreal, Rue Saint-Denis, near Bishop's Church, 1852."

or service nor have they or either of them contributed to the purchase of the ground upon which the synagogue and pastor house are built, or the building thereof." Everything had been financed by the few "Portuguese Jews in this city," who had lost control of their congregation "at the instance of the said president." In the future, Dr. David would have to refrain from such manoeuvres, or Benjamin Hart would issue a "writ of mandamus against the corporation."[28]

My sources are silent on the outcome of the quarrels started by Hart. It is likely that the terrible typhus epidemic that hit in the summer of 1847 diverted attention toward infinitely more serious problems. In his *Histoire populaire du Québec*,[29] Jacques Lacoursière summarizes the situation: according to a report by the Montreal emigration committee, out of the 100,000 immigrants who arrived in the colony by river, "5,293 died at sea;

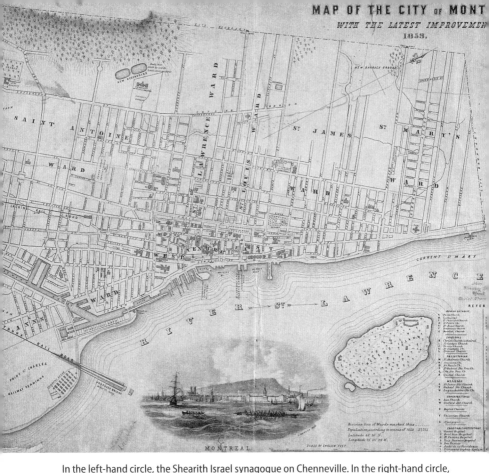

In the left-hand circle, the Shearith Israel synagogue on Chenneville. In the right-hand circle, the Shaar Hashomayim synagogue on Saint-Constant.

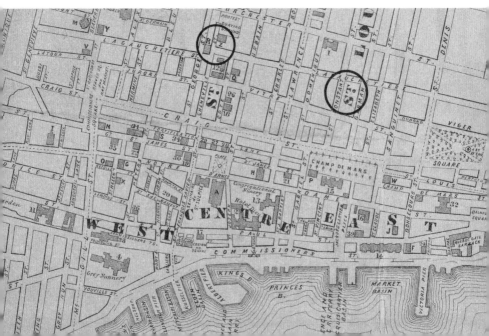

3,389 at Grosse-Île; 1,137 at Quebec City; 3,862 at Montreal; 130 at Lachine; 39 at Saint-Jean; total: 13,850 not including those who died in other parts of the country or once they reached either Upper Canada or the United States." The figure of 100,000 may surprise some readers. As the above suggests, these immigrants were headed not only for Canada, but also for the United States. The St. Lawrence was the gateway to North America for the poorest immigrants; the crossing was longer but less expensive, as the immigrants set sail on ships that were making a return trip after dropping off a cargo of wood. The figures vary from source to source. For instance, the *Canadian Encyclopedia* gives 9,232 deaths at sea and 5,424, at Grosse-Île. André Charbonneau and André Sévigny, who seem to me to be the most reliable sources, estimate that "about 18% (17,477) of the emigrants who set out for Quebec City (98,469) died during their voyage in 1847."[30]

David Rome quotes Moses Judah Hays who, as the person responsible for security, wrote a report in which he noted the extreme seriousness of the situation that he had to confront with the assistance of a small police force of forty-five people, half of whom had fallen ill. Hays wrote that he was lucky to have escaped the epidemic, while "so many of my co-labourers fell around me."[31] According to Rome, Hays also mentioned the devotion of public leaders and religious leaders of all denominations, particularly members of the Catholic hierarchy. The disease struck without pity: doctors, bureaucrats, hospital staff, and others. Dr. Aylwin, immigration agent Buchanan, and many others fell ill and recovered; as they had been in good health, they had a better chance of survival. However, immigration agent McEldery, for instance, succumbed.[32]

The years 1847, 1848, and 1849 were particularly difficult. Not only did the ships bring typhus, they brought news that rocked the business world. London had just opted for a free-trade policy. The "corn laws" that provided preferential tariffs for Canadian wheat were to be phased out. The British were to lose their monopoly on shipping, and Americans were to be free to compete with Canadians.

Going Broke

In 1848, the Montreal Savings Bank had difficulties that affected Hays's pocketbook. All indications are that Benjamin Hart was also caught up in a quagmire of bad business, for he declared bankruptcy in 1848 or early 1849.

We know this by the steps that his wife took in the courts to force him to respect the financial obligations set out in their marriage contract.*

Benjamin Hart had other problems. He apparently put an end to his battle with the congregation in order to concentrate on salvaging his business, which seems to have been an import-export concern. He was almost seventy years old, and he had to admit that he no longer had the energy and flexibility necessary to make the required adjustments. His morale was also sinking. The vote on the Rebellion Losses Bill was the last straw. In 1849, he joined the annexationist movement and, logically, he chose to end his days in the United States.

Benjamin's apprehensions about the progress made by the Ashkenazim were confirmed.** The historian Louis Rosenberg has estimated that the Jewish population in Canada was 154 in 1841; 451 in 1851, and 1,350 in 1861.[33] Who were the newcomers, and where did they come from?

I decided to consult the Jewish register from 1842 on. I noted the arrival of a Samuel Benjamin, who was elected a municipal councillor in 1849;[34] Samuel's brother, Goodman; members of the Moss family; Gottschalk Issac Asher; Wolf Monk; and others. Between 1850 and 1874, eighteen names were entered in the register, including Sternberg, Silverman, Hoffnung, Kortosk, Ollendorf, and Rubenstein. Among these were two "Portuguese Jews," as Benjamin Hart called them. In his view, "Portuguese" was synonymous with "Sephardic," and their rites did not fit well with the majority of the newcomers, who were clearly in the Ashkenazi tradition.

* This document, prepared for the Court of Bankruptcy for the District of Montreal, lists the living children: Frances (born 1807), Samuel Arthur Wellington (born 1813), Frederick Webber (born 1814), Jonathan Theodore (born 1816), Henry (born 1817), Benjamin Moses (born 1820), Emily Abigail (born 1822), Constance Hatton (born 1826), and Dorothea Catherine (born 1828). To this list must be added Aaron Philip, who may have been the oldest son and who died in 1843. Six other children apparently died in infancy: Henrietta (1808–09), Ephraim (1809–10), Helen (1819), Julia (1823), Reuben (1824–25), and a sixth, unidentified child. Six of Benjamin and Harriott Judith's children got married; they all emigrated to the United States. I found evidence of Frederick in Louisiana and of Wellington in Michigan and New York.

** In the congregation's minutes, there were nevertheless applications for admission in the ensuing months: David Nathan and Edward Moss in September 1847; Alex Levy, Isaac Jacobs, and Lawrence Moss in September 1848. The Benjamins, Aschers, and Wenks packed the meeting in June 1847. Pierre Anctil specifies that Benjamin was anxious about non-British Ashkenazim—that is, those of Eastern European origins.

THE SHAAR HASHOMAYIM SYNAGOGUE, MONTREAL

The Shaar Hashomayim synagogue inaugurated in 1922 at the corner of Kensington and the chemin de la Côte Saint-Antoine.

It should be noted that the synagogue has been modified considerably in recent years. It is the third Shaar Hashomayim Synagogue: the first was on rue Saint-Constant (1860) and the second was on McGill College (1886).

Just to the east, also on the chemin de la Côte Saint-Antoine, are two houses (168 and 178) built in about 1840 by Moses Judah Hays. On one house, an additional floor with a roof and attic was built and the stones on the front wall were covered with yellow stucco. In the beginning, these two houses were part of a group of four houses on the Terrasse Mecalfe.

Anne Joseph compiled all of the documents related to the Josephs and their relatives and presented the results of her research simply in chronological order. It is an easy book to use thanks to an extensive index.

One day, a woman named Anne Joseph contacted me. She wanted to publish a book on the Joseph family. Born into a Catholic family, she had been baptized Anne Evelyn Goulding. She had converted to Judaism before marrying Bill Joseph, who was a not-very-observant Jew. It was his third marriage. She was curious about his past, and about the Joseph family history; she decided to put together a short document about his family for his seventieth birthday. Bill was born in 1920, so the birthday celebration took place in 1990. Bill's five children found out, with a mixture of curiosity and pride, about their ancestry. Anne was in seventh heaven! She was hooked on this story and wanted to continue her research. Her enthusiasm was contagious. My colleague at the time, Marcelle Cinq-Mars, adopted Mrs. Joseph and vice versa. She compiled an extraordinary body of work, which she chose to present in chronological order. Marcelle, who is an excellent historian, was quite sceptical and wondered if I would go all the way with the project. As a start-up publisher, the investment seemed quite risky and the genre a bit limited. Here is the colophon of the 562-page tome titled *Heritage of a Patriarch: A Fresh Look at nine of Canada's Earliest Jewish Families* (Septentrion, 1995): "Typeset in Garamond 11/upon a page design developed by Marcelle Cinq-Mars/and Diane Trottier/printed in April 1995/ by Veilleux of Boucherville/to record The Heritage of a Patriarch/of which William Kenneth Joseph and Denis Vaugeois/are respectful heirs/ the first by blood as a direct descendant/the second by intellect through prolonged study of the Harts and/éditeur à l'enseigne du Septentrion."

The issues that Benjamin Hart raised were not without foundation, and the Ashkenazim did not wait to be shown the door. In September 1846, they formed the Congregation of English, German and Polish Jews, which became the Shaar Hashomayim Congregation; this congregation opened a magnificent synagogue on Rue Saint-Constant on 22 May 1860. Until that time, they had not had a place of worship. According to Arthur Daniel Hart, on 12 September 1858, at a large meeting held "in the rooms on Great St. James Street," a core group led by Louis Ollendorf, Solomon Silverman, C. Blankensen, and several others made the decision to provide their community with a synagogue. They immediately received subscriptions for $2,856.[35] The following month, they met again and created a council:

M. A. Ollendorf, president; Edward Himes, treasurer; A. Hoffnung, honorary secretary; and Lewis Anthony, *parnas*. They were authorized to acquire a plot of land on Rue Saint-Constant "for the exclusive religious use of German and Polish Jews, it being understood that this building or this land may never be put up for sale, except to reinvest the profits in a similar work."

One hundred years after the first Jews arrived in Lower Canada, both streams of Jewish tradition were well established in Montreal, but in very different ways. Had Benjamin Hart gotten his way? Perhaps. And yet an enigma persists. The product of a family from Germany, Aaron Hart was probably an Ashkenazi, which may explain why he was not a member of the Shearith Israel Congregation formed in December 1768 on the model of the Spanish and Portuguese Synagogue in New York.[36] This synagogue had adopted the Sephardic rite even though, it seems to me, most of its members were Ashkenazim.

None of Aaron's sons attended the Montreal synagogue until Benjamin, in a mysterious religious impulse, decided to throw his energy into it, breaking his family's tradition. He was timidly imitated by several Harts of the third generation, including Aaron Hart David, who was more under the influence of the Davids than the Harts, despite his given name.

History is full of unanswered questions.

מעשה המנרה מקשה זהב זה הוא על ירכה ער

ויעשה את המנרה וכמנורה אר

Conclusion

THE MOST STRIKING FACT about this first century of the Jewish presence in Quebec is no doubt the election of a Jewish representative to the House of Assembly of Lower Canada. Elected in 1807 in the riding of Trois-Rivières, Ezekiel Hart was never able to take his seat. His victory came at a bad time.

A parliamentary system had been instituted in 1791. The British prime minister, William Pitt the Younger, and his minister responsible for the colonies, Lord Grenville, felt that the time had come to give in to ever-stronger pressures in favour of a "chamber of representatives of the people indistinctly composed of old and new subjects of His Majesty freely elected by the inhabitants of the towns and countryside or parishes of the Province." These details, contained in a 1784 petition, were not in vain. The British merchants, among whom were not only Englishmen but also Scots, Huguenots, and several Jews, had demanded a House of Assembly immediately after the Treaty of Paris (1763). At first, they wanted a House under their control, so that they could dominate the conquered population and limit the governor's powers. Little by little, however, the tone of the petitions became more reasonable and the notion of according suffrage to Canadiens, who were designated as "new British subjects," was introduced.

The Tablet of Law and furnishings of the Temple

This book offers an opportunity to present the main symbols of Judaism. This parchment is from a Hebrew manuscript written by Salomon ben Raphael in May 1299. A verse taken from Numbers (8: VIII.4) forms the frame: "And this work of the candlestick was of beaten gold, unto the shaft thereof, unto the flowers thereof, was beaten work: according unto the pattern which the LORD had shewed Moses, so he made the candlestick." The menorah in the upper right is the perfect symbol for the continuity of Judaism. Portrayed with it are associated tools: chalices, ash shovels, candle snuffers, and stepladders. "Below, the vase in which the manna is kept is flanked by the flowered branch belonging to Aaron, Moses's brother, and the sterile branch of the elders" (Fellous, 208: 22). Those who studied, in their long-ago courses, a bit of religious history will remember that manna is the food sent miraculously to the Hebrews when they were crossing the Sinai Desert. In the left-hand column, two above on the Ark of the Covenant rest on the Tablets of Law on which are written the Ten Commandments, each represented here by its first word. Below, a pair of spoons tops two stacks of six moulds shown "in cross section to let their contents be seen: loaves of bread dedicated to the priests of the Temple, all placed on a table."

ANNO REGNI

GEORGII III.

R E G I S

MAGNÆ BRITANNIÆ FRANCIÆ ET HIBERNIÆ

TRICESIMO PRIMO.

Au Parlément commencé et tenu à *Weftminfter*, le Vingt-cinquième jour de Novembre, l'an de notre Seigneur 1790, et dans la Trente-unième année du Règne de notre Souverain Seigneur GEORGE Trois, par la grace de DIEU, Roi de la *Grande Bretagne*, de *France* et d'*Irlande*, Défenfeur de la Foi, *&c.* étant la première Seffion du dix-feptième Parlement de la *Grande Bretagne*.

A · Q U E B E C:
IMPRIMÉ PAR GUILLAUME VONDENVELDEN,
IMPRIMEUR DE LOIX DE SA TRÈS EXCELLENTE MAJESTÉ LE ROI,
M.DCC.XCVII.

Petitions for a House of Assembly

In 1764, Eleazar Levy and twenty other Quebec merchants signed a petition. Around 1770, a petition signed by thirty merchants was presented for a House of Assembly. Aaron Hart signed it. A few years later, Samuel Jacobs, Levy Solomons, and Ezekiel Solomons put their names to another petition with 100 signatures. After 1774, some 200 people demanded the abrogation of the Quebec Act, which maintained French civil law, the seigneurial regime, and certain privileges of the Catholic Church. Among those signing were Samuel Jacobs, Simon Levy, Mesach Levy, Andrew Hays, David S. Franks, Ezekiel Solomons, Isaac Judah, Lazarus David, Aaron Hart, and Levy Solomons. Most of these names reappeared on the major petition of 1784, along with some new ones, including Aaron Hart's oldest sons, Moses and Ezekiel Hart, and his brother-in-law, Uriah Judah, as well as Elias Solomon, John Franks, Abraham Hart, Isaac H. Abrams, and Hyam Myers. Thus, twenty or so Jewish subjects were seriously involved in public affairs.

Finally, the "British" petitioners conceded that Canadiens might be elected, but not in urban ridings, where business that Canadiens didn't understand took place, as they told each other in private. Then, all of these conditions were dropped. Among the "new subjects," voices were heard in favour of

This is the royal coat of arms of British sovereigns. King Richard I had chosen "Dieu et mon droit" as a motto to signify that he held his title of Sole God. As for the motto "Honni soit qui mal y pense," the history is charming. The Countess of Salisbury was said to have lost her garter while dancing; King Edward immediately picked it up to place the blue ribbon around his own knee. The rest, I leave to your imagination.

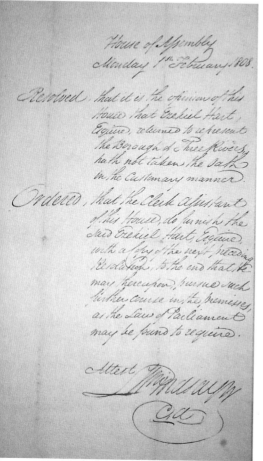

The creation of parliamentary institutions was widely celebrated. The artist François Baillairgé, given responsibility for designing the mace for the House, gave free rein to his enthusiasm at the beginning of his personal diary for 1792: "The new bil of quebec or rather the amendment of the old one was put in force last 26 December. It gives us a house of assembly and divides the province into two governments those of upper and lower Canada, but in quebec will reside the main authority in the governor general to which the one in upper Canada will report and 1792 is the first free year of the country."

The Harts were among the signatories of the numerous petitions that led to this big day. In 1796, Moses thought about running for office in William Henry (Sorel). The stature of the candidate Jonathan Sewell and the warnings of his father dissuaded him. After Aaron Hart's death, his sons decided to run on the first occasion. The opportunity was the general election of 1804. Defeated, Ezekiel took advantage of the death of member John Lees to try his luck again. He was successful this time, but his father's doubts were to be confirmed.

On 1 February 1808, the clerk of the House, W. Lindsay, made it known that Ezekiel "hath not taken the oath to the customary manner." This question of the wording of the oath would be debated for years. On the Internet, I found an article published in *The Jurist* (vol. 15, part, 26 July 1851) in which there is still discussion of "the right of a Jew to take the abjuration oath without the words upon the true faith of a Christian. . . . The persons referred to shall take the 'oath hereinafter mentioned' words which, in plain English, mean the oaths set forth, and no others." The author adds that it would take great tact to find an argument that would allow the wording of the oath to be set aside. In London, the debate resurfaced with the election of Lionel Nathan de Rothschild, in 1847. The House of Commons had voted in a statute to circumvent the difficulty posed by the wording of the oath, but the House of Lords rejected it. In 1850, Rothschild was elected again, and this time he asked to take the oath on the Old Testament rather than on the Bible. This wish was granted, but the wording of the oath was retained. In 1858, both chambers were allowed to decide on the wording of its own oath. Rothschild took the oath with his head covered and said in Hebrew the words that suited him for "So help me God." He was finally able to take his seat.

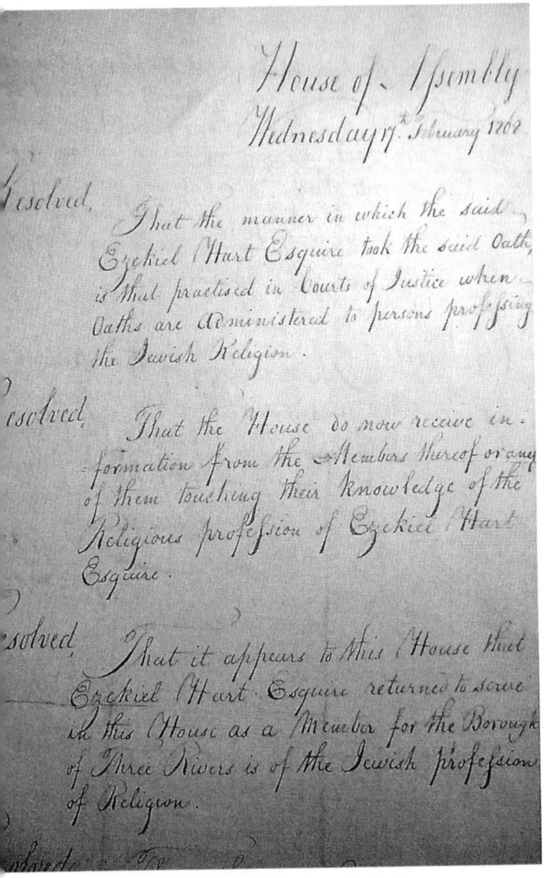

[Handwritten document on left:]

House of Assembly
Wednesday 17ᵗʰ February 1808

Resolved, That the manner in which the said Ezekiel Hart Esquire took the said Oath, is that practised in Courts of Justice when any Oaths are administered to persons professing the Jewish Religion.

Resolved, That the House do now receive information from the Members thereof or any of them touching their knowledge of the Religious profession of Ezekiel Hart Esquire.

Resolved, That it appears to this House that Ezekiel Hart Esquire returned to serve in this House as a Member for the Borough of Three Rivers is of the Jewish profession of Religion.

Resolved, ...

Contrary to popular opinion, Lionel Nathan Rothschild was not the first Jew to sit in the House of Commons. His cousin David Solomons could technically claim this honour. Elected in 1851, after a number of attempts, Solomons pronounced his oath omitting the words "on the true faith of a Christian." He participated in three votes before the question was raised. The debate became complicated when some claimed that not only had he not taken the oath "in the form appointed by law," but in any case a Jew could not be a member of a parliament in the British Empire, a "Christian nation." Things went bad for Solomons, who was sentenced to pay fines. He was to return to Parliament in 1859 and sit at Rothschild's side; however, he was a very active MP, whereas Rothschild abstained from all discourse during his fifteen years in Parliament.

There is no doubt that Ezekiel had been a precursor. He was very aware of it, and his father had clearly had the intuition of the inevitable debates to come.

On 17 February 1808, the House examined the Hart case, establishing that he was "of the Jewish Profession of Religion." The question was raised to introduce a distinction between the requirements of the courts and those of Parliament. Hart "took the said oath is that practiced in Courts of Justice when oaths are administered to persons professing the Jewish Religion."

Justice Foucher "added that as a Judge, he knew the said Hart to be a Jew, as he had lately in person pleaded before him for certain privileges to which he conceived he had a right to wit that of not being summoned to appear in the Courts of Justice on Saturday, it being his Sabbath day and that of the Jews." Deposition made by W. Lindsay.

free elections and the creation of parliamentary institutions. The evolution occurred gradually; it took some twenty years to reach a consensus that brought together "old" and "new" subjects—contrary to the myth perpetrated by some, such as the intellectual Pierre-Elliott Trudeau, that democracy had been imposed on the Canadiens. This may have been ignorance or bad faith—or a mixture of the two—on Trudeau's part, and on the part of a certain English Canadian historiographic current that gave rise to the image of Quebec as a "priest-ridden society" that kept democratic principles at bay.

The independence of the United States[1] had forced the authorities in London to pause and reflect, and the Loyalist refugees accustomed to a parliamentary regime in the Thirteen Colonies increased the pressure to create an elected House, although they demanded a "separate district" in which English-language subjects would be in the majority. They were the first separatists! In response, in 1791 London gave in and passed the Constitutional Act, which divided the "Province of Quebec" resulting from the Conquest into Upper and Lower Canada, and it announced the creation of a House of Assembly and then the formation of a Legislative Council and an Executive Council for each of the Canadas.[2]

This separation into two Canadas ensured the "English" (many of them Loyalists) of a majority in Upper Canada, and the Canadiens of a majority in Lower Canada, where they elected an average of thirty-five members out of fifty, at least in the early years of the parliamentary regime. The members had to learn about how parliamentarianism works; they quickly understood that, logically, they could vote in laws and control the budget. Theoretically, this is still true today. Theoretically.

Pitt and Grenville showed much optimism by granting such powers to the conquered of 1760. In the early sessions, the vote was divided along ethnic lines on questions as innocuous as assistance for the poor, the homeless, and families; regulations regarding roads, bridges, and courts; and bills respecting transportation, customs duty, permits, and trade. Finally, each side founded a newspaper to explain and promote its interests. The *Mercury* was founded in 1805; *Le Canadien*, the following year. By 1807, it seemed that just about every parliamentary motion led to confrontation.

Ezekiel Hart had studied in the United States and his native tongue was English. Although he was elected by a French Catholic population, he was perceived as a potential member of the British Tory Party. His manner of taking the oath of office was a pretext for keeping him from taking his seat both in 1807 and when he was re-elected the following year. The prediction by his father, Aaron Hart, seemed to be coming true: "You will be opposed as a Jew."

"Citizens of No Country"

Embarrassed by the debate that had taken place over the election of Ezekiel Hart, Pierre Bédard, the leader of the Parti canadien, at first was silent. He took to his books and, several weeks later, came to some sad conclusions. In *Le Canadien*, on 2 March 1808, he was quoted as saying, "The Jews themselves wanted to be citizens of no country." He continued, "They were waiting for the Messiah, their Prince, and while they waited they could not give their loyalty to any other Prince but the one for whom they were reserving themselves." It was not his best speech, and he had not yet gotten to know the Harts of Trois-Rivières. The Hart family had more than become citizens of a country!

Imprisoned during the tumult that surrounded the mandate of Governor Craig, including the Hart affair, Bédard had ample time (more than a year) to reflect and gather documentation on the situation of Jews in the world, and particularly in England. He was not surprised to find that London had stood behind the members who had kept Ezekiel Hart from taking his seat in the House. Lord Castlereagh, the Secretary of State for the Colonies, had confirmed that Jews were not eligible. Bédard must have wondered what would have happened if Hart had sided with his party, if he had voted in favour of its candidate for Speaker of the House, Jean-Antoine Panet? Hart was a strange character, Bédard thought. What would his party's position have been then? After all, the second time he was in the House, in 1809, Hart had changed his attitude regarding the vote prescribed by tradition. The Canadiens would have then had no reason to exclude him; they had no prejudices against Jews; they simply saw them as foreigners who were slowly becoming part of the family.

What did this statement to the effect that Jews were "citizens of no country"

The mace was essential to the work of the House of Assembly. It represented royal power; today, this power is conferred upon members. The sergeant at arms brings the mace to the opening of each session. The Web site the Assemblée nationale du Québec notes, "The . . . mace is also a symbol of the power of the Assembly to protect its constitutional rights and those of the MNAs from external threat, a responsibility conferred upon the Sergeant at Arms." On 8 May 1984, René Jalbert, the sergeant at arms at the time and himself a former soldier, managed to subdue Corporal Denis Lortie, who went on a shooting spree in the throughout the Parliament.

refer to? Obviously, Bédard had read it somewhere. He was rubbing up against the legend of the wandering Jew.

Pierre Bédard Facing Reality

Soon after he left prison, Pierre Bédard was appointed a magistrate in Trois-Rivières. When he arrived in his judicial district, in 1812, he immediately realized how important the Harts were. The ancestor, Aaron Hart, had settled in. He had clearly become the "citizen of a country." His oldest son, Moses, was well established in this small town and the nearby fiefs. Ezekiel, a member of the House for one day, had inherited the Bécancour seigneury facing Trois-Rivières. The family ran the town. Apparently, a powerful dynasty was taking shape.

Bédard had barely unpacked his boxes when he witnessed an unexpected conflict: Thomas Coffin, a militia officer and important figure, refused to admit Benjamin Hart into his self-styled battalion because he didn't want to offend the population in general, and Catholics in particular. Coffin was obsessed by the Harts. Of course, Benjamin, who was a scrappy fellow, openly protested and even gained the support of the vicar, F. Noiseux, and Justice Louis Foucher, who had run against Benjamin's brother Ezekiel in 1807–08. In a memorandum that was made public, Benjamin emphasized that the question of religion could not be used since Isaac Phineas, of Louiseville (Rivière-du-Loup), had just been appointed an ensign by Coffin.[3] On 26 August 1812, a petition signed by forty-seven people backed Benjamin Hart: "We the undersigned certify that we have no objection or repugnance to serve in the militia with Mr. Benjamin Hart either as officer or otherwise." Thirty-five of the signatories were Canadiens, French speaking and Catholic.

Coffin refused to budge, and Benjamin joined a Montreal battalion. At first a simple soldier, he quickly rose to the rank of lieutenant, and then lieutenant-colonel. During this time, Coffin, to show off his power, integrated Ezekiel into his own battalion. To my knowledge, throughout this dispute, the word "Jew" was never used, although both sides alluded indirectly to Benjamin Hart's religion.

Jews had been settled in the St. Lawrence Valley for exactly half a century. Although, at the time of the American invasion of 1775, some had sympathized with the American rebels, they presented a united front in defending the British Crown during the War of 1812. When it came to the rebellion of 1837, however, they were once again divided. Some were sympathetic to the Patriotes, whereas others stood with the Tories. In short, little by little, the Jews of Lower Canada adapted, integrated, and went their own ways.

The Absence of Prejudices against Jews

At the beginning of this book, I quoted a hasty judgment by Dr. Jacob Rader Marcus denouncing "a great deal of anti-Jewish sentiment" that he thought Aaron Hart had encountered during his forty years in Trois-Rivières, suffering the insults of frustrated, drunken individuals and the mistrust of the local aristocracy. In his assessment of my master's thesis, Marcus was critical of my nationalism. And yet, nationalism raised its ugly head in his own work. Where did he find this "anti-Jewish sentiment"? I searched long and hard for it, in vain. And that, in fact, was the reality of "Canadian" Jews: there was not an ounce of anti-Jewish sentiment around them.

Aaron Hart snapped up seigneuries* and dominated local commerce. The Canadiens resigned themselves to the fact. His son Ezekiel solicited their support; they voted for him, but he voted against them. His other son Moses acted scandalously: he dragged people into court on any pretext; he openly criticized their religion and laws; he attacked their language and insisted on using English. Benjamin played the heavy during the rebellion, and it was at this time that I found a report of a plot against Jews, hatched by a certain Joseph Bourdon—a plot that was lost in the swath of silence created by the execution of the Patriotes.

Rather than "anti-Jewish sentiment," all doors were open to Jews, including those of the Catholic Church and, it seems, the Anglican Church. In fact, the real problem of the Jews of that time, and perhaps of all times, was their indifference to religion or their conversion, often for the purpose of marriage.

---

* Chevalier de Niverville and Chevalier de Tonnancour had to give up their land. The Conquest did its work. Aaron Hart was as much one of its artisans as were William Grant and Malcolm Fraser. In one sense, Aaron was a victim of the circumstances that led him to play the role of the local moneylender. He didn't need to do this to be successful. He supplied arms to the competitors of Valdombre, Claude-Henri Grignon and his son, Séraphin. The parallel was inevitable, and it tripped up the authors Laurendeau, Douville, and even Tessier.

Choosing a Title for This Book

I thought long and hard about an appropriately descriptive title for this book. I considered "A Hundred Years of Jewish Presence" with "The Saga of the Harts" as a subtitle. The main story of the book is clearly about the Hart Family, but I wanted to set it against the background of the history of Quebec and the broader background of North America. The traditional reference points are not well known to the general public.[4]

The key moments of the history of the Jews in Quebec have been integrated into this historical overview. I wanted to place the Harts within a wider context by describing their relationships with the Judahs, Josephs, Davids, Solomonses, Hayses, Levys, Franks, Jacobs, and other Jewish families. One might think that the ties woven among the first Jewish families in North America would not be a surprise, but it was a surprise to me. Perhaps a good subtitle would have been "A Close-knit Community."

Of course, another common expression came to mind: "promised land." This title has often been used, including by the wonderful Israeli film director Amos Gitai. I had already given a very popular title to one of my books, *America,* but I am not certain that it was a good idea. And then my publisher would have an opinion; what would his reaction be to "Quebec, the Promised Land: A Hundred Years of Jewish Presence." "New Land," "Host Land," "Land of the Future." I liked the last one. Quebec was indeed a land of the future for the Jews. The hundred years described in this book provide an abundant illustration of this. The only problem that they encountered, I repeat, was the absence of prejudice against them. Had not new waves of immigrants arrived starting in the mid-nineteenth century, the Jewish pioneers of Quebec might have become French Catholics or English Protestants.

Survival

Ezekiel Moses Hart, one of the founders of the Séminaire de Trois-Rivières, was perceived as a Catholic Canadien, even though he was the natural son of Moses Hart, a non practising Jew and impenitent philanderer. His fellow citizens saw Ezekiel Moses Hart as the husband of Marie-Joséphine-Domithilde Pothier, member of an honourable Trois-Rivières family. He was baptized and married in the cathedral. His children, of course, went to French Catholic schools, including the Ursuline convent. In chapter 10,

I mentioned a number of similar cases, whence the question of survival for Jewish families of the time.

It is a more delicate matter to give contemporary examples. In the introduction, I mentioned Suzanne Houde, who was a descendant of Moses Hart's. She had no idea. When I told her about her family's wealth, she was pensive. What had she been told by her father, Frédérick Houde, who fashioned himself after a French movie star with a scarf flung around his neck and a convertible to tool around in? Affable and elegant, he had married a remarkable woman and they had five daughters and two sons. Frédérick liked to say that his best heirloom was his daughters. And he was right. The heirloom left by Moses—his son Areli Blake, and his daughters Amelia Henrietta Hart, who married C. M. Perry, and Caroline Emma Perry, who married Ernest Houde—was among the family's best-kept secrets.

I have also mentioned René Hart, the son of Jos Hart, also a descendant of Moses Hart. René married Fleurette Carrier. His mother was Éva Hamel; his grandmother, Marie-Louise Brûlé. Unlike Frédérick Houde, René Hart was interested in his ancestry. In his case, there was no financial estate but a vague cultural heritage, at least a real curiosity. Before he died, René had begun a return to Judaism.

A number of Hart descendants whom I met told me that they were not certain they would find pride in their ancestors. Finding out that they were Jewish by ancestry surprised people who had for so long thought they were "old-stock Quebecers," but knowing that Moses Hart was their forebear was too much for some of them. All the same, the curiosity was there, and the pride not far behind. Why not? Perhaps also "old-stock Quebecer" is itself a misnomer. In fact, research on the Hart family and their descendants complements other vast areas of research showing that French Canada has always been a melting pot since Champlain arrived. People could very well be "French Canadian" and also have Aboriginal, Irish, Scottish, German, Arab, African, Italian, or Jewish ancestors, or some of each.

One day, I took the Israeli consul to the archives at the Séminaire de Trois-Rivières. René Hart came with us, and a photograph was published in the local daily, *Le Nouvelliste*. Someone wrote me soon afterward that if I wanted to present true descendants of the Harts, there were better examples to be had than René Hart. The letter was unsigned.

What Became of the Harts?

An essential question arises: what became of this extraordinary family? Quebec demographers are accustomed to pioneers with many descendants. In *Naissance d'une population*, published by the Presses universitaires de France in 1987, Hubert Charbonneau and his colleagues at the department of demographic studies at the Université de Montréal came up with impressive figures. By 1729—that is, in less than a century after they had arrived— Jean Guyon (Dion), Zacharie Cloutier, Jacques Archambault, Marin Boucher, and Noël Langlois left, respectively, 2,150, 2,090, 1,825, 1,454, and 1,388 descendants. Aaron Hart and Dorothea Judah were similarly prolific. At least eight children survived them, and each also had a large family.

Almost all of Moses's children were born out of wedlock. Some converted to Catholicism; others disappeared without a trace. Alexander Thomas, although his mother wasn't Jewish, left a Jewish branch of the family thanks to the religion of his wife, Miriam Judah. The case of the children of Ezekiel and of Frances Lazarus is exemplary of the fate of Aaron's descendants. Seven children survived them: four sons and three daughters. The daughters remained single except for Esther's short relationship with Justice Vallières de Saint-Réal. Two of the sons married cousins: Aaron Ezekiel married Phoebe David, the daughter of his aunt Sarah, the wife of Samuel David, and Adolphus Mordecai married Constance Hatton Hart, one of his uncle Benjamin's daughters. The oldest son of Ezekiel and Frances, Samuel Bécancour, died in 1859, and Ira Craig in 1883; both were single. The observation is obvious: the Harts had trouble finding spouses in their religion; the pool of cousins had its limits. Benjamin's many children went to the United States; Alexander's branch ended with the third generation.

That said, Aaron and Dorothea are the ancestors of hundreds of people, but very few of them were, or are, Jewish by religion or tradition. Although it is a little-known fact, Quebec was definitely a melting-pot.[5]

Posterity

Aaron Hart dispossessed the most influential people in Trois-Rivières. De Niverville and de Tonnancour fell on the field of honour. Both could have given a course titled "Conquest 101."

In the third generation, the Harts were divided between business and law, between loyalty to their origins and assimilation. The memory of the

The Star of David and the coat of arms of the kings of England can be found on this sword signed by someone named Troved and adorned with many motifs. This object deserves the final word. On it appear loyalty to the king and attachment to Judaism. It may have belonged to Ezekiel Hart, who, despite his bitter political aftertaste, fought with determination a fight that would take another fifty years to be resolved in the British Parliament.

Harts remained, fragile but still as present—if not more so—as that of their contemporaries.

The best tribute to this family was made by the editors of the *Dictionary of Canadian Biography*. Three generations of Harts are written about in that work—Aaron, three of his sons, and three of his grandsons—which is absolutely exceptional. All Jewish encyclopedias have an entry on Aaron Hart.

In Trois-Rivières, two historical plaques are devoted to Ezekiel Hart—appropriately enough, on Rue Hart.

There are dozens of Jewish pioneers who should interest researchers. They were found in every field of human activity. They were not all in business, they were not all wealthy, but many of them were bold and innovative. John Franks, chimney inspector, was one of them. He was an exceptional person, a multifaceted man. Moses Judah Hays was another remarkable entrepreneur, who helped to shape the face of Montreal. New waves of immigration would bring to the shores of the St. Lawrence people such as the painter William Raphael and the engineer Sigismund Mohr, my favourites![6] These are people who also made Quebec.

Beyond the Hart family, this first century of Jewish presence is an opportunity to discover Quebec as a wonderful land of welcome. The dramas are few and far between—so much so that for some intellectuals these pages of history will be quite dull. My objective was to demonstrate that there is more of interest than meets the eye.

Notes

Introduction

1. The historian Maurice Séguin wrote of a fifteenth colony, Nova Scotia, which had already been added to the original thirteen colonies.

2. Jacob Rader Marcus, *Early American Jewry: The Jews of New York, New England, and Canada, 1649–1794* (Philadelphia: Jewish Publication Society of America, 1951), p. 275. About Aaron's warning, S. J. Godfrey and J. C. Godfrey propose an explanation in *Search Out the Land* (Montreal: McGill-Queens University Press, 1995), p. 324, note 1.

3. Immediately after the English victory in 1760, the French-speaking inhabitants of Canada were still "Canadiens." "In 1763," writes the historian G. Frégault (*Histoire du Canada par les textes* [Montreal: Fides, 1963], 15, our translation), "there were still Canadians, but there was no longer a Canada." When the British started calling themselves Canadians some seventy years later, they began calling the *Canadiens* French Canadians.

4. Albert Tessier, *Souvenir en vrac* (Trois-Rivières: Éditions du Boréal Express, 1974), pp. 171–72. Quotations from this work are our translation.

5. The collection was acquired in 1934 from the lawyer Édouard Bureau, son of Senator Jacques Bureau (1860–1933) and grandson of Joseph-Napoléon Bureau (1827–97), who had been one of the Harts' lawyers. When his father died, Édouard inherited the Hart papers and handed them on to Father Tessier. Curiously, the Hart collection contains no document concerning Joseph-Napoléon Bureau, who was a very active politician and a man of initiative. A one-time journalist and printer, he helped to relaunch *L'Ère nouvelle*, a Trois-Rivières district newspaper, in 1884.

6. *Bulletin des recherches historiques*, vol. 51 (1945), 47–50 (quotation our translation).

7. Arlette Corcos, *Montréal, les Juifs et l'école* (Sillery: Septentrion, 1997), pp. 75–113.

8. Jean-François Nadeau, *Adrien Arcand, Führer canadien* (Montreal: Lux, 2010), pp. 91–95.

9. Ibid., p. 95 (our translation).

10. Vaugeois, *Les Juifs et la Nouvelle-France* (Trois-Rivières: Boréal Express, 1968), p. 39 (our translation).

11. Raymond Aron, "De Gaulle, Israël et les Juifs," *L'Express*, no. 874 (18–24 March 1968), 47 (our translation). Also in 1968, Aron published a book with the same title with Plon.

12. See note 1.

13. With the abolition of the seigneurial system in 1854, the seigneurs were compensated. Those under the seigneur were no longer subordinated to the seigneurs, but they had to pay the price of their land and this gave rise to seigneurial rents paid to the former seigneur or to a moneylender.

14. Raymond Douville, *Aaron Hart. Récit historique* (Trois-Rivières: Le Bien public, 1938), p. 9 (our translation).

15. Denis Vaugeois, "Aaron Hart," *Dictionary of Canadian Biography*, vol. 4.

16. Ibid.

17. No doubt the daughter of Emanuel Manuel, who had married Dorothea's sister.

18. Douville, *Aaron Hart*, p. 98, our translation.

19. Ibid., p. 99, our translation.

20. Ibid., p. 168, our translation.

21. Ibid., p. 136, our translation.
22. David Rome, comp., "On the Early Harts, Part I," CJA, new series no. 15 (1980), p. 72.
23. *Le Bien public,* 16 February and 13 April 1939.
24. *Action nationale,* vol. 13 (1939), p. 271–72 (our translation).
25. "Les opinions politiques et religieuses de Moses Hart," *Les Cahiers des Dix* (1952), 137–51.
26. "Les années de jeunesse et vie familiale de Moses Hart," *Les Cahiers des Dix* (1958), 195–216 (our translation).
27. Ibid., p. 196–97 (our translation).
28. Denis Vaugeois, "Sigismund Mohr," DCB, vol. 12.

CHAPTER I
The Arrival of Aaron Hart: A Dynasty Is Born
1. See Raymonde Litalien, Jean-François Palomino, and Denis Vaugeois, *Mapping a Continent: Historical Atlas of North America, 1492–1814,* translated by Käthe Roth (Montreal and Quebec City: McGill-Queens University Press and Septentrion, 2007), pp. 27-32.
2. McCord Museum, McGill University, Hart papers, M 18642.
3. Jacob Rader Marcus, *Early American Jewry: The Jews of New York, New England and Canada, 1649–1794* (Philadelphia: Jewish Publication Society of America, 1951), p. 24.
4. I know very little about these men, although this price list led me to discover an error committed by the Supreme Court of Canada in accepting a modified version of the safe-conduct given by General James Murray to the chief of the Huron tribe of Lorette on 8 September 1760. On the document printed in 1752, the "long s," a normal typographic character for the period, is used. But this character was not used in Murray's document presented to the Supreme Court. Only one conclusion is possible: the printed version of this document was made later. I proved this in another book; the subsequent discovery of the original confirmed that my proof was valid. See Denis Vaugeois, *The End of the French-Indian Alliance,* translated by Käthe Roth (Sillery: Septentrion, 2001).
5. Marcus, *Early American Jewry,* p. 73.
6. Benjamin Sack, *History of the Jews in Canada* (Montreal: Canadian Jewish Congress, 1945), p. 51.
7. Douglas Borthwick, *History and Biographical Gazetteer of Montreal* (Montreal, 1892), p. 475.
8. Martin Wolff, *The Jews of Canada* (New York, 1926), p. 156.
9. Anne Joseph, *Heritage of a Patriarch* (Sillery: Septentrion, 1995), p. 387.
10. See Denis Vaugeois, *Les Juifs et la Nouvelle-France* (Trois-Rivières: Boréal Express, 1968), pp. 107–16.
11. Douville, *Aaron Hart, récit historique* (Trois-Rivières: Éditions du Bien public, 1938), pp. 12–13.
12. Ibid., p. 13.
13. Michel Solomon, *Aaron Hart, sieur de Bécancour* (Montreal: Humanitas nouvelle optique, 1992).
14. Ibid., pp. 108, 126.
15. Irving Abella, *The Coat of Many Colours: Two Centuries of Jewish Life in Canada* (Toronto: Lester & Orpen Dennys, 1990), p. 15. The author reproduced the miniature as portraying Aaron Hart.
16. Two painters had offered their services. William Berczy wrote to his wife from Quebec on 18 August 1808, "Mr. Hart of Trois-Rivières, who I saw here last Sunday, also asked me

to spend some time with him upon my return to Montreal to make a portrait of his wife and of him" (RAPQ, 1940–41, p. 42 [our translation]). In the Hart archive (0009-B-f), there is a letter from portraitist Gerome Fassio responding to a letter that he had received. He proposes to go to Trois-Rivières and offer his services to the family, and he asks about the number of members.

17. A number of years ago, Jacques Lacoursière transcribed on a typewriter various files in the Ursuline nuns' archives, including this letter by Adolphus Mordecai Hart. During a more recent visit to the Ursuline nuns, the archivist Claude Jutras was not able to find the letter or the nun's notes.

18. Gerald Ephraim Hart, *The Fall of New France, 1755-1760* (Toronto and New York: W. Drysdale & Co., R. W. Douglas, and G. P. Putnam's Sons, 1888), pp. 141–47.

19. Ibid., p. 147.

20. Vaugeois, *Les Juifs*, pp. 87–94.

21. David S. Jones, *Rationalizing Epidemics: Meanings and Uses of American Indian Mortality since 1600* (Cambridge: Harvard University Press, 2004), 95–98. Parkman was the first to bring to light Amherst's "detestable suggestion" to Bouquet. Only recently has the Trent-Ecuyer affair really been brought to light. Parkman had indicated, in a footnote, that the captain had reported the appearance of a smallpox epidemic around Fort Pitt in July 1763. Jones took up this information and uncovered the horror of this tactic designed to "extirpate this Execrable Race." Parkman's references are in *The Conspiracy of Pontiac*, 1899, vol. 1, 42–47.

22. Quoted in David S. Jones, *Rationalizing Epidemics: Meanings and Uses of American Indian Mortality since 1600* (Cambridge: Harvard University Press, 2004), p. 97, ref. P. 255.

23. Vaugeois, *Les Juifs*, p. 97.

24. Sheldon J. Godfrey and Judith C. Godfrey, *Search Out the Land: The Jews and the Growth of Equality in British Colonial America* (Montreal: McGill-Queens University Press, 1995), p. 82.

25. DC, 1911, p. 140 (our translation).

26. Ibid., p. 45-46 (our translation).

27. Ibid., p. 142 (our translation).

28. Godfrey and Godfrey, *Search Out the Land*, pp. 283–84; see also Vaugeois, *Les Juifs*, pp. 138–39.

29. Godfrey and Godfrey, *Search Out the Land*, p. 133.

30. DC, 1911, p. 52.

CHAPTER 2

"The Little Jew of Trois-Rivières": Secrets to Success

1. In an entertaining novel, *Fort sauvage* (Pantin: Le Castor astral, 1996), Claude Beausoleil speculates on what might have happened if a French resistance movement had been combined with an Indian revolt.

2. One was called "the battle of the Plains of Abraham"; the other, the "battle of Sainte-Foy." Both took place at more or less the same spot. The battle of the Plains of Abraham, on 13 September, has gone down in history as the more significant. The historian Guy Frégault (*La Guerre de la Conquête* (Montreal: Fides, 1955, p. 343), however, has called it the "day of errors" (our translation). On the strictly military level, there were two important battles in Quebec in 1759–60, one at Montmorency in late July of 1759 and the battle of Sainte-Foy in the spring of 1760, both won by French and Canadien troops with Lévis second in command to Montcalm at the former and commander at the latter.

3. Haldimand replaced Burton from May 1762 to March 1763.

4. FC 411, H159 A4 (our translation).

5. Raymond Douville, *Aaron Hart, récit historique* (Trois-Rivières: Éditions du Bien public, 1938), p. 24–25; Denis Vaugeois, *Les Juifs et la Nouvelle-France* (Trois-Rivières: Boréal Express, 1968), p. 117. The lease is dated 9 July 1762. Hart is identified as "English by nation."

6. Marcel Trudel, *Le Régime militaire dans le gouvernement des Trois-Rivières, 1760-1764* (Trois-Rivières: Éditions du Bien public, 1952).

7. Ibid., 76. See Haldimand's correspondence, which mentions a number of purchases of furnaces and iron bars.

8. Ibid.

9. FC 411, H159 A4 (our translation). Haldimand often wrote his reports in French. He also wrote to Amherst in French on the subject of clarifying the borders of Canada. The trustee whom he mentions below is probably Hart, and the ironic tone is deliberate.

10. Document transmitted by Claude Kaufholtz-Couture and taken from Haldimand's correspondence, 16 February 1780 (Corr. No. 22518; our translation).

11. The revenge of the Huguenots. See Jacques Lacoursière, Jean Provencher, and Denis Vaugeois, *Canada-Québec: synthèse historique* (Sillery: Septentrion, 2004), pp. 171–72,

12. ASTR, Fonds Hart, J-A-2. It should be noted that Aaron Hart's spelling was execrable in general.

13. In the seventeenth century, the word "Jew" took on the meaning of "miser." In the nineteenth century, the word "Israelite" was used instead of "Jew." With the creation of the state of Israel, some Jews turned away from the word "Israelite," which was often confused with "Israeli," a word designating a nationality that included Muslims, Christians, Druzes, agnostics, atheists, and people of other religions. In the Province of Quebec in the eighteenth century, the word "Juif" or "Jew"was rarely used. Cramahé was an exception. In 1774, the notaries Dillet and Badeaux styled the French version of the word "jouïv." See the very interesting essay by Jacob Rader Marcus, "Rejection of the Jew: The People. The Extent of Prejudice, the Word 'Jew' as an Epithet, the Smear Tactic," chapter 14 in *United States Jewry 1776–1985* (Detroit: Wayne State University Press, 1989), vol. 1, pp. 525–58.

14. But fish, apparently, was even more important. Jonathan Dull pays great attention to it in his masterful study *The French Navy and the Seven Years' War* (Lincoln: University of Nebraska Press, 2007). In Dull's view, the Grand Banks off Newfoundland were a source of wealth but also a valuable training ground for French sailors.

15. Adam Shortt, *Documents Relating to Canadian Currency, Exchange and Finance during the French Period*, vol. 2 (Ottawa, 1925), p. 972 (our translation).

16. The archives now conserved at LaCourneuve contain political correspondence concerning North America filed under the title "Mémoires et documents." In 1760–61, even before the war ended, "His Majesty" announced the payment of bills of exchange drawn from Canada in the fairest manner. Instructions were given on how to evaluate them.

17. Marcel Trudel, *Le Régime militaire dans le Gouvernement des Trois-Rivières, 1760-1764* (Trois-Rivières: Éditions du Bien public, 1952), pp. 170–71 (our translation).

18. These were *livres tournois* (French pounds). In English, *sols* became shillings (abbreviated "s") and *deniers* became pennies (abbreviated "d"). The pound sterling that came to be used widely when the British arrived had a variable value and was aligned with three different exchange rates: Halifax, New York, and Quebec.

19. Fernand Ouellet, *Histoire* économique *et sociale du Québec, 1760-1850* (Montreal: Fides, 1966), p. 59.

20. Ibid., p. 58 (our translation).

21. Such sales were public and the highest bidder won. In the BAnQ are records of "sheriff's sales" for which the steps are set out: judgment against an individual, public notice, sale of the property, and distribution of the money brought in. In New France, the sheriff's tasks were shared by judges, king's procurers, and bailiffs. Rénald Lessard, personal communication.

22. Douville, *Aaron Hart*, pp. 27–28. There are several contracts of agreements among the unclassified papers in the Hart archive (ASTR).

23. F. Antaya, "Chasser en échange d'un salaire. Les engagés amérindiens dans la traite des fourrures du Saint-Maurice, 1798–1831," *Revue d'histoire de l'Amérique française*, vol. 63, no. 1 (2009): 7; Claude Gélinas, "La traite des fourrures en Haute-Mauricie avant 1831. Concurrence, stratégies commerciales et petits profits," *Revue d'histoire de l'Amérique française*, vol. 51, no. 3 (1998): 394.

24. Douville, *Aaron Hart*, pp. 41–50. On 14 May 1767, Aaron himself hired Michel Salois (in a contract made before notary J. B. Badeaux). This was no doubt shortly before he left for England. From 20 April to 11 May 1768, Moses Hart, "as money holder for Aaron Hart, his brother, absent from this province," hired Joseph Chevalier, Henri Biron, Jean Clair, Augustin Provençal, Louis Baulac, and Joseph Coursel *dit* Chevalier.

25. He was also in contact with Isaac Levy, John Franks, and Ezekiel Solomons, to whom he recommended *engagés* for trading in the Upper Country. In 1773, Badeaux's registry showed three *engagements*: Antoine Courville, Charles Letourneau, and Lousi Chefdevergue dit Laroze. The Trois-Rivières region was always a large recruitment pool for *voyageurs*.

26. Douville, *Aaron Hart*, p. 36.

27. Translator's note: At the time, spellings of family names were not standardized. In this document, Pommereau's name was spelled "Pemmereau," and elsewhere it was spelled "Pommerleau." For clarity's sake I have standardized the name to Pommereau.

28. Ralph Burton was in love with Marguerite Bruyères. She followed him to Trois-Rivières, and they married soon after. He made her brother, Jean Bruyères, his secretary; Jean had an open relationship with Catherine-Elisabeth Pommereau. They married before a Protestant minister in 1764. She was co-seigneuress of the Bécancour seigneury that Ralph Henry Bruyères inherited. Raymond Douville, "Jean Bruyères," DCB, vol. 4. The sources for this article point to articles by Gérard Malchelosse and by Marcel Trudel, who was particularly interested in mixed marriages during that period. See Marcel Trudel, "Les mariages mixtes sous le régime militaire, *Revue d'histoire de l'Amérique française*, vol. 7, no. 1 (1953): 7–31.

29. Sale at auction of the Marquisat du Sablé on 23 September 1800, "containing about ten arpents in area." Ceded by Joseph Boucher de Niverville, senior and junior (same name), to Aaron Hart for the price of £21 cash. Sheriff Henry Blackstone. Albert Tessier, "Deux enrichis: Aaron Hart et Nicolas Montour," *Cahier des dix*, vol. 18, no. 3 (1938): 224; BRH, 1900, p. 248; BRH, 1915, p. 46; P. G. Roy, *Inv. Des concessions en fiefs et seigneuries*, vol. 1 (1927), pp. 289, 291.

30. Aaron Hart had the Sainte-Marguerite seigneury seized on 17 March 1800. On 23 September, "Aaron Hart being the last and highest bidder became the purchaser thereof at the price of two-hundred and thirty pounds current money of the Province of Lower Canada." Joseph Boucher de Niverville and his son had been vanquished a second time. The papers were written in English by Sheriff Henry Blackstone. ASTR, Fonds Charles Boucher de Niverville, FN-0166-B.2.

31. "Around 1800, most than one third of the seigneurial land belonged to English seigneurs." Michel Lavoie, *C'est ma seigneurie que je réclame* (Montreal: Boréal, 2010), p. 199 (our translation). For an idea of the British control of seigneurial lands, see R. Cole Harris and Louise Deschênes (eds.), *Atlas historique du Canada*, vol. 1, *Des origines à 1800* (Montreal: Presses de l'Université de Montréal, 1987), plate 51.

32. ASTR, Fonds Hart, 0009-F-a.

33. See Jean-Baptiste's journal "Invasion du Canada par les Américains en 1775," published in Montreal in 1870.

34. On 4 July 2009, upon the occasion of the 375th anniversary of the foundation of Trois-Rivières, the Ursuline order received symbolic payment for the services that the nuns had rendered from the United States via the consul to Quebec City. During a short ceremony after a reconstruction of the battle of 1776, the consul, David F. Fetter, gave Sister Yvette Isabelle $132 in cash, the debt due by the U.S. Congress since 1776. The Ursulines appreciated the gesture, even though inflation and interest had not been included!

35. In March 1766, Aaron Hart obtained "a business licence for the sale of liquor in Trois-Rivières." Levy Solomons and B. Frobisher signed as endorsers. In 1768, Isaac Levy and John Franks were the endorsers of a new licence. LAC, Shop Licences, RG 4B28, vol. 120. Every year, Aaron applied to renew his licence.

36. Sometimes spelled Woorster; standardized to Wooster here.

37. Aaron Hart quoted in Douville, *Aaron Hart*, p. 61 (our translation).

38. ASTR, 0009-F-A-3.

39. This name was sometimes spelled Aaron Philipp. Here it has been standardized to Aaron Philip.

40. See the comments by Lewis A. Hart accompanying his genealogical notes conserved at the McCord Museum. He gives interesting information on the financial assistance that Samuel Judah gave Washington. The Hart family long hoped for reimbursement.

41. These had to do with his marriage to Marie-Catherine Delezenne. See Robert Derome's excellent biography of Delezenne in DCB, vol. 6.

42. The new arrivals, the "old subjects," all speculated on the paper money in circulation. "Taking advantage of the situation," wrote Rénald Lessard, "some English merchants got their hands on considerable sums at a discount" (*L'Ancêtre*, vol. 34 [2008]: 357-360, our translation). This question, though important, has not been widely studied. André Côté, in *Joseph-Michel Cadet, 1719-1781, négociant et munitionnaire du roi en Nouvelle-France* (Sillery: Septentrion, 1998), is one of the few exceptions. Fernand Ouellet, who, obviously, deals with the question in his *Histoire économique et sociale,* admitted to me that he didn't really know how the story ended. There does not seem to have been real reimbursement, at least for paper money in circulation in Canada. France constantly pushed back the date and changed the terms of reimbursement. See pp. 56–57.

43. Douville, *Aaron Hart*, p. 74 (our translation).

44. Ibid., pp. 76–88.

CHAPTER 3
The Hart Clan: Introductions

1. *Histoire des Ursulines des Trois-Rivières* (P. V. Ayotte, 1892), vol. 2, p. 380.

2. Ibid., p. 381 (our translation).

3. Sheldon J. Godfrey and Judith C. Godfrey, *Search Out the Land* (Montreal: McGill-Queens University Press, 1995), p. 324. On the contrary, notes Pierre Anctil, Jews are encouraged to become involved in lay affairs. He noted on the manuscript, "There is no real basis for this statement" (our translation).

4. Irving Abella, *Coat of Many Colours: Two Centuries of Jewish Life in Canada* (Toronto: Lester & Orpen Dennys 1990), p. 13.

5. On 6 September 1793, Mother Thérèse de Jésus reported, "We owe to Mr. Aaron Hart, our merchant, eight thousand pounds, upon which he has asked for no interest. Every

year, he advances us credit. However, we take from his store only what is indispensable to us." Things were going poorly: "almost nine thousand pounds" were owed to the seigneury owned by the Ursulines. Nevertheless, on 12 March 1795, Mother Thérèse announced proudly that she had reimbursed Mr. Hart £4,000. "The name of Mr. Hart," wrote the author in 1888, "remained very popular in the house; our elder nuns still tell us today about hot dinners that he sent to the community." In a note, she adds, "A native of Germany, Jewish by nation and religion, Mr. Aaron Hart came to Canada, attached to the account of the army of General Wolfe, and in 1760 he held the military funds of Trois-Rivières." *Les Ursulines des Trois-Rivières*, vol. 1 (1888), pp. 414–15 (our translation).

6. ASTR, 0009-J-a-3.

7. ASTR, 0009-D-b.

8. With some reservation, I recommend *Aaron's Covenant*. The author paints a harsh portrait of Aaron, accusing him of forcing his wife to have many pregnancies.

9. Historical demographic studies comparing rates of infantile mortality among Catholics, Protestants, and Jews show that Jews had the lowest rate.

10. Aaron and Dorothea's eight children who reached adulthood were Moses, Ezekiel, Benjamin, Alexander, Catherine, Charlotte, Elizabeth, and Sarah.

11. Luce Jean Haffner, *Quatre frères Jean. De La Rochelle à Québec* (Sillery: Septentrion, 1989).

12. David Rome, comp., "On the Early Harts, Part 1," CJA, new series no. 15 (1980): 16.

13. Anne Joseph, *Heritage of a Patriarch: Canada's First Jewish Settlers and the Continuing Story of These Families in Canada* (Sillery: Septentrion, 1995), pp. 22–25.

14. ASTR, 0009-J-L-1 and 0009-K-0-1.

15. Denis Vaugeois, "Samuel Jacobs," in DCB, vol. 4.

16. ASTR, 0009-J-C-3 and J-C-5.

17. The ASTR file is complemented by the one at the BAnQ.

18. Law suggests that there was an affair between Dorothea and Aaron's brother Moses. I think that this was unlikely.

19. Some of this correspondence is conserved at the McCord Museum, cote 18655. David Rome reproduced the important parts in "On the Early Harts, Part 2," CJA, new series no. 16 (1980): 199–214.

20. Rome, "On the Early Harts, Part 2," p. 199.

21. McCord, M18653.

22. Raymond Douville, *Aaron Hart. Récit historique* (Trois-Rivières: *Le Bien public*, 1938), p. 118 (our translation).

23. McCord, M18659; Rome, "On the Early Harts, Part 2," p. 206.

24. "Perhaps not the least, because he didn't marry her," comments Sophie Imbeault (our translation). We will never know. Vallières was an elusive character, brimming with talent and deliberately provocative. On the subject, I recommend Raymond Douville, "La Maison de Gannes," *Cahiers des Dix*, No. 21 (1956).

25. This is true especially for Moses Hart's children born out of wedlock—at least the sons, who are easier to find. I note that four of Ezekiel's six children never married. Why? And yet this family seems to have been very well integrated, even if wealth created a real distance.

26. BAnQ, registry of notary Joseph Badeaux (our translation).

27. There was another son, Samuel, present at Ezekiel's wedding. He was apparently born in 1774.

28. Harriott was sometimes spelled Harriot; here it has been standardized to Harriott.

29. Photocopies of all of these documents, which are in my possession, will be given to the Archives du Séminaire de Trois-Rivières after this book is published.

CHAPTER 4
Aaron Hart's Estate
1. Executors included his two oldest sons, Moses and Ezekiel, and a family friend, Robert Lester, who replaced Judah Joseph, named in the 1793 will.
2. ASTR, 0009-J-a-6, our translation.
3. ANC (today LAC), coll. Duchesnay, 3 October 1692 (dossier 37) (our translation).
4. In *Les Anonymes* (Sonatine, 2010, p. 148, our translation), R. J. Ellory has Inspector Robert Miller say, speaking of his colleague Albert Roth, "Jews don't make families. They make dynasties."
5. ASTR, 0009-I-g.
6. I have not been able to establish any connection between Charles Blake and the Hart family in Trois-Rivières. Moses named his oldest son Areli Blake, and he in turn named his oldest son William Blake.
7. ASTR, 0009-J-A-9.
8. ASTR, 0009-J-A-10a.
9. David Rome, comp., "On the Early Harts, Part 2," CJA, new series no. 16 (1980): 166.
10. Marcel Trudel, *Le terrier du Saint-Laurent en 1663* (Ottawa: University of Ottawa Press, 1973), pp. 368–69 (our translation). "The depth of the land called 'Marquisat du Sablé' (although conceded by a commoner by birth and remaining held by a commoner) was 10 arpents: it extended from the future Rue des Forges and la Commune, to the foot of Côteau des Pères, or Côteau Saint-Louis; given the sites that were between this lot and Rue Notre-Dame, its frontage would give today on Rue Badeaux and its depth, bordered on one side by Rue des Forges and on the other by Rue Saint-Antoine and by a line extending it, went as far as the junction of Rue des Forges, Rue Sainte-Marie, and Rue Saint-Georges." This is the heart of downtown Trois-Rivières.
11. There are few details on the lawsuits brought between mother and sons. What was at stake is not clear –the pension, the division of goods, or their value. An agreement dated 14 January 1801 was signed before the notary by Dorothea and her sons: "A doubt having arisen with regard to the merchandise left in the deceased's store, the parties agree to constitute a capital of £1,500 for the widow, who renounces the merchandise" (ASTR, A-10-A/5, our translation). See also the acceptance signed before notary Joseph Badeaux the previous day in the presence of Pierre Vézina and Robert Lester (ASTR, 0009-J-A-10a/4). However, the affair didn't end there. A new agreement was made on 26 November 1802 between Dorothea and her two older sons following a lawsuit that she brought at the Court of King's Bench.
12. ASTR, 0009-J-A-10c.
13. ASTR, 0009-J-A-10a.
14. ASTR, 0009-I-a-1.
15. ASTR, 0009-I-a-2.
16. Sophie Imbeault had the impression that Moses had assassinated her. The evidence showed that Moses harassed Dolly and she committed suicide.
17. Aaron wrote a letter to Moses indicating that he wanted to replace Jane. He asked Moses to look for a female black slave in the United States, noting that the cost was lower there.
18. On 15 March 1788, before notary Badeaux, there was a transaction between Godefroy de Tonnancour and John McPherson: "A Negress aged about 29 years, named Gennie, and her daughter named Marie, aged about 3 years, belonging to the Lord seller for having purchased from Mr. Aaron Hart, merchants of this city" (our translation). In *Figures tri-*

fluviennes, short note signed A.T. The mother and daughter had been purchased in March 1786 and were apparently sold on to de Tonnancour in May or June 1787.
19. Alfred Dubuc, "John Molson Sr.," DCB, vol. 7.

CHAPTER 5
Ezekiel Hart, House of Assembly Member from Trois-Rivières
1. For any activity for which they did not have to swear an oath, Jews had free rein. They could start a wholesale or retail business, run an inn or hotel, and own land with the corresponding titles. In fact, Aaron Hart was a seigneur several times over. He even had his own pew in more than one church!
2. He also refused to let Benjamin Hart join his militia in 1812.
3. Benjamin Sulte has described Ezekiel Hart's 1807 victory (*Revue canadienne*, vol. 7 [1870], 432 ff). He noted that beer (courtesy of the Harts) flowed freely "without any disorder being seen." He quoted *Le Canadien* and *The Mercury*, which, respectively, endorsed and opposed Ezekiel's election. Ezekiel became an agent for *The Mercury* in Trois-Rivières.
4. ASTR, 0009-L-d-67.
5. Twice, the Parti canadien failed in its attempt to vote in an expense allowance for representatives from outside the Quebec City region. See Jean-Pierre Wallot, *Un Québec qui bougeait. Trame socio-politique au tournant du XIXᵉ siècle* (Montreal: Éditions du Boréal Express, 1973), p. 149.
6. Another word for the Torah, the teachings transmitted by Moses. The term "Pentateuch," from the Greek for "five coffers," designates the five books of Moses that tell the history of the people of Israel and presents a set of prescriptions that constitute the basis of Judaism, including the Kosher food laws.
7. *Les Ursulines des Trois-Rivières depuis leur établisssement jusqu'à nos jours* (P. V. Ayotte, 1892), vol. 2, p. 380 (our translation). "In the summer of 1809, a distinguished visitor presented himself in the classes: His Excellency Governor Craig. He was passing through our town and wanted to honour with his visit our Reverend Father the chaplain and the community. While in town, he was the host of Mr. Ezekiel Hart, who lived on Rue des Forges. The land behind his house formed a lovely terrace, where the music of the Canadian Regiment played its most joyous fanfares while the distinguished guests ate dinner. It is in memory of this visit by the Governor that Mr. Hart gave the name Craig to one of his sons who was born that summer." The nun then described the elections of 1807 and 1808 in which Ezekiel was elected but was not able to take his seat: "The parliament having been prorogued again, the governor went in person to Trois-Rivières to support the election of Mr. Hart (October 1808), but Mr. Hart abandoned the fight and Mr. Bell and Mr. Badeaux were elected." After that, the governor approved "a generous subsidy for the reconstruction of the monastery." Jean-Pierre Wallot (in *Un Québec qui bougeait. Trame socio-politique du Québec ou tournant du XIXᵉ siècle* [Sillery: Septentrion, 1973], p. 164) confirms Craig's brief campaign tour in 1809, but specifies that Moses, not Ezekiel, was the candidate.
8. Wallot, *Un Québec qui bouge*, p. 164. Wallot gives specific references to A. D. Hart, P. G. Roy, Benjamin Gult Sack, B. Sulte, and D. Creighton.
9. Unless otherwise indicated, the information and quotations in this section are from the Journal of the House of Assembly of Lower Canada.
10. It is important to note that the two members who sounded the alarm were Tories. Sewell was well enough informed to know that Jews could not sit in Parliament in England. Did De Bonne also know this, or did he simply want to ingratiate himself to the powerful Sewell?

11. LAC, G7, G15c, vol. 13: 99.

12. ASTR, 0009-E-B.

13. Wallot, *Un Québec qui bougeait*, p. 164, note 59. Wallot was very clear and quite exasperated (our translation): "Simplistic and far-fetched explanations abound in historiography." Wallot demolished them without pity. I noted this: Craig "had expressed his thanks to Hart with an engraving of himself, found later in Hart's effects. J. Neilson printed it and sold several hundred in 1810–11." About the Harts, Wallot added, "A long monograph could be written on this family of entrepreneurs and on their relatively important role in the Lower Canadian economy of the time: exports of wheat, potassium, and furs; various imports; wholesale and retail sales; brewery; speculation on lands in the seigneurial zone and the townships; and so on." Wallot explained, "The Hart sons . . . were not necessarily attractive and popular individuals: ambitious, enterprising, cornering markets, unscrupulous in business, creditors and employers of a good part of the population of Trois-Rivières. . . . They dominated the electorate at a time when votes were held by a show of hands." He even added up the number of seizures made and sales at auction held by the Harts in 1807, 1808, and 1809 (twenty-nine, twenty-tree, and thirty, respectively).

CHAPTER 6
Jews Win a Victory Thanks to the Patriotes: The Laws of 1831–32
1. The Public Archives of Canada was well equipped. I quickly became familiar with reprography by photostat, the ancestor of the photocopy. The document to be reproduced was exposed for ten seconds, and then the photographic paper was immersed in a fix bath that produced a negative. There was an extra charge for a positive. Even today, I feel sentimental about my old photostats. Sometimes, I allowed myself the luxury of a positive, as I did for the first Jewish register conserved at the Archives judiciaires de Montréal. Jacques Lacoursière and I soon invested in a portable device with a transparent cushion designed to protect the document to be reproduced. We were using this primitive device around 1963, when we produced the journal Boréal Express.

2. RG 1, E 11, vols. 1–2.

3. Canada became a country in 1867. Before that, this term designated a part of New France or the two provinces of British North America.

4. DC, 1911: 141–43.

5. Denis Vaugeois, Québec 1792. Les acteurs, les institutions et les frontières (Montreal: Fides, 1992), pp. 47–53.

6. There has been a long debate over this hypothesis. I believe that the Sephardic rite was imposed in Montreal under the influence of the New York and London communities. I will return to this in the final chapter.

7. Jacques Lacoursière, formerly a member of the Commission de toponymie du Québec, notes that today Dominion Square has been divided into Place du Canada and Dorchester Square.

8. As Pierre Anctil remarked, however, they could purchase land, on which they could build a synagogue and create a cemetery. I believe that individuals, and not the congregation, acted on behalf of the community before the legislation of the 1830s.

9. Sheldon J. Godfrey and Judith C. Godfrey, *Search Out the Land* (Montreal: McGill-Queens University Press, 1995), p. 294, note 14.

10. Another remark by Pierre Anctil: Although Jews were allowed to keep separate official registers only later, nothing kept them from keeping a register of marriages, births, and burials in the synagogue. The lack of Jewish leaders was the problem.

11. At the time, "Israelite" was preferred to "Jew," which seemed to have a negative connotation.

12. ASTR, 0009-A-H-3.

13. David Rome, comp., "Benjamin Hart and 1829," CJA, new series no. 24 (1982): 7.

14. Journals of the House of Assembly of Lower Canada, 4 December 1828, pp. 84–85 (our translation).

15. Siméon Pagnuelo, *Études historiques et légales sur la liberté religieuse en Canada* (Beauchemin & Valois, 1872), p. 164) (our translation).

16. Fernand Ouellet, "Louis-Joseph Papineau," DCB, vol. 10.

17. Without explanation, of course.

18. Journals of the House of Assembly, 26 January 1830, p. 26.

19. Journals of the House of Assembly, 12 March 1830, p. 311.

20. Report of the Public Archives for 1830, Ottawa, p. 175.

21. Journals of the House of Assembly, 7 February 1831, p. 102–03 (our translation).

22. Godfrey and Godfrey, *Search Out the Land*, p. 188.

23. Irving Abella, The Coat of Many Colours: Two Centuries of Jewish Life in Canada (Toronto: Lester & Orpen Dennys, 1990), p. 181.

24. Godfrey and Godfrey, *Search Out the Land*, p. 57.

25. Elinor Kyte Senior, *Les habits rouges et les patriotes* (Montreal: VLB, 1997), p. 276. E. B. O'Callaghan was a close friend of Papineau's. This book is available in English: *Redcoats and Patriotes: The Rebellions in Lower Canada*, 1837–38 (Toronto: Canada's Wings, Inc., 1985).

26. See Senior, Habits rouges, p. 276. After searching through countless documents at the BAnQ, I found only one deposition mentioning this presumed plot. It was made before Pierre-Édouard Leclère, chief of the Montreal police, who also headed a secret police force that hounded Patriote sympathizers. See the excerpt of the deposition made by Joseph Bourdon on 2 November 1838 on page 160. In *O Canada, O Quebec*, Penguin, 1992, Mordecai Richler disingenuously wrote "It is worth noting that in [Léandre] Bergeron's history, subtitled a Patriote's Handbook, he fails to point out that one of the stated aims of the Patriotes' rebellion of 1837-38 was that all Jews in Upper and Lower Canada be strangled and their goods confiscated." More on this on page 160.

27. "Le procès," Le Boréal Express. *Journal d'histoire du Canada*, vol. 3, p. 542 (our translation).

28. David Rome, comp., "On the Jews of Lower Canada and 1837-38, part 2," CJA, new series no. 29 (1983): 156–57.

29. David Rome, comp., "On the Jews of Lower Canada and 1837-38, Part 3," CJA new series no. 30 (1983): 283, 290–96.

30. Arthur Wellington Hart, sent to London to protest on his father's behalf, accused the "Lord Bishop of Quebec" of blocking his appointment to the Special Council. Finally, Poulett Thomson, the future Lord Sydenham, was asked to give a ruling. First, Thomson's answer read, "the Lord Bishop of Quebec died before special Council came into existence." Second, "I freely admit," Thomson wrote, "that his religious persuasion ought not to be a barrier to his admission to the special Council, I must at the same time consider that it gives no claim, independent of other consideration, to be admitted to that Body." LAC, MG 11, Series Q, vol. 242 part 3: 86–87. In other words, "Being a Jew did not prevent his being put into the House, but cannot be a reason for finding him there," as Lord Russell summarized in a letter to Thomson.

31. In London, the Little Englanders movement was calling for the imperial government to scale back its commitments to the colonies. Westminster responded by moving towards

free trade and putting an end to protectionist measures known as the Corn Laws. This in turn prompted some in Canada to favour annexation with the United States.

32. Raymond Arthur Davies, *Printed Jewish Canadiana*, 1685-1900 (Montreal, 1955), p. 24.

CHAPTER 7
Moses Hart: Morality and Religion

1. Voluminous file at BAnQ in Trois-Rivières. See Court of King's Bench, 1807 and 1816 (068, 0124).

2. Apparently, Moses, like his father and his brother Ezekiel, was small in stature, whereas the youngest son, Alexander, was not as short.

3. *Gazette de Québec*, 2 January 1825.

4. ASTR, Fonds Hart, 0009-J-H-1.

5. Raymond Douville, "Les années de jeunesse et vie familiale de Moses Hart," *Cahiers des Dix*, no. 23 (1958): 211–13.

6. Anne Joseph, *Heritage of a Patriarch: Canada's First Jewish Settlers and the Continuing Story of These Families in Canada* (Sillery: Septentrion, 1995), pp. 130, 166.

7. ASTR, Fonds Hart, C-g. There may have been two Aaron Moses Harts.

8. In his will, Moses left small bequests to Henry and Benjamin, the sons of Anne Galarno.

9. Raymond Douville, "Années de jeunesse et vie familiale," *Cahiers des dix*, no. 23 (1958), 195–216.

10. ASTR, Fonds Hart 0009-J-C-7 (our translation). This very moving letter was written phonetically in French.

11. Douville, handwritten notes conserved at BAnQ in Trois-Rivières (our translation). Douville, in "Années de jeunesse et vie familiale de Moses Hart," *Les Cahiers des Dix*, no. 23 (1958), mentions this marriage at p. 215.

12. ASTR, Fonds Hart 0009-J-C-6 and 0009-J-C-8.

13. ASTR, Fonds Hart 0009-C-0. I know nothing else about the son named Ezekiel. Moses warned that he must not go to town. Finally, the child was to be sent back to his parents (?).

14. ASTR, Fonds Hart, 0009-L-H-5/4.

15. ASTR, Fonds Hart 0009-L-h-5.

16. See "The Record Book of the Reverend Jacob Raphael Cohen, Compiled with an Introduction by Alan D. Corré with Biographical Annotations by Malcolm H Stern," *American Jewish Historical Quarterly*, vol. 49, no. 1 (September 1969), 23–82.

17. ASTR, Fonds Hart 0009-A-F-1.

18. ASTR, Fonds Hart, 0009-A-E-1

19. ASTR, Fonds Hart 0009-A-E-2.

20. ASTR, Fonds Hart 0009-A-f-2, three pages.

21. ASTR, Fonds Hart 0009A-G-6.

22. ASTR, Fonds Hart 0009-A-G. In this file are what remain of three copies of *General Universal Religion* that were saved, as well as various documents concerning the printing and distribution of the three editions.

23. Raymond Douville, "Jean-Baptiste Badeaux," *Dictionary of Canadian Biography*, vol. 4.

24. Denis Vaugeois, "Les positions religieuses de Moses Hart," *Canadian Catholic Historical Association, Study Sessions*, 33 (1966), 41–46.

25. Jacob Rader Marcus, "The Modern Religion of Moses Hart," *Hebrew Union College Annual*, vol. 20, 585–615.

26. Ibid., p. 612.

27. Ibid., p. 615.

CHAPTER 8
Moses Hart in Business
1. ASTR, Fonds Hart 0009-Q-c-1 to Q-c-20.
2. He took a trip to England in 1792 that enabled him to establish direct contacts. Between 1795 and 1835, he dealt with some twenty different trading companies in London, Liverpool, Bristol, Glasgow, Birmingham, Stourbridge, Wolverhampton, and Leeds. He imported mainly raw sugar, coffee, woollens, fabrics, and Jamaican rum, and exported mainly potash and wheat. His cousin, Judah Joseph, frequently went to London between 1803 and 1834 and served as an intermediary as needed. (ASTR, 0009-P-a-1 to P-a-55; about 900 documents.)
3. Moses's son offered £4 to £5, Molson indicated in his letter of 10 January. "The offer was so absurd that we did not conceive you could be serious." In return, Molson offered the motor at £900, specifying that it was not to be installed in a ship that would compete with the Molsons between Quebec City, Trois-Rivières, William Henry, and Montreal—"in fact in any manner in opposition to our present line." (ASTR, Fonds Hart 0009-Q-2 and Q-E.)
4. ASTR, Fonds Hart 0009-Q-M-1 and Q-M-2.
5. ASTR, Fonds Hart 0009-Q-N-2 and Q-N-8.
6. Anne Joseph, *Heritage of a Patriarch: Canada's First Jewish Settlers and the Continuing Story of These Families in Canada* (Sillery: Septentrion, 1995), p. 200. Aaron Hart David wrote that he had travelled, in May 1840, on the "Hart steamer . . . and nothing was broken."
7. This quotation is from notes transcribed from drafts in the Ursulines' archives (our translation) for publication of *Les Ursulines des Trois-Rivières*, vol. 4 (Quebec City: Imprimerie L'Action Sociale, 1911), p. 429. The nun's account continues (our translation): "Feeling that he was mortally wounded, he cried, 'A priest! A priest!' He was transported to the hospital, where religious aid was given to him as art and science tried to preserve a life that was about to be extinguished. Mr. Hart died as a result of his injuries, but as a good Christian."
8. ASTR, Fonds Hart 0009-N-b-1 to N-b-3. Quotation from Denis Vaugeois, "Ezekiel Hart," DCB, vol. 7.
9. BAnQ, Trois-Rivières, Badeaux register, 30 August 1797. See also Douville, 1938, pp. 126–34.
10. See Catherine Ferland's original and useful work, *Bacchus en Canada: Boissons, buveurs et ivresses en Nouvelle-France* (Sillery: Septentrion, 2010).
11. Raymond Douville, *Aaron Hart, récit historique* (Trois-Rivières: Éditions du Bien public, 1938), p. 130 (our translation).
12. ASTR Fonds Hart 0009-N-c-4.
13. Denis Vaugeois, "Ezekiel Hart," DCB, vol. 7.
14. Ibid.
15. ASTR Fonds Hart 0009 N-b.
16. Gerald Tulchinsky, "William Dow," DCB, Vol. 9.
17. ASTR, Fonds Hart 0009-M-b-7.
18. ASTR, Fonds Hart 0009-M-b-3.
19. ASTR, Fonds Hart 0009-M-b-10.
20. ASTR, Fonds Hart 0009-M-b-8. Voluminous file.
21. ASTR, Fonds Hart 0009-M-b-5.

CHAPTER 9
Moses Hart: Reformist or Agitator?

1. ASTR, 0009-Q-1.

2. ASTR, 0009-K-L-3.

3. ASTR, 0009-L-F-51.

4. ASTR, Fonds Hart 0009-L-G-14. A number of documents were printed and therefore carefully written. The archivist Evelyn Kolish of the BAnQ in Montreal told me (on 21 December 2010) that there are few studies on appeals to the Privy Council before 1867. The lawsuit had to involve a value over £500. Kolish told me that usually the parties "were pigheaded enough to do battle and had the means to do so" (our translation). A legal principle was rarely at issue, and so these appeals were not of interest to experts.

5. BAnQ (Trois-Rivières), Legal Papers, year 1827, no. 1325.

6. BAnQ, T.-R., Legal Papers, 1827: 1326, our translation.

7. Ibid., no. 1331, our translation.

8. ASTR, 0009-A-G.

9. BAnQ (Trois-Rivières), Annual Register 1835, p. 94.

10. It should be noted that this name was spelled Levitt, Leavitt, and sometimes Levit.

11. Because of the names mentioned, René Hardy believes that it was the grand jury.

12. René Hardy, however, says that he has found a number of trials involving blasphemy. Jacques Lacoursière found some under the French régime.

13. ASTR, 0009-A-G-6.

14. The rise of swearing in French Canadian working-class society in the mid-nineteenth century caused enough of a scandal for the courts to reintroduce prison sentences for blasphemers. But this strict law did not last long, as the new type of blasphemy, inspired by the vocabulary of the sacristy, spread quickly. The will of the authorities, particularly bishops, did not prevail. René Hardy interprets the popularity of swearing as a form of protest against the religious authority that came to the fore after the failure of the 1837–38 rebellion. "Blasphemy has a history," Hardy said in a speech to the Amis de la Maison Saint-Gabriel, 21 November 2006 (our translation). See also René Hardy, *Contrôle social et mutation de la culture religieuse au Québec, 1830-1930* (Montreal: Boréal, 1999).

15. ASTR, 0009-E-G.

16. ASTR, 0009-E-i.

17. ASTR, 0009-J-C-7.

18. ASTR, 0009-J-C-10.

19. ASTR, 0009-E-H.

20. His reform plans appear throughout his correspondence. Most are presented among the legal papers. ASTR, 0009-L-a-1 to L-a-9.

21. ASTR, 0009-L-a-1.

22. ASTR, 0009-L-a-2.

23. The Act of Union assented to in London on 23 July 1840 was uncompromising: section 41 decreed that all written or printed documents emanating from the legislature would be "only in the English language." Any translations would have no legal value and would not be conserved. Article 41 of the Act of Union was revoked in 1848 with the adoption of a general act that provided no specifications about use of languages other than English. In January 1849, Lord Elgin, Governor General of the United Canadas, inaugurated the Parliamentary session speaking first in English and then in French. Some people protested the Governor General's use of a "foreign" language.

24. This was no doubt true. He was born in 1768. David David (1764–1824) was apparently the first Jew born in Canada.

25. ASTR, 0009-E-c and E-d.

26. Louis-Hippolyte La Fontaine and Robert Baldwin, two reformers, had been invited to be part of the "ministry" by Governor Bagot. On 13 September 1842, La Fontaine stated the conditions for his participation. He began his speech in French. He was asked to speak English. He reacted as follows (in French): "Even if I knew English as well as French, I would still make my first speech in the language of my French Canadian countrymen, if only to protest solemnly the cruel injustice of that part of the Act of Union which aims to proscribe the mother tongue of half of the population of Canada. I owe it to my country-men. I owe it to myself." Translation in Jacques Monet, "Louis-Hippolyte La Fontaine," DCB, vol. 9.

27. Appendix EE of the Journal of the House of Assembly (1836–37).

28. David Rome, comp., "On the Early Harts—Their Contemporaries, Part 2," CJA, new series no. 20 (1980): 154–80.

29. Ibid., p. 156.

30. David Rome, comp., "On the Early Harts, Part 4," CJA, new series no. 18 (1980): 326–27.

31. He entrusted his petition (undated, but c. 1844) to Aaron Moses Hart, whom he pre-sented as his natural son (ASTR, 0009-L-a-9). Aaron Moses came into Moses's good graces under the obvious influence of Mary McCarthy and her sister Margaret, Aaron Moses's wife. In a letter of 3 August 1846 addressed to Henry Judah, who was living in New York, Moses said that he was "very weak and can scarcely do business." He continued, "I cannot read not without spectacles at my advanced age 77 the 28th nov. last." The letter was not in his handwriting (0009-J-P-1). He said that he had not had news of Orobio and added that he no longer spoke to Areli: "He is so passionate, impudent and foolish." This letter gives a glimpse of Moses's state of mind as he was preparing to write his will. The McCarthy sisters had clearly taken control and were manipulating Aaron Moses.

32. ASTR, Fonds Hart, unclassified. Personal file: P1060430.

33. Those who are curious may read the ten letters from J. Davison to Moses Hart between 1835 and 1837 (0009-J-c-10), accusing him of having had her husband imprisoned in order "to have his way with his wife," or those of a certain Catherine O'Connor, who wrote him from prison, first to offer assistance and then to threaten him (0009-J-C-7).

34. Mary McCarthy asked the notary J. A. Berthelot to settle some affairs in Montreal. They exchanged a number of letters. He wrote her in French, and she answered, or had her answer prepared, in English. In fact, it is obvious that she dictated her letters. "You have forgotten once again to send me the death certificate of the late Mr. Moses Hart," he wrote her, in French, on 24 October 1854. "I cannot send you as you desire M. Hart Extract Mortuaire as the Jews keep no register of Births marriages and deaths in this District," she responded on 31 October. She specified that "the revd M. De Sola officiated at the burial," but that an excerpt from a Montreal register was not valid in Trois-Rivières. No doubt a bit exasperated, she reminded him that the death of Mr. Hart "took place at the 15th day of october 1852, but has been proved in my law business here, by parol [?] evidence." (ASTR, 0009-L-D-8.)

35. Or was the trembling due to age? She was no doubt in her fifties, as Reuben Moses was born in October 1840.

CHAPTER 10
The Pleasure of an Inquiry: An Open Church

1. Pierre Lepape, Preface, in Claude Manceron, *Les Hommes de la liberté* (Omnibus, 2009), p. vi (our translation).

2. "That same year [1847], the festival of our gentle patron, St. Ursula, was marked by an event that brought joy and happiness to the entire monastery. Mathilda Hart, born to Jewish parents, converted the day before, made her first communion on that day." *Les Ursulines des Trois-Rivières*, vol. 4 (1911), p. 69 (our translation).

3. Will written by hand, dated and signed by the testator.

4. Margaret Armstrong was also likely the mother of Aaron Moses, who was to marry Margaret McCarthy.

5. Moses also lost track of him. ASTR, 0009-J-P-1.

6. In the codicil, both were said to be "daughters of Moses Hart, merchant," but the space for the mother's name was left blank. Several days before each was married, she was baptized, and a date of birth is given in parentheses on the baptismal certificates.

7. Moses had affairs with several Irish women. I think in particular of Marguerite Long, whom he had thrown in prison in order to get rid of her and who wanted nothing but to return to her homeland.

8. Among the students registered between 1752 and 1806 were Anne Hart, Esther Hart, Henriette Hart, Emma Hart, and Caroline Hart.

9. Around 1844, letters began to be addressed to Mrs. Moses Hart. I suspect that her relatives had realized that her new spouse was not without means. Since I have found no trace of Peter Brown, I deduce that she was already a widow when she arrived in North America. ASTR, Fonds Hart, 0009-J-M.

10. Will of 1847. Moses left part of his estate to "Edward Hart and Moses Aaron Hart, children issuing from the marriage of Aaron M. Hart and Marguerite McCarthey [*sic*] and Henry Moses Hart, child of Benjamin Moses Hart, son of the testator, currently in the United States." This Benjamin Moses has not been previously mentioned in this book, but he did well and truly exist.

11. Strictly speaking, it was a separation. The first federal statute on divorce dates from 1968. Before that, Quebecers who wanted to divorce had to have a private bill adopted by Parliament.

12. Marcel Trudel, *Le régime militaire dans le gouvernement des Trois-Rivières, 1760-1764* (Le Bien public, 1952), p. 76, note 75.

13. ASTR, 0009-J-M-7.

14. Raymond Douville, *Aaron Hart, récit historique* (Éditions du Bien public, 1938), p. 187 (our translation).

15. "Undershot chin!" Frégault cried, referring to the famous portrait of Cartier. Other clues to the identity of the skull were missing teeth due to scurvy and scars due to plague. Moral: it is better to forget searching about the remains of both Cartier and Champlain. Of course, Frégault's mockery had other motives.

16. Our translation. This is the first indication I found of her age. She therefore gave birth at the ages of about thirty-six and thirty-eight years.

17. Archives of the diocese of Trois-Rivières. Register of the subscription campaign for construction of a cathedral. It is to be noted that the authorities avoided using the name McCarthy.

18. Here are the final lines of the biography of Aaron Hart that I wrote for the Dictionary of Canadian Biography (vol. 4, 1980 p. 358-359): "Hundreds of Aaron Hart's descendants,

who were firmly attached to their properties, refused to lose everything by leaving a region which resolutely remained French and Catholic. They chose to remain there, though threatened with slow but inexorable assimilation by the local majority. Today some of them jealously guard the secret of their origins and of their relative prosperity; many others are completely ignorant of them. Aaron Hart could not foresee this curious historical reversion in which those defeated in 1760 would gradually become vehicles of assimilation. The Harts of the Trois-Rivières region would have the same experience as the Burnses, Johnsons, and Ryans: mingling with the 'long-time Canadians' [the Canadiens] they too would become the progenitors of the Québécois of today."

CHAPTER 11
The Evanescence of a Great Family and a Founding Community: Sephardim vs. Ashkenazim

1. By chance, I laid my hands on the *engagement* contract (29 July 1806) between Moses Nathan and Benjamin and Alexander Hart for trade in the West (RAPQ, 1945–46: 243). At the time, *engagements* of this type were numerous.

2. These children were born of his marriage contracted in 1806 "with separation of goods" to Harriott Judith Hart, Ephraim Hart's daughter. A court case in March 1849 gives a good idea of the family's situation at that time. Harriott Judith was claiming the pension set out in their marriage contract, as Benjamin had gone bankrupt.

3. They were raised in the same family even though they weren't sisters.

4. The synagogue was demolished, but the date is not known.

5. Louis Rosenberg, *Chronology of Canadian Jewish History* (National Bicentenary Committee of the Canadian Jewish Congress, c. 1960).

6. Anne Joseph, *Heritage of a Patriarch* (Sillery: Septentrion, 1995), pp. 176–77.

7. Between 8 June and 2 July 1832, 1,558 people died of cholera in Quebec City alone.

8. I know nothing about Isaac Aaron except that he "made trouble" and was very voluble. He disappeared as mysteriously as he had appeared. In a letter of 31 August 1847, Isaac Aaron, known as Bucklesbury (England), indicated his choice of seat in the synagogue. L.R. [Louis Rosenberg], comp., CJA, vol. 1, no. 2 (1956): 20. See also ASTR, L-D-1.

9. Dany Fougères, *L'approvisionnement en eau à Montréal. Du privé au public, 1796-1865* (Sillery, Quebec: Septentrion, 2004), p. 281. Fougères gives a detailed description of the challenges facing Hays.

10. David Rome, comp., "On the Early Harts—Their Contemporaries, Part 2," CJA new series no. 20 (1980): 250. See also Joseph, *Heritage*, pp. 173–74. In Annette Wolff's unpublished biography of Moses Judah Hays, she writes that he proposed a "steamboat ferry" between Montreal and Longueuil. Goods and passengers would be loaded at the Bonsecours market and transported to "a wharf erected on the flats or Islet, about two acres above the south-westerly end of the island of saint Hélène, where a bridge communicating with the mainland should be constructed." In Hays's opinion, given the shallowness of the water as far as St. Helen's Island, a "drawbridge" wasn't necessary; a "truss bridge" would suffice.

11. CJA, vol. 1, no. 1 (1955): 4–5.

12. Ibid., pp. 6–8.

13. Although the formulation is awkward, Benjamin was obviously worried about something. I am unaware of any manifestation of aggression toward the Jews. There may have been some tension within the Jewish community, but Benjamin was reading too much into it. Violence wasn't on the agenda, except perhaps on the political level between Tories and Patriotes. Augustin Cuvillier, who had presided at the founding meeting, was himself

at the centre of a controversy. He was accused of having ordered the troops to open fire on those who were protesting against the government—protests that were about to foment the rebellion. See James Jackson, *The Riot That Never Was* (Montreal: Baraka Books, 2009).

14. *CJA*, vol. 1, no. 1 (1955): 9.

15. Cotté died in 1795 and this marriage took place in 1818. Larocque took me back to the path of Lewis and Clark. See Denis Vaugeois, *America: The Lewis & Clark Expedition and the Dawn of a New Power* (Montreal: Vehicule Press, 2005), pp. 66–67. This research interested me enough to divert me temporarily from the Harts. Cotté and Larocque have biographies in the *Dictionary of Canadian Biography*.

16. The contract was signed by Lucie-Angélique, Marie-Josephte, and Marie-Catherine-Émilie, and their mother, the widow Cotté. Aside from Hays, Valentine, and Hart, the contract was also signed by Isaac Aaron, who was following things closely—sometimes too closely for Benjamin's taste. CJA, vol. 1, no. 2 (1956): 6–9.

17. ASTR, 0009-A-h.

18. This honour cost him £200. M. E. David was the son of Moses David and Charlotte Hart, Benjamin's sister.

19. As we have seen, at the height of the rebellion, they were very active as magistrates.

20. Fougères, *L'approvisionnement en eau*, pp. 282–83. Hays sold his company to the city of Montreal in 1845 and remained in the city's employ for one year to provide a transition.

21. CJA, vol. 1, no. 6 (1962): 12, 26.

22. In 1837, the name "Congregation of Portuguese Jews in Montreal" was changed to "Corporation of Spanish and Portuguese Jews, Shearith Israel of Montreal."

23. On 17 September 1846, Abraham de Sola wrote to A. H. David, president of the K. K. Shearith Israel, to accept the position of *hazan*. CJA, vol. 1, no. 3 (1957): 8–9.

24. "The Legislative Assembly," reported the *Montreal Herald*, "took over the ballroom, and the Legislative Council the apartment above, used for Freemasons' meetings and decorated with their emblems." Quoted in Jacques Lacoursière, *Histoire populaire du Québec*, vol. 3, *1841 à 1896* (Sillery: Septentrion, 1996), p. 52 (our translation). Like most Jews of his times, Hays was a Freemason.

25. Rosenberg, *Chronology*, p. 8.

26. CJA, vol. 1, no. 3 (1957): 9–10.

27. Aaron Hart David was the son of Samuel David and Sarah Hart, and thus Benjamin's nephew. In 1840, he moved to Trois-Rivières, where he lived for four years. He explained that life was too expensive in Montreal and, on top of that, prejudices against Jews deprived him of sufficient patients. See Joseph, *Heritage*, pp. 199–200.

28. A writ of mandamus is a court order for an organization or an individual to perform a duty that is imposed by law or to take an action required by law.

29. Jacques Lacoursière, *Histoire populaire du Québec*, vol. 3, *1841 à 1896* (Sillery: Septentrion, 1996), p. 36 (our translation).

30. André Charbonneau and André Sévigny, *1847, Grosse-Île au fil des jours* (Parcs Canada, 1997), pp. 17 and 24 (our translation). For a gripping description of a crossing, see Peter Behrens, *The Law of Dreams* (Toronto: House of Anansi, 2007).

31. David Rome, comp., "On the Early Harts - Their Contemporaries, Part 2," CJA, new series no. 20 (1980): 256.

32. André Charbonneau and André Sévigny, *1847, Grosse Île au fil des jours* (Ottawa: Parcs Canada, 1997), pp. 272, 274.

33. Rosenberg, *Chronology*, pp. 8–10. These data are very difficult to verify. See also [Louis

Rosenberg], CJA, vol. 1, no. 6 (1962): 3.

34. Benjamin Gult Sack, *History of the Jews in Canada: From the Earliest Beginnings to the Present Day*, vol. 1, *The French Regime* (Montreal: Canadian Jewish Congress, 1945), p. 141.

35. Arthur Daniel Hart, *The Jew in Canada* (Montreal, 1926), p. 93.

36. Pierre Anctil believes that the model is, rather, the Bevis Marks synagogue in London. In any case, the Sephardic Jews had had a step up on the more recently arrived Ashkenazim, who were no doubt of more modest means.

Conclusion

1. The United States became independent in a context of internal divisions. With the Proclamation of Independence came a settling of accounts and the flight of tens of thousands of Loyalists—colonists who remained faithful to the British Crown—into exile. Many of them settled in Canada, which, in the view of historians, became British North America. Loyalists arriving in Nova Scotia in 1784 caused the division of this colony—or province, the words are synonymous—into Nova Scotia and New Brunswick.

2. See Denis Vaugeois, *Québec 1792. Les acteurs, les institutions et les frontières* (Fides, 1992). In this book, I trace the origins of our parliamentary institutions through the political context and the game of hide-and-seek that surrounded certain petitions that historian Pierre Tousignant uncovered in his doctoral dissertation. I take a new look at the border between Quebec and Ontario and at the composition of these two councils. Instead of following the Ottawa River to its mouth, the border went west of the seigneuries of Nouvelle-Longueuil and Vaudreuil that belonged to two seigneurs who had defended Quebec in 1775 and were taken captive. Lord Dorchester rejected the idea of including the two seigneuries in Upper Canada.

3. CJA, no. 23, 113–14.

4. That is why I have included an appendix with a chronology of the political history of Quebec with references to the text. It is my fond hope that the events of the years 1763, 1774, 1775, 1792, 1810, 1822, 1837, 1838, 1840, 1848, and 1849 will become better known. It is difficult to venture down the path of history without reference points.

5. See my article "Le Québec, un creuset méconnu," *Mémoire de la Société généalogique canadienne-française*, vol. 39, no. 4 (1988), 277–90. This was the text of a speech that I gave at the Congress for the Société généalogique canadienne-française's forty-fifth anniversary, on 8 October 1988. Following the speech, many of the genealogists present agreed with the points I made. This was following a controversy created by the broadcast of a television series called *L'étoffe d'un pays* (directed by Michel Audy, broadcast on Télé-Québec) in which we examined the diverse origins of French Canadians. The title makes a clear allusion to the expression "pure laine."

6. See their biographies in the *Dictionary of Canadian Biography*, vols. 14 and 12, respectively.

PLAN OF THE CITY OF THREE RIVERS

DEDICATED BY PERMISSION

TO THE

MAYOR AND CORPORATION

J.E. TURCOTTE ESQ. MAYOR.

BY

ARCHIBALD MACDONALD

CIVIL ENGINEER

1865

The "legendary" portrait of Aaro Hart and the real one of his wife, Dorothea Judah.

One hundred years after Aaron Hart's arrival, the family owned much of the town and district of Trois-Rivières. The descendants have considerable amounts of real estate stretching as far as the Eastern Townships. I abandoned the idea of compiling the list myself; those interested can consult the after-death inventories of Moses Hart, Ezekiel Hart, and Benjamin Hart.

The Pachirini fief, below, evaded the grasp of the Harts. Situated between the Jesuits' property, Rue Notre Dame, and Le Platon, this fief became the small parade ground and the site where the heart of the parish was established. The Algonquin chief Charles Pachirini had received this site in 1684. A few Algonquin families had settled there, surrounded by lots conceded to Europeans. The name Pachirini appears frequently in the baptism and marriage registers, particularly in that of Pierre Couc and Marie Mite8meg8k8e, who are the ancestors of the Montours of North America. Linctot and Hertel (the fiefs on the map above right) were among the famous Trois-Rivières pioneers.

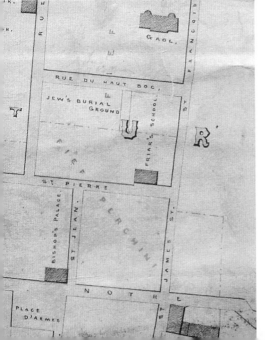

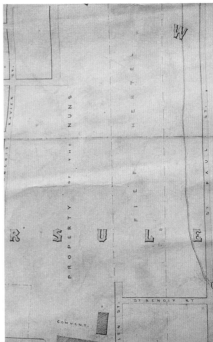

Real Estate Heritage (1760-1860)

When the seigneurial system was abolished, in 1854, the authorities summed up the situation. Here is an overview of the real estate holdings of Aaron's and Dorothea's descendants:

- Fief Boucher (20 arpents): Ezekiel Moses Hart (cense and rents: $1.00; lods and sales: $279.50)
- Fief du Vieuxpont: Julia Seaton, widow of Areli Blake Hart (cense and rents: $133.33; lods and sales: $1,275)
- Fief Hertel et Marsolette belonging to the heirs of Moses Hart (cense and rents: $783.83; lods and sales: $282.16)
- Fief Hertel et Linctot: Mary McCarthy, heir of Moses Hart
- Seigneurie or Fief Dutord: heirs of Moses Hart (cense and rents: $2,820; lods and sales: $2,693.04)
- Seigneurie de Godefroy: heirs, Charlotte Mathilda and Sarah Dorothea Hart (cense and rents: $4,783.12; lods and sales: $4,672.75)
- Seigneurie de Rocquetaillade: heirs: Charlotte Mathilda and Sara Dorothea Hart (cense and rents: $3,388.17; lods and sales: $2,896.66)
- Seigneurie de Sainte-Marguerite: Mrs. A. B. Hart (Julia Seaton) (cense and rents and annual levies: $1,393.66; and lods and sales: $4,147 and common mill $2,000)
- Seigneurie de Belair: heirs of Moses Hart (cense and rents: $577.83; lods and sales: $973.34 and common mill: $1,000)
- Seigneurie de Bruyères: Theodore Hart (Benjamin's son) (cense and rents: $4,591.50 and lods and sales: $3,396.08 + $101.08 and common mill: $5,000)
- Seigneurie de Bécancour: heirs of Samuel Bécancour Hart (Cense and rents: $2,703.25; lods and sales: $1,327.92)
- Seigneurie de Courval: Miriam Judah (cense and rents: $19,521.50 and $4,113.33, seigneurial manor $2,000, and non-granted land $9,428)

The amounts of the cense and rents and the lods and sales give an idea of the value of the properties in question. The lods and sales was a tax of one twelfth due to seigneurs on all sales or exchanges of buildings effected by a *censitaire*. Because the 1854 statute did away with seigneurs and *censitaires*, the seigneurs were compensated by the government. The *censitaires*, incapable of purchasing their land, continued to pay rents to their seigneurs or lenders until their debts were transferred to municipalities (1945). Today, though rare, seigneurial rents are still being paid.

Appraisal roll of the city and suburbs of Trois-Rivières, November 1845

The names of owners are accompanied by the names of neighbours, a description, and an appraisal.

Moses Hart owned twenty-two properties distributed as follows: Rue Sainte-Marguerite (4), Rue Notre-Dame (5), Rue Saint-Paul (1), Rue du Platon (1), Rue des Forges (5), Rue Saint-Georges (1), Rue des Champs (1), Rue Haut-Boc (2), and Rue Alexandre (2). His main property was appraised at $500. In comparison, Samuel Bécancour, Ezekiel's oldest son, owned one house appraised at $1,000, and he owned thirteen houses. Alexander Thomas owned one house appraised at $225, which is very decent, and Areli Blake owned one house appraised at $200. Mathew Bell, a major landowner, owned a house appraised at $1,500. This was the most valuable one. The total appraisal was for $97,632. To this amount must be added the fiefs and seigneuries, valued at $41,454. Moses Hart owned four seigneuries: Marquisat du Sablé ($4,750), Vieuxpont ($2,338), Sainte-Marguerite ($5,080), and Hertel ($45).

In La Commune are the names of the representatives or heirs of Ezekiel Hart (no. 25), Moses Hart (no. 30), Aaron Hart (no. 70), then Joseph Abraham (no. 130) and Edward Abraham (Hart) (no. 131), Ira Craig Hart (no. 151), Aaron Moses Hart (no. 161), Ezekiel M. Hart (no. 163), the heirs of Ezekiel Hart (nos. 222, 306, and 307), Aaron Moses Hart (no. 232), Ezekiel Moses Hart (no. 333), Caroline Hart (no. 237), Samuel Bécancour Hart (no. 308).

Ezekiel Hart's Intellectual and Social Heritage

Thanks to Ezekiel Hart's inventory after death, we can take stock of the large house on Rue des Forges from top to bottom. The inventory, started on 30 November 1843, was completed in late February of the following year, and was complemented that September by the examination of various business papers, accounts payable and receivable, and the list of his many properties.

Marie Godin, the wife of Louis Langlois, a former servant of Frances Lazarus's, was present to identify the goods that were from Lazarus estate; Frances had died eighteen years before. I deduce that she had made her own will but left usufruct to her husband. In a very simple will, a stark contrast with that written by his brother Moses, Ezekiel left his estate to his children, Samuel Bécancour, Aaron Ezekiel, Ira Craig, Adolphus Mordecai, Esther Elisa, Harriet, and Caroline Athalia. His daughters inherited some land, "if single" (they did remain single, except for Esther, who lived for some time with Vallières de Saint-Réal). The house had sixteen well-furnished rooms. In a "large room at the top of said house," a "Turkish carpet estimated at six *livres courant*." That was a tidy sum. Further on, "a piano estimated at twenty *livres courant*," a chessboard, and other items. This inventory can be consulted at the Archives nationales de Trois-Rivières (cote L.D. Craig, 30-11-1843). The will is in the registry of notary Joseph-Michel Badeaux. The will is in English and the inventory in French.

Ezekiel was wealthy, but above all he was a "good husband and father. In addition to large holdings in real estate, he had given his children a refined and careful upbringing that would be passed on to his descendants" (DCB, vol. VII). Ezekiel was no doubt proud of his library, which the notaries spent three days inventorying. It comprised more than four hundred books, including a two-volume history of Judaism, the laws of Moses, a German bible, a critical history of the Old Testament, a Hebrew-Latin dictionary, books on history, geography, and law, plays, and travel accounts, including by Lahontan and John Lambert. Through Lambert, Ezekiel entered the history books. Lambert gave a long description of his visit to Trois-Rivières, introduced the Hart family, and gave his interpretation of the Hart affair. Lambert struck the right tone, which no doubt pleased Ezekiel. At the risk of boring you, here are the titles found in the first section of the room identified as the "library."

Descendants of Ezekiel Hart and Frances Lazarus

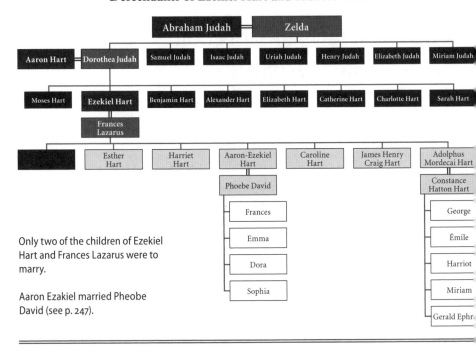

Only two of the children of Ezekiel Hart and Frances Lazarus were to marry.

Aaron Ezakiel married Pheobe David (see p. 247).

Adolphus Mordecai Hart married Constance Hatton Hart, his cousin. Here is her family tree.

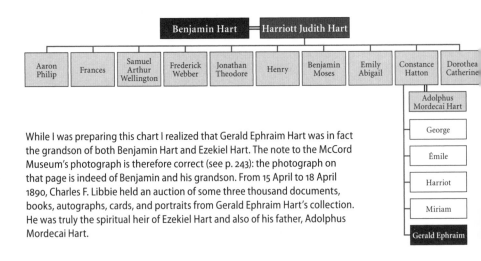

While I was preparing this chart I realized that Gerald Ephraim Hart was in fact the grandson of both Benjamin Hart and Ezekiel Hart. The note to the McCord Museum's photograph is therefore correct (see p. 243): the photograph on that page is indeed of Benjamin and his grandson. From 15 April to 18 April 1890, Charles F. Libbie held an auction of some three thousand documents, books, autographs, cards, and portraits from Gerald Ephraim Hart's collection. He was truly the spiritual heir of Ezekiel Hart and also of his father, Adolphus Mordecai Hart.

I examined the after-death inventories of Moses and Ezekiel—a bit peremptorily, I must admit—without finding any mention of monogrammed pieces. Given certain factors that lawyers would call circumstantial evidence, I hypothesized that some such pieces belonged to Ezekiel and Frances Hart. By the education that they gave their children and the social network that I know they had, they could easily have ordered plates and glasses in their effigy. The children may have shared these pieces when their mother died in 1821. The Harts loved to host parties and show off their success. Ezekiel was aware of being a part of history. John Lambert (2006, 305–08) confirmed this.

The carafe and small glasses bear a monogram: a stylized H. Both are donations from the founder of the McCord Museum, David Ross McCord. The dates 1820–25 are given for the carafe and glasses, and 1810–30 for some dishes. No provenance is indicated. Similar dishes are found in the Château Ramezay collection. There is no provenance given for those dishes either, but, as this museum has a bill from the Hart Bank and a portrait that is believed to be of Moses or Ezekiel Hart, a link has been established between the dishes and the two other objects.

On 6 January, the notaries were in the kitchen, the hall, a laundry room, and finally the library, where they found:

"A glass-fronted armoire estimated at ten shillings; a Latin-French dictionary; a volume from Goddons Book Keeping; an English-French dictionary by N. G. Dufief; a book by Smith Wealth of Nations in two volumes; a dictionary by Guthries; a volume by Fergusons lectures; a volume of operati by Dionis; a volume of Walker Gazetteer; a Latin book; Spirit of laws, in two volumes; Puclids doctor; a volume by Laws of New York, second volume; Zimmerman Survey; a work on domestic medicine by G. Buchan in five volumes; a universal dictionary latino gallicum; a geographic dictionary by Vosgien; a French-Latin dictionary by M. Lallemant; a second book by Telamae; Histoire d'Écosse by Robert Lindsay; a fisrt volume of Porcupine Works by Thomas Bradford; History of Poland; Smiths

Geography in two volumes; Robertsons navigation in two volumes; New Dispensatory, one volume; a Blume de Dorval chronicle, being number twenty; a volume by Delia? A Romance by Mademoiselle Longeville; a French-Italian dictionary by François Dolberti; a volume by Horati Flacci opera; an Italian-French dictionary; Bouchette geography; Sheridans dictionary in two volumes; MacKenzies Voyages; Books of the Encyclopedia Britannica in seventeen volumes estimated at 17 *livres courant.*"

On 7 December 1843, the inventory of the library continued. To give an idea of the size of Ezekiel's collection, the above list covered two and a half pages. There were thirteen and a half to come, or more than three hundred titles.

Ezekiel was fascinated by history and geography. He owned books on the history of a number of countries: England, Scotland, Siberia, Picture of Quebec, Life of Washington, History of the Reign of George the Third, Universal History in twenty volumes, and so on. And then there were The Crusaders, Pope Works, and other books of the sort.

Practical books: book of politeness, every man his own brewer, portable dictionary of health, Alexanders History of Women, and so on.

Classics: The Thousand and One Nights, Don Quixote, The Hermit, The Gentleman of the Old School, Ambrioso or the Monk, and so on.

Various periodicals and magazines, including a five-volume collection of the *Quebec Mercury* and many issues of *European magazine.*

Many lots of old books generally assembled at the end of a day of inventorying.

On 12 December, the notaries attacked the shed, where they found a four-wheel buggy, a four-wheel wagon, a cabriolet, a caleche, sleigh, an open buggy, a sled, and other items. In the stable were two horses and other animals.

All after-death inventories are fascinating documents, and Ezekiel and Frances's is particularly so. I give it a five-star rating.

Tug-of-war!
Superior Court and Court of King's Bench
(District of Quebec, 1809–1900)

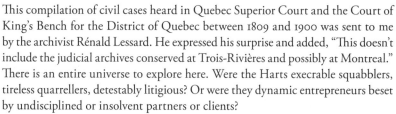

This compilation of civil cases heard in Quebec Superior Court and the Court of King's Bench for the District of Quebec between 1809 and 1900 was sent to me by the archivist Rénald Lessard. He expressed his surprise and added, "This doesn't include the judicial archives conserved at Trois-Rivières and possibly at Montreal." There is an entire universe to explore here. Were the Harts execrable squabblers, tireless quarrellers, detestably litigious? Or were they dynamic entrepreneurs beset by undisciplined or insolvent partners or clients?

It remains a story to be told. For the moment, I will mention that Moses Hart alone initiated 213 trials, and his partners, Ira Craig (73 trials) and Alexander Thomas (4), also took recourse to the courts. Thomas was more peaceable, which doesn't surprise me, but he took his uncle Ezekiel to court when the latter was over seventy years old. Ezekiel, ever tenacious, sued his nephew in return. Those familiar with the Harts will note that there are occasionally problems of spelling with the first names of the Harts: Adolphat N. for Adolphus M, Arele Blake or Avelie for Areli Blake, Renben for Ruben, and so on.

Order	File no	Last name	First name	Year	Last name	First name
01401	1732	HART	AARON EZEKIEL	1832	PERREAULT	JOSEPH FRANCIS
01402	338	HART	AARON EZEKIEL	1834	PERREAULT	JOSEPH FRANCOIS
01403	1283	HART	AARON EZEKIEL	1836	FONTAINE	JEAN BTE
01404	2254	HART	AARON EZEKIEL	1837	BURROUGH	EDWARD
01405	442	HART	AARON EZEKIEL	1838	BURROUGH	EDWARD
01406	2254	HART	AARON EZEKIEL	1838	BURROUGH	EDWARD
01407	367	HART	AARON EZEKIEL	1839	PADEN	CHARLES R.
01408	442	HART	AARON EZEKIEL	1839	BURROUGH	EDWARD
01409	443	HART	AARON EZEKIEL	1845	BURROUGH	EDWARD
01410	1387	HART	AARON PHILIP	1840	KEMPT	JOHN
01411	1275	HART	AB	1827	CHAPMAN	H. S.
01412	1275	HART	AB	1827	REVASS	JOHN
01413	2034	HART	AB	1836	TAYLOR	GEORGE
01414	1116	HART	ABRAHAM	1865	MICHON	ETIENNE
01415	110	HART	ABRAHAM	1875	JOURDAIN	THOMAS GORDON
01416	58	HART	ABRAHAM	1878	BOUDREAU	PIERRE ALPHONSE
01417	122	HART	ABRAHAM	1880	HALL	WILLIAM
01418	115	HART	ABRAHAM	1881	HALL	WILLIAM
01419	487	HART	ABRAHAM SAMUEL	1877	LASALLE	BENONI
01420	297	HART	ABRAHAM SAMUEL	1878	MILOT	ADOLPHE
01421	58	HART	ABRAHAM SAMUEL	1879	BOUDREAULT	PIERRE A.
01422	443	HART	ADOLPHAT N.	1845	BURROUGH	EDWARD
01423	429	HART	ALEXANDER	1826	SÉGUIN	FRANCOIS J.
01424	429	HART	ALEXANDRE	1814	SÉGUIN	FRANCOIS JACQUES

Order	File no	Last name	First name	Year	Last name	First name
101425	133	HART	ALEXANDRE	1815	SÉGUIN	FRANCOIS JACQUES
101426	222	HART	ALEXANDRE	1815	LEMAY	PIERRE
101427	367	HART	ALEXANDRE	1816	HAIG	JOHN
101428	103	HART	ALEXANDRE	1817	BARLOW	JOSEPH
101429	567	HART	ALEXANDRE	1817	SÉGUIN	FRANCOIS JACQUES
101430	1563	HART	ALEXANDRE	1833	SÉGUIN	FRANCOIS JACQUES
101431	1563	HART	ALEXANDRE	1833	HAMILTON ROBINSON	JOHN
101432	1563	HART	ALEXANDRE	1833	STEIN	ADOLPHUS
101433	1004	HART	ALEXANDRE THOMAS	1835	O'BRIEN	WILLIAM
101434	56	HART	ALEXANDRE THOMAS	1837	DUBORD	HYPOLITE
101435	1769	HART	ALEXANDRE THOMAS	1841	HART	EZEKIEL
101436	766	HART	ALEXANDRE THOMAS	1843	WILLIAM	CHARLES
101437	2034	HART	ARELLE BLAKE	1835	TAYLOR	GEORGE
101438	2034	HART	ARELLE BLAKE	1835	DAVIE	ALLISON
101439	1149	HART	AUGUSTIN	1842	LAGUEUX	PIERRE
101440	56	HART	AVELIE	1851	FILMER	EDMUND
101441	410	HART	BENJAMIN	1814	HENDERSON	JAMES
101442	410	HART	BENJAMIN	1814	HENDERSON	WILLIAM
101443	429	HART	BENJAMIN	1814	SÉGUIN	FRANCOIS JACQUES
101444	133	HART	BENJAMIN	1815	SÉGUIN	FRANCOIS JACQUES
101445	152	HART	BENJAMIN	1816	LEBLANC	ETIENNE
101446	567	HART	BENJAMIN	1817	SÉGUIN	FRANCOIS JACQUES
101447	947	HART	BENJAMIN	1822	SEIXAS	EDWARD
101448	1128	HART	BENJAMIN	1838	GUGY	B. C. A.
101449	1394	HART	BENJAMIN	1842	GLASS	HENRY
101450	1364	HART	BENJAMIN	1842	GLASS	HENRY
101451	754	HART	BENJAMIN	1842	BUTEAU	FRANCOIS
101452	1376	HART	BENJAMIN	1843	CLARKE	WILLIAM
101453	1322	HART	BENJAMIN	1843	KERR	GEORGE
101454	1322	HART	BENJAMIN	1843	GLASS	HENRY
101455	754	HART	BENJAMIN	1843	BUTEAU	FRANCOIS
101456	1034	HART	BENJAMIN	1845	DUBORD dit LAFONTAINE	CHARLES
101457	1058	HART	BRIDGET ANN	1873	HART	JOHN
101458	184	HART	BRIDGET ANN	1880	WURTELE	RICHARD HENRY
101459	1548	HART	BRIDGET ANN	1895	ROBITAILLE	ALFRED
101460	443	HART	CAROLINE ATHALIA	1845	BURROUGH	EDWARD
101461	270	HART	CAROLINE ATHALIA	1864	DEROUIN	CHARLES
101462	8	HART	CAROLINE ATHALIA	1877	BÉCANCOUR	SAMUEL
101463	8	HART	CAROLINE ATHALIA	1877	SEIGNEURIE DE BÉCANCOUR	
101464	662	HART	CATHERINE	1899	PHOÉNIS INSURANCE	
101465	595	HART	CHARLES	1848	O'BRIEN	MICHAEL
101466	1231	HART	CHARLES ADOLPHUS	1846	PORTER	HENRY HOWARD
101467	81	HART	CO	1812	JONES	JOSEPH
101468	81	HART	CO	1812	MELVIN	ROBERT
101469	81	HART	CO	1812	WHITE	THOMAS
101470	974	HART	DANIEL	1841	DREYFOUR	SIMÉON
101471	443	HART	ESTHER ELOSA	1845	BURROUGH	EDWARD
101472	712	HART	EZEKIEL	1812	SMITH BAYARD	WILLIAM
101473	106	HART	EZEKIEL	1824	BRUNET	LOUISE
101474	672	HART	EZEKIEL	1825	BRUNET	PHILIPPE
101475	672	HART	EZEKIEL	1825	BINET	LOUIS
101476	19	HART	EZEKIEL	1825	BRUNET	LOUISE
101477	19	HART	EZEKIEL	1825	ROY	JOSEPH
101478	103	HART	EZEKIEL	1825	CHAPERON	LEWIS
101479	117	HART	EZEKIEL	1825	FRASER	HUGH
101480	867	HART	EZEKIEL	1825	HERPHINS	JAMES
101481	189	HART	EZEKIEL	1825	LAUNIERE	LÉGER
101482	672	HART	EZEKIEL	1826	BRUNET	PHILIPPE
101483	672	HART	EZEKIEL	1826	BINETTE	LOUIS
101484	421	HART	EZEKIEL	1826	COFFIN	THOMAS
101485	95	HART	EZEKIEL	1826	MC CALLUM	JAMES
101486	95	HART	EZEKIEL	1826	MC CALLUM	JOHN
101487	851	HART	EZEKIEL	1827	DE GOUFFE	BAPTISTE
101488	867	HART	EZEKIEL	1827	EPHINS	JAMES
101489	986	HART	EZEKIEL	1828	BADEAUX	JOSEPH

Order	File no	Last name	First name	Year	Last name	First name
101490	1685	HART	EZEKIEL	1829	LARUE	OLIVIER
101491	1383	HART	EZEKIEL	1829	VASECK	STANISLAS
101492	32	HART	EZEKIEL	1809	MORROGH	ROBERT
101493	127	HART	EZEKIEL	1810	OLDINY	MICHAEL G.
101494	320	HART	EZEKIEL	1811	DE LA NAUDIÈRE	CHARLES
101495	7	HART	EZEKIEL	1817	ROUSSEAU	PIERRE
101496	36	HART	EZEKIEL	1833	ROLLAND	JEAN ROCK
101497	1543	HART	EZEKIEL	1835	KERR	JAMES HASTING
101498	1769	HART	EZEKIEL	1841	HART	ALEXANDER THOMAS
101499	1056	HART	EZEKIEL	1841	HART	ISRAEL
101500	1056	HART	EZEKIEL	1845	HART	ISA C.
101501	725	HART	FRÉDÉRICVK	1841	YOUNG	GEORGES
101502	1727	HART	GEORGE	1857	MIDDLETON	ELIZA
101503	2383	HART	GEORGE	1875	MC CALLUM	DANIEL
101504	801	HART	GEORGE EZEKIEL	1875	HOULD	JEAN BTE LUDGER
101505	1700	HART	GEORGE EZEKIEL	1876	CASEY	THOMAS
101506	122	HART	GEORGE EZEKIEL	1880	HALL	WILLIAM
101507	1689	HART	GEORGE EZEKIEL	1880	MC GREEVY	THOMAS
101508	78	HART	GEORGE EZEKIEL	1881	GERVAIS	ARMAND ED.
101509	115	HART	GEORGE EZEKIEL	1881	HALL	WILLIAM
101510	115	HART	GÉRALD E.	1881	HALL	WILLIAM
101511	384	HART	GÉRALD E.	1885	BEAUDRY	LOUIS Z.
101512	1348	HART	GÉRALD E.	1890	HUOT	JACQUES E.
101513	443	HART	HARRIET	1845	BURROUGH	EDOUARD
101514	122	HART	HARRIET JUDITH	1880	HALL	WILLIAM
101515	115	HART	HARRIET JUDITH	1881	HALL	WILLIAM
101516	250	HART	HENRY E.	1885	MILETTE	AUG
101517	1572	HART	HENRY L.	1844	MEAD	JOSEPH H.
101518	187	HART	IRA CRAIG	1838	DYDE	JOHN
101519	1154	HART	IRA CRAIG	1836	REINHART	JONATHAN
101520	1154	HART	IRA CRAIG	1836	REINHART	GEORGE
101521	1128	HART	IRA CRAIG	1837	GAGNON	BENJAMIN
101522	1393	HART	IRA CRAIG	1837	PORTER	JOHN
101523	1393	HART	IRA CRAIG	1837	HUNTER	CHARLES
101524	352	HART	IRA CRAIG	1839	MC LEOD	JOHN
101525	2355	HART	IRA CRAIG	1839	THOMPSON	JOHN
101526	2354	HART	IRA CRAIG	1839	THOMPSON	JOHN
101527	1676	HART	IRA CRAIG	1840	VALOIS	FELIX
101528	493	HART	IRA CRAIG	1840	BOUCHER	CAROLINE
101529	1336	HART	IRA CRAIG	1841	FALLIS	MATTHEW
101530	869	HART	IRA CRAIG	1841	PAQUET	MICHEL
101531	1154	HART	IRA CRAIG	1841	GRANT	JAMES
101532	532	HART	IRA CRAIG	1841	HADDAN	ROBERT
101533	532	HART	IRA CRAIG	1841	HADDAN	ALEXANDER
101534	1376	HART	IRA CRAIG	1841	MC LEAN	ALEXANDER
101535	1056	HART	IRA CRAIG	1841	HART	EZEKIEL
101536	472	HART	IRA CRAIG	1842	WEIPPERT	HUBERT
101537	1336	HART	IRA CRAIG	1842	FALLIS	WILLIAM
101538	864	HART	IRA CRAIG	1843	HOBROUGH	JOSHUA
101539	1301	HART	IRA CRAIG	1843	LYNCH	MARTIN
101540	584	HART	IRA CRAIG	1843	HENDERSON	MATTHEW
101541	1100	HART	IRA CRAIG	1843	HART	MOSES
101542	1056	HART	IRA CRAIG	1843	HART	EZEKIEL
101543	449	HART	IRA CRAIG	1843	TOURANGEAU	JOSEPH
101544	273	HART	IRA CRAIG	1843	HOBROUGH	JOSHUA
101545	1172	HART	IRA CRAIG	1844	THORNTON	ROBERT
101546	1100	HART	IRA CRAIG	1844	HART	MOSES
101547	2061	HART	IRA CRAIG	1844	HOBROUGH	JOSHUA
101548	1056	HART	IRA CRAIG	1844	HART	EZEKIEL
101549	443	HART	IRA CRAIG	1845	BURROUGH	EDWARD
101550	683	HART	IRA CRAIG	1845	FALCONBRIDGE	WILLIAM
101551	683	HART	IRA CRAIG	1845	PLEAICK	MARY
101552	1056	HART	IRA CRAIG	1845	HART	EZEKIEL M.
101553	676	HART	IRA CRAIG	1845	PLEAICK	MARY
101554	380	HART	IRA CRAIG	1846	Canada FIRE ASSURANCE CO.	
101555	1154	HART	IRA CRAIG	1846	GREEN	MARY
101556	1154	HART	IRA CRAIG	1846	PEMBERTON	WILLIAM

Order	File no	Last name	First name	Year	Last name	First name
101557	1154	HART	IRA CRAIG	1846	LARUE	EDOUARD
101558	1172	HART	IRA CRAIG	1846	THORNTON	ROBERT
101559	1154	HART	IRA CRAIG	1847	REINHART	JONATHAN
101560	1154	HART	IRA CRAIG	1847	GREEN	MARY
101561	1154	HART	IRA CRAIG	1847	PEMBERTON	WILLIAM
101562	1154	HART	IRA CRAIG	1847	LARUE	EDOUARD
101563	1154	HART	IRA CRAIG	1847	REINHART	GEORGE
101564	1172	HART	IRA CRAIG	1847	THORNTON	ROBERT
101565	1172	HART	IRA CRAIG	1847	MC LIMONT	RICHARD
101566	1172	HART	IRA CRAIG	1847	HENDERSON	WALTER CHARLES
101567	1172	HART	IRA CRAIG	1847	SINCLAIR	JOHN
101568	395	HART	IRA CRAIG	1848	VENIÈRE	NARCISSE
101569	1059	HART	IRA CRAIG	1848	PAQUET	MICHEL
101570	1154	HART	IRA CRAIG	1848	REINHART	JONATHAN
101571	1154	HART	IRA CRAIG	1848	GREEN	MARY
101572	1172	HART	IRA CRAIG	1848	THOSTON	ROBERT
101573	1172	HART	IRA CRAIG	1848	MC LIMONT	RICHARD
101574	1172	HART	IRA CRAIG	1848	HENDERSON	WALTER
101575	1172	HART	IRA CRAIG	1848	SINCLAIR	JOHN
101576	1059	HART	IRA CRAIG	1849	GAGNON	MARGUERITE
101577	1056	HART	IRA CRAIG	1850	HUNT	EZEKIEL M.
101578	1059	HART	IRA CRAIG	1850	LABRECQUE	CHARLES
101579	1059	HART	IRA CRAIG	1850	TURGEON	EMÉRANCE
101580	1154	HART	IRA CRAIG	1850	LARUE	WILBROD
101581	1154	HART	IRA CRAIG	1851	REINHART	JONATHAN
101582	1154	HART	IRA CRAIG	1851	GREEN	MARY
101583	1154	HART	IRA CRAIG	1851	PEMBERTON	WILLIAM
101584	1154	HART	IRA CRAIG	1851	LARUE	EDOUARD
101585	1154	HART	IRA CRAIG	1851	REINHART	GEORGE
101586	1154	HART	IRA CRAIG	1851	LARUE	WILBROD
101587	1154	HART	IRA CRAIG	1851	REINHART	GEORGE THOMAS
101588	395	HART	IRA CRAIG	1854	VENIÈRE	NARCISSE
101589	8	HART	IRA CRAIG	1877	BÉCANCOUR	SAMUEL
101590	8	HART	IRA CRAIG	1877	SEIGNEURIE DE BÉCANCOUR	
101591	590	HART	JAMES	1821	SWIFT	MATHEW
101592	415	HART	JONATHAN	1817	MC LISH	DAVID
101593	876	HART	JONATHAN	1817	RITCHIE	ROBERT
101594	199	HART	JONATHAN	1819	JONES	JOSEPH
101595	199	HART	JONATHAN	1819	WHITE	THOMAS
101596	299	HART	JONATHAN	1819	DICK	JAMES
101597	413	HART	JONATHAN	1819	GAGNON	JACQUES
101598	529	HART	JONATHAN	1819	GAGNON	JACQUES
101599	1290	HART	JONATHAN	1820	GAGNON	JACQUES
101600	660	HART	J. C.	1836	THOMPSON	FRÉDÉRICK
101601	1260	HART	JOHN	1847	O'BRIEN	MICHAEL
101602	677	HART	JOHN	1847	MILLER	LOUIS
101603	1058	HART	JOHN	1873	HART	BRIDG
101604	1273	HART	JOHN	1874	QUÉBEC GULF STEAMSHIP	
101605	705	HART	JOSEPH	1848	BRADLEY	SAMUEL
101606	946	HART	KATIE ANN	1895	GERVAIS	LOUIS BPT
101607	172	HART	LOUIS NAPOLÉON H.	1891	HOWESTON	GEORGES B.
101608	2556	HART	MARIE ARLINE	1885	JULIEN	PIERRE
101609	122	HART	MIRIAM H.	1880	HALL	WILLIAM
101610	115	HART	MIRIAM H.	1881	HALL	WILLIAM
101611	377	HART	MIRIAM H.	1883	CARLE	CHARLES
101612	384	HART	MIRIAM H.	1885	BEAUDRY	LOUIS
101613	68	HART	MIRIAM H.	1885	BRUNELLE	GASPARD
101614	263	HART	MIRIAM H.	1885	MAILHIOT	HENRY G.
101615	248	HART	MOSES	1809	MILLER	ROBERT
101616	22	HART	MOSES	1809	KER	JAMES
101617	260	HART	MOSES	1809	BURNS	WILLIAM
101618	43	HART	MOSES	1810	VALLERAND	FRANCOIS
101619	50	HART	MOSES	1810	VALLERAND	FRANCOIS
101620	97	HART	MOSES	1810	MARCHAND	NICK
101621	184	HART	MOSES	1810	SMITH	WILLIAM
101622	46	HART	MOSES	1811	MARCHAND	NICOLAS

Order	File no	Last name	First name	Year	Last name	First name
01623	447	HART	MOSES	1811	BURNS	WILLIAM
01624	537	HART	MOSES	1811	LABRECQUE	JACQUES
01625	400	HART	MOSES	1811	DAUFIN	GENEVIEVE
01626	81	HART	MOSES	1812	JONES	JOSEPH
01627	81	HART	MOSES	1812	WHITE	THOMAS
01628	81	HART	MOSES	1812	MELVIN	ROBERT
01629	525	HART	MOSES	1813	BURN	TH
01630	525	HART	MOSES	1813	BURN	MARGARET
01631	632	HART	MOSES	1813	MARCHAND	NICOLAS
01632	131	HART	MOSES	1815	MARCHAND	NICOLAS
01633	287	HART	MOSES	1816	GAUVREAU	LOUIS CLAUDE
01634	748	HART	MOSES	1816	PARKER	WILLIAM
01635	600	HART	MOSES	1817	BURN	THOMAS
01636	784	HART	MOSES	1817	JONES	EWDWARD
01637	704	HART	MOSES	1818	CARRIER	ETIENNE
01638	1136	HART	MOSES	1818	BARNARD	JAMES
01639	1146	HART	MOSES	1818	DELISLE	MAGDELEINE
01640	1146	HART	MOSES	1818	MERCURE	AUGUSTIN
01641	522	HART	MOSES	1819	PARKER	WILLIAM
01642	159	HART	MOSES	1820	DUQUET	LOUIS
01643	184	HART	MOSES	1820	WHITNEY	JOSHIA
01644	197	HART	MOSES	1820	CARRIER	ETIENNE
01645	219	HART	MOSES	1820	HAY	JEAN BPT
01646	294	HART	MOSES	1820	WILSON	WILLIAM
01647	391	HART	MOSES	1820	MONGRAIN	LOUIS
01648	467	HART	MOSES	1820	GAUVREAU	LOUIS CLAUDE
01649	575	HART	MOSES	1820	WHITNEY	JOSHUA
01650	617	HART	MOSES	1820	HAY	JEAN BPT
01651	193	HART	MOSES	1821	LANG	JAMES
01652	17	HART	MOSES	1821	SHEPPARD	PETER
01653	159	HART	MOSES	1822	DUQUET	LOUIS
01654	345	HART	MOSES	1822	HAY	JEAN BPT
01655	219	HART	MOSES	1822	HAY	JEAN BPT
01656	1077	HART	MOSES	1822	NOEL	JEAN BPT
01657	609	HART	MOSES	1822	WILSON	WILL
01658	609	HART	MOSES	1822	WILLIAM	ANN
01659	812	HART	MOSES	1823	DUQUET	ISAIE OL.
01660	605	HART	MOSES	1823	GAUVREAU	LOUIS CLAUDE
01661	605	HART	MOSES	1823	CHANDONNAIS	MARIE A.
01662	345	HART	MOSES	1823	HAY	JEAN BTE
01663	1459	HART	MOSES	1823	JOURDAIN	CHARLES
01664	1077	HART	MOSES	1823	NOEL	JEAN BTE
01665	1286	HART	MOSES	1823	PLAMONDON	LOUIS
01666	1381	HART	MOSES	1823	PLAMONDON	LOUIS
01667	843	HART	MOSES	1823	ROBINSON	WEBB
01668	1299	HART	MOSES	1823	THOMAS	LEWIS A.
01669	1339	HART	MOSES	1823	TREMAIN	BENJAMIN
01670	566	HART	MOSES	1824	REX	DOMINUS
01671	465	HART	MOSES	1824	REX	DOMINUS
01672	17	HART	MOSES	1824	SHEPPARD	PETER
01673	339	HART	MOSES	1825	BLUMHART	GEORGE
01674	532	HART	MOSES	1825	BLUMHART	GEORGE
01675	669	HART	MOSES	1825	CHARAY	PIERRE
01676	1339	HART	MOSES	1825	GOODHUE	CHARLES FRANCOIS XAVIER
01677	382	HART	MOSES	1825	NORIS	THOMAS
01678	406	HART	MOSES	1825	OLIVA	THOMAS CASIMIR
01679	406	HART	MOSES	1825	FORTIER	FRANCOIS
01680	843	HART	MOSES	1825	ROBINSON	WEBB
01681	843	HART	MOSES	1825	GUICHAUX	HENRY
01682	843	HART	MOSES	1825	PRIMROSE	E. W.
01683	843	HART	MOSES	1825	CASAULT	ANTOINE
01684	843	HART	MOSES	1825	EAST	FRÉDÉRICK
01685	843	HART	MOSES	1825	DAUTON	ROBERT
01686	843	HART	MOSES	1825	STILSON	JOSEPH
01687	843	HART	MOSES	1825	JONES	JOSEPH
01688	843	HART	MOSES	1825	DESALABERY	M. C.
01689	843	HART	MOSES	1825	COULSON	FRANCOIS

Order	File no	Last name	First name	Year	Last name	First name
101690	843	HART	MOSES	1825	MACKIE	WILIAM
101691	843	HART	MOSES	1825	URSULINES OF QUÉBEC	
101692	1284	HART	MOSES	1825	TREMAIN	HENRY H. X.
101693	503	HART	MOSES	1825	VOYER	PIERRE
101694	442	HART	MOSES	1825	VOYER	PIERRE
101695	585	HART	MOSES	1826	BLUMHART	GEORGE
101696	585	HART	MOSES	1826	LACOMBE	ROSALIE
101697	409	HART	MOSES	1826	DESBARATS	PIERRE E.
101698	364	HART	MOSES	1826	DUQUET	LÉO
101699	364	HART	MOSES	1826	DUQUET	JOSEPH
101700	272	HART	MOSES	1826	HAMEL	JOSEPH
101701	563	HART	MOSES	1826	JOURDAIN	CHARLES
101702	843	HART	MOSES	1826	HADDAN	ALEX
101703	843	HART	MOSES	1826	CHINIC	MARTIN
101704	1339	HART	MOSES	1826	TREMAIN	BENJAMIN
101705	766	HART	MOSES	1826	VANFELSON	GEORGE
101706	503	HART	MOSES	1826	VOYER	PIERRE
101707	503	HART	MOSES	1826	MUNRO	ANGELIQUE
101708	442	HART	MOSES	1826	VOYER	PIERRE
101709	442	HART	MOSES	1826	SAUVAGEAU	ALEX
101710	364	HART	MOSES	1827	DUQUET	LOUIS
101711	364	HART	MOSES	1827	DUQUET	JOSEPH
101712	1339	HART	MOSES	1827	GOODHUE	CHARLES FRANCOIS XAVIER
101713	508	HART	MOSES	1827	JULIEN ELOT	MARY
101714	335	HART	MOSES	1827	KERR	JAMES
101715	1587	HART	MOSES	1827	KERR	JAMES
101716	406	HART	MOSES	1827	OLIVA	THOMAS C.
101717	406	HART	MOSES	1827	FORTIER	FRANCOIS
101718	843	HART	MOSES	1827	ROBINSON	WEBB
101719	843	HART	MOSES	1827	GUICHAUX	HENRY
101720	843	HART	MOSES	1827	PRIMROSE	F. X.
101721	843	HART	MOSES	1827	CASAULT	ANTOINE
101722	843	HART	MOSES	1827	EAST	FRED.
101723	843	HART	MOSES	1827	DAUSTON	ROBERT
101724	843	HART	MOSES	1827	STILSON	JOSEPH
101725	843	HART	MOSES	1827	JONES	JOSEPH
101726	843	HART	MOSES	1827	DESALABERY	M.
101727	843	HART	MOSES	1827	CHINIC	MARTIN
101728	843	HART	MOSES	1827	MACKIE	WILIAM
101729	843	HART	MOSES	1827	URSULINES OF QUÉBEC	
101730	843	HART	MOSES	1827	HADDAN	ALEX
101731	1562	HART	MOSES	1828	BOUCHETTE	JOSEPH
101732	1246	HART	MOSES	1828	BEAULIEU	JOSEPH
101733	355	HART	MOSES	1828	MORROGH	ROBERT L.
101734	39	HART	MOSES	1829	ANDERSON	JOHN
101735	1484	HART	MOSES	1829	GAUVREAU	MARIE ANNE
101736	1654	HART	MOSES	1829	GÉRARD	SAMUEL
101737	563	HART	MOSES	1829	JOURDAIN	CHARLES
101738	1483	HART	MOSES	1830	TROTTIER	ZACHARIE
101739	1483	HART	MOSES	1830	MÉRAN	JOSEPH
101740	1483	HART	MOSES	1830	LEQUIER	JOSEPH
101741	1679	HART	MOSES	1832	CALDWELL	JOHN
101742	585	HART	MOSES	1832	DENIS dit LAPIERRE	ETIENNE
101743	1689	HART	MOSES	1833	EXPARTE	
101744	1539	HART	MOSES	1834	FROST	THOMAS
101745	1208	HART	MOSES	1834	MILLER	JOHN
101746	47	HART	MOSES	1834	O'BRIEN	WILLIAM
101747	1778	HART	MOSES	1834	O'BRIEN	WILLIAM
101748	1004	HART	MOSES	1834	O'BRIEN	WILLIAM
101749	2021	HART	MOSES	1834	OLIVIER HAILMILTON	THOMAS
101750	2201	HART	MOSES	1835	BLACK	GEORGE
101751	1654	HART	MOSES	1835	GÉRARD	SAMUEL
101752	718	HART	MOSES	1835	LASSISERAIE	JOSEPH LOUIS
101753	1654	HART	MOSES	1836	GERRARD	SAMUEL
101754	1081	HART	MOSES	1836	MARCOUX	JOSEPH
101755	68	HART	MOSES	1836	DEFOY	EDOUARD
101756	2297	HART	MOSES	1836	NICHOLSON	JOHN

Order	File no	Last name	First name	Year	Last name	First name
101757	2304	HART	MOSES	1836	TWEDDLE	THOMAS
101758	2021	HART	MOSES	1836	ST OLIVIER	THOMAS
101759	2291	HART	MOSES	1836	NICHOLSON	JOHN
101760	2201	HART	MOSES	1836	BLACK	GEORGE
101761	982	HART	MOSES	1836	DUVAL TAYLOR	GEORGES
101762	662	HART	MOSES	1836	SATLAND	JOHN
101763	2322	HART	MOSES	1837	DUQUET	ISAIE OLIVIER
101764	1570	HART	MOSES	1837	MC LEAN CARTER	ISABELLA
101765	1081	HART	MOSES	1837	MARCOUX	JOSEPH
101766	1081	HART	MOSES	1837	MARCOUX	JOSEPH
101767	1081	HART	MOSES	1837	VOYER	PIERRE
101768	2297	HART	MOSES	1837	NICHOLSON	JOHN
101769	1654	HART	MOSES	1837	GERRARD	SAMUEL
101770	982	HART	MOSES	1837	TAYLOR	GEORGE
101771	1867	HART	MOSES	1837	BROWN	WILLIAM
101772	1654	HART	MOSES	1838	GERRARD	SAMUEL
101773	2014	HART	MOSES	1838	ANTRABUS	EDMOND W. R.
101774	254	HART	MOSES	1840	MARTIN BEAULIEU	LOUIS
101775	2304	HART	MOSES	1840	TWEDDLE	THOMAS
101776	2242	HART	MOSES	1840	DEMERS	ALEXANDRE
101777	1239	HART	MOSES	1840	STUART	JAMES
101778	911	HART	MOSES	1840	PERREAULT	JOSEPH
101779	1570	HART	MOSES	1840	MC LEAN CARTER	ISABELLA
101780	1570	HART	MOSES	1840	POTHIERS	TOUSSAINT
101781	2201	HART	MOSES	1837	BLACK	GEORGE
101782	68	HART	MOSES	1837	DEFOY	EDOUARD
101783	2304	HART	MOSES	1837	TWEDDLE	THOMAS
101784	2322	HART	MOSES	1838	DUQUET	ISAIE O.
101785	2322	HART	MOSES	1838	NOEL	JEAN BTE
101786	1081	HART	MOSES	1838	MARCOUX	JOEPH
101787	1570	HART	MOSES	1838	MC LEAN CARTER	ISABELLA
101788	1867	HART	MOSES	1838	BROWN	WILLIAM
101789	862	HART	MOSES	1838	JONES	JOHN
101790	610	HART	MOSES	1838	JONES	JOHN
101791	862	HART	MOSES	1839	JONES	JOHN
101792	1081	HART	MOSES	1839	MARCOUX	JOSEPH
101793	2014	HART	MOSES	1839	ANTRABUS	EDMUND W. R.
101794	1332	HART	MOSES	1839	MARTIN dit BEAULIEU	LOUIS
101795	1654	HART	MOSES	1839	GERRARD	SAMUEL
101796	1570	HART	MOSES	1839	MC LEAN	ISABELLA
101797	2304	HART	MOSES	1839	TWEDDLE	THOMAS
101798	2244	HART	MOSES	1839	DEMERS	ALEXANDRE
101799	1213	HART	MOSES	1841	SEWELL	AUGUSTUS ROBERT
101800	739	HART	MOSES	1842	NICHOLSON	JOHN
101801	1213	HART	MOSES	1842	SEWELL	AUGUSTUS ROBERT
101802	1727	HART	MOSES	1842	GIBB	JAMES
101803	1727	HART	MOSES	1842	LANE	ELISKA
101804	725	HART	MOSES	1842	WILLIAM	CHARLES
101805	937	HART	MOSES	1843	JOHNSON	RICHARD
101806	911	HART	MOSES	1843	PERREAULT	JOSEPH
101807	1727	HART	MOSES	1843	GIBB	JAMES
101808	1727	HART	MOSES	1843	LANE	ELISKA
101809	1654	HART	MOSES	1843	GÉRARD	SAMUEL
101810	1100	HART	MOSES	1843	HART CRAIG	IRA
101811	725	HART	MOSES	1843	WILLIAM	CHARLES
101812	739	HART	MOSES	1843	NICHOLSON	JOHN
101813	1100	HART	MOSES	1844	HART CRAIG	IRA
101814	1024	HART	MOSES	1844	CURATE CHURCH WARDENS OF FABRIQUE ST JEAN DESCHAILLONS	
101815	937	HART	MOSES	1844	SEWELL	AUGUSTUS ROBERT
101816	1416	HART	MOSES	1845	BERGERON	AUGUSTIN
101817	951	HART	MOSES	1847	MONTIZAMBERT	EDWARD L.
101818	663	HART	MOSES	1847	RUSSEL	WILLIAM GEORGE
101819	1221	HART	MOSES	1849	BILODEAU	PIERRE
101820	951	HART	MOSES	1850	MONTIZAMBERT	EDWARD L.
101821	1654	HART	MOSES	1851	GERRARD	SAMUEL

Order	File no	Last name	First name	Year	Last name	First name
101822	1376	HART	MOSES	1851	PAINCHAUD	JOSEPH
101823	1654	HART	MOSES	1852	GARAND	SAMUEL
101824	1654	HART	MOSES	1853	GERRARD	SAMUEL
101825	10	HART	MOSES	1874	BAILLARGEON	CHARLES F.
101826	328	HART	MOSES	1875	LEMAIRE	FRANCOIS
101827	464	HART	MOSES	1877	LASALLE	BENONI
101828	302	HART	MOSES ALEXANDRE THOMAS	1891	BOUDREAULT	PIERRE ALP.
101829	64	HART	MOSES E.	1881	BOUDREAU	P. A.
101830	1834	HART	ORLÉANS	1847	COOK	JOHN
101831	1999	HART	PATRICK	1844	CLEAROHUE	JAMES
101832	1999	HART	PATRICK	1844	SYMMES	ROBERT
101833	791	HART	PATRICK	1845	DAVIDSON	JAMES
101834	374	HART	PATRICK	1846	DEFOY	JULIE LÉOCADIE
101835	457	HART	PATRICK	1846	DEFOY	JULIE LÉOCADIE
101836	1856	HART	RENBEN M.	1865	DESROCHERS	LÉON
101837	248	HART	ROBERT	1809	MILLER	ROBERT
101838	443	HART	SAMUEL BÉCANCOUR	1845	BURROUGH	EDWARD L.
101839	266	HART	SAMUEL BÉCANCOUR	1845	PRATTE	MODESTE
101840	16	HART	SAMUEL JUDAH	1879	KING	CHARLES
101841	16	HART	SAMUEL JUDAH	1879	KING	JAMES
101842	1863	HART	THÉODORE	1850	HENRY	WILLIAM
101843	803	HART	THÉODORE	1855	MORGAN	JOSEPH
101844	803	HART	THÉODORE	1855	MORGAN	EDWARD L.
101845	67	HART	THÉODORE	1857	PELLETIER	HENRI
101846	690	HART	THÉODORE	1857	PELLETIER	HENRI
101847	1801	HART	THÉODORE	1873	LEVEY	CHARLES E.
101848	72	HART	THOMAS	1833	BETHEL	WILLIAM
101849	1150	HART	THOMAS	1833	LABRIÈRE DE MONTARVILLE BOUCHER	FRANCOISE
101850	1636	HART	THOMAS	1833	WOLF	ALEX. JOS.
101851	1008	HART	THOMAS	1836	WOLF	ALEXANDER JOSEPH
101852	1368	HART	THOMAS	1839	AHERN	JOHN V.
101853	1311	HART	THOMAS	1844	THE QUEEN	
101854	689	HART	THOMAS	1845	CORRIGAN	WILLIAM
101855	1211	HART	THOMAS	1845	ROSS	WILLIAM
101856	1211	HART	THOMAS	1845	FRASER	SIMON
101857	22	HART	THOMAS	1859	MOORE	JOSEPH BALDOCK
101858	32	HART	THOMAS	1859	MOORE	JOSEPH BALDOCK
101859	47	HART	TIMOTHY	1811	PATTERSON	TIMOTHY
101860	47	HART	TIMOTHY	1811	MALANECK	JOHN M.
101861	47	HART	TIMOTHY	1811	WALKER	WILL
101862	47	HART	TIMOTHY	1811	HOPKINS	SAM
101863	246	HART	WILLIAM	1824	FAIRDILD	DAVID

The petition that circulated in support of Benjamin Hart in 1812 spurred me to take a look at the files from that period. I decided to examine the register of judgments for the years 1812–14 (see p. 200). Like all documents of this nature, the register was impeccably kept and the names are entered in alphabetical order. Alas, my photos are not very good, but I can nevertheless pick out some thirty cases registered in Benjamin's name; twenty-five in Ezekiel's name; and ten in Moses's name. In Moses's files in the Archives du Séminaire, I found a number of invoices presented by lawyers. On 19 October 1835, Thomas H. Judah gave him a statement of account for thirty-four cases between 1829 and 1834 (ASTR, 0009-L-D-44); on 14 March 1836, there was another statement for forty-two different cases pleaded from 1830 to 1835. Of course, Moses Hart took the time to examine and annotate each of the items listed. On 7 November 1851, Judah presented yet another statement of account for fifteen cases in 1841–42. No, this is not a typo, these are the actual dates. Many of these statements were found in the heirs' papers (see the case of notary Burn, p. 218).

The directory of the Hart collection includes a list of eighty-three "advocate prosecutors for the Harts." A quick examination leads me to believe that these were not all lawyers, but this number is not far off the mark. There is also a list of 244 cases instigated by the Harts against other people and 78 instigated against the Harts. In general, these cases concern Moses. There are few of Ezekiel's and Benjamin's papers in the Hart collection. That said, to have an idea of the nature of the cases, one must consult the judicial archives; the papers in the Hart collection with regard to this subject contain mainly invoices and exchanges of letters. Moses Hart had problems with both religion and justice. One must be surprised at the many drafts for reforms that he wrote, his petitions in favour of increasing the number of judges and the reduction of legal fees (ASTR, 0009-1-a-1 to L-a-9). He sometimes denounced the French legal system, but he did have some regrets: "In the times of the French, justice was administered by the intendant, without lawyers. It is time that we stop considering London as the last recourse for Canadian law. . . . Seeking justice three thousand miles away is ludicrous" (0009-L-a-7). Someone once wrote, "In New France, justice worked well, there were no lawyers"!

In the Berthelot file, I found a letter dated 6 December 1799 from the young Trois-Rivières lawyer Amable Berthelot to Moses Hart: "I have just received two *piastres* that you sent me by the mail . . . Do not believe that this is the way one acts with honest people and that I am satisfied with what you have sent me. When a lawyer takes the trouble to examine a case and to exempt you from a trial that could only have turned to your disadvantage, he must in all regards be better paid. If you do not send me £1.3.4 the amount owed expect that I will pursue you in court" (ASTR, 0009-L-D-7). Moses Hart was always bad at paying his bills. There are dozens of accounts by lawyers who demand fees for years' worth of services. Some are in the heirs' papers.

Bibliography

List of abbreviations

ASTR	Archives du Séminaire de Trois-Rivières
BRH	Bulletin de recherches historiques
BAnQ	Bibliothèque et Archives nationales du Québec
CJA	*Canadian Jewish Archives*
DCB	*Dictionary of Canadian Biography*
DC	*Documents relatifs à l'histoire constitutionnelle*
LAC	Library and Archives Canada
PRDH	Programme de recherche en démographie historique
RAPQ	*Rapport de l'archiviste de la province de Québec*
RG	Record Group

Archives

Archives du Séminaire de Trois-Rivières (ASTR), mainly for the Hart Collection.

McCord Museum, mainly for the Hart Papers.

American Jewish Historical Society (AJHS), Center for Jewish History, mainly for The Hart Family Papers. Now in New York, before at Brandeis University (Waltham).

American Jewish Archives (AJA), Cincinnati.

Archives of the Canadian Jewish Congress. Montreal: mainly their wonderful collection in the Canadian Jewish Archives (*CJA*) (Vol. 1, No. 1) published by the Congress starting in August 1955 on the initiative of M. H. Myerson, Louis Rosenberg and David Rome.

BAnQ, TR for Centre d'archives de la Mauricie et du Centre-du-Québec, Bibliothèque et Archives nationales du Québec, Superior Court collection, District judiciaire de Trois-Rivières. Also BAnQ, Québec.

Library and Archives Canada (LAC). Ottawa.

Université de Montréal, Collection Baby.

Bibliothèque de l'Assemblée nationale for the collection of *Journaux de la Chambre d'Assemblée*.

Main works cited

ABELLA, Irving (1990). *A coat of many colours: two centuries of Jewish life in Canada*. Lester & Orpen Dennys.

ANTAYA, F. "Chasser en échange d'un salaire. Les engagés amérindiens dans la traite des fourrures du Saint-Maurice, 1798-1831," *Revue d'histoire de l'Amérique-française*, Vol. 63, No. 1.

ARON, Raymond. "De Gaulle, Israël et les Juifs," *L'Express*, No. 874, 18-24 March 1968.

BEAUSOLEIL, Claude (1996). *Fort sauvage*. Pantin, Le Castor astral.

BIRON, Hervé (1947). *Grandeurs et misères de l'Église trifluvienne, 1615-1947*. Trois-Rivières: Éditions Trifluviennes.

BOULET, Gilles, Jacques LACOURSIÈRE and Denis VAUGEOIS (2010). *Le Boréal Express. Journal d'histoire du Canada*, tome III, 1810-1841. Québec: Septentrion.

CHARBONNEAU, André and André SÉVIGNY (1997). *1847, Grosse Île au fil des jours*. Ottawa: Parcs Canada.

CORCOS, Arlette (1997). *Montréal, les Juifs et l'école*. Sillery: Septentrion.

CORRIVEAU, Claude (1991). *Les Voitures à chevaux au Québec*. Septentrion.

Côté, André (1998). *Joseph-Michel Cadet (1719-1781), négociant et munitionnaire du roi en Nouvelle-France*. Sillery: Septentrion.

DAHL, Edward H. (2000) and Jean-François GAUVIN. *Sphaerae Mundi*. Septentrion.

DAVIES, Raymond Arthur (1955). *Printed Jewish canadiana, 1685-1900. Tentative check list of books, pamphlets, pictures, magazine and newspaper articles and currency written by or relating to the Jews of Canada*. Montreal: Lillian Davies.

DEROME, Robert. "Marie-Catherine Delezenne," *Dictionary of Canadian Biography*, VI.

DESCHÊNES, Gaston (1999). *Une capitale éphémère. Montréal et les événements tragiques de 1849*. Sillery: Septentrion.

DOUVILLE, Raymond, "Les opinions politiques et religieuses de Moses Hart." *Les Cahiers des Dix*, No. 17 (1952), p. 137-151.

DOUVILLE, Raymond (1938). *Aaron Hart, récit historique*. Trois-Rivières: Éditions du Bien public.

DOUVILLE, Raymond. "La Maison de Gannes," *Les Cahiers des Dix*, No. 21 (1956), p. 105-136.

DOUVILLE, Raymond. "Années de jeunesse et vie familiale de Moses Hart," *Les Cahiers des Dix*, No. 23 (1958), p. 195-216.

DOUVILLE, Raymond. "John Bruyères," *Dictionary of Canadian Biography*, IV.

DUBUC, Alfred. "John Molson," *Dictionary of Canadian Biography*, VII.

DULL, Jonathan R. (2009). *La guerre de Sept Ans, histoire navale, politique et diplomatique*, Bécherel, Les Perséides.

ELLORY, R. J. (2010). *Les Anonymes*. Paris: Sonatine.

FELLOUS, Sonia. "Histoire du judaïsme," *La Documentation photographique*. Paris: La Documentation française, No. 8065, September-October 2008.

FERLAND, Catherine (2010). *Bacchus en Canada. Boissons, buveurs et ivresses en Nouvelle-France*. Québec: Septentrion.

FOUGÈRES, Dany (2004). *L'approvisionnement en eau à Montréal. Du privé au public, 1796-1865*. Sillery: Septentrion.

FRÉGAULT, Guy (1955). *La Guerre de la Conquête*. Montreal: Fides.

FRÉGAULT, Guy (1963). *Histoire du Canada par les textes*. Montreal: Fides, 2 vol.

GAGNON, Serge (1987). *Mourir hier et aujourd'hui : de la mort chrétienne dans la campagne québécoise au xix⁰ siècle à la mort technicisée dans la cité sans Dieu*. Québec: Presses de l'Université Laval.

GÉLINAS, Claude. "La traite des fourrures en Haute-Mauricie avant 1831. Concurrence, stratégies commerciales et petits profits," *RHAF*, Vol. 51, No. 3, p. 394.

GÉLINAS, Claude (2000). *La gestion de l'étranger. Les Atikamekw et la présence eurocanadienne en Haute-Mauricie, 1760-1870*. Sillery: Septentrion.

GODFREY, Sheldon J. and Judith C. GODFREY (1995). *Search out the Land. The Jews and the Growth of Equality in British colonial America, 1740-1867*. Montreal: McGill-Queen's University Press.

GREER, Allan (2000). *Habitants, marchands et seigneurs, La société rurale du bas Richelieu, 1740-1840*, Septentrion.

GRIGNON, Claude-Henri (2002). *Les Pamphlets de Valdombre*. Montreal: Stanké.

HAMELIN, Marcel (1961). "Jacques Terroux et le commerce entre 1760 et 1865." Thèse de licence, Université Laval.

HARDY, René (1999). *Contrôle social et mutation de la culture religieuse au Québec, 1830-1930*. Montreal: Boréal.

HARDY, René, Normand SÉGUIN et al. (2004). *Histoire de la Mauricie*. Sainte-Foy: Institut québécois de la recherche sur la culture.

HART, Arthur Daniel (1926). *The Jew in Canada. A complete record of Canadian Jewry from the days of the French Régime to the present time*, Toronto: Jewish Publications Ltd.

HART, Gerald E. (1888), *The Fall of New France, 1755-1760*. Montreal, Toronto and New York: W. Drysdale & co, R. W. Douglas and G. P. Putnam's Sons.

HARRIS, R. Cole et Louise DECHÊNE (dir.). (1987), *Atlas historique du Canada*, Vol. 1, *Des origines à 1800*. Montreal: Presses de l'Université de Montréal.

IMBEAULT, Sophie (2004). *Les Tarieu de Lanaudière. Une famille noble après la Conquête, 1760-1791*. Sillery: Septentrion.

JACKSON, James (2009). *The Riot that Never Was: The Military Shooting of Three Montrealers in 1832 and the Official Cover-up*. Montreal: Baraka Books.

JARVIS, Ruth R. "Gabriel Cotté," *Dictionary of Canadian Biography*, IV.

JEAN HAFFNER, Luce (1994). *Les quatre frères Jean. De la Rochelle à Québec. Sillery*: Septentrion.

JONES, David S. (2004). *Rationalizing Epidemics. Meanings and Uses of American Indian Mortality since 1600*. Harvard University Press.

JOSEPH, Anne (1995). *Heritage of a patriarch. Canada's First Jewish Settlers and the Continuing Story of these Families in Canada*. Sillery: Septentrion.

LACOURSIÈRE, Jacques (1996). *Histoire populaire du Québec*, tome III, *1841 à 1896*. Sillery: Septentrion.

LACOURSIÈRE, Jacques, Jean PROVENCHER and Denis VAUGEOIS (2004). *Canada-Québec : synthèse historique*. Sillery: Septentrion.

LAMALICE, André L. J. "François-Antoine Larocque," *Dictionary of Canadian Biography*, IX.

LAMBERT, John (2006). *Voyage au Canada dans les années 1806, 1807 et 1808*. Septentrion. (English edition, 1810: *Travels through Lower Canada*...)

LAVOIE, Michel (2010). *"C'est ma seigneurie que je réclame." La lutte des Hurons de Lorette pour la seigneurie de Sillery, 1650-1900*. Montreal: Boréal.

LAW, Charles (2006). *Aaron's Covenant. Seeding the Hart Dynasty*. Trafford Publishing.

LESSARD, Rénald. "Les papiers du Canada," *L'Ancêtre*, Vol. 34 (summer 2008)" p. 357-360.

LEVITTE, Georges and David CATARIVAS (1964). *Les Juifs*. Paris: Robert Delpire.

LITALIEN, Raymonde, Jean-François PALOMINO and Denis VAUGEOIS (2008). *Mapping a continent: Historical Atlas of North America 1492-1814*. Septentrion.

MANCERON, Claude (2009). *Les hommes de la liberté*, tome I, *Les vingt ans du roi*. Paris: Omnibus.

MARCUS, Jacob Rader (1951). *Early American Jewry. The Jews of New York, New England and Canada, 1649-1794*, Vol. 1. Philadelphia: The Jewish Publication Society of America.

MARCUS, Jacob Rader, "The Modern Religion of Moses Hart," *Hebrew Union College Annual*, Vol. XX, p. 585-615.

MARCUS, Jacob Rader (1898). *United States Jewry 1776-1985*, Vol. 1. Detroit: Wayne State University Press.

MARCUS, Jacob Rader (1952), *Early American Jewry. The Jews of Pensylvania and the South, 1655-1790*. Philadelphia.

MARCUS, Jacob Rader (1959). *American Jewry. Documents eighteenth Century*. The Hebrew Union College Press.

MARGUERITE-MARIE, sœur (1888-1911), *Les Ursulines des Trois-Rivières depuis leur établissement jusqu'à nos jours*. Trois-Rivières: P.V. Ayotte, Vol. 1 et 2.

McCULLOUGH, A.B. (1987). *La monnaie et le change au Canada des premiers temps jusqu'à 1900*. Environnement Canada.

MILLER, Carman. "Moses Judah Hays," *Dictionary of Canadian Biography*, Vol. IX.

MÜNCH, André (2000). *L'Expertise en écritures et en signatures*. Septentrion.

MOUSSETTE, Marcel (1983). *Le chauffage domestique au Canada des origines à l'industrialisation*. Québec: Presses de l'Université Laval.

NADEAU, Jean-François (2010). *Adrien Arcand, führer canadien*. Montreal: Lux.

OUELLET, Fernand (1966), *Histoire économique et sociale du Québec 1760-1850: structures et conjoncture*. Montreal: Fides.

OUELLET, Fernand. "Louis-Joseph Papineau," *Dictionary of Canadian Biography*, X.

PAGNUELO, Siméon (1872). *Études historiques et légales sur la liberté religieuse en Canada*. Montreal: Beauchemin & Valois.

PARKMAN, Francis (1899). *The Conspiracy of Pontiac and the Indian War after the Conquest of Canada*, Toronto: George N. Morang & Company Limited, tome I.

PLOURDE, Michel (dir.), (2000). *Le Français au* Québec: *400 ans d'histoire et de vie*. Québec and Montréal: Publications du Québec eandFides.

RHEAULT, Marcel J. and Georges AUBIN (2006). *Médecins et patriotes, 1837-1838*. Sillery: Septentrion.

ROME, David. "Adolphus Mordecai Hart," *Dictionary of Canadian Biography*, X.

ROSENBERG, Stuart E. (1970). *The Jewish Community in Canada*, Vol. I. Toronto and Montréal: McClelland and Stewart.

SACK, Benjamin Gult (1945). *History of the Jews in Canada. From the Earliest Beginnings to the Present Day*, Vol. I, *The French Regime*. Montreal: Canadian Jewish Congress.

SAMSON, Roch (1998). *Les Forges du Saint-Maurice. Les débuts de l'industrie sidérurgique au Canada, 1730-1883*. Ottawa and Sainte-Foy: Parcs Canada et Presses de l'Université Laval.

SENIOR, Elinor Kyte (1997). *Les habits rouges et les patriots*. Montreal: VLB éditeur.

SHORTT, Adam and Arthur G. DOUGHTY (1911). *Documents relating to the constitutional history of Canadac 1759-1791*. Ottawa: C. H. Parmelee.

SHORTT, Adam (1925). *Documents relating to Canadian currency, exchange and finance during the French period*, Vol. II.

SOLOMON, Michel (1992). *Aaron Hart, sieur de Bécancour. La vie mouvementée du premier juif établi au Québec au XVIIIᵉ siècle*. Montreal: Humanitas nouvelle optique.

TESSIER, Albert. "Deux enrichis : Aaron Hart et Nicolas Montour," *Les Cahiers des Dix*, No. 3 (1938), p. 217-242.

TESSIER, Albert (1974). *Les Forges Saint-Maurice*. Sillery: Éditions du Boréal Express.

TRUDEL, Marcel (1952). *Le Régime militaire dans le Gouvernement des Trois-Rivières, 1760-1764*. Trois-Rivières: Éditions du Bien public.

TRUDEL, Marcel (1968). *Initiation à la Nouvelle-France*, HRW.

TRUDEL, Marcel (1973). *Le terrier du Saint-Laurent en 1663*. Ottawa: Éditions de l'Université d'Ottawa.

TRUDEL, Marcel (1999). *Histoire de la Nouvelle-France*, tome X, *Le régime militaire et la disparition de la Nouvelle-France, 1759-1764*, Fides.

TULCHINSKY, Gerald. "William Dow," *Dictionary of Canadian Biography*, IX.

VAUGEOIS, Denis. "Les positions religieuses de Moses Hart," *Société canadienne de l'histoire de l'Église canadienne*, session d'études 33 (1966), p. 41-46.

VAUGEOIS, Denis (1968). *Les Juifs et la Nouvelle-France*. Trois-Rivières: Éditions du Boréal Express.

VAUGEOIS, Denis. "Aaron Hart," *Dictionary of Canadian Biography*, IV; "Samuel Jacobs," IV; "Ezekiel Hart," VII; "Aaron Ezekiel Hart," VIII; "Moses Hart," VIII; "Sigismund Mohr," XII.

VAUGEOIS, Denis (1992). *Québec 1792. Les acteurs, les institutions et les frontiers*. Saint-Laurent: Fides.

VAUGEOIS, Denis (2002). *The Last French and Indian War*. McGill's Queen's University Press.

VAUGEOIS, Denis (2005). *America. The Lewis & Clark Expedition and the Dawn of a New Power*. Véhicule Press.

WALLOT, Jean-Pierre (1973). *Un Québec qui bougeait. Trame socio-politique du Québec au tournant du XIXᵉ siècle*. Sillery: Éditions du Boréal Express.

Sources of illustrations

p. iii, Service des Archives du Congrès juif canadien. Comité des Charités; **p. v**, author's coll.; **p. 2**, author's coll.; **p. 4**, ASTR, FN-0021-M6-42-07; **p. 7**, American Jewish Archives; **p. 8**, ASTR, 0009-J-A-2; **p. 9**, ASTR FN-0014-Q3-42-14; **p.10**, AUQTR, Fonds Hervé Biron, photo 124, crayon de Gérald Montplaisir, *Le Nouvelliste*, 20 juin 1954; **p. 12**, author's coll.; **p. 14**, author's coll.; **p. 16-17**, ASTR, FN-0014-Q3-42-19, Studio Lumière de Cap-de-la-Madeleine, 5 mars 1956; **p. 21**, CJCCCNA-PC1-4-22A-9; **p. 23**, CJCCCNA-PC1-4-21K; **p. 26**, photo Jan Lukas; **p. 29 ????? CARTE; 30**, McCord Museum M18642; **p. 31**, tiré d'Arthur Daniel Hart, *The Jew in Canada*, Jewish Publications Limited, 1926; **p. 34**, McCord Museum MP-000 154.34; **p. 35**, McCord Museum M18640; **p. 36**, McCord Museum 1-38984.1; **p. 37**, author's coll.; **pp. 39-40 ????? LEVY-TRENT; p. 43**, LAC "S" Series, RG4, A1, vol. 17; **p. 45**, coll. Claude Bouchard; **p. 45**, LAC, C-002006; **p. 46**, photo Claude Michaelidès; **p. 48**, ASTR, 0009-J-A-1; **p. 50**, Canada Post; **p. 52**, drawing attributed to Henri Bleau, LAC, C-17059; **p. 53**, McCord Museum M8355; **p. 55**, Archives diplomatiques françaises, Microfilm Mémoires et Documents, Amérique, vol. 10, bobine P.12092, coin from the collection of the Société numismatique de Québec; **p. 56-57**, same as for p. 55; **p. 59**, ASTR, N1-F34; **p. 61**, detail from atlas by H.W. Hopkins and published by Walter S. Mac Cormac, 1879; **p. 62**, ASTR, 0009-F-A-2, F-A-3 and F-A-5; **p. 65**, author's coll.; **p. 67-68**, detail of Bouchette's1815 map; **p. 68**, ASTR, FN-0064-61-05; **p. 70**, ASTR,unclassed; **p. 73**, engraving from *Les Ursulines des Trois-Rivières*, second tome, P.V. Ayotte, 1892; **p. 75**, Metropolitan Museum of Art, New York; **p. 76**, author's coll.; **p. 79**, BAnQ, TR, 2-AC-4; **p. 80**, Internet; **p. 82**, ASTR, 0009-J-a-12; **p. 83**, BAnQ, TR, Fonds Cour du banc du roi (TL20, S2, SS1); **p. 88**, McCord Museum M18660; **p. 89**, author's coll.; **p. 92**, McCord Museum M327; **p. 96**, detail of an ancient piece of paper from Poland, photo Roger Roche, colour Pierre-Louis Cauchon; **p. 98**, BAnQ, TR, greffe de Joseph Badeaux, CN401, S6; **p. 100**, detail of Archibald Macdonald's plan (BAnQ, Fonds Ville de Trois-Rivières V2, S2, P1242), photo of Hart monument, Rue Hart by the author and document about opening of Rue Hart, ASTR, 0009-I-g-1; **p. 102-103**, coll., Société de numismatique de Québec; **p. 106**, codex Rossiana 555, folio 127, bibliothèque apostolique du Vatican. Illustration from Sonia Fellous, *Histoire du judaïsme*, p. 43; **p. 108**, illustration from Roch Samson, *Les Forges du Saint-Maurice*, PUL, 1998: 233; **p. 114**, illustration from Edward Dahl and Jean-François Gauvin, *Sphaerae Mundi*, Septentrion, 2000, p. 24, based on detail of Coronelli's globe, below detail of purchase contract of Pompée, BAnQ, TR, greffe de J. B. Badeaux, 23-09-1774; **p. 115**, ASTR, 0009-I-A-1 et I-A-2; **p. 116**, detail of painting by Agostino Brunias, Marché de Saint-Domingue, coll. Barbados Museum; **p. 118**, author's coll.; **p. 121**, detail from atlas by H.W. Hopkins and published by Walter S. Mac Cormac, 1879; **p. 122**, American Jewish Historical Society, Brandeis, Miscellaneous material, box 2; **p. 124**, AJHS, Brandeis, *ibid.*; **p. 126**, LAC, C-024888; **p. 129**, BAnQ, C-111156 and BAnQ, P600-6/476/6; **p. 132**, photo by Francesco Bellomo; **p. 133**, coll. Yves Beauregard; **p. 136**, LAC, House of Commons; **p. 137**, Château Ramezay; **p. 140**, author's coll.; **p. 143**, LAC, RG 1, E11, vol. 1-2 and coll. Baby, Université de Montréal; **p. 147**, *CJA*; **p. 149**, ASTR, 0009-A-H-3; **p. 151**, author's coll.; **p. 152**, Archives judiciaires de Montréal; **p. 154**, author's coll.; **p. 156**, private coll.; **p. 159**, McCord Museum M8034; **p. 160**, author's coll.; **p. 162**, LAC, C-013493; **p. 163**, author's coll.; **p. 164**, Château Ramezay, 998.1891; **p. 169**, MP-000 154.14; **p. 178**, ASTR, 0009-A-g; **p. 181**, ASTR 0009-A-G-12; **p. 184**, LAC, C-031247; **p. 187**, collection Arthur Robidoux; **p. 190-91**, BAnQ, Bouchette's map; **p. 194-95**, private coll. and Château Ramezay; **p. 198**, BAnQ, TR, Fonds

Cour du banc du roi pour le district de Trois-Rivières, TL20, S1.SS1; **p. 202**, BAnQ, TR, dépositions judiciaires, 1827; **p. 203**, private collection; **p. 210**, McCord Museum, M981.207.4; **p. 211**, BAnQ, P1000, S4, D83, PB98-1; **p. 215**, ASTR, 0009-A-I-2; **p. 216**, ASTR, 0009-A-I-2; **p. 217**, ASTR, 0009-A-I-1 and A-H-3; **p. 220**, McCord Museum M2003. 106.3; **p. 224**, photo Edouard Hillel from *Stones that Speak* by David Rome and Jacques Langlais, Septentrion, 1992: 26; **p. 228-229**, greffe de William Burn, BAnQ, Sherbrooke; **p. 231**, McCord Museum, 1-5091.1; **p. 233**, ASTR, 0009-J-M-7-1 and J-M-3; **p. 234**, photo Édouard Hillel from Rome and Langlais, 1992: 27; **p. 237**, ASTR; **p. 240**, ASTR, 0009-J-M-7-1; **p. 241**, ASTR, 0009-J-M-7-4; **p. 242-43**, McCord Museum, MO-0000 154.2; **p. 244**, McCord Museum MP-000 154.3; **p. 245**, ASTR, 0009-A-G-12; **p. 246**, detail Bouchette's map; **p. 247-48**, private coll.; **p. 250**, LAC C-000117, George Gipps, 1835; Hays, private coll.; **p. 252**, McCord Museum M970.67.23; **p. 254-55**, 3 photos, private coll.; list and budget, ASTR 0009-A-H-3; **p. 257**, CJCCCNA; **p. 258**, McCord Museum M930.51.1.52; **p. 259**, McCord Museum M2001.30.3 et M11588; **p. 260**, LAC, C-013340; **p. 261**, priv. coll.; **p. 262**, coll. Bernard Duchesne; **p. 263**, McCord Museum M310 et M7411.1.1; **p. 264**, McCord Museum M15902; **p. 267**, A.D. Hart; **p. 268**, publisher's coll.; **p. 270**, manuscrit hébreu 7, folio 12, BNF, Fellous, 2008: 23; **p. 272**, priv. coll.; **p. 273-74**, AJHS, BNQ, fonds G.-Morriset (auj. BAnQ) and AJHS, Brandeis; **p. 276**, BNQ, *ibid.*; **p. 282**, A.D. Hart; **p. 284**, Ezra, miniature of codex Amiantino, 5th century BC., bibliothèque Laurentienne, Florence and from Marek Halter, *Histoire du peuple juif*, Arthaud, 2010; **p. 304**, détails from atlas by H.W. Hopkins; above right, McCord Museum 18640 and Metropolitan Museum of Art; **p. 309**, McCord Museum M2450.53 et M24190; **p. 311**, photo Francesco Bellomo, from Gaston Deschênes, *Hôtel du Parlement*, Stromboli, 2007, p. 170.

The work of the personnel from the following institutions has been very helpful: McCord Museum, Library and Archives Canada, the Archives du séminaire Saint-Joseph de Trois-Rivières and the Archives of the Canadian Jewish Congress. Without the competence and generosity of Nicole Vallières, Christian Vachon, Stéphanie Poisson, Janice Rosen, and Christian Lalancette, it would have been impossible to produce the book as you see it.

Index

Preparing this index raised a problem I meet whenever I write about the Harts. In the absence of birth certificates or even registers, spelling inevitably becomes a problem. Fortunately, most first names, such as Aaron, Moses or Benjamin, raise no problems. That is not the case for Ezekiel/Ezechiel/Ézéchiel or Alexandre/Alexander. Some variations in the text are tolerated and note in the index. The best example is surely that of Dorothée, Dorothé, Dorothea, Dorothy, etc. Another case appeared that I had not foreseen, the use of hyphens. Hyphens are rare in first names in English. However, applying that rule generated unexpected problems. One of Moses Hart's last children was given the name Samuel-Judah, yet Samuel is the first name of many Judahs. I therefore followed King Solomon. To avoid confusion, which became even more likely since Jews often use first names as surnames, I often used hyphens to put two first names together or to link two family names, which French Canadians are also known to do. Variations were tolerated in the text and are noted in the index but clarity has trumped rigidity. Moreover, for several people details are also provided in the index to situate them better in light of the repetition of many first names.

MORE NONFICTION FROM BARAKA BOOKS

Barack Obama and the Jim Crow Media
The Return of the Nigger Breakers
Ishmael Reed

A People's History of Quebec
Jacques Lacoursière & Robin Philpot

An Independent Quebec
The past, the present and the future
Jacques Parizeau, former Premier of Quebec

Trudeau's Darkest Hour
War Measures in Time of Peace, October 1970
Edited by Guy Bouthillier & Édouard Cloutier

The Riot that Never Was
The military shooting of three Montrealers in 1832 and the official cover-up
James Jackson

The Question of Separatism
Quebec and the Struggle over Sovereignty
Jane Jacobs

Soldiers for Sale
German "Mercenaries" with the British in Canada during
the American Revolution 1776-83
Jean Pierre Wilhelmy

America's Gift
What the World Owes to the Americas and Their First Inhabitants
Käthe Roth and Denis Vaugeois

Inuit and Whalers on Baffin Island Through German Eyes
Wilhelm Weike's Arctic Journal and Letters (1883-84)
Ludger Müller-Wille & Bernd Gieseking
(Translated from the German by William Barr)

Joseph-Elzéar Bernier
Champion of Canadian Arctic Sovereignty
Marjolaine Saint-Pierre (translated by William Barr)